Papias

and the

New Testament

Erik cervantes

Papias
and the
New Testament

MONTE ALLEN SHANKS

PICKWICK *Publications* · Eugene, Oregon

PAPIAS AND THE NEW TESTAMENT

Pickwick Publications
An Imprint of Wipf and Stock Publishers
199 W. 8th Ave., Suite 3
Eugene, OR 97401

www.wipfandstock.com

ISBN 13: 978-1-61097-693-0

Cataloguing-in-Publication data:

Shanks, Monte Allen.

Papias and the New Testament / Monte Allen Shanks, with a foreword by John Polhill.

xiv + 310 pp. ; 23 cm. Includes bibliographical references.

ISBN 13: 978-1-61097-693-0

1. Papias, Saint, Bishop of Hierapolis, -approximately 120. 2. Christian literature, Early. 3. Bible. Matthew—Criticism, interpretation, etc. 4. Bible. Mark—Criticism, interpretation, etc. 5. Bible. John—Criticism, interpretation, etc.. I. Polhill, John B., 1939–. II. Title.

BS2970 M768 2013

Manufactured in the U.S.A.

To Amy, my beloved wife.

To my Dad.

To the glorious Lord Jesus Christ

Contents

Contents

Foreword

THE MOST COMMON ASSOCIATIONS with the name Papias held by contemporary scholars are the early patristic writer's comments that the Gospel of Mark is based on the reminiscences of Peter and that Matthew wrote a collection of Jesus' "logia" in a "Hebrew dialect." In Johannine studies, Papias is often seen as the prime evidence for there being two contemporaneous "Johns" in Ephesus, the apostle and the "Elder."

What is often *not* recognized is that these references to Papias' witness are generally gleaned from one source, a single section of Eusebius' *Church History*. Also to be noted is that Eusebius' comments should not be taken uncritically. For instance, serious questions exist as to whether Eusebius misunderstood Papias' remarks about the apostle John and erroneously concluded there were two by that name. Such issues are treated thoroughly in this book. More significantly, Shanks draws from a much more extensive base of source material on Papias than the witness of a single Father.

Papias was an important early father, a member of the generation that immediately followed and was acquainted with some of the apostolic eyewitnesses to Jesus and his teachings. He belonged to that group of writers referred to as the "Apostolic Fathers," and he is included within the major collections of these writers. Unfortunately none of his writings have survived to the present. We do, however, have extensive references to Papias in later church fathers. These attest to a five-volume work by Papias entitled *An Exposition of the Oracles of the Lord*. Though we no longer have this work, we have numerous statements alluding to its contents within the writings of such fathers as Irenaeus and Jerome and many others. Eusebius claims to be quoting this work in his remarks about Mark and Matthew and the two Johns of Ephesus. These references to Papias are referred to as the Papian "fragments."

Shanks covers all of the major issues involved in an investigation of Papias. He provides a thorough presentation of all the major editions of the Apostolic Fathers and their treatment of Papias, giving a balanced evaluation of the editors' agreements and differences in their discussions of the early father. Relatively little is known of the life of Papias. Shanks devotes a whole chapter to the subject, providing as full a treatment as is available anywhere. The largest segment of Shanks' research is his treatment of the fragments. He devotes a considerable number of pages to the Eusebian statement alone. Each fragment is cited in English translation, followed by a critical evaluation of its accuracy and value in the discussion of Papias' contribution to the study of the early Christian literature.

Shanks' work covers a wide scope of issues related to Papias and the early development of the New Testament. It deals with canonical questions, such as which books Papias was aware of and what evidence Papias provides for their authorship. Some of the Papian fragments raise text-critical issues, such as his seeming awareness of the pericope of the adulterous woman now found in manuscripts of Luke and John. Shanks covers these and many similar issues in detail. Perhaps his book's greatest value is in bringing together all the strands of research on Papias' life and writings into a single volume, making it an invaluable reference tool.

John Polhill
Professor of New Testament
Southern Baptist Theological Seminary

Preface

THE FOLLOWING EFFORT COULD not have been possible without the labors of many others. Scholars such as Adolf Harnack, J. B. Lightfoot, J. R. Harmer, A. Cleveland Coxe, James Kleist, William Schoedel, Josef Kürzinger, Ulrich Körtner, Bart Ehrman, Michael Holmes, and Richard Bauckham have all labored to collate and/or research the extant evidence of Papias and his *magnum opus*, which is commonly known as *An Exposition of the Oracles of the Lord*. Having gathered these fragments, they made it possible for others to research them, which many have done, predominately giving special attention to one or several at a time. With so many having focused their attention on these fragments one might wonder if there is anything new to write about Papias and his writings. I think yes; thus, the book you have before you. Regardless of your evaluation of this effort, and although I have taken issue with the conclusions of some of those mentioned above, it is important that I acknowledge their labors since their efforts were so foundational to this book.

I also wish to thank the many men and women who have personally invested in me. While I have partnered with many from churches and ministries, the individuals that I have in mind are predominately from the faculties of Dallas Theological Seminary and The Southern Baptist Theological Seminary. Without their investment this book would not have been possible. Some individuals that I especially wish to thank from these faculties are Drs. Darrell Bock, Craig Blaising, Mark Bailey, Walt Baker, Howard Hendricks, Robert Stein, William Cook, Michael Haykin, and most importantly Dr. David Puckett and Dr. John Polhill. I thank Dr. Puckett for allowing me to learn a great deal about academic administration, and I especially wish to thank Dr. Polhill for graciously agreeing to supervise me throughout my Ph.D. program. I am forever in their debt. I also want to thank Professor Marsha Omanson for her interaction with this manuscript while it was a dissertation, and Dr. Adam McClendon for his proof reading efforts. May your tribes increase. Additionally, I want to thank Dr. Robin Parry for his encouragement and input, and the good people at

Pickwick Publications for their efforts as well. May the Lord richly bless all while drawing all nearer to himself.

Lastly, and most importantly, I want to thank two very important people in my life. The first is my dad, who regularly keeps me grounded in the things that truly matter in life. I also want to thank my wife, who has partnered with me through thick and thin every step of the way. My life would be absent of love and so many other wonderful blessings without her gracious touch. May the Lord richly bless all who have labored before me and all who have graciously enriched my life with their own.

A search for the truth,
by the doggedness of the Holy Spirit
with the conviction to hold firm,
for the glory of Almighty God
in the matchless name of His wonderful Son,
the Lord Jesus Christ.

Monte A. Shanks
Georgetown, Indiana
December 2012

Abbreviations

ABD	*The Anchor Bible Dictionary*
AJT	*The American Journal of Theology*
ANF	Anti-Nicene Fathers
BAGD	W. Bauer, W. F. Arndt, F. W. Gingrich, and F. W. Danker *Greek-English Lexicon of the NT*
Bib	*Biblica*
CBQ	*Catholic Biblical Quarterly*
CP	*Chronicon Paschale*
CTRV	*Contemporary Review*
Exp	*The Expositor*
ExpTim	*Expository Times,* a.k.a. *The Expository Times*
Herm	*Hermathena*
HTR	*Harvard Theological Review*
JBL	*Journal of Biblical Literature*
JECS	*Journal of Early Christian Studies*
JETS	*Journal of the Evangelical Theological Society*
JRPS	*Journal of Religion and Psychical Research*
JSNT	*Journal for the Study of the New Testament*
JTS	*Journal of Theological Studies*
LCL	Loeb Classical Library (Cambridge: Harvard University Press/ London: William Heinemann, 1912–)
LSJ	Liddell-Scott-Jones, *Greek–English Lexicon*
NPNF2	Nicene and Post-Nicene Fathers
NovT	*Novum Testamentum*
NTS	*New Testament Studies*
PG	J. Migne, *Patrologia Graeca*
SBJT	*The Southern Baptist Journal of Theology*
SJT	*Scottish Journal of Theology*

Abbreviations

SP	*Studia Patristica*
TDNT	*Theological Dictionary of the New Testament*
TS	*Theological Studies*
TZ	*Theologische Zeitschrift*
VC	*Vigiliae Christianae*

1

Introduction

The Need for Research

François Bovon suggested, "As the dividing line between *Urchristentum* and ancient Christianity becomes more and more artificial, New Testament scholarship and the discipline of patristics must join hands."[1] In theory his exhortation is commendable; however, it is unlikely that such a colloquium would bring a significant agreement or clarity to either field simply due to the diversity of approaches and presuppositions within each discipline. Nevertheless, this book is a modest attempt towards Bovon's bold suggestion. A survey of New Testament and patristic studies concerning the origins of the apostolic writings finds a particular individual repeatedly referenced—he is Papias, an early second-century bishop of Hierapolis. Few if any patristic figures are quoted and/or marginalized as often as Papias, especially with the advent of "higher" critical scholarship. What makes this marginalization so intriguing is that very little can be objectively known about him and his work, yet he demands the attention of any scholar who desires to understand the origins of the New Testament.[2]

1. Bovon, *Early Christianity*, 225.

2. It is acknowledged that to some this book's title may appear rather anachronistic since one could infer from it that this study argues that the New Testament canon was "completed" by the middle of the second century AD. While that is a thesis worthy of research, it will not be the focus of this book. Instead, it focuses upon Papias's witness to and attitudes toward certain apostolic writings that inevitably were included within the canonical New Testament. Consequently, this is a study that focuses upon *a particular period* in which the literature of the New Testament was developing into a canon.

1

This book researches Papias and what his surviving literary fragments communicate about the apostolic writings, as well as what other patristic and medieval authors understood about him and what he meant concerning the origins of certain books of the New Testament. Its thesis is that the surviving "Fragments of Papias"[3] are a valuable resource because they document that some of the New Testament writings originated from some of the original followers of Jesus Christ (i.e., the apostles). Regarding the importance of this thesis with respect to the Papian fragments, Clayton Jefford wrote,

> Undoubtedly the most important materials from the witness of Papias related to reminiscences concerning the development of New Testament literature. It was Papias, for example, who preserved the tradition that Mark made note of the recollections of the apostle Peter as a written testimony to the words and deeds of the Lord. And it was also Papias who documented that Matthew recorded the sayings of Jesus in Hebrew in order that each person could translate them into their own language and context. Additionally, the witness of Papias provides a unique link between apostolic tradition and the post-apostolic church, since Eusebius argues Papias had heard John (the apostle) and was a companion of Polycarp. Such fragmentary traditions and testimony to ancient links between scattered Christians have gone a long way toward the development of historical assumptions about the evolution of our New Testament canon and the apostolic witness that it reflects.[4]

The surviving Papian fragments are also important because they reveal that Papias had an attitude of value and respect toward certain New Testament writings, and that his attitude was consistent with the attitudes of other known leaders of the early orthodox church (e.g., Polycarp). This thesis is worthy of focus because a segment of modern and post-modern scholarship, both liberal and conservative, has depended far too heavily upon Eusebius's questionable interpretation of Papias's preface in order to

3. Hereafter, this collection of literature or portions within it will regularly be referred to as "Papian fragments."

4. Jefford, *Apostolic Fathers*, 25–26. It should be noted that the Papian fragment that Jefford alluded to does not say that Matthew wrote his Aramaic Gospel *so that* anyone could translate it into his own language and context, but rather that is was after he wrote his Aramaic Gospel that individuals later attempted to translate his work into their own language and context. Eusebius believed that Matthew initially wrote a Gospel for those of his own native tongue. See Eusebius *Ecc. Hist.* III.24.6 (LCL 153:250–51).

identify who Papias was, those that he might have known, and his knowledge of certain portions of the New Testament. The result of this limited and biased exposure enables some scholars to make conjectures about Papias that are at odds with other patristic statements concerning him, conjectures that ironically are also inconsistent with statements made by Eusebius himself.

This book surveys the selection of patristic and medieval literature commonly referred to as "The Fragments of Papias" in order to address the many misconceptions involving Papias's knowledge of the apostolic writings. Its thesis regarding Papias's value for obtaining a greater understanding of the development of the canonical New Testament is defended through a rigorous investigation of the Papian fragments, an investigation that had two goals in mind: The first was to identify the context in which Papias lived and those with whom he associated; and then having identified his proper place within the patristic period it examined his witness concerning the existence of certain New Testament writings and their origins. It is recommended that those who are familiar with Eusebius's opinion of Papias and his exegesis of Papias's preface read appendix 1 before proceeding with the rest of this book.

METHOD OF RESEARCH

This effort relies significantly upon the Papian fragments as they are found in J. B. Lightfoot's *The Apostolic Fathers*, which was edited and revised by Michael W. Holmes in 1999,[5] and the edition of the "Fragments of Papias and Quadratus" found in the Loeb Classical Library series.[6] It does not, however, completely follow Holmes's ordering of these fragments. This research also employs additional critical editions that supply and examine individual Papian fragments that are not found in either of these editions.[7]

---

5. Holmes, *Apostolic Fathers: Greek Texts and English Translations* (Grand Rapids: Baker, 1999), 562–90. Holmes has edited and revised several different editions of the Papian Fragments with similar titles. Consequently, hereafter, this particular edition will be footnoted as Holmes, *The Apostolic Fathers: Diglot Edition*. The ordering of the Papian material by Lightfoot and Holmes has its weaknesses since it is not chronological (e.g., Eusebius's preservation of Papian material comes before Irenaeus's reference to Papias). A more comprehensive explanation for the ordering of the Papian material in this book will follow.

6. *Papias and Quadratus* (LCL 25: 85–118).

7. Baker Academic recently published a 3rd edition of the *The Apostolic Fathers*, of which Holmes was again the editor. Holmes, however, changed the presentation of the

As stated previously, this effort had two goals. The first was to discern the time frame in which Papias lived, while the second was to identify Papias's knowledge and attitude towards any apostolic writings. Identifying Papias's context is important for determining how close he was to the apostolic period and, consequently, the general trustworthiness of his knowledge and statements about their writings. Some argue that Papias's proximity or lack thereof to the apostolic generation does not necessarily affect the trustworthiness of his testimony or of the traditions he received regarding the origins of the apostolic writings.[8] The fact remains, however, that generally speaking the closer one is to an event or source the more credible that one is perceived, especially if his testimony is contemporaneous with the event to which he testifies. Regarding the importance of contemporaneous testimony in historical studies, James Donaldson wrote, "In regard to testimony, we set out with the principle, that the only proper historical evidence is contemporary testimony. . . . We receive the statements of contemporaries as true, unless there is some reason to look upon them as false. As we move away from the particular period into testimony of a later period, we are not warranted in rejecting it entirely, for the testimony of a later period may be and generally is the testimony of contemporaries handed down from one generation to another. But we must be more cautious."[9]

Consequently, Papias's proximity to the apostolic generation is valuable in determining his credibility as a witness to it and its literature; literature that eventually became part of the New Testament canon. Having determined the likely time period of Papias's life and ministry, the second goal will be addressed, which is discerning his knowledge of and attitude towards the certain writings of the New Testament. This is accomplished by analyzing specific Papian fragments with special attention given to

---

Papian texts in this edition. Consequently, the format of the 1999 edition (referred to in this book as the "diglot edition") is preferred for the purposes of this book. Nevertheless, the 3rd edition is regularly referenced and footnoted when appropriate.

8. For an example of some who concluded that Papias did not personally know any apostles but defended him as a credible witness to the origins of New Testament see Perumalil, "Papias and Irenaeus," 332–37. Vernon Bartlet believed that Papias converted to Christianity after the apostle John's death but was still a credible witness to the origins of New Testament. Bartlet, "Papias," 2:311. For an explanation of why a late date for Papias witness weakens his importance see Yarbrough, "The Date of Papias," 181–86.

9. Donaldson, *A Critical History*, 1:10–11.

Papias's employment, references, or allusions to New Testament passages, as well as his understanding of their origins and his attitudes toward them.[10]

The reason for predominantly employing the editions of Lightfoot and Holmes is that they provide the most comprehensive collection of Papian material since they not only include actual Papian quotes, but also many other patristic and medieval references and allusions to him and his writings. These additional citations are important because Papias's work is no longer extant; therefore, this material provides an important witness to the church's understanding and attitudes towards Papias, as well as their understanding of his writings.[11] Although all Papian fragments are found in secondary sources, such as those found in the writings of Irenaeus and Eusebius, they remain valuable sources for discovering the church's understanding of who Papias was and what he wrote. An added benefit of the editions of Lightfoot and Holmes, and Loeb Classical Library, is that they provide the Greek and Latin texts of the Papian fragments whenever possible.[12]

Holmes's order of these fragments, however, is not be entirely employed because it, whether intentionally or unintentionally, inappropriately provides an unjustifiable aid to the bias that has for long plagued a proper understanding of Papias and his meanings. This is observable in Holmes's decision to begin his compilation of the Papian fragments with three that were preserved by Eusebius, while Irenaeus's reference to Papias is fourteenth, in spite of the fact that it is considerably earlier than those preserved by Eusebius. Instead, this book enumerates and discusses the Papian fragments chronologically.[13]

This survey, as stated earlier, also includes additional Papian fragments not included in Holmes's edition. An example is the reference to Papias's martyrdom in the *Chronicon Paschale*.[14] Holmes did not include

---

10. This subject has been briefly addressed by scholars such as Heard, "Papias' Quotations," 130–34; Schoedel, "Papias," 235–70. It is hoped, however, that this book provides a more holistic and thorough approach to this topic, thus shedding greater light on this rather obscure period of the development of the New Testament canon.

11. While many of these fragments originate from the patristic period, a few are from the medieval period.

12. A few of the fragments are only available in Armenian and Arabic.

13. An aim of this book is to provide research that possesses the strengths of both the synchronic and diachronic approaches to this material.

14. *Chronicon Paschale* (PG 92:628). Hereafter, throughout this book the *Chronicon Paschale* will generally be referred to as *CP*.

this Papian fragment from the *Chronicon Paschale* because he agreed with Lightfoot that the original source of this fragment did not actually refer to Papias, but instead was the product of a copyist's error.[15] Lightfoot, however, provided no textual support for his theory; therefore, his decision to reject this fragment is entirely based upon conjecture. Consequently, because his decision concerning this important fragment is tenuous at best, it is included and discussed in detail within the biographical chapter of this book (i.e., chapter 3). Additionally, any Papian fragment that only holds value for understanding Papias's life receives greater focus in the biographical chapter of this book, and although they are also included within the chapter that lists all of the Papian fragments they do not there garner a significant amount of discussion.

This book, as mentioned previously, also focuses upon the life of Papias and his knowledge and attitudes towards writings that are now found in the canonical New Testament. It does not address the full spectrum of Papias's theology embedded within these fragments, although this would be an endeavor worthy of greater attention.[16] His theology is only addressed as it directly relates to his attitude toward and knowledge of any apostolic writings. Additionally, this book will only examine extensively the Papian fragments that significantly impact its thesis. Fragments that are ancillary and do not greatly impact its thesis will only be addressed briefly. This effort also ignores material that is generally referred to as "The Traditions of the Elders."[17] While these fragments are also valuable sources for understanding the theology and development of the early church, directly connecting them with Papias is tenuous at best—although it can be argued that in many ways they are consistent with theological tenants that are often associated with Papias.[18] These fragments, however, provide little support or challenge to the thesis of this book; therefore, they are not

15. Lightfoot, *Essays on Supernatural Religion*, 147–49.

16. For an example of research that focused upon one aspect of Papias' theology see Gregory, *The Chiliastic Hermeneutic of Papias of Hierapolis*.

17. For examples of these fragments see Holmes, *Apostolic Fathers*, 3rd ed., 768–73. The Fragments of Papias, in vol. 5 of *The Apostolic Fathers*, trans. Schoedel, 124–27. Hereafter, this edition will be footnoted in the following manner: Schoedel, *The Fragments*.

18. There have been some who attribute certain of the fragments of the "elders" to Papias, but in most cases their attempts are largely based upon arguments from silence. For this reason Holmes aptly recommended that they be consigned to studies concerning Irenaeus. Holmes, *Apostolic Fathers*, 3rd ed., 727. For examples of attempts to attribute some of these fragments to Papias see Hill, "Papias," 311; Deeks, "Papias Revisited," 296–30;. Deardorff, "Is It Papias' Logia?" 115–26.

included within the scope of its research. Lastly, unless otherwise stipulated, all references to the dates and/or centuries discussed in this book should be understood to be *anno Domini,* and all biblical quotations are taken from either the NASB or NIV translations of the New Testament.

2

A Survey of the History of Research

INTRODUCTION

THE ASSEMBLING OF THE fragments of Papias into a single collection is not an original endeavor. It is not uncommon to find compilations of these fragments as part of larger works devoted to the writings of the apostolic fathers. Such works, however, often come with little or no critical analysis of Papian material. Commentary is provided in some cases, but as helpful as they may be they are consistently too broad or superficial to be of any in-depth aid to the researcher, although their bibliographies are extremely helpful. A comprehensive history of all the research touching upon Papias and his writings is not the purpose of this book. Such an endeavor would go well beyond its stated objective. Consequently, this book only surveys the essential publications and research germane to its restricted thesis, as well as a few additional critical works intimately related to its subject matter. While this chapter does provide evaluations and in some cases critiques of the theories and arguments of the scholars addressed in it, hereafter, in general, more substantial interaction with their positions will occur during times of direct analysis of the Papian fragments.

PRIMARY WORKS

Philip Schaff reported that the seventeenth-century Jesuit Halloix was the first to write a "fanciful" biography on the life of Papias, which was published in 1633 and titled, *Vita S. Papiae*.[1] Halloix's book apparently comprised only several folios; regrettably, it was not available for the research for this book. In 1846 Martin Joseph Routh published a compilation of the Papian fragments in Latin in the first volume of the *Reliquiæ Sacræ*.[2] Routh's work contains a brief introduction that is followed by eleven Greek fragments, with a few Latin parallels, which is followed by a lengthy commentary on these fragments, which was also in Latin.

A brief treatment of Papian fragments, translated by Alexander Roberts and James Donaldson, was included within the first volume of the Ante-Nicene Fathers series. A. Cleveland Coxe provided an introduction to this material in the American edition of this series published in 1885, in which he stated that his collection largely depended upon Routh's work.[3] He placed Papias's lifespan from 70–155, and believed that Papias knew both Polycarp and the apostle John.[4] Coxe is one of the few scholars who included the fragment concerning Papias's martyrdom in 163 found in the *Chronicon Paschale*, as well as Eusebius's contradiction of himself in stating that Papias was both a "man most learned in all things" and someone of "small capacity."[5] His list of Papian material contains only ten fragments, about which he provided only a few comments in the form of footnotes.

A book by Edward H. Hall titled, *Papias and His Contemporaries: A Study of Religious Thought in the Second Century* was published in 1899. A legitimate question concerning this work is why Hall even mentioned Papias in his title at all since his book only tangentially discussed this apostolic father. Instead, his book was largely devoted to the assertion that Marcion as a significant and inspirational leader of the early church and that Gnosticism was a foundational component of Christianity. A more appropriate title for Hall's book would have been *Gnosticism and Its Influence upon the Early Church during the First Two Centuries*. The appropriateness of this title is evident from the subject matter found in chapters 5 and 6, which are the last two chapters of the book and are comprised of more than a hundred pages. The titles of these chapters are "Theological Speculations" and "The Mystic Gospel" respectively. In these decisive chapters there is virtually not a single reference to Papias, but a prolonged explanation of Hall's theory that Gnosticism had a deep and lasting impact

1. Schaff, *History of the Church*, 2:693.
2. Routh, *Reliquiæ Sacræ*, 1: xl–44.
3. *Fragments of Papias* (ANF 1:151–55).
4. Ibid., 151.
5. Ibid., 152.

the development of Christianity. Regarding Gnosticism's influence upon Christianity Hall wrote, "Christianity had done its best, as we have seen, to purge itself of the virus of Gnosticism. But it was too late. It might cast out its Marcions and Valentines, but it could not undo the work they had wrought. Gnosticism had become bone of its bone. To read the pages of what was soon to be known as the New Testament is to come upon these hated doctrines again and again."[6]

Hall did not argue that the apostolic fathers were defending the Christian faith against the heresies of Gnosticism,[7] but rather that from the beginning Gnosticism was deeply embedded, and thus has been forever woven into the fabric of what is accepted today as orthodox Christianity. Concerning the second-century debates between the orthodox church and gnostic heretics, he contended that "at that time, it must be remembered, there could be no genuine heresy, for there was no established faith. No Councils had yet rendered their decisions. There was no accepted Christian canon."[8]

Hall's work, however, is not without its merits. His fourth chapter, titled "The Millennial Reign," is a helpful survey of chiliastic theology as found in Jewish and Christian writings ranging from the first century BC through the second century AD. He believed that the preaching of Jesus and his followers was decidedly chiliastic, which in his opinion explains why chiliasm is so systemic throughout the New Testament. Concerning Papias's chiliasm and his knowledge of any writings of the New Testament, Hall contended that there was warrant for believing that the book of Revelation was "well known to Papias."[9] Hall, however, only briefly acknowledged the Papian fragment embedded in Irenaeus's *Against Heresies* V.33.3–4 for support of this assertion.[10] Regarding Papias's eschatology, Hall contended that his millennialism should not be surprising since it was the "prevailing" view during the late first century and early second century.[11] Unfortunately, his treatment of Papian material in this chapter, as well as throughout his book, is sparse. The majority of Hall's fourth

---

6. Hall, *Papias*, 199.

7. Hall recognized that Gnosticism existed in multiple forms rather than a single monolithic movement. Ibid., 186–87.

8. Ibid., 193.

9. Ibid., 123.

10. See the discussion on fragment 1 in this book, p. 106.

11. Ibid., 121.

chapter in fact deals with the millennial views of Jesus, Paul, and Irenaeus rather than that of Papias.

That Hall was convinced that Gnosticism was a foundational influence of the apostolic church is clearly evident in his third chapter, which is titled, "Two Learned Doctors." In this chapter he speculated that Justin Martyr and Marcion were early leaders who vied for the soul of a confused and developing religion, arguing that both were perceived as peers by the church at large. Regarding Marcion's integrity and fidelity to the authoritative texts of the church, or what Marcion argued most accurately reflected their autographs, Hall wrote, "Marcion was at worst a falsifier only in the sense in which Matthew and Luke can be called falsifiers. Everything indicates that he was a conscientious and scrupulous student of the early records, convinced that they were much corrupted, and anxious to purify them."[12]

Hall analyzed in chapter 2, which is titled "Primitive Christian Literature," some of the literature of certain apostolic fathers by providing brief surveys of *First Clement*, the epistles of Ignatius, *The First Epistle of Barnabas*, *The Epistle of Polycarp*, the *Shepherd of Hermas*, and *The Teaching of the Twelve Apostles*. He argued concerning these writings that many of them actually preceded the composition of the canonical Gospels, as well as other literature of the New Testament. Regarding his late dating of Gospel literature, whether canonical or spurious, Hall contended that the first "known" Gospel was the *Gospel of Peter*, which he believed originated from the "early part of the second century"![13] His thesis in this chapter was that the literature of the apostolic fathers reveals not just a developing canon drawn from the original writings by the apostles, but of evolving materials that had not yet solidified into what eventually became known as the canonical New Testament.

It is in chapter 1 that Hall devoted most of his attention to the subject of Papias, concluding that he was "an early investigator" of apostolic traditions, which is his title for the chapter. His treatment of Papias is largely superficial without any real investigation of his historical context, or a discussion of those who either knew him or had read his writings, with Eusebius being the lone exception. Concerning Papias's five-volume work, Hall interpreted its title as *Interpretations of the Lord's Sayings*.[14] His

12. Ibid., 94.

13. Ibid., 56.

14. Ibid., 5. There are many different translations of Papias's title. This book will refrain from an in-depth discussion on its proper translation until chapter 4. Hereafter,

defense for interpreting the word "λόγιον" as "sayings" is superficial and lacks an appreciation of its use when referring to teachings or pronouncements that were believed to be of divine origin.[15] Hall discussed Papias's context and how he should be understood by depended almost entirely upon Eusebius's exegesis and evaluation of Papias. His discussion regarding Papias's reference concerning the original writings of Mark and Matthew has some thoughtful insights regarding the church's context in the first century, but in the end he contended that Papias's reference to these writings provides today's scholar with only limited information about the final composition of what are now recognized as the canonical Gospels of Mark and Matthew.[16] Hall asserted concerning Mark's original composition that Papias's preface does not speak of the Gospel of Mark, but rather a disorderly arrangement of Peter's sermons.[17] Whereas with Matthew's initial work, Hall affirmed that it was written in Hebrew, and that its relationship to the Greek Gospel that bears his name is unclear at best.[18]

In spite of the fact that Hall appears to have been the first person to attempt to address Papias's place within the apostolic period in a lengthy book, he unfortunately strayed dramatically from his declared subject, and thus provided little original insight into the man, his context, his writings, and his views. Hall's work reveals that he was deeply influenced by the presuppositions of the Tübingen School's philosophy of religion rather than a disciplined approached to the historical data. His indebtedness to positions consistent the Tübingen school of thought is observable in his initial assertions found on the first few pages of his book,

> The easiest questions to ask are sometimes the hardest to answer, especially where religions are concerned, whose infancy is so sure to be obscure and unrecorded, and which conceal so carefully the secrets of their early growth,—not intentionally, of course, but of necessity. Before the world has awoke to their significance, or the actors themselves become aware of the role they are filling, the incidents that attended their birth have already been lost, *and it is impossible to recover them.* In the case

---

for the sake of brevity and when appropriate, Papias's work will generally be referred to as *Exposition*.

15. Ibid., 242. For a more comprehensive discussion of the significance of this word in both Jewish and Christian literature of the patristic period see Warfield, *Inspiration and Authority*, 351–407.

16. Hall, *Papias*, 18–20.

17. Ibid., 13.

18. Ibid., 14–17.

of Christianity, more than a century passed before it gained that consciousness of itself or sense of individuality which made its early hours sacred to its thought, or even the story of its founders. Then it was too late; *too late, that is to recall with any vividness such far-away occurrences, or the personalities engaged in them.* Even the twelve Apostles, with two or three exceptions, are mere names to us; still more the obscure chroniclers who so laboriously gathered for us, here and there, *whatever had survived from distant half-forgotten times.*[19]

Regrettably, any detailed analysis of the Papian fragments is conspicuously lacking in Hall's three-hundred page book. What is often present is his lack of appreciation of historical evidence, as well as his twisting of the data. One example is his assertion concerning Eusebius's statement regarding Papias's knowledge of the Johannine writings. Hall contended that "this involves many assumptions: as that Papias actually cites 1 John by name, which Eusebius does not assert."[20] What Eusebius actually wrote was, "Κέχρηται δ' ὁ αὐτὸς μαρτυρίαις ἀπὸ τῆς Ἰωάννου προτέρας ἐπιστολῆς," which Lake translated as, "The same writer used quotations from the first Epistle of John."[21] If Eusebius did not believe Papias "cited" 1 John then what did Hall believe Eusebius was possibly attempting to communicate? Was it his position that since Eusebius failed to provide a direct quote from Papias citing a Johannine fragment with chapter and verse then one cannot confidently assert that Eusebius believed that Papias knew of John's first epistle? Such a position shows that Hall possessed either very little knowledge of patristic handling of the Scriptures, or a modern standard for measuring literary dependence that is at best unwarranted or at worst biased.

Hall believed that Papias was an important apostolic figure, who was the "first church official to occupy himself in studying or collecting the records of the past."[22] He often asserted, however, that the historical data concerning Papias provided few facts from which historians and scholars could make solid conclusions. He was also convinced that Papias's search for apostolic writings was in vain, writing that "in his search for materials Papias seems to have found no written documents which covered the

19. Ibid., 1–2. Italics mine.

20. Ibid., 310.

21. A more literal translation would be, "The same [author] has employed testimonies from the prominent epistle of John." Eusebius *Ecc. Hist.* III.39.17 (LCL153: 298–99).

22. Hall, *Papias*, 4–5.

ground, or none at least that carried official weight."[23] Given the totality of Hall's convictions, one is left to wonder how he could make such sweeping conclusions while in his own opinion there appears to be only scant historical data from which to draw? With respect to his theories, however, a survey of disciplined scholars who came after him reveals that many of his conjectures could not withstand their more thorough investigations of the historical evidence. Consequently, Hall's effort has received little attention from both his peers and current scholarship.

At the turn of the twentieth century Oscar de Gebhardt, Adolf Harnack, and Theodore Zahn published a small volume titled, *Patrum Apostolicorum Opera*.[24] This work, along with other writings of the apostolic fathers, provides nineteen Papian fragments in only their original Greek and Latin texts. No introduction or analysis to Papias or his writings were provided. Similarly, Edgar J. Goodspeed also published an edition of thirteen Papian fragments in a work titled, *The Apostolic Fathers: An American Translation*.[25] Goodspeed, following the Funk-Bihlmeyer edition,[26] only provided a very brief introduction and did not provide any text of these fragments in their original languages, nor did he provide any critical commentary concerning them.

Another edition of the fragments of Papias was translated by James A. Kleist and published in 1948 as part of the sixth volume of Ancient Christian Writers series.[27] This work was edited by Johannes Quasten and Joseph C. Plumpe and produced by Newman Press. Kleist's translation is typical of other treatments of these fragments in that he does not provide any texts in the original languages, although he does provide a helpful introduction to his edition. He believed that Papias knew the apostle John and was born before 80, and more probably sometime between 61 and 71.[28] He also interpreted the title of Papias's work as *Exegesis of the Lord's Gospel*.[29] It was his opinion, although without explanation, that Papias was familiar with the "whole New Testament," and that he wrote after the

23. Ibid., 5.

24. Gebhardt, Harnack and Zahn, *Patrum Apostolicorum Opera*, 69–78.

25. Goodspeed, *The Apostolic Fathers*, 261–71.

26. Ibid., xi. The Funk-Bihlmeyer edition is a critical text of the apostolic fathers published in German in 1924 and updated in 1956. Bihlmeyer, *Die Apostolischen Väter*, 133–40.

27. *The Fragments of Papias*, trans. James C. Kleist, 6:105–24. Hereafter, this edition of the fragments of Papias will be footnoted in the following manner: Kleist, *Papias*.

28. Kleist, *Papias*, 105, 204.

29. Ibid., 105.

deaths of most of the apostles, with the possible exception of the apostle John.[30] Kleist thought that Papias's attitude toward the written word was generally Greek, meaning that when given a preference he valued first person dialogue delivered with artful rhetoric rather than simply reading a manuscript that provided no opportunity for thoughtful discourse.[31] Having authored a five-volume work, however, proves to a significant degree that Papias believed there was some merit and educational benefit to be found in the written word.[32] His translation of Papias's preface as found in Eusebius's *Ecclesiastical History* III.39.1–17 is insightful and has much to commend it, although he understood the reference to "the presbyter John" as meaning "the Old Man John."[33] He also suggested that the pre-Papian tradition concerning Mark's lack of "τάξει" should be interpreted as "verbatim" instead of "order."[34] Kleist assembled thirteen Papian fragments, giving some textual references for the more obscure fragments, while providing no commentary on any individual fragment.

Thomas Nelson and Sons also published a patristic series in 1967 containing the Papian fragments titled, *The Apostolic Fathers: A New Translation and Commentary*. The fifth volume of this series is titled *Polycarp, Martyrdom of Polycarp, Fragments of Papias*, and was translated by William Schoedel. Schoedel provided a brief introduction, and some commentary contained within footnotes throughout his translation of the Papian fragments. He questioned Papias's association with the apostle John because he doubted Irenaeus's association with both Papias and Polycarp. Based upon a superficial analysis of Irenaeus's description of his relationship to Polycarp, Schoedel concluded that "the fact remains that Irenaeus's information of Polycarp is thin indeed."[35] Regarding Irenaeus's knowledge of the apostle John, Schoedel believed that he seemed to have confused the apostle John with another highly debated character who is often referred to as "elder John."[36] He also questioned whether Polycarp and Papias were even close associates or that they shared common theological perspectives,

30. Ibid., 107.

31. Ibid., 107, 204–5 n. 7.

32. A. F. Walls wrote a very insightful article regarding Papias's obvious value and attitude toward the written word; see Walls, "Papias," 137–40.

33. Kleist, *Papias*, 106–12. See also Bauckham, *The Eyewitnesses*, 21–24.

34. Kleist, *Papias*, 112.

35. Schoedel, *The Fragments*, 89–90. Schoedel doubted that Irenaeus had any real contact with Polycarp. Consequently, he argued that Irenaeus's "misunderstanding" of the apostle John was based upon his misreading Papias.

36. Ibid., 90.

basing his conjecture on the extant writings of the two.[37] This is a common position of some scholars, which is largely based upon an argument from silence. Only meager fragments from Papias's writings have survived along with a single epistle from the hand of Polycarp; consequently, such a small literary pool is an insufficient reservoir from which to definitively prove that these two bishops were in any sense theological opponents. Polycarp and Papias have always been historically linked together. Consequently, for one to conclude that these two leaders of the Asiaic church did not share the same basic theological perspectives one would have to reject Irenaeus's personal testimony, as well as ignore the reality that their surviving works are completely different genres with different authorial purposes in order to meet the needs of different audiences. Consequently, in the absence of any objective statements implying hostility or tension between these two bishops, one should not assume or conjecture with any confidence that they were of different theological camps.

Schoedel contended that Papias knew three of the four Gospels, as well as 1 Peter and 1 John, while also asserting that he probably had no direct contact with "the apostles."[38] However, he dated Papias to have written his books ca. 110, which is early compared to some scholars, and does not prohibit the possibility that Papias might have had credible associations with some apostles. Schoedel also contended, contrary to Hall's conjectures, that Papias's work shows no knowledge of a gnostic threat.[39] This too is an unwarranted but common assumption of some scholars that will be discussed later. His edition of Papian material contains sixteen fragments, which is followed with a section containing "The Traditions of the Elders." He gave a reasonable explanation for his translation of the title of Papias's work, which was, "*An Exposition of Dominical Oracles.*"[40]

Schoedel's handling of Papian material in this series is generally very helpful. His analysis of Papias's preface as preserved by Eusebius is especially thorough and will be referenced often throughout this book. It is unfortunate, however, that his remarks are restricted to only footnotes since many of his insights and conclusions deserve a more thorough examination. The format of his footnotes is equally ill-designed since they appear in the form of a running commentary with no clear identification

37. Ibid., 90–91.

38. Ibid., 91.

39. Ibid., 91–92.

40. Ibid., 96. Papias's title and its possible interpretations are more thoroughly discussed in chapter 4.

of his progression to different Papian fragments. This format makes his treatment of Papian material difficult to follow. Schoedel republished and expanded his treatment of Papias and his writings in a chapter titled "Papias," in *Principat* 27,1. *Vorkonstantinisches Christentum; Apostolische Väter und Apologeten*, which was published in 1993. He reaffirmed in this book many of his positions while also interacting with more current scholarship on the subject of Papias. He expanded his research to cover topics such as "Papias and the Canon;" some new Papian fragments that have been translated from Armenian sources by F. Siegert; the dating of Papias's *Exposition*; the form and purpose of his work; and finally a section titled "The Theological World of Papias." While this chapter greatly enhances Schoedel's treatment of Papias, it ironically does not include majority of the fragments of Papias.[41] Schoedel's treatment of the Papian material in these two works is commendable. It is unfortunate, however, that they are provided in such disjointed formats, not to mention in two entirely different books.

Schoedel also contributed the article on Papias in the *Anchor Bible Dictionary*, which provides the clearest explanation of his positions concerning this apostolic father.[42] He clearly affirmed in this article his support of Eusebius's exegesis of Papias's preface, contending that the term "presbyter refers not to church officials but to followers of the disciples (notably John) who handed on the orthodox theological tradition."[43] The argument that this individual (i.e., the apostle John) who possessed the responsibility of preserving and transmitting orthodox traditions did not possess an "official" title or recognized status within the hierarchy of the church is a tenuous position at best, especially given that the biblical witness demonstrates that some apostles applied the term "elder" to themselves. The apostle Peter (1 Pet 5:1) and the apostle John (2 John 1; 3 John 1) both employed the term to themselves with the view that they possessed authority not only over other "presbyters" and leaders within churches, but over entire churches as well. While it may be true that they were not a certain type of "church official" (i.e., a local pastor of a specific congregation); nonetheless, they did consider themselves to be "presbyters."

Contrary to his earlier decision, Schoedel translated the title of Papias's work in the *Anchor Bible Dictionary* as "Exposition of the Lord's

41. Schoedel only provided Papias's preface as preserved by Eusebius. Schoedel, "Papias," 248–50.

42. Schoedel, "Papias," in *ABD* 5:140–42.

43. Ibid., 140.

Logia."[44] He provided no explanation for this change. He did comment, however, that Papias used the term "logia" in his title with the same sense as his reference to Mark's recording of Jesus' words and deeds, which Schoedel believed to be our canonical Gospel of Mark.[45] Unfortunately, "logia" is not really a translation at all, but only a transliteration that does not provide today's reader with a proper understanding of Papias's meaning, or the impact that such a word would have had upon his audience, both secular and Christian. Given these weaknesses, therefore, "oracles" is a better translation of the word "logia."[46]

It is in this article that Schoedel also provided one of the more objective overviews regarding Papias's five-volume work, writing that

> We do not know to what extent (if any) the shape of the book was determined by the written sources used by Papias (Mark and Matthew). We do not know what the scope or structure of the book was. We do not know whether the five divisions of the work represent anything more than perhaps an imitation of the Pentateuch, the Psalms, or some other collection. We cannot specify the genre of the work with any confidence (though perhaps the relevant parallel is offered by the *apomnemoneumata*—the memoirs—of antiquity). It is not known whether any polemical intent informs the writing of the work.[47]

If Papias's preface is to be given any weight, however, it seems that a possible "polemical intent" for his work would be to accurately identify and explain the sayings of Jesus, which implies that in some settings that the proper interpretations of Jesus' teachings were in flux. Schoedel's admission offers a helpful reminder with respect to speculations about the content and purposes of Papias's *magnum opus*, given the absence of any substantial material from his hand.

Schoedel also addressed the possible sources of Papias's traditions, and while this will be a major topic throughout this book now would be an appropriate time to broach this subject. Schoedel confidently asserted that Papias's reference to the "presbyters" is not a reference to the apostles, writing that,

> Papias mentions "the presbyters"—or more precisely, those "who had actually attended the presbyters"—as his oral sources.

44. Ibid.

45. Ibid., 142.

46. Again, on this issue see Warfield, *Inspiration and Authority*, 351–407.

47. Schoedel, "Papias," in *ABD* 5:140–41.

. . . These lines from Papias' preface can be read in a way that identifies the presbyters with the disciples. But it is more likely that Papias regarded the presbyters as followers of the disciples. If the latter is correct, Papias claims to have had his information from the disciples at third hand (*sic*). It is also possible to read the passage in a way that identifies the apostle John with the presbyter John. *But this reading also seems very doubtful* (Schoedel 1967: 98). Presumably, then, Aristion and the presbyter John were regarded as personal "disciples" of Jesus who were not among the twelve; and presumably John was called "the Presbyter" (whereas Aristion was not) to distinguish him from the apostle, who had just been named[48]

This interpretation of Papias's preface originated with Eusebius (a writer whose native tongue was Greek) and is a commonly accepted by some. Consequently, to argue that this interpretation cannot possibly be correct would be a vain endeavor. Nevertheless, the essential question regarding Eusebius's exegesis is whether it provides the most natural reading of Papias's preface. Schoedel and others who accept Eusebius's exegesis base their argument that Papias meant to distinguish the character known as "John the elder" from the apostle John upon Papias's employment of the article ὁ before the term πρεσβύτερος. Generally speaking, their position is that Papias meant to distinguish John the elder from the previously mentioned apostle John by his employment of the article. What is so ironic about this position is that it is promoted in the face of normal Greek grammar that dictates that such syntax be interpreted to mean the exact opposite of Schoedel's position. Incredibly, the use of an article (i.e., "ὁ" before "πρεσβύτερος Ἰωάννης") would mean that Papias actually meant to identify "the presbyter John" as the same John from among the previously mentioned group of presbyters, which is an interpretation that even Schoedel himself recognized. Such syntax is referred to as an "anaphoric article." Regarding this use of the article, Daniel Wallace wrote, "The anaphoric article is the article denoting previous reference. (It derives its name from the Greek verb ἀναφέρειν, 'to bring back, to bring up.') The first mention of the substantive is usually anarthrous because it is merely being introduced. But the subsequent mentions of it use the article, for the article is now pointing back to *the* substantive previously mentioned. *It is the most common use of the article and the easiest usage to identify.*"[49]

48. Ibid., 141. Italics mine.

49. Wallace, *The Basics*, 98. Italics mine. A. T. Robertson describes the anaphoric use of the article as "very frequent." Robertson, *A Grammar*, 762. Wallace identified

Arguing, therefore, that Papias was simply identifying the character known as John the elder from the apostle John, or that the article is a reference to his office and not a reference to the previously mentioned John is a poorly defended position. Regarding the syntactical use of simple identification with the article, Wallace wrote, "Simple Identification. *Definition*: The article is frequently used to distinguish one individual from another. *This is our 'drip-pan' category and should be used only as a last resort.* Pragmatically, unless the article fits under one of the other six categories of the individualizing article or under the generic use (or one of the special uses), it is acceptable to list it as 'the article of simple identification.'"[50] The salient point regarding this common use of the article with respect to substantives is that when scholars base their interpretations of Papias's preface upon Eusebius's exegesis, they ironically adopt the least defensible position because it ignores the common function of the article in the context of previously mentioned substantives. In reality, Papias's employment of the article should lead the exegete directly back to the John who was a prestigious member of the previously mentioned group of presbyters who were also apostles.[51] Schoedel is not alone in this unusual exegesis. Similarly, Johannes Munck failed to recognized Papias's employment of the anaphoric article, stating that

> But the attempts that have been made to identify John the apostle with "John the presbyter" must be rejected. It would be *unnatural* to describe the same person in this way with an interval of barely more than a line. There seems to be no reason for such an artificial device, when it would have been quite sufficient for Papias to have referred to the apostle together with Aristion. . . . We must assume that the other John, who was both a "disciple of

---

other common uses of the article as "Monadic ('One of a Kind' or 'Unique' Article); "Well-Known ('Celebrity' Article)," both of which could apply to Papias's context. It may be that Papias's employment of the definite article served double duty. Some, however, argue that Papias was simply distinguishing the character often referred to as "the elder John" from the apostle John. Lightfoot, *Essays*, 146. But then one is left to ask, who would have been this "one of a kind" or "well known" elder that Papias might have referred, and about whom no other late first-century or early second-century record has been preserved? Moreover, it seems very unlikely that Papias, an actual disciple of the apostle John, would have referred to any "John" of the churches in Asia Minor as "John, *the well known* elder" in "contradistinction" to the even more well known apostle John.

50. Wallace, *The Basics*, 96. Italics mine.

51. Eusebius himself employed an anaphoric article upon his second mentioning of Aristion, see Eusebius *Ecc. Hist.* III.39.4–5 (LCL 153: 292).

the Lord" and a "presbyter," but not an apostle (nor an apostle's disciple) *being the only duplicate in the list of names*, had to be distinguished from his great namesake by a description that indicated that this was John the non-apostle.[52]

It defies explanation that people educated in Greek syntax might argue so confidently the exact opposite of what normal Greek syntax dictates regarding use of the definite article within the context of repeated substantives. Contrary to Munck's confident assertion, what may seem "unnatural" to some would seem extremely natural, if not expected, to Papias's audience. If the character known as "John the elder" was in fact simply a presbyter of a local church in Asia Minor and not the apostle John, then it would have been completely natural for Papias to have distinguish him by referring to the city of his bishopric (e.g., bishop John of Ephesus, or elder John of Smyrna), while in the process *not* employing a definite article at all.[53] But if Papias wanted to identify John as a member of the previously mentioned apostolic colloquium, then identifying him as "*the* presbyter John" would be the most natural grammatical construction to do so. Although both Schoedel and Munck[54] recognized the possibility that Papias was identifying the elder John as the apostle John, they both reject this interpretation and described it as "very doubtful" and "unnatural," the result being that it is they, while relying upon Eusebius, who have unjustifiably and unnaturally distanced this important apostolic father from any associations with the apostolic generation.

Schoedel concluded his article with a discussion regarding "Papias and the New Testament." He believed that Papias's preface referred to the canonical Gospels of Mark and Matthew. He also rejected the theory that Matthew wrote his Gospel in an Aramaic style rather than in the Aramaic language.[55] He insightfully discussed the possibility that other Gospels existed and may have competed for equal authority with the canonical Gospels. He also addressed the question of whether Papias knew of the other two canonical Gospels, concluding that the evidence that Papias knew of the Gospel of Luke "is fragile."[56] Regarding the question of whether Papias knew of the Gospel of John, Schoedel speculated that the possibility of the

52. Munck, "Presbyters," 238. Italics mine.

53. John J. Gunther referred to Eusebius's John as "John of Patmos." Gunther, "The Elder John," 13.

54. Munck, "Presbyters," 236.

55. Schoedel, "Papias," in *ABD* 5:141–42.

56. Ibid., 142.

existence of the character commonly referred to as "John the elder" (i.e., a bishop named John who was not one of the twelve apostles) provides "legitimate" questions for "assessing claims made for the authorship of the various writings attributed to John in the NT."[57] Lastly, Schoedel briefly addressed the *pericope adulterae* and Eusebius's claim that Papias made use of the epistles of 1 Peter and 1 John. Regarding Papias's exposure to these two epistles, he concluded that, "It seems unlikely that the theology of either of these two writings influenced Papias deeply."[58] It seems rather odd that one who previously concluded that we know virtually nothing at all about the scope, genre, and purpose of Papias's five-volume work would make such a confident assertion.[59] What is knowable is that Eusebius, who presumably had access to Papias's books, observed that Papias "used quotations" from Peter's "prominent" epistle, thus indicating its existence.[60] Whether Papias was influenced heavily, slightly, or negatively is simply unknowable, although one might infer from Eusebius's comment that Papias derived some benefit from 1 Peter (as well as from 1 John). Schoedel also speculated that "Papias' Christianity was evidently non-Pauline, but it was not necessarily anti-Pauline."[61] Similarly to his position concerning the possible influence or lack thereof of 1 Peter upon Papias, his assertion concerning Paul's influence on Papias is entirely based upon silence because of the lack of available material from the hand of Papias, a paucity that Schoedel himself recognized. Regardless the speculative nature of a few of his positions, Schoedel is an important Papian scholar and many of his conclusions and theories are insightful and worthy of consideration; consequently, he is regularly referenced throughout this work.

Josef Kürzinger wrote a book in 1983 titled, *Papias von Hierapolis und die Evangelien des Neuen Testaments*. His book is the fourth volume of the *Schriftenreihe der Katholischen Universität Eichstätt* series from the University's department of Philosophy and Theology. Kürzinger provided in this volume twenty-five Papian fragments,[62] as well as an extensive bibliography of research published from 1960 to 1981 that to some extent concerned Papias and his writings.[63] Kürzinger's book begins with four

57. Ibid.

58. Ibid.

59. Ibid., 140–41.

60. Eusebius *Ecc. Hist.* III.39.17 (LCL 153: 298–99).

61. Schoedel, "Papias," in *ABD* 5:142.

62. Kürzinger, *Papias*, 91–138.

63. Ibid., 145–227. This bibliography also includes a few annotations on certain works.

chapters; each being a previously published article by Kürzinger on related issues concerning Papias's comments on the Gospels of Matthew and Mark.

One of the more significant contributions from Kürzinger's work is found in his third chapter titled, "The Statement of Papias of Hierapolis as to the Literary Form of the Gospel of Mark." Kürzinger demonstrated in this chapter that as Papias discussed Mark's Gospel he was engaging in literary and/or rhetorical criticism, which was a common academic practice within educated Grecian circles of his day.[64] However, the contribution that Kürzinger is most noted for is his theory that when Papias discussed the "*Erstgestalt*" or "first-form" of Matthew's Gospel, he did not mean that Matthew wrote in Aramaic, but rather that he composed his Gospel in Greek with a Jewish rhetorical style. He defended his position in this manner:

> Wenn man beachtet, daß Papias in all seinen Ausdrücken in der Terminologie des zeitgenössischen hellenistischen Schrifttums sich bewegt, wird man keinen Zweifel mehr haben, daß er auch den Terminus διάλεκτος im Sinn der Rhetorick gebraucht. Nicht um das Interesse an der anderen Sprache geht es ihm, wenn er mit Ἑβραΐδι διαλέκτῳ die σύνταξις der Logien des Mt kennzeichnen will, also nicht etwa um das Aramäische oder Hebräische im Unterschied zum Grieshischen des Mk, sondern um die andere—ἑρμηνεία, eben jene, wie sie nach seiner Auffassung und Kenntnis der Literatur des Judentums eigentümlich ist.[65]

Some scholars find Kürzinger's theory attractive, primarily because they believe it solves the problem of the relationship between the canonical Greek Gospel of Matthew and Papias's reference to an Aramaic Gospel of Matthew. However, his theory does not adequately account for Eusebius's understanding of the origin and language of Matthew's initial Gospel. Eusebius wrote concerning it that "Yet nevertheless of all those who had been with the Lord only Matthew and John have left us their recollections, and tradition says that they took to writing perforce. Matthew had first preached to Hebrews, and when he was on the point of going to others *he transmitted in writing in his native language the Gospel according to himself,*

---

64. Ibid., 43–67.

65. Ibid., 21, see also 39. This theory was also adopted by Robert Gundry; see Gundry, *Matthew*, 618–20. Throughout this book "Hebraic" and "Aramaic" will be used as synonyms when discussing the language of Matthew's initial Gospel.

and thus supplied by writing the lack of his own presence to those from whom he was sent."[66]

Regarding this tradition Eusebius stated that it was not his assumption that Matthew had written an Aramaic Gospel, but rather that it was the church's tradition that undoubtedly reached back into the first century as corroborated by Papias. Consequently, Kürzinger's theory appears to not only be based upon questionable exegesis, but upon the assumption that later patristic scholars who read Papias and/or other early church sources concerning the origin of Matthew's Aramaic Gospel (e.g., Eusebius, Irenaeus,[67] and Jerome[68]) simply misunderstood those sources.

Kürzinger, in his second chapter, attempted to address Irenaeus's understanding on the composition of Matthew's first Gospel. He believed that while Irenaeus depended upon Papias for his understanding of this work, Irenaeus also had access to other sources knowledgeable about its origins.[69] Irenaeus's comments (albeit in Latin) about Matthew's Aramaic Gospel can be found in *Against Heresies* III.1.1. Fortunately, however, his statements, which were originally written in Greek, have also been preserved in Eusebius's *Ecclesiastical History* V.8.1–2.[70] Irenaeus's comments do not mention Papias or anyone else for that matter as his source for this tradition, whether literary or oral. Kürzinger's position that Irenaeus had depended upon Papias *as a source* for his impressions about this early Gospel is certainly reasonable, his discussion, however, seems to imply that Irenaeus had relied *exclusively* upon Papias's writings in order to form his opinions about Matthew's early work. Consequently, he appeared to ignore the important fact that Irenaeus also had personally interacted with Polycarp, and probably others who were well aware of the church's tradition regarding the composition of Matthew's initial Gospel. Such an interaction would mean that Irenaeus's understanding of this Aramaic work was not only based upon his reading of certain trustworthy sources (e.g., Papias), but also upon the private discussions he had and/or the public lectures he heard from at least one other apostolic father (i.e., Polycarp).

Concerning his theory that Matthew wrote his only Gospel in a Jewish literary style, Kürzinger himself acknowledged that at times Irenaeus

---

66. Eusebius *Ecc. Hist.* III.24.5–6 (LCL 153:251). Italics mine.

67. Ibid. V.8.2 (LCL 153:455).

68. Jerome *Illustrious Men* III (NPNF2 3:362).

69. Kürzinger, *Papias*, 36.

70. Regrettably, *Against Heresies* predominately survives to this day only in Latin and Armenian manuscripts.

understood the phrase Ἑβραΐδι διάλεκτῳ to refer to a spoken language rather than a rhetorical style. He argued, however, that with respect to Irenaeus's comments about the composition of Matthew's initial Gospel, modern scholars have simply failed to appreciate Irenaeus's shift in meaning. Concerning this misunderstanding, Kürzinger wrote, "Gewiß, es finden sich bei Irenäus auch Stellen, in denen διάλεκτος in erster Linie den Sinn von Sprache hat. . . . Und da sich für Papias doch überzeugend die Verwendung von διάλεκτος als Ausdruck der Rhetorick aufzeigen läßt, wird ihn auch Irenäus so verstanden haben. Ja, man möchte aus dem betonten τῇ ἰδίᾳ αὐτῶν διαλέκτῳ | heraushörne, daß auch Irenäus damit die Besonderheit des Stils der—Εβραῖοι, das ist der Juden, im Auge hat."[71] The reason why many ancient and modern scholars have failed to appreciate the strength of Kürzinger's theory regarding Irenaeus's (as well as Papias's) apparent shift in meaning is that his explanation simply does not reflect the most obvious interpretation of Irenaeus's or Papias's words. Moreover, since Kürzinger failed to provide other examples where similar shifts in meaning have occurred his position, while notable, has not received a considerable following. Concerning this particular theory of Kürzinger D. A. Carson and Douglas Moo wrote, "But however possible, it is not the natural way to read the passage, and it is certainly not what later church fathers understood. Without exception, they held that the apostle Matthew wrote canonical Matthew and that it was first written in Semitic. That is true, for instance of Irenaeus (*Adv. Haer.* 3.1.1, quoted in Eusebius, *H.E.* 5.8.2), Tertullian (*Adv. Marc.*, 4.2), Origen (quoted by Eusebius, *H.E.* 6.25.3–6), Eusebius himself (*H. E.* 3.24.5–6), and Jerome (*De vir. ill.* 3)."[72]

Kürzinger's fourth chapter discusses the title and purpose of Papias's *Exposition*. He additionally interacted with the work of well known scholars such as Preuschen, Schwartz, and Harnack. Kürzinger translated Papias's title as: *Sammlung der Logien über den Herrn.*[73] Although aware that ἐξήγησις is normally translated as "an explanation,"[74] Kürzinger translated ἐξήγησις as "Sammlung," which in English is usually translated "collection." He based his argument for this translation upon Grecian linguistic usage, the rhetorical function of titles, and word ordering; nevertheless, his explanations failed to provide a satisfactory defense for this

71. Ibid., 35–36.

72. Carson and Moo, *An Introduction*, 145.

73. Kürzinger, *Papias*, 83. In English his translation of Papias's title reads as *A Collection of the Oracles of the Lord*.

74. Ibid., 70–71.

translation, for none of them sufficiently explains why ἐξήγησις should be interpreted as "a collection" instead of *"An Exposition" of the Oracles of the Lord.*[75] Moreover, given that Papias already possessed or knew of at least two canonical Gospels, i.e., Mark and Luke[76] (and more likely all four) what possible function would a simple "collection" of sayings from the Lord serve the Asiatic church. If Papias's purpose, however, was to explain the history of the Lord's oracles, as well as the meaning of specific sayings, then interpreting ἐξήγησις as "an explanation" would make perfect sense for the title of such a work.

While some of Kürzinger's positions are debatable, his research has shed considerable light on Papias through his analysis of Papias's preface as preserved by Eusebius. One of the more important contributions of his work is that it adequately demonstrates that Papias felt competent enough to discuss in rhetorical terms the credibility and value of the Gospels of Mark and Matthew. Consequently, one could infer from Papias's effort that he had achieved a respectable level of academic training. Such an inference is supported by the fact that Papias's literary abilities enabled him to compose a five-volume work that not only influenced his own generation, but continued to influence Christian pastors, theologians, and apologists in the centuries that followed. Although Papias's *Exposition* and the theology it contained fell out of favor with those who inevitably became important leaders in the later patristic era (e.g., Eusebius, Jerome, et al.), one should not conclude with Eusebius that Papias's fall from favor necessarily proves that he was a man of little intellectual power or academic training.

A book titled *Papias von Hierapolis* by Ulrich H. J. Körtner was also published in 1983. Since Körtner's work was published in the same year as Kürzinger's it should not be surprising that he shows little awareness of Kürzinger's book.[77] Körtner's compilation of Papian material contains twenty-two fragments.[78] Similarly to this book, Körtner's monograph attempts to address themes relating to Papias and the extant fragments of his writings. Unlike the book before you, however, Körtner supplied in Greek his own version of the collection of Papian fragments along with their translations in German. Unfortunately, however, his Greek texts are

75. Ibid., 76–77.

76. An explanation of Papias's possible knowledge of Luke's Gospel will come in the following chapters.

77. Körtner did occasionally cite articles by Kürzinger that later became part of Kürzinger's book.

78. Körtner, *Papias*, 50–71.

handwritten, which modern readers may find as somewhat of a distraction. Similarly to the Papian list of Lightfoot and Holmes, Körtner placed Eusebian material at the head of his compilation, while placing Irenaeus's reference to Papias as his twelfth fragment. Körtner also provided a history of the many different editions of the fragments of Papias, beginning with Halloix's edition and ending with the list of Funk-Bihlmeyer; additionally he compared the order of the fragments as they are found in each of these editions.[79] He was of the opinion that Papias wrote much earlier then some assume, writing that "vor allem die Analyse der polemischen Funktion der Papiasbücher hat gezeigt, daß der Hierapolitaner eher um 110 n.Chr. als gegen Mitte des 2. Jh.s seine Darstellung der Jesusgeschichten geschrieben hat."[80] He also did not believe that Papias wrote his five-volume work before the compositions of the canonical Gospels.[81] Believing that Papias wrote early in the second century, he contended that Papias was not a hearer of the apostle John but rather was a hearer of Eusebius's John the elder, basing much of his position upon Eusebius's exegesis and opinions about Papias.[82] He additionally argued that Irenaeus also confused the son of Zebedee with Eusebius's John the elder; thus confusing church historians and theologians for centuries to follow. He explained his theory in this manner, "Daß Andreas v. Cäsarea im 6./7. Jh. von einem Presbyter Johannes neben dem Apostel nichts weiß, ist nun andererseits leicht erklärlich, da schon Ireanäus den Presbyter Johannes mit dem Zebedaiden identifizierte, ferner schon Justin, Clemens Alexandrinus und Meilto v. Sardes den Apokalyptiker für den Apostel hielten.[83] Clearly, therefore, Körtner's view of Papias's possible knowledge of the apostle John was significantly influenced by Eusebius, while also marginalizing Irenaeus's personal testimony about Papias.[84]

Körtner should be commended for his monograph and his attention to detail with respect to important issues surrounding the fragments of Papias. Examples of such are his attention to exegetical and textual issues found within his list of twenty-two Papian fragments, and his word studies of significant vocabulary such as πρεσβύτερος and λόγια.[85] Körtner also

79. Ibid., 44–49.
80. Ibid., 225.
81. Ibid., 227.
82. Ibid., 122–29.
83. Ibid., 128.
84. Ibid., 44–49.
85. Ibid., 114–22.

addressed many other issues regarding Papias, such as his chiliasm, the history of Christianity throughout the second century, and the "Johannine Circle,"[86] just to mention a few. Although a reader may be distracted by the use of handwritten Greek texts found throughout his monograph, this should not cause one to regard his work lightly. Consequently, it is a helpful aid to any who wish to research Papian material.

More recently the Loeb Classical Library has added collections of the Apostolic Fathers to its series. Volume 25 contains a section devoted to Papian material under the title "Fragments of Papias and Quadratus," which was translated by Bart Ehrman.[87] Ehrman also provided a brief introduction to his translations in which he stated that Papias lived from 60 to 130. He translated the title of Papias's five-volume work as, *Expositions of the Sayings of the Lord*, which he believed to have been written between 110–140.[88] Although without providing any detailed explanation, Ehrman doubted that Papias knew any of the Lord's disciples. His introduction, however, does address Papias's chiliastic theology and its relation to Irenaeus.[89] Following the normal format for the Loeb series, Ehrman provided the Papian fragments in their original languages along with their English translations in a chronological order. He also provided brief notes regarding the textual families of Eusebius's *Ecclesiastical History* with respect to chapter 39 of book three, which is where the majority of Eusebius's discussion about Papias is found. Ehrman, as indicating by the title, also included a fragment from Quadratus that was also preserved by Eusebius together with his assembling of Papian material. The edition of the Loeb Classical Library Series is a particular helpful tool for anyone who desires direct access to the Greek and Latin texts of the more well known Papian fragments.

Lastly, but certainly not of the least importance, is the spectrum of work complied by J. B. Lightfoot, J. R. Harmer, and Michael W. Holmes.[90] A three-volume work titled *Supernatural Religion: An Inquiry into the Reality*

86. Ibid., 197–202.

87. *Papias and Quadratus* (LCL 25:85–118).

88. Ibid., 86–87. Ehrman's introduction provides little critical discussion of the generally recognized dating of Papias and his writings. Clearly, if Papias lived from 60 to 130 then he could not have written his *Exposition* as late as 140.

89. Ibid., 88.

90. These works are addressed at this point because they should be discussed together in spite of the fact that they span more than a century. For a more thorough explanation of the history of the editions of *The Apostolic Fathers* from these scholars see Holmes, *The Apostolic Fathers: Diglot Edition*, ix–xii.

of Divine Revelation was anonymously published in England in 1874.[91] This book and its subsequent revisions were most likely the efforts of Walter Richard Cassels, although he never publicly claimed responsibility for being its author.[92] This particular book touched upon many topics dealing with the history of the early church and its leaders. In response to *Supernatural Religion*, J. B. Lightfoot wrote a series of articles addressing conjectures found throughout these volumes. These articles were published in *The Contemporary Review* in intervals, beginning in December 1874 and continuing until May 1878, and afterwards, with the help of J. R. Harmer, they were combined, edited, and published into a single volume work in 1889 under the title *Essays on the Work Entitled "Supernatural Religion."*[93] In response, the author of *Supernatural Religion* also wrote another work titled, *A Reply to Dr. Lightfoot's Essays*, which was also published in 1889.[94] Lightfoot's *Essays on the Work Entitled "Supernatural Religion,"* contained two chapters solely dedicated to the subject of Papias and the assumptions made about him by the author of *Supernatural Religion*. Before his response to *Supernatural Religion*, Lightfoot had previously published a two-volume work, which was originally printed in 1869 and titled, *The Apostolic Fathers Part I. S. Clement of Rome. A Revised Text with Introductions, Notes, Dissertation, and Translations.*[95] This series was expanded in 1885 to five volumes with the addition of Lightfoot's work on the letters of Ignatius and Polycarp.[96] Material from and about Papias, however, was not included in any of these volumes. A couple of years after Lightfoot's death, J. R. Harmer abridged Lightfoot's work on the apostolic fathers into a single book. Along with Lightfoot's writings, "Harmer also contributed the texts with translations of the *Epistle of Barnabas*, the *Shepherd of Hermas*, and the *Epistle of Diognetus*."[97] He was also responsible for introducing twenty Papian fragments into this volume, doing so by selecting fragments from and about Papias that Lightfoot discussed in *Essays on the Work Entitled "Supernatural Religion."*[98] Michael W. Holmes joined the work of Lightfoot

---

91. *Supernatural Religion: An Inquiry into the Reality of Divine Revelation* (London: Longmans, Green, 1874). Hereafter, *Supernatural Religion*.

92. Nash, "Supernatural Religion," 166–67.

93. Lightfoot, *Essays*, vii–ix.

94. *A Reply to Dr. Lightfoot's Essays* (London: Longmans, Green, 1889).

95. Lightfoot, *The Apostolic Fathers Part I*, v.

96. Ibid., *The Apostolic Fathers Part II*.

97. Holmes, *The Apostolic Fathers: Diglot Edition*, x.

98. Lightfoot and Harmer, *Apostolic Fathers*, 513–24.

and Harmer in 1989 when he revised and updated the English of their one-volume book.[99] The need to revise Lightfoot's version of *The Apostolic Fathers* also provided the opportunity to include expanded introductions and new information from discoveries of additional texts and material.[100] Holmes also added within this new edition six new Papian fragments to the collection of Lightfoot and Harmer.[101] Holmes was invited to reformat the single-volume version of *The Apostolic Fathers* into a diglot edition, a format that is a significant improvement to earlier editions of Lightfoot and Harmer.[102] This edition is a significant improvement primarily because it allows the Greek texts to be immediately compared with their English translations without having to turn a page.[103] The latest version of this work was released as a third edition in 2007.[104] Holmes is to be commended for his part in keeping Lightfoot and Harmer's work current and convenient for those interested in researching this earlier portion of the patristic period, as well as the development of the New Testament canon.

The influence of Lightfoot's scholarship in New Testament and patristic studies can hardly be overestimated. It is his two chapters on Papias in his book *Essays on the Entitled Supernatural Religion* that are of significant importance to this subject. Lightfoot had no trouble believing that Papias in fact had been "a hearer of John."[105] Concerning the evidence of Papias's relationship to John and his importance as a witness to the apostolic generation, Lightfoot wrote, "These two fathers are closely connected together in the earliest tradition. Papias, writes Irenaeus, was 'a hearer of John and a companion of Polycarp.' On the latter point we may frankly accept the

99. Lightfoot and Harmer, *Apostolic Fathers*, 2nd ed., viii–ix. Holmes also admitted that in some cases interpretations/translations of certain texts had been changed, and in such cases Lightfoot's interpretation had been relegated to footnotes.

100. Holmes, *The Apostolic Fathers: Diglot Edition*, x.

101. Lightfoot and Harmer, *Apostolic Fathers*, 2nd ed., 325–27.

102. Holmes, *The Apostolic Fathers: Diglot Edition*, x.

103. Ibid., 556–91. Some fragments are in Latin, Armenian, and Arabic. Fragments in both Armenian and Arabic were not provided in this edition even though their English translations are provided.

104. Holmes, *Apostolic Fathers,* 3rd ed., 307–29. Along with Greek and Latin texts, this edition also includes Armenian and Arabic texts of certain Papian fragments.

105. Lightfoot, *Essays*, 142. Throughout this book the identification of a "John the elder" (unless otherwise clearly stated) will not refer to the John who was a son of Zebedee and one of the original twelve apostles who followed Jesus. Instead, "John the elder" will refer to the person Eusebius claimed to have discovered but for whom no credible historical reference can be found. For the purpose of variety, John the elder may also be referred to as "elder John," "the elder John," or "Eusebius's elder John."

evidence of Irenaeus. A pupil of Polycarp was not likely to be misinformed here. . . . Yet, even if Papias was not a personal disciple of St. John, still his age and country place him in more or less close connection with the traditions of this Apostle; and it is this fact which gives importance to his position and teaching."[106]

Lightfoot translated the title of Papias's writings as "*Exposition of Oracles of the Lord*," which he argued was composed ca. 130 or later.[107] He also believed that not only did Papias personally know John the son of Zebedee, but that he also knew Eusebius's "John the elder," which Lightfoot believed was a name the primitive church gave this individual in "contradistinction" to the apostle John.[108] The apostle John was not the only member of Jesus' original twelve disciples that Lightfoot believed Papias had met. He also believed that Papias possibly knew the apostles Philip and Andrew as well.[109] He estimated Papias to have been born ca. 60–70, and that he was slightly older than Polycarp.[110] Lightfoot doubted, however, that Papias was martyred in 164 as indicated in the *Chronicon Paschale*, or that he had even lived to see the death of Polycarp,[111] arguing that if Eusebius had any information regarding Papias's death then he would have been obliged to provide it.[112]

Lightfoot was of the opinion that the dominant purpose of Papias's *magnum opus* was to exegete and explain, or give commentary, on the sayings of Jesus found in a body of work already in circulation.[113] What makes

106. Ibid., 142.

107. Ibid., 150. Lightfoot also suggested that a more literal translation of Papias's title would be "*Exposition of Dominical Oracles*." Ibid., 155.

108. Ibid., 146.

109. Ibid., 146, 149 n. 3.

110. Ibid., 150.

111. Lightfoot argued that if Papias had died in 164, then his birth "could hardly" have been before 80, which in his estimation would have made Papias too young to have known the apostle John, or to have remembered anything about him with any credibility. Ibid., 147. He admitted, however, that these dates did not demand that it was impossible for Papias to have known the apostle John (ibid., 147 n. 3). It should be noted that the *CP* places Papias's death in 163. See fragment 16, p. 233, of this book for further analysis.

112. Ibid., 147–50. A significant weakness in Lightfoot's treatment of Papias was his assumption that if Eusebius had possessed additional information concerning Papias that he would have been willing to provide it. Such optimism in Eusebius's treatment of Papias is clearly unwarranted. For a discussion regarding this subject see appendix 1.

113. Ibid., 155–58.

Lightfoot's analysis interesting is that he believed Papias felt compelled to write his commentary of explanations in order to provide "correct interpretation of an existing narrative."[114] In other words, Papias was concerned with securing orthodoxy as he had received it from the apostles.[115] Lightfoot did not ignore the fact that Papias had discussed oral traditions, rather he contended that Papias employed such traditions to "confirm and illustrate his explanations" of them.[116] Consequently, he believed that if Papias's work had survived to this day it would be "highly important" since it would have provided information about what the early church viewed as "false exegesis," as well as exegesis that Papias viewed as "true."[117] Lightfoot speculated that gnostics were a possible major opponent of orthodox Christianity that provided imperfect or false exegesis on the oracles of the Lord.[118]

Lightfoot was also of the opinion that Papias possessed our canonical Gospels.[119] More specifically, he understood Papias's cryptic quote concerning Matthew's original Hebraic Gospel to imply that it was translated and in circulation until an "official" Greek version of Matthew's Gospel went public.[120] Additionally, he believed that Papias's reference to the "oracles of the Lord" not only referred to the Gospel narratives, but that it was also Papias's affirmation that these narratives were commensurate with the rest of the Scriptures since the Greek term λόγιον was used by both Jewish and Christian authors to refer to the divine pronouncements of God before, during, and after the composition of the New Testament.[121]

Lastly, Lightfoot provided an insightful discussion regarding the *pericope adulterae*.[122] He theorized that this pericope was not originally contained in John's Gospel, but was later added by a "transcriber" who was familiar with Papias's work and provided the *pericope adulterae* in the form of a "catena" as an illustration of Jesus' statement in John 8:15, which was Jesus' critical evaluation that Jewish leaders were unable to make proper moral judgments. His theory regarding the placement of this

114. Ibid., 157.
115. Ibid., 160.
116. Ibid., 158.
117. Ibid., 160.
118. Ibid., 160–61.
119. Ibid., 163–69.
120. Ibid., 169–70.
121. Ibid., 172–74.
122. Ibid., 203–5.

pericope as found in John's Gospel is attractive, and while it will not be addressed in this book, his conjecture is worthy of further consideration.[123] Lightfoot concluded his second chapter about Papias with a discussion on the subject of Papias's possible awareness of the Fourth Gospel and the book of Revelation.[124]

Lightfoot's treatment of Papias in these two chapters is insightful. While reading his work, however, it is important for the reader to look beyond its polemical nature. Lightfoot was not merely providing his research on Papias, he was also attempting to defend English Christianity from the quickly encroaching influences of the Tübingen School as promoted by the author of *Supernatural Religion*. Many of Lightfoot's arguments are weighty, while others are as speculative as those of his adversary. Regardless of the polemic arguments found in *Essays on the Work Entitled "Supernatural Religion*, his work provides a wealth of information and ideas about the nature of Christianity at the close of the apostolic generation and the beginning of the second century. Consequently, both Harmer and Holmes have done Lightfoot a great service by adding "The Fragments of Papias" to the body of work he initiated.

SECONDARY WORKS

While the above primary works are essential to any research concerning the fragments of Papias, there are other works that also provide significant contributions to developing a proper understanding of Papias and his place in the patristic period. These secondary works may not deal directly with Papias, or they may only deal with a single element regarding him and/or his material. Their contributions, however, are valuable. One such work is Frank Grant Lewis's book titled, *The Fourth Gospel: Its Extent, Meaning, and Value*, published in 1908. A better title for the book would have been *Irenaeus's Knowledge of the Fourth Gospel and Its Extent, Meaning, and Value*, for one of Lewis's primary focuses in his book was to analyze Irenaeus's knowledge of the author of the Gospel of John, even though he clearly stated that he did not intend to answer a "single

123. Ibid., 204–5. I would add to Lightfoot's hypothesis only that it is possible that Papias may have been the author of this catena, which he might have placed in the vicinity of John 8.15 in his personal copy of the Fourth Gospel. Regarding the possibility that Papias may have served as the personal amanuensis of John see the discussions of fragments 19 and 26.

124. Ibid., 202–16.

question" concerning its "authorship."[125] While this may have been his intent, nevertheless, his work has much to offer for answering this question. The "critical" issue for Lewis was: "Did Irenaeus have actual knowledge of Christian affairs in Asia at the close of the first century?"[126] In order to answer this question, he systematically reviewed and analyzed all references to the Gospel of John in Irenaeus's *Against Heresies* along with all references to any John found within the context of quotes, references, and allusions to the Fourth Gospel.[127]

On the basis of his research Lewis contended that Irenaeus clearly knew of the Fourth Gospel (including chapter 21); that he saw it as authoritative; and that it was the work of a John of Asia who lived during the late apostolic period. Consequently, Lewis argued that Irenaeus "recognized only one John of apostolic times," and that this John was a "disciple of the Lord," and an "apostle;" and finally, that he was "John, the son of Zebedee."[128] Regarding these observations and conclusions Lewis wrote, "This cumulation(*sic*) of evidence places Irenaeus' opinion beyond doubt. The author of the fourth gospel was as certainly an apostle for him as though he had taken a page, to state, to argue, and prove the point. He would have been astonished if he could have known that any reader would ever think otherwise. One can hardly believe that those who have been in doubt about the matter have read Irenaeus."[129]

Consequently, Lewis argued that "Accordingly, when we take into account that he (Irenaeus) recognized only one John other than John the Baptist and John Mark and that this one John, on the basis of Irenaeus' own testimony rightly understood, was an 'apostle,' the conditions which his testimony as a whole imposes are satisfied only by the conclusion that the son of Zebedee was, for Irenaeus, the author of the fourth gospel."[130] Given the thoroughness of his research, however, some may have trouble accepting his theories regarding the final composition of the Gospel of John as it is known today.[131] Regardless of these theories, Lewis concluded

125. Lewis, *Fourth Gospel*, 5.

126. Ibid.

127. Ibid., 10–15.

128. Ibid., 17–18. Lewis also acknowledged Irenaeus's awareness of John Mark and John the Baptist.

129. Ibid., 19.

130. Ibid., 23.

131. Ibid., 33–38, 60–62. Lewis speculated that the Gospel of John as it is known today was published in the middle of the second century and was drawn from a pool of literature compiled from sermons and "booklets" authored by the apostle John. He

in the affirmative that because of his relationship with Polycarp, Irenaeus was a well versed and trustworthy witness to the affairs of the church in Asia Minor at the end of the first century.[132] Lewis's work, consequently, is not only a powerful tool for investigating Irenaeus's attitude toward the Gospel of John or his knowledge of its author, but also for developing a clearer picture of Irenaeus's relationship to the history of the church and its leaders at the close of the apostolic period.

John Chapman wrote in 1911 a book titled *John the Presbyter and the Fourth Gospel*, which was published by Clarendon Press. Chapman's book attempted to answer the Johannine question by an analysis of Papias's preface as preserved by Eusebius. His work largely focused upon what Papias meant by the word "presbyter." In order to correctly understand Papias's meaning, he argued that one must also investigate Irenaeus's employment of the term.[133] While this might be helpful for understanding the meaning of this word in the late second-century church, to rely exclusively upon Irenaeus for understanding Papias's meaning has its perils. The most obvious problem with this approach is that it is clearly anachronistic since Irenaeus wrote after the period in which Papias ministered. Consequently, Chapman's theory ignores the possibility of any morphological evolution in the term "presbyter" during one of most important periods of the church's development.

Chapman, with respect to Papias's use of this word, theorized that he did not employ it to refer to an office of the church but rather in a strictly general sense, such as when referring to one's age. Chapman argued that, "It is clear that Papias means 'οἱ πρεσβύτεροι' in the etymological sense, not in the ecclesiastical, and the same use is common in St. Irenaeus."[134] Based

---

theorized that Irenaeus knew of this material, and when it was finally brought together in the form of a Gospel (which Lewis speculated may have been composed by Polycarp or other disciples of John) Irenaeus naturally recognized it as originating from the apostle John, and thus referred to it as the apostle's work. A major challenge to Lewis's theory is there is no historical record to verify any such chain of events. Lewis himself recognized this silence, stating that such a record "was too unimportant . . . to warrant its preservation." His theory is also challenged by historical references to John as being alive during the composition of the Gospel that bears his name. Even if Lewis's theory is granted, there is nothing prohibiting that such a compilation did not occur under the supervision of the apostle John himself. Regardless of Lewis's speculation concerning the final composition of John's Gospel, his work is a thorough and powerful tool for researching Irenaeus's attitude and knowledge regarding the authorship of the Fourth Gospel.

132. Ibid., 24–30.

133. Chapman, *John the Presbyter*, 12.

134. Ibid., 13.

upon this assumption, he concluded that for Irenaeus the term presbyter "never" referred to the apostles, but to their followers.[135] Subsequently, he asserted that since Papias used this word with the same sense then he must have not known any of the apostles.[136] Chapman was so confident in his position that he stated, "It seems that no parallel is to be found for the supposed πρεσβύτεροι = ἀπόστολος of Papias,"[137] This is a conjecture that even Eusebius did not feel confident to assert.[138] Additionally, Chapman failed to recognize that such a "parallel" existed well before the beginning of the second century as can be observed in 1 Peter 5:1, in which the apostle Peter referred to himself as a "fellow elder" (συμπρεσβύτερος), and described himself as one who possessed definitive authority over other presbyters because of his firsthand witness to the sufferings of Christ. The context of this passage, not to mention that of the entire epistle, clearly indicates that he perceived himself as an official of the church (both as an apostle, 1 Peter 1:1; and as an elder 1 Peter 5:1), and as one who possessed authority over the church, and who exercised control over her doctrines and traditions. First Peter 5:1, therefore, clearly demonstrates that Peter was not simply referring to himself as an elderly man. The same can be said for the use of the title "presbyter" in the second and third epistles of the apostle John.[139] The author of these epistles identified himself in 2 John 1 as "Ο πρεσβύτερος ἐκλεκτῇ κυρίᾳ,"[140] and clearly perceived himself as one who possessed authority to distinguish between orthodoxy and heresy, and thus possessed the right to command others to adhere to correct doctrine (2 John 7–11). He also perceived himself as one who possessed the right to exercise authority over other leaders in the church (3 John 9–10). Regarding this author's perceived authority, Harnack wrote, "Yet these letters were composed by a man who, whatever he may have been, claimed and exercised apostolic authority over a large number of the churches."[141]

135. Ibid., 16.

136. Ibid., 18.

137. Ibid., 19.

138. Regarding Papias's two references of "John" Eusebius wrote, "It is here worth noting that he twice counts the name of John, and reckons the first John with Peter and James and Matthew and *the other Apostles, clearly meaning the Evangelist.*" Eusebius *Ecc. Hist.* III.39.4–5 (LCL 153:293). Italics mine.

139. It is recognized that the authorship of these epistles is often debated. For the moment, I will simply assume that the apostle John is the author of these epistles. A more thorough analysis will follow throughout this book.

140. This is literally translated as "The Elder to the elect lady."

141. Harnack, *Expansion of Christianity*, 320.

Consequently, it is indefensible to argue that the authors of these epistles only employed the term "presbyter" as a reference to their ages.

Ironically, the best argument against Chapman's primary thesis, which was that Papias employed the term πρεσβύτεροι only in the "etymological" sense, was provided by Chapman himself, for in a footnote on page 19 he wrote, "It may be urged that the word 'Presbyters' in the sense of 'Fathers' might include apostles, in the mouth of a very early writer. It might but apparently it does not. It seems rather to have a technical meaning—primitive sub-apostolic witness who were not apostles nor disciples of the Lord but usually disciples of apostles. They are witnesses to tradition and links. The Apostles are not regarded as links; they are the authentic teachers, the originator of tradition and not a part of it."[142]

Chapman severely damaged his own thesis by this very admission. If Papias employed the word "elder" with a "technical meaning," then one is left to ask, what other possible "technical" sense could be meant? Chapman answered this question most adeptly when he admitted that in the environment of the early church an elder would be one who was an original "witness" to the church's traditions. His argument that an apostle would never be referred to as an elder is simply indefensible since he himself contended that the apostles were the "authentic teachers" and "originators of tradition."[143] The title of elder as referring to an office of the church and as being applied to the apostles fits perfectly well with the biblical witness as found in 1 Peter, and 2 and 3 John.[144] While Irenaeus, writing in the last quarter of the second century, and today's scholars regularly feel the necessity to distinguish between the apostles and their disciples and associates, congregates of the church at the end of the first century would not have felt any such compulsion. In fact, it appears that the term "apostle" did not carry the same clout at the end of the first century as it did for Irenaeus, and as it does for today's church. Ironically, at the end of the first century the church in Asia Minor had to deal with the problem of "false apostles" as indicated in Revelation 2:2. These types of imposters

142. Chapman, *John the Presbyter*, 19.

143. For a better explanation of this possibility see Bornkamm, "πρεσβύτερος," in *TDNT*, 6:676, and Coenen, "Bishop, Presbyter, Elder," in *NIDNT*, 1:200.

144. First Peter 5:1; 2 John 1; 3 John 1. Another important biblical reference is Acts 15:9, where it is clear that Luke desired to identify those who were apostles and those who were not. His segregation of the apostle from other church officials, however, does not prove that the apostles did not view themselves as "elders" who possessed the supreme authority within the church to promote and defend its doctrines and traditions (i.e., orthodoxy).

presented a problem for the church even as early as Paul's own day (cf. 2 Cor 11:13). Additionally, the problem of false apostles was also a major concern for the author of the *Didache*.[145] While it seems that the early church struggled with the problem of erroneously appointed itinerant "apostles," (whether by self promotion or by rogue churches) there seems to be little evidence that one could designate themselves as an "elder," nor is there evidence that "false elders" plagued the early church at the end of the first century.

Chapman recognized the possibility that Papias had received his knowledge of the "Lord's actions and words" secondhand, meaning his sources were "disciples of the Lord." Additionally, he also conceded that there is no compelling argument that Papias's knowledge of Jesus' activities and teachings was thirdhand.[146] It is not uncommon to find some who assume that because Papias testified that he had known those who knew the "apostles" and "disciples of the Lord," then he himself must not have known the "apostles" and/or "disciples of the Lord." This is an unwarranted assumption as illustrated by the following equation demonstrating Papias's possible relationship to any apostle, as well as other possible channels of communication by which oral traditions probably traveled to Papias. Allowing for "A" to represent the apostles, and "B" to represent their followers and contemporaries,[147] and "C" to represent Papias: If group A knew group B, and group B knew C, then there is nothing that prohibits the possibility that C also knew group A; for if A and B were contemporaries, and group B and C were contemporaries then the possibility that C was a contemporary of group A becomes even stronger. In spite of this possibility, there are some who contend that Papias not only did not know any apostles, but that he also did not know any of their followers as well.[148]

While Chapman's book provides some helpful insights, it is severely undermined by his unwarranted assumption that in order to understand Papias's use of the term "presbyter" one must depend upon Irenaeus's later use of the term. At times, however, even Chapman seems to contradict himself, as seen in his statement that "The whole question (of) what Papias

145. See *Didache* 11 (LCL 24: 434–35). Ehrman dated the *Didache* as originating in the late first century or early second century.

146. Chapman, *John the Presbyter*, 22. Schoedel, however, doubted that Papias had direct contact with Aristion and the character Eusebius referred to as "the elder John." Schoedel, *The Fragments*, 98; Schoedel, "Papias," 252.

147. Bauckham, *The Eyewitnesses*, 15. "Followers" were students of disciples, while "contemporaries" were those who only tangentially knew the apostles.

148. Bacon, "An Emendation," 183.

meant, and what his readers would understand, depends upon their previous knowledge of who the Presbyters were. Examples will make this clear. For the possibly ambiguous word 'Presbyter' let us substitute first 'disciple', which will naturally be understood as equivalent to apostle, and then 'bishop', which will naturally appear to exclude the Apostles."[149] Such apparent contradictions and baseless assumptions can be found throughout his book. Consequently, although he is often cited by others with respect to Papian research, his arguments should not be uncritically accepted as the final word regarding the identity of the character commonly referred to as "John the elder," or of Papias's use of the word πρεσβύτερος.

A brief but salient article by A. F. Walls was published in 1967 titled "Papias and Oral Tradition," in the twenty-first volume of *Vigiliae Christianae*. As the title suggests, the article focuses on Papias's attitude towards oral traditions. Concerning Papias's preface as preserved by Eusebius, Walls stated that "the frequent preoccupation of the modern reader of Papias with gospel origins has perhaps favored the assumption that in this famous passage Papias is expressing a uniform preference for oral as *against* written tradition and reflecting a contemporary lack of interest in the literary preservation of tradition."[150] Walls made several very important observations regarding the validity of this assumption; the first was that Papias was so concerned with preserving and explaining oral traditions, both from Jesus and others who saw him, *that he wrote a book* and, as Walls so aptly pointed out, "a very large one" at that.[151] Nevertheless, Papias's interest in oral traditions is hardly questionable. Papias's preference for first-person rhetoric over written works is understandable given his Greek culture and the opportunities he had to listen to individuals who were both apostles and/or hearers of Jesus, as well as their followers. If given the choice between reading the Gospel of John or listening to the apostle John, very few would choose the former, whether that one be a first-century Greek speaking bishop of Asia Minor or a twenty-first-century American layman. Contending, however, that Papias disdained the written word and only valued the spoken word is a proposition doomed to embarrassment by the very quill of Papias.

A second important observation of Walls concerns Papias's selection and subsequent preservation of material. The source of a tradition was essential for Papias because it was the guarantor of its orthodoxy. Regarding

149. Chapman, *John the Presbyter*, 10–11.

150. Walls, "Papias," 137. Italics mine.

151. Ibid.

the value that he placed upon a tradition's source and his desire for orthodoxy, Walls wrote,

> [Papias] delights in those who teach the truth and in those who provide commandments given by the Lord to the faith, and deriving from the Truth itself. . . . That is, in orthodoxy and authenticity as guaranteed by pedigree—in fact, apostolicity. Instead of taking all traditions at face value, he has carefully noted the accounts of reliable people with known access to apostolic teaching. Papias, then, is thinking of works of whose apostolic origin there is no proof. With Matthew, Mark, and any other demonstrably apostolic work he is not here concerned. For Papias, what matters is the quality of the source, not whether it is oral or written. A written work known to be apostolic provides the "oracles of the Lord", which may be taken as authentic, ready for exposition. . . . For him, authenticity meant apostolicity; and apostolicity was patient of historical verification. Far from being uninterested in the literary preservation of the tradition, he was wrestling manfully with the problems involved in it.[152]

Walls is not alone in the assertion that Papias valued literary sources. Schoedel in a similar fashion also agreed that Papias was not averse to relying upon written traditions, stating that "Papias discloses his preference for oral tradition in good rhetorical style as a preference for a 'living and abiding voice' (*Hist. Eccl.* 3.39.4), yet he clearly is also well disposed to his written sources."[153]

Walls's observations are important because they effectively challenge the notion held by some (e.g., Hall, Bauer) that orthodoxy was a late development in the early church. Some scholars have argued that orthodoxy developed late in the second century, for others orthodoxy was not identified until the late fourth century. Robert Stein, in reference to form critics Rudolf Bultmann and Martin Dibelius, explained that "For some form critics, however, a *non sequitur* often takes place that assumes that the *Sitz im Leben* that preserved and molded the gospel traditions also gave them their birth. As a result, the needs of the early church are seen not only as the preserver but also as the creator of the traditions. The tradition was not only *to* the church and *for* the church but also *from* the church."[154]

---

152. Ibid., 139.

153. Schoedel, "Papias," in *ABD* 5:141. Richard Bauckham has a particularly excellent explanation regarding the Greek value for education that was directly from one's teacher rather than a written text; see Bauckham, *The Eyewitnesses*, 21–24.

154. Stein, *Synoptic Gospels*, 185.

Stein, however, concerning the biblical evidence validating such a hypothesis concluded that "[u]pon closer examination, there seems to be little objective evidence to support such a view."[155] It is true that the refinement of the parameters and nuances of orthodoxy was a constant challenge in the early church; nevertheless, discerning the spring from which it flowed seems to have been decided relatively early, as Walls observed and Papias's preface verifies.

More recently, an important scholar for Papian research and the development of the New Testament is Richard Bauckham. Bauckham wrote an article in 1993 titled "Papias and Polycrates on the Origin of the Fourth Gospel," and in 2006 he wrote a book titled *Jesus and the Eyewitnesses: The Gospel as Eyewitness Testimony*, within which he also addressed the subject of Papias. Bauckham's earlier article expands on Martin Hengel's theory that the character known as "John the Elder" was actually the "beloved disciple and the author of the Fourth Gospel (as well as of the Johannine letters)."[156] He, however, in contrast to Hengel contended that "In the present article, we shall proceed on the basis of the view that the Gospel portrays the beloved disciple, not as one of the twelve, but as a Jerusalem disciple of Jesus. This view is accepted by many of those recent scholars who hold that the beloved disciple is portrayed in the Gospel as a historical individual, not as a purely ideal figure."[157] Bauckham posited that one of the benefits of his theory, as opposed to that of Hengel's, was that "it can explain the attribution to John the son of Zebedee, which eventually prevailed in the early church, as the result of an assimilation of John the Elder, a disciple of Jesus who was not one of the twelve, to the better known and more prestigious apostle John the son of Zebedee."[158] Bauckham, in harmony with Eusebius, depended upon Papias's preface to support this theory, arguing that

> In the period when the authorship of the Gospel by John the Elder was quite often canvassed, the possibility that he could also be the beloved disciple was rarely raised, even though it was usually rightly recognized that according to Papias he had been a personal disciple of Jesus. . . . In this article we shall argue that the best external evidence in fact supports the internal evidence in seeing the beloved disciple, the author of the Gospel, as the

155. Ibid.
156. Bauckham, "Papias and Polycrates," 24.
157. Ibid., 25.
158. Ibid., 26.

disciple of Jesus who was not one of the twelve. This coincidence with the best reading of the internal evidence strongly suggests that this external evidence is also reliable when it calls this disciple John, indicating a John of Ephesus who must be, not the son of Zebedee, but Papias' John the Elder. . . . The only Church, so far as we know, which ever(*sic*) claimed to be the place of origin of the Fourth Gospel was Ephesus. This means that if any of the external evidence is of any value, the most reliable is likely to be that of writers who can witness to the local tradition of Ephesus and its neighbourhood in the second century. Such writers are Papias of Hierapolis and Polycrates of Ephesus.[159]

In the first half of his article, Bauckham attempted to explain Polycrates's "erroneous" testimony regarding the authorship of the Gospel of John. Bauckham argued in a rather strained fashion that Polycrates implied that he was related to the "John" who leaned back upon Jesus during the Passover. Bauckham believed that Polycrates was quite proud of his familial pedigree of orthodox bishops, all of whom served in the early to mid second century (although he recognized that Polycrates never explicitly called them his "ancestors"). He postulated, however, that Polycrates, who wrote in the late second century, had to depend heavily upon the local tradition of the church in Ephesus to construct his ancestral heritage and "took it for granted" that his relative was the apostle John instead of a different John who was supposed to have been the elder of the Ephesian church.[160]

Armed with nothing but conjectures, Bauckham contended that the true identity of Polycrates's John is in reality the unnamed disciple of John 18:15, but who was later identified as the "John" in Acts 4:6.[161] To support this conjecture he cited a reference to an Ephesian bishop named "John" in the *Apostolic Constitutions* 7.46, who was reportedly appointed to the bishopric of Ephesus by none other than the apostle John. It challenges the limits of reasonable objectivity to contend that Polycrates, (who presumably was quite proud of his "possible" family tree), was in error when he believed that his ancestor was the apostle John, but who in reality was the unnamed disciple in John 18:15, who is later identified as the "John" mentioned in Acts 4:6 (and who was also the "beloved disciple"), and that the seventh chapter of the *Apostolic Constitutions* (a fourth-century

159. Ibid., 26, 28.
160. Ibid., 28–33.
161. Ibid., 42–44.

document) corrects the "erroneous" testimony of both Polycrates and Irenaeus regarding the authorship of the Fourth Gospel.

Having attempted to explain Polycrates's confusion regarding his ancestors and the authorship of the Gospel of John, Bauckham turned his attention to Papias. His discussion regarding Papias and his meanings contains many insightful comments. He believed, in spite of Eusebius's silence on the subject, that Papias was aware of the Gospel of John and the book of Revelation.[162] He based his argument upon Papias's listing of the apostles, which he aptly observed to be Johannine in chronology, and upon evidence drawn from other Papian fragments. He insightfully recognized that Eusebius's quotations of Papias regarding the origins of the Gospels of Matthew and Mark may have come from different contexts, but that Eusebius had probably brought them together thematically in a manner that was consistent with their original contexts.[163] He also posited that Papias's comments concerning these Gospels affirm that they were based upon eyewitness accounts, a thesis which is central to his recently published book. Bauckham contended, however, that Papias's comments could be inferred to mean that he "appears to be acknowledging the fact that the Greek Gospel of Matthew which he and his readers knew had suffered something in the translation from Matthew's original Hebrew. . . . Quite probably Papias went on to make this more explicit in a further comment which Eusebius omitted, because he did not like the notion that the Greek Gospel of Matthew used by the church diverged rather considerably from Matthew's original Hebrew Gospel."[164]

Bauckham's conjecture that Papias "possibly" referred to our Greek Gospel of Matthew, and that Eusebius "probably" censored his reference, are completely based upon silence and, therefore, should not be uncritically accepted. His observations, however, about the proliferation of Greek Gospels produced from faulty translations of Matthew's original Aramaic work is attractive because it does not contradict the historical record concerning the existence of "Gospel" literature during the last half of the first century. Regarding the existence of multiple literary accounts about Jesus, Bauckham posited, "From what we know Papias to have said about Matthew, it is clear that he thought there had been more than one translation of the original Hebrew Gospel into Greek. Probably he knew something about Greek Gospels, under the name of Matthew and related to our

162. Ibid., 44–45.

163. Ibid., 46.

164. Ibid., 47–48.

Matthew, which were used by Jewish Christians in Palestine and Syria. He knew they exhibited major divergences from the Gospel of Matthew used in Hierapolis and neighbouring churches."[165]

He supported this theory by an analysis of the vocabulary that Papias employed in his preface concerning the Gospels of Matthew and Mark. Papias stated that Mark had been Peter's interpreter (ἑρμηνευτής) while others had interpreted (ἡρμήνευσεν) Matthew's Aramaic Gospel according to their ability or lack thereof. The possibility of there being multiple spurious or faulty gospels, or other gospels that may have competed with our canonical Gospels is not inconsistent with the historical record as preserved in Luke's Gospel (Luke 1:1–4) and Papias's preface (τὰ ἐκ τῶν βιβλίων).[166]

If Matthew wrote a Gospel that contained the teachings and deeds of Jesus for an Aramaic speaking audiences, then such a document would certainly have been highly prized since it would be viewed as containing the actual words and teachings of the one whom the audience believed was both the Savior and Messiah. Such a document would have been perceived as significant—if not priceless for predominantly Greek-speaking diasporic Jews who had made pilgrimages to "the holy land" and had subsequently converted to Christianity. The result of such conversions would be that many would have acquired a copy of Matthew's Aramaic work before returning home. Once such a document reached cities throughout the Diaspora, other Jews and "God fearing" Gentiles alike would certainly have desired to have it read to them (as well as possess their own copies). Understandably, they would have preferred to read or hear this document in their native tongue. The result would be that some unqualified ("as each was able"; [ὡς ἦς δυνατὸς ἕκαστος]), and/or possibly some unorthodox translators may have been employed for the purpose of translating Matthew's text. Such a translation process would have at times required interpretive decisions to be made regarding the various possible meanings of the author's text, whether intentionally or unintentionally. These translators may have been asked or hired to translate the entire document or possibly only small portions it. Given the differing and at times competing philosophical worldviews within the intellectual, academic, and

165. Ibid., 48.

166. Papias's statement concerning "things from the books" was given in the context of his desire to learn of the teachings of the Lord through the teachings of the apostles and those who had personally followed the Lord, and his evaluation of the teachings of those who claimed to have associated with those who had been disciples of the Lord.

spiritual milieu of both the Gentile and Jewish communities throughout the Roman Empire during the first century, one can only wonder at the potential problems such a document would have caused young orthodox churches desiring to maintain fidelity to the actual teachings of the apostolic colloquium.[167]

Bauckham explained Papias's statement about the fidelity of Matthew and Mark to their sources, and the apparent lack of fidelity of those who attempted to translate Matthew's Aramaic Gospel in this manner, "Whereas Mark's accuracy and scrupulosity in recording everything he had heard from Peter, leaving nothing out and falsifying nothing, is stressed, those who interpreted Matthew as best they could were evidently much less careful and competent."[168] Bauckham's discussion focused predominantly upon the differences in the ordering of the material found in the Gospels of Matthew and Mark. His analysis, however, introduces important questions concerning the impact that competing epistemologies and theologies could have had upon Christian communities during the last half of the first century.

---

167. This discussion is indifferent to the question of whether Mark's Greek Gospel or Matthew's Aramaic Gospel came first. Eusebius quoted Papias's reference to Mark's Gospel before the statement about Matthew's Aramaic Gospel, which might imply (assuming that Eusebius quoted these passages in the order that he found them) that Mark's Greek Gospel preceded Matthew's Aramaic work, but this is not a certainty, nor does it need be, for this question is not significant. Whether Matthew's Aramaic Gospel was written before or after Mark's Greek Gospel is negligible with respect to questions involving the credibility of an Aramaic Gospel since first-century Christians, both Jewish and Gentile, would have thought that such a work contained the very words of Jesus (i.e., his *Ipsissima verba*). Consequently, it would have presented a serious challenge to the value of any Greek translation of Jesus' words and deeds, regardless of the reputation of its eyewitness source(s). However, it does not seem unreasonable to think that if Matthew composed an Aramaic Gospel before his Greek version, such a work probably predated Mark's Gospel as well. Such a chronology fits Irenaeus's tradition, which stated that Matthew wrote his Hebraic Gospel while Peter and Paul were evangelizing Rome (see Eusebius *Ecc. Hist.* V.8.2 (LCL 153:454–55). This places the composition of Matthew's Hebraic Gospel in the early 50's. This book does not seek to answer questions about what might have been the relationship of Matthew's Aramaic Gospel to the *Gospel according to the Hebrews*, the *Gospel of the Ebionites*, or speculations concerning "Q," "M," "L," or other possible sources of the synoptic Gospels. For a thorough discussion of the synoptic problem see Stein, *Synoptic Gospels*, 29–152. Vernon Bartlet broached the important subject of the complexities concerning the clash between Hebraic and Grecian approaches to epistemology, theology, and hermeneutics. Bartlet, "Papias's 'Exposition,'" 18–20.

168. Bauckham, "Papias and Polycrates," 49.

A glaring weakness in Bauckham's article is his frequent speculations with respect to what Papias may have said and what Eusebius might have censored concerning the Gospel of John and other books of the New Testament. His assertion that "Eusebius did not record everything his sources said about the origins of the Gospels" is not unreasonable.[169] It is hardly questionable that Eusebius employed Papias's preface to explain the origin and defend the authenticity of the Gospel Mark. Speculating, however, about what Eusebius might have censored or what Papias may have written concerning other Gospels, such as that of John and Luke, is simply an exercise in academic shadow boxing. Constantine Tischendorf has aptly argued that Eusebius's silence with respect to what Papias may have said about the origin of the Gospel of John, and subsequently the origins of other New Testament books, is of little weight. Concerning Eusebius's silence about the origin of John's Gospel, Tischendorf wrote, "Now, it is difficult to conceive a statement more utterly groundless and arbitrary than this, that the silence of Papias as to the Gospel of John is a proof against its genuineness. . . . We have no right to conclude, from Eusebius' extracts out of Papias' book, that there was no reference to St. John's Gospel in the entire book."[170] He buttressed this assertion by highlighting Eusebius's references to Polycarp's epistle to the Philippians, as well as his reference to Theophilus's letter to Autolycus in order to explain Eusebius's silence concerning certain New Testament books, writing that, "Eusebius only says one thing of Polycarp's letter to the Philippians—that it contains passages taken from the First Epistle of Peter; and yet the letter is full of quotations from St. Paul! He also mentions (iv.26), that Theophilus, in his letter to his friend Autolycus, made use of the Apocalypse, and yet he does not so much as notice that these books contain a citation of a passage from the Gospel of St. John, and even with the name of the apostle given. Now, the blind zeal of the adversaries of the Gospel has either chosen not to see this, or has passed it over in silence."[171]

Tischendorf cogently explained Eusebius's silence by arguing that "no one in the early Church era doubted these writings [i.e., The Gospel of Luke, The Gospel of John, and the Pauline epistles], and so it never occurred to Eusebius to collect testimonies in their favor."[172] Tischendorf,

---

169. Ibid., 53.

170. Tischendorf, *When?* 88. Concerning the weight that should be given to Eusebius's silence regarding the New Testament canon see also Lightfoot, *Essays*, 2–58.

171. Tischendorf, *When?* 89.

172. Ibid., 88. The bracketed comment is provided to identify the context in which

therefore, has sufficiently explained the relevance of Eusebius's silence by arguing that his primarily concern was with providing the origins of certain questionable catholic epistles, not with books that fell within his *homologoumena* (e.g., the Gospel of John). While today's New Testament and patristic scholars desperately hunger for historical explanations of the origins of all the books of the New Testament, Eusebius and his audience, on the other hand, suffered from no such appetite. Consequently, Eusebius's silence is a poor catapult from which to launch conjectures about what Papias may or may not have said about the Gospel of John or about any other New Testament books for that matter.

Bauckham also speculated about the possible relationship of the *Muratorian Canon* and the writings of Papias. He posited that the tradition found in the *Muratorian Canon* regarding the Gospel of John was possibly dependent upon Papias.[173] His explanation highlighted several interesting similarities between existing Papian fragments and the *Muratorian Canon*, but very few of them can be objectively verified. Bauckham argued that because the *Muratorian Canon* distinguished the author of the Gospel of John as a "John" who was only one of the "disciples" from Andrew who was referred to as one of the "apostles," then we should assume that the writer of the Gospel of John could not have been a son of Zebedee. While this distinction is interesting, it alone does not prove Bauckham's thesis. Bauckham moved from his discussion of the *Muratorian Canon* to Irenaeus, whom he contended came to his understanding of the Gospel origins "by intelligent deduction rather than because he had additional information."[174] He is generally silent in this article, however, about Irenaeus's confessed relationship to Polycarp, who was himself a student of the apostle John.

Bauckham concluded his article with these startling assertions:

> The Fourth Gospel was never anonymous. As Hengel has shown, as soon as Gospels circulated in the churches, they must have been known with author's names attached to them. The Fourth Gospel was known as John's. In Asia, the tradition from Papias early in the second century to Polycrates at its end was that this John, the beloved disciple and the author of the Gospel, was John the Elder, a disciple of the Lord but not one of the

---

the quote is given.

173. Bauckham, "Papias and Polycrates," 53–58. For a more thorough discussion of the possible relationship of the *Muratorian Canon* and the writings of Papias see Hill, "What Papias Said," 582–605.

174. Bauckham, "Papias and Polycrates," 61.

twelve, who had died in Ephesus. *We known* [sic] *of no dissent from this tradition in Asia before the third century. . . .*

The writings of Irenaeus help to show us why this ascription would prove acceptable. It has been commonly assumed and sometimes argued that Irenaeus identified the author of the Fourth Gospel with John the son of Zebedee. . . . Decisive evidence is surprisingly and significantly elusive, despite Irenaeus' frequent references to the Fourth Gospel and its author. Irenaeus knew of John of Ephesus both from Papias and independently from Asian traditions he learned in Smyrna as a young man. . . . He refers to John (regarding him as the author of all Johannine writings, including the Apocalypse) sixteen times as "the disciple of the Lord" (and thirty-one times as just "John"), *never as "John the apostle."*[175]

Although Bauckham is "technically" correct that Irenaeus never referred to the author of the Fourth Gospel as "John the apostle," Bauckham failed to fully respect Irenaeus's identification of the apostle John as the author of the Fourth Gospel in *Against Heresies* I.9.2. The descriptions within this passage clearly indicate that Irenaeus confidently believed that the John who authored the Fourth Gospel was in fact also an apostle, writing that "So that, according to them in all these terms *John* makes no mention of the Lord Jesus Christ. For if *he* has named the Father . . . by thus speaking, (he) referred to the primary Ogdoad, in which there was as yet no Jesus, and no Christ, *the teacher of John*. But that *the apostle* did not speak concerning their conjunctions, but concerning our Lord Jesus Christ, whom *he* also acknowledges as the Word of God, *he himself has made evident*. For, summing up *his statements* respecting the Word previously mentioned by *him he further declares*, "and the Word was made flesh, and dwelt among us."[176]

The entire context of Irenaeus's statement makes it perfectly clear that he identified the author of John 1:14 as the John who was not only "the apostle" (in contradistinction to an "elder") but who also had Jesus Christ as his "teacher." Consequently, Lewis has more than adequately defended the conclusion that Irenaeus did in fact believe that it was John—a son of Zebedee and one of the original twelve disciples—that authored the canonical Gospel bearing his name.

Bauckham poorly defended his assertions by postulating that in the face of the gnostic threat Irenaeus was concerned to maintain the "apostolicity" of the "Scriptures" and orthodoxy as coming from "eyewitness

175. Ibid., 65, 67. Italics mine.
176. Irenaeus, *Against Heresies* I.9.2 (ANF 1:329). Italics mine.

tradition from the ministry of Jesus in his native Asia. . . . But since Irenaeus can treat the seventy as 'other apostles' in addition to the twelve (*Haer.* 2.21.1), there is no need to suppose he included the Fourth Evangelist among the twelve."[177] It was Bauckham's position that the church has simply misunderstood Irenaeus as attributing the Gospel of John to the John who was an apostle and a son of Zebedee. Instead, it was Irenaeus's intent to communicate that the John who authored the Fourth Gospel was in fact the "John" who Bauckham identified as Eusebius's John the elder.

Bauckham's article, "Papias and Polycrates on the Origin of the Fourth Gospel" contains many insightful observations, although it is equally plagued with unwarranted conjectures. While Bauckham recognized that Papias's preface could be interpreted in such a way that completely undermines his thesis that the Johannine writings are from a John who was not the son of Zebedee,[178] he constantly assumes his own poorly defended premises and then continues to build on them. His article, however, is valuable to the discussion regarding the participation of eyewitnesses in the composition of the Gospels. Concerning this thesis, Bauckham is well versed and argues competently, and it is this thesis that is the central theme to his recently published book, to which I now turn.

Bauckham's book *Jesus and the Eyewitnesses* is a compelling answer to the many unwarranted assumptions of form critics who generally argue that the canonical Gospels originated from gospel traditions that developed over a prolonged period and were ultimately authored by those who had little credible knowledge of the events about which they wrote. While disagreeing with several of Bauckham's presuppositions and conclusions, as a whole his work is impressive. Many of his arguments are well written and based upon a reasonable reading of the historical data. Consequently, his work is a breath of fresh air that is bound to have a considerable impact upon New Testament studies in the coming decades.

Bauckham devoted significant attention to Papias's preface as preserved by Eusebius, giving considerable focus to his statements regarding the Gospels of Matthew and Mark. What makes his comments so salient is that he offered them in light of recent historical research that focuses upon the literary styles of ancient histories and biographies. His survey and synthesis of this research and its application to the Gospels sheds new light upon their purposes, as well as the possible purposes of

---

177. Bauckham, "Papias and Polycrates," 68. See also Bauckham, *The Eyewitnesses*, 458–63.

178. Bauckham, "Papias and Polycrates," 61.

Papias's five-volume work. Bauckham addressed Papias and his statements regarding the origins of Matthew's and Mark's Gospels in chapter 2, which he titled "Papias on the Eyewitnesses." In this chapter he reaffirmed his unwarranted assumption regarding what Papias may have said regarding the canonical Gospel of Matthew.[179] As previously explained, it was his opinion that Papias had written a rather a disparaging comment regarding the Greek translation of Matthew's Aramaic Gospel, a Gospel that Bauckham believed was in circulation in Hierapolis. It was this statement about which Bauckham speculated that Eusebius did not approve of and, consequently, censored in his discussion of the origins of Matthew's Gospel. There is, however, no record of Papias as having ever said anything disparaging regarding the canonical Gospel of Matthew. Bauckham also addressed the question of when Papias wrote his five-volume work, which he translated as, *Expositions of the Logia of the Lord*.[180] Bauckham only transliterated the term "Logia" because he believed that its meaning is too "disputed." He speculated, however, that it probably referred to the "accounts of what Jesus said and did."[181]

Bauckham made an important observation regarding the debate concerning when Papias wrote his work, which was that as Papias wrote he was writing about an earlier period in his life, but while doing so he wrote as if it were in real time (i.e., employing the historical present). He explained his observation in this manner, "For our purposes it is much more important that, whenever Papias actually wrote, in the passage we shall study he speaks *about* an earlier period in his life, the time during which he was collecting oral reports of the words and deeds of Jesus."[182] This is an important observation because if correct, and there is no reason to demand that it is not, then it expands the time frame of Papias's witness with respect to the origins of the apostolic writings.

The debate regarding when Papias wrote has been well documented by Robert Yarbrough, who explained that scholars estimate the date of Papias's writings as early as AD 80 to as late as 160.[183] One of Yarbrough's

179. Bauckham, *The Eyewitnesses*, 12–13, 225. Rupert Annand went to a different extreme and doubted that the canonical Gospel of Matthew even existed at the time Papias wrote. Annand, "Four Gospels," 57.

180. Bauckham, *The Eyewitnesses*, 12.

181. Ibid.

182. Ibid., 14.

183. Yarbrough, "The Date of Papias," 181. For a more thorough analysis and discussion on the subject of date of Papias's *Exposition* see Yarbrough, "The Date of the Writings of Papias of Hierapolis" (M.A. thesis, Wheaton College, 1982).

main concerns in his article was to address the arguments of those who unnecessarily distance Papias from the apostolic generation. Regarding these attempts he wrote, "Thus Papias is important as an early witness to portions of the NT canon and their authors and to the life and development of the post-apostolic, or even late apostolic, Church. . . . The further removed temporally Papias is from the facts he relays, the less credible his testimony becomes."[184] Yarbrough contended that Papias wrote ca. 95–110 and not ca. 130 or later, a period which is adopted by a few scholars.[185] Similarly, Bauckham also argued that the position that Papias wrote ca. 130 was based upon "unreliable evidence";[186] consequently, he apparently dated Papias's work as having been written ca. 110.[187]

The opinion that Papias wrote ca. 110 generally rests on the rejection of the importance that some place on a historical reference made by Philip of Side and the significance of Papias's use of present tense verb (i.e., λέγουσιν) as found in his preface. Regarding the historical reference made by Philip, those who attribute an early date to Papias's writings are of the opinion that Philip's reference is completely unreliable for pinpointing when Papias wrote.[188] The historical reference in question is Philip's statement that Papias referred to those who were resurrected by Christ as having survived "until the time of Hadrian."[189] It should be observed that Philip did not actually quote Papias, but rather he only summarized

184. Yarbrough, "The Date of Papias," 181.

185. For an exhaustive list see ibid., 182.

186. Bauckham, *The Eyewitnesses*, 13.

187. Ibid., 14.

188. Bacon, *Studies*, 441. Schoedel, *The Fragments*, 120–21. Yarbrough, "The Date of Papias," 185. The discussion regarding the present tense verb "λέγουσιν" will be addressed at a later point. For now it is recognized that it is certainly possible to understand that the period that Papias was referring to was the actual time in which he wrote.

189. Holmes, *Apostolic Fathers*, 3rd ed., 745. A similar statement by Quadratus is found in Eusebius *Ecc. Hist.* IV.3.2–3 (LCL 153:309). This statement makes it clear that these were people who had actually been resurrected by Jesus, and not resurrected some years later by his followers. Hadrian reigned from 117 to 138. It is generally held that Jesus' ministry occurred approximately sometime between 26–33. If Jesus had resurrected a small child (e.g., two years old or younger, cf. Mark 5:21–43; Luke 7:11–15; John 11:1–46) who was born ca. 30, then such a child would have been approximately eighty-seven when Hadrian began to rule. This is not to argue that Jesus did in fact raise a small child who survived until Hadrian's ascension, for there is no record of Jesus having raised a child of two years old or younger from the dead. It is only to demonstrate that it would not be impossible for someone who was born ca. 30 to have lived to see the beginning of Hadrian's reign.

what Papias wrote, which was that some who were raised from the dead by Christ had survived until Hadrian's "time." Benjamin Bacon explained his hesitancy for trusting Philip's statement in this manner:

> It is perhaps not superfluous to add that the date once advocated on the basis of an alleged fragment of Papias in Philip of Side, declaring that some of the subjects of Jesus' life-restoring power had "survived till the time of Hadrian," has no value. It would indeed seem to be implied that the author of the statement was himself writing under a later emperor; but it is now generally recognized that Philip merely rests, as usual, on Eusebius, and that in transcribing the material of Eusebius regarding Papias and *Quadratus*, whom Eusebius reports as making statements of this kind immediately after his statements in regard to Papias, Philip of Side has confused the two. For in delivering his Apology to Hadrian at the time of the emperor's visit to Athens (125 A.D.) *Quadratus* did in fact declare that some of these subjects of Jesus' healing power had survived "even to our times." These are the actual words of Quadratus given in the verbatim extract of Eusebius (*HE*, IV,3). Eusebius' order is misleading; for he places the activity of Papias before that of Quadratus, dating the latter correctly in the reign of Hadrian.[190]

While not attempting to defend Philip as an great historian or denying that he depended heavily upon Eusebius, there is evidence that should encourage scholars to take a closer look at Philip's treatment of Papias and his writings, for he shows knowledge of Papias's work that is found nowhere in the extant writings of Eusebius. Philip stated that Papias's reference to the martyrdom of James and John could be found in the "second book" of Papias's five-volume work, which is a referent not supplied by Eusebius.[191] He also stated that Papias wrote that it was "Manaim's" mother who was raised from the dead, which again is a detail not documented by Eusebius. It can be argued that these references indicate that Philip had at least read some excerpts of Papias's writings or possibly had access to an entire manuscript.

Regarding Bacon's speculation that in a moment of confusion Philip attributed a statement to Papias that was originally made by Quadratus,[192] it should be recognized that there is not sufficient evidence to date proving

190. Bacon, *Studies*, 441.

191. The accuracy of this statement and the question of whether Philip actually wrote anything about Papias will be addressed later.

192. This view is not original to Bacon; see Chapman, *John the Presbyter*, 98.

that it was not Quadratus who had depended upon Papias for his apologetic claim about the life-giving power of Jesus and the supremacy of the Christian faith rather than Papias depending upon Quadratus. Consequently, it is an argument from silence to postulate that Philip was simply confused about whether it was Papias or Quadratus who first made the statement concerning the longevity of those who had received Christ's miraculous touch. Additionally, it is just as possible that neither depended upon the other, but rather that they both employed a popular polemic of the late first-century and early second-century church for proving the superiority of Jesus. The absences of more substantial textual evidence regarding this reference to Hadrian makes conclusions concerning it difficult. Contending, however, that Philip was confused with respect to everything that Papias wrote, and, therefore, is completely unreliable for providing aid concerning anything else he wrote is unwarranted. Philip at times may have been a poor historian and writer; however, that is not to prove that he was completely incompetent or that he provided no important historical data or independent witness regarding Papias and his writings.[193]

One last important observation should be made with respect to both Philip's allusion to what Papias wrote, as well as Eusebius's quote of Quadratus, which is that neither demonstratively stated that the recipients of Jesus' miraculous power survived until the time of Hadrian's "reign," which is an inference some assume.[194] Philip stated that Papias wrote that those who were raised by Jesus survived until "ὅτι ἕως Ἀριανοῦ ἔζω,"[195] while Eusebius quoted Quadratus as contending before Hadrian that, "καὶ εἰς τοὺς ἡμετέρους χρόνους τινὲς αὐτῶν ἀφίκοντο,"[196] neither of which mentions Hadrian's "reign" per se. Hadrian was born in 76 and was pronounced emperor in 117 at the age of 41. Using the resurrection of Jarius's daughter for a yard stick (Mark 5:21–43), a girl born ca. 20 could certainly have survived until 76 or even to 100. Consequently, it is possible that both Papias's and Quadratus's focus was upon Hadrian's "lifetime" rather

---

193. Quasten, *Patrology*, 3:528–30. Regarding the potential value of Philip's work, Quasten wrote, "Despite Socrates' and Photius' criticisms it is to be regretted that it [i.e., Philip's *Christian History*] did not come down to us because it must have contained much information lacking in Eusebius's Church History."

194. Deeks, "Papias Revisited: Part II," 324.

195. Holmes, *Apostolic Fathers*, 3rd ed., 744. Literally translated, this text states, "that until (the time) Hadrian was living," which more fluently would read, "until Hadrian's lifetime."

196. Eusebius *Ecc. Hist.* IV.3.2–3 (LCL 153:309). Literally translated, this text states: "and some of them extend into our times."

than his "reign." In the absence of any clear reference to Hadrian's ascension to the throne, therefore, one should not assume with certitude that his reign was their intended point of reference. This is not to argue, however, that Papias *must* have written his work ca. 130 or later, or that he actually wrote sometime between 95 to 110, but only that there is no definitive reason to discount Philip as a viable witness to some of the contents in the writings of Papias. As Yarbrough has written, however, it does suggest that Philip provides no definitive aid in pinpointing the time in which Papias wrote, for if Papias was merely referencing Hadrian's lifetime then a date of ca. 95–110 is still possible, as is a date after 117.

Placing the discussion of the dating of Papias's work aside, Bauckham's observation is still very important, which was that in his preface Papias appeared to have written about an earlier time in his life, rather than what was actually occurring in his life at the time of his writing.[197] While it is possible that Papias wrote ca. 95–110 or sometime between 117–38, or possibly even later (although this seems less likely), if he wrote anytime between 95 through 138 it would make him a credible source for transmitting the traditions received from the eyewitnesses of Jesus' ministry regarding the origins of the books of the New Testament. Bauckham contended that the period which Papias was writing about was ca. 80, which in his opinion was the approximate time in which the Gospels of Matthew (presumably the Greek Gospel), Luke, and John were also written.[198] This means that some of the traditions that Papias received, such as the origin of Mark's Gospel, reached all the way back into the middle of the first century.

Bauckham rightly suggested that Papias was part of the second generation of the orthodox church.[199] Some scholars fail to recognize that the apostolic generation reached until the end of the first century, ending with the death of the apostle John. There is also confusion as to whether Papias received his traditions and "stories" about Jesus' ministry second or thirdhand. Bauckham argued that Papias received traditions regarding the Lord's deeds and teachings directly from eyewitnesses of the Lord's ministry.[200] It is the position of this book that Papias was a leader in the

197. Yarbrough believed that Papias was describing the period in which he wrote. Yarbrough, "The Date of Papias," 187–88.

198. Bauckham, *The Eyewitnesses*, 14.

199. Ibid., 16.

200. Bauckham's employment of the phrase "eyewitness" is a tremendous improvement such terms as "secondhand" and "thirdhand," which can be misleading with respect to one's credibility. For example, if Papias received from the apostle John the

generation that followed the apostles, and that he received his traditions of the contents the Lord's teachings directly from some of the apostles (eyewitnesses), as well as from their disciples and contemporaries who knew the apostles but not the Lord (secondhand), as well as those who claimed to have known only the associates of the disciples of the apostles (thirdhand). Regarding this last group who claimed to have known some original apostles, whether they called themselves "apostles," or prophets, or evangelists, or "elders"[201] it was from this group that Papias rigorously evaluated their "messages" in order to see if they conformed to that which he had "carefully learned" and "carefully remembered" from his own first-hand exposure to certain apostles.[202]

Bauckham also made an unwarranted conjecture that has also been assumed by a few other scholars concerning Papias's access to members of the apostolic colloquium (e.g., the apostle John). He assumed for no apparent reason that Papias's travels were severely restricted, arguing that "Papias, living in Hierapolis, did not normally have the opportunity to hear these Asiatic elders himself, but when any of their disciples visited Hierapolis he asked what they were saying. In particular, of course, he wanted to hear of any traditions that the elders had from the Lord's disciples: Andrew, Peter, and the others. The apparent ambiguity in Papias's words really derives from the fact that he takes it for granted that the words of the elders in which he would be interested are those that transmit tradition from Andrew, Peter, and the other disciples of the Lord."[203]

It is tenuous at best to assume that Papias avoided the well-worn road that allowed many to freely travel to from Hierapolis to Ephesus. That Papias interrogated those who visited his jurisdiction can hardly be challenged. Papias's reference to his investigations, however, should not

---

contents of the discussion between Jesus and Nicodemus concerning what constitutes being born again (cf. John 3:1–15) then John's testimony of that discussion is considered "secondhand," even though the apostle John may have been present during the discussion. However, John's eyewitness accounting of Lazarus's resurrection (cf. John 11.1–44) is considered "firsthand" testimony of that event since John witnessed it rather than simply being present but not a participant of a conversation. Consequently, because of the confusion concerning the credibility of first and secondhand testimony, Bauckham's use of the term "eyewitness" provides greater clarity concerning the reliability of the Gospel narratives as passed on to the following generation.

201. As previously explained, by the beginning of the second century the terms "elder" and "apostle" were in flux; consequently, these terms had various understandings attributed to them when used in different contexts.

202. Holmes, *Apostolic Fathers*, 3rd ed., 735.

203. Bauckham, *The Eyewitnesses*, 17.

be understood to demand that he never left Hierapolis. Papias claimed to have "carefully learned" and "carefully remembered" the traditions of the apostles, thus "guaranteeing their truth."[204] He could hardly have made such a guarantee if he had to depend exclusively upon thirdhand sources that occasionally drifted through Hierapolis. If he was in fact a contemporary of those who were students of the last living apostle (e.g., as Polycarp was to the apostle John) who spent his final years in Ephesus, then it is almost certain that Papias would have made the same effort as Polycarp (who was the Bishop of Smyrna) to sit and learn at the feet of this most trustworthy eyewitness of life and ministry of Jesus, and in all probability he would have made multiple attempts. Why should any objective person contend that while others traveled Papias did not?[205]

It is also just as possible that the apostle John may have made a trip or two to enjoy the "healing" springs at Hierapolis. Hierapolis was not some back water town in Asia Minor, but rather it was a kind of resort town that lay only six miles from its slightly larger sister city Laodicea.[206] The book of Revelation described the members of the Laodicean church as economically thriving. It appears that the people of Asia Minor often had business in that part of the region, and if not for business then some also traveled to Hierapolis for religious and/or health reasons.[207] Within and around these two thriving cities there were at least three separate church networks with-

204. Holmes, *Apostolic Fathers*, 3rd ed., 735.

205. Bauckham, *The Eyewitnesses*, 33. Bauckham acknowledged that Christian leaders who were eyewitnesses of Jesus and his teachings had "special positions" and ministries that "spanned decades," and were "often very mobile." He believed that Christian Jews who were leaders of the church in Asia Minor traveled to Jerusalem and met with these eyewitnesses before 70. Such pilgrimages would have been essential for guaranteeing the transmission of orthodox traditions. After the fall of Jerusalem, however, the eyewitnesses of Jesus ministry would have been compelled to leave Palestine and locate elsewhere (e.g., Asia Minor or Syria). See also Metzger, *The Canon*, 51–56. Bauckham's admission regarding the mobility of early Christian leaders is interesting and seems to harmonize with the historical data. Because of their status as eyewitnesses, however, the need for these leaders to travel and minister to other regions would not have abated after the fall of Jerusalem, nor would the need for regional bishops to travel to the locations of these eyewitnesses in order to hear and learn from them. Consequently, it is a complete mystery as to why Bauckham and others think that Papias was less mobile than any other average leader of the church in Asia Minor, or that he would have apparently neglected to take advantage of any opportunities to travel and receive valuable instruction from important apostolic source(s).

206. For a more thorough discussion of this region see chapter 3 of this book.

207. A more comprehensive description of the city of Papias bishopric is found the following chapter.

in a day's walk of each other, one in both Laodicea and Hierapolis, and a third in Colossae. Why, therefore, should we assume that the apostle John refrained from journeying to this particular area of Asia Minor? Jerome wrote that the apostle John "founded and built churches throughout all Asia" with Ephesus serving as his base of operation.[208] Similarly, Eusebius recorded on the authority of Clement of Alexandria that after the apostle John returned from his banishment on Patmos he had a rather active ministry that required him to travel to "neighboring districts."[209] Regardless of whether the apostle John traveled to Hierapolis, there is no reason to think that Papias suffered under some form of "house arrest" that prohibited him from the firsthand education that he so dearly valued.[210] Contrary to Bauckham's assertion, therefore, it is unlikely that distance education was Papias's only source for obtaining apostolic traditions, especially those originated from the apostle John.

Bauckham concluded his initial chapter on Papias (which is chapter 2) with a discussion focused on the purpose of Papias's work. It is here that Bauckham cogently explained the value that authors of ancient histories placed upon sources that were firsthand or eyewitnesses to the subject matter of the historian. Bauckham believed Papias's reference to "a living and surviving voice" was not metaphorical, but rather it was his assertion that he had access to eyewitnesses as he gathered material for his *magnum opus*, eyewitnesses who were still "surviving" as he wrote.[211] The importance of this allusion, he contended, is significant with respect to distinguishing between what constituted "oral tradition" and what was regarded as "oral history." Bauckham convincingly argued that Papias viewed his work as a historical endeavor, although he unnecessarily believed that Papias was "unable to interview participants directly."[212] It was his theory that the time between when the eyewitnesses of Jesus communicated their traditions concerning his ministry to their followers and when Papias's gained access to those hearers of said "oral" traditions concerning Jesus was extremely brief, lasting no longer than the time it took for one to travel from Ephesus to Hierapolis. This brief period, Bauckham argued, is missed by those who hold to the "inappropriate model" developed by

---

208. Jerome *Illustrious Men* 9 (NPNF2 3:364–65).

209. Eusebius *Ecc. Hist.* III.23.6 (LCL 153:243).

210. Munck had no problem believing Papias often traveled in order to learn the traditions of the elders that he highly valued and trusted. Munck, "Presbyters," 229.

211. Bauckham, *The Eyewitnesses*, 27.

212. Ibid., 31.

many form critics regarding the transmission of traditions within the first-century church.[213] He ended this insightful chapter with a discussion of the concept of "tradition," which he explained was often found in ancient histories as a reference to a "written record" rather than to the "collective and cross-generational nature of oral traditions."[214] In spite of a few of Bauckham's unwarranted assumptions, such as Papias's apparent distaste for travel, this early chapter provides research that effectively calls into question the traditional model of many form critics concerning the transmission and recording of "oral" traditions and histories of the early church.

Bauckham again focused upon Papias in chapter 9, devoting his attention towards Papias's comments concerning the origins of the Gospels of Matthew and Mark drawn from Papias's preface. Bauckham's discussion in this chapter may well be the most insightful discourse to date regarding this topic, a topic about which much ink has been vainly spilt. He initiated his discussion by addressing the manner in which Eusebius arranged Papias's comments regarding the origins of the Gospels of Matthew and Mark. He rightly observed that it is not certain that Papias's source concerning his tradition about Matthew's Aramaic "Gospel" was in fact the "Elder John." Eusebius's contextualization of Papias's comment on this work, however, suggests that the same person was Papias's source for the origins of both Mark's Greek Gospel and Matthew's initial Aramaic Gospel.[215] Bauckham also briefly addressed the "widespread view" that John Mark (Barnabas's cousin) was the author of the Gospel of Mark. Concerning this view, he argued that "there is no reason to suppose that this was the John Mark of the New Testament."[216] While it is true, as Bauckham

213. Ibid., 31–32.

214. Ibid., 36–37.

215. Ibid., 202. Matthew Black rejected this conjecture, writing that "we cannot, therefore, be certain that the two statements were juxtaposed in this way by anyone other than Eusebius, nor can we assume (as many have done) that both are 'traditions' of 'the elder.'" Black, "Rhetorical Terminology," 32. Although, as Black stated, we cannot be certain regarding the context in which both these statements were originally found in Papias's writings, Eusebius appears to have brought them together in a respectable fashion. Black's contention, however, regarding the source of Papias's statement about Matthew's Aramaic Gospel should be duly noted. This is not to argue that Papias's tradition regarding this Gospel did not predate Papias or was from a less reliable source, only that we simply cannot be as certain about Papias's source for his tradition concerning Matthew's Aramaic Gospel as we might be of Papias's tradition regarding Mark's Gospel.

216. Bauckham, *The Eyewitnesses*, 203.

suggested, that the Greek name *"Markos"* and the Latin *"Marcus"* were common first-century names, and therefore, one cannot be "certain" that John Mark was the author of the Gospel bearing his name. Nevertheless, it is also a poorly defended position to assert that scholars have "no reason" to hold the opinion that the Mark found in 1 Peter 5:13 is not the same John Mark who helped compose what many believed to be the canonical Gospel of Mark.[217] Regardless of Bauckham's opinion concerning which Mark may have composed the Gospel bearing his name, he affirmed that it was the elder John who was Papias's source regarding the origin of the "first" Greek Gospel, and that Papias only quoted the epistle 1 Peter 5:13 as "corroboration of what the Elder said."[218]

Having established that "a" Mark authored the first Greek Gospel, Bauckham aptly discussed his function as a "translator" for the apostle Peter. His argument respects Papias's vocabulary and broadly analyzes what part Mark may have played in assisting Peter in the composition of the "first" Gospel. He believed that Mark was primarily Peter's interpreter (i.e., translator from Aramaic to Greek) rather than one who provided commentary on Peter's messages. Concerning this important distinction, Bauckham wrote,

> The Greek noun *hermēneutēs* is related to the verb *hermēneuō*, which Papias uses later in his statement about Matthew's Gospel. Both words can refer to interpretation in the sense of either (1) translation from one language to another, or (2) explanation and exposition. Does Papias (reporting the Elder) mean that Mark acted as Peter's translator or as an expositor who explained what Peter's teaching meant? Although many scholars have opted for the latter possibility, what Papias goes on to say about Mark makes this option unlikely. The whole paragraph seems designed to assert that Mark reproduced in his Gospel exactly what he heard Peter say. This is how Papias excuses what would otherwise be a serious deficiency in Mark's Gospel: its lack of "ordered arrangement." Mark intended to do no more than write down what Peter said just as he recalled it. This emphasis coheres much more naturally with calling Mark Peter's "translator" than with conceding Mark freedom to interpret what Peter said.[219]

217. Ibid. Bauckham appeared to marginalize this very assertion in a later footnote (cf. ibid., 206, n. 10).

218. Ibid., 205.

219. Bauckham, *The Eyewitnesses*, 205.

Bauckham aptly recognized concerning the issue of how Mark may have functioned as Peter's translator—whether during Peter's preaching or in the process of composing Mark's Gospel—that while Peter may have been bilingual (as many have suggested), that is not to say that he was as proficient as he wished, or as eloquent as Roman audiences may have demanded.[220] Anyone who has ever attempted to preach or compose an important document into a non-native language to an unfamiliar audience knows that such a task can be very daunting. Regarding Mark's primary role as Peter's interpreter, Bauckham asserted that Mark functioned as such while helping Peter to transition his sermons from oral communication to a literary record. Bauckham wrote concerning Mark's involvement in the "translation" of Peter's preaching into a document(s) of some form that

> Peter might be content with his own rough Greek in his oral teaching, but when it came to having his words recorded he preferred to express himself in his native Aramaic and allow Mark to translate into more accurate and readable Greek. It is worth recalling that even the Jewish historian Josephus, who could certainly speak Greek well, used secretaries to assist him with writing good literary Greek (*C. Apion.* 1.50). Mark's Greek has no literary pretensions, but it could well have been sufficiently better than Peter's for his role as translator to have been thought useful in recording Peter's teaching in writing.[221]

It was Bauckham's contention, therefore, that "Mark translated and wrote as Peter spoke," but that when this material was finally brought together in the form of a Gospel it was "Mark, not Peter, (who) was responsible for the order in which they were compiled to form the Gospel."[222] Bauckham's analysis of the relationship between Mark and Peter during the development of the Gospel of Mark is compelling. While it is difficult to be absolutely certain as to how these two related during the composition of the Gospel of Mark, Bauckham has cogently argued that Papias's language affirms that the apostle Peter was the dominant source for the content of Mark's Gospel, and that the source of this tradition was the individual that Papias referred to as "the Elder," who Papias also stated was "a disciple of the Lord."

220. Gundry was of the opinion that Peter was sufficiently bi-lingual; he could, therefore, speak for himself. Gundry, *Mark*, 1035.

221. Bauckham, *The Eyewitnesses*, 206.

222. Ibid., 207.

Bauckham also made another interesting observation regarding Papias's comment about the fidelity of Mark's Gospel with respect to Peter's teachings, which was that Papias employed language that was common for describing ancient historiography.[223] It was Papias's main concern to defend Mark's fidelity to his eyewitness source, as well as to defend his integrity as Peter's "translator." The importance of Bauckham's observation is that to a significant degree Papias viewed Mark's work as a faithful history of Jesus' life, and not simply as a theological treatise that originated from the mind of Mark, about which its historical basis had little purpose or value, let alone its accuracy. Some radical form and redaction critics speculate about what may have been the spiritual or moral needs of early communities for which the Gospels were original composed, or what might have been the spiritual milieu that generated these initial Gospel traditions. They fail to consider the very real possibility that in the minds of the Gospel writers a very pressing need of early Christian communities was *to know with certainty what Jesus actually said and did*, and, consequently, that an accurate history of his life was composed by them in order to meet this most essential need. Moreover, this primary purpose for the canonical Gospels is confirmed not only in Papias's preface, but also in the preface of Luke's Gospel as well (cf. Luke 1:1–4).

While Bauckham's thesis regarding Papias's comments about Mark's fidelity to Peter's traditions is compelling, there is one component of his position that some scholars may find objectionable, which is his position that the subject of the verbs *"emnēmoneusen"* and *"apemnēmoneusen"* (found in Papias's preface regarding the origin of Mark's Gospel) may in fact be Peter and not Mark.[224] Bauckham argued that Mark translated into writing what *Peter* remembered, rather than Mark wrote down what *he* remembered Peter to have preached. While Bauckham's translation is grammatically "possible" (if for no other reason than he could conceive of it) it is not likely. The more natural interpretation is that it was Mark's memory of Peter's messages and teachings that was employed as he compiled the Gospel that bears his name.[225] This, however, should not detract from Bauckham's main thesis that Mark's composition is an accurate history about the life and teachings of Jesus Christ with Peter being his eyewitness source. If Mark had participated in Peter's ministry, either as an in-

---

223. Ibid., 208–9.

224. Ibid., 210–11.

225. Gundry, *Matthew*, 619. Regarding this possible interpretation see also Mullins, "Papias," 217.

terpreter as Peter preached, or as Peter's tutor who helped him translate or
refine his original Aramaic message and its meanings into the appropriate
Greek words and rhetorical style, then Peter was still Mark's source for his
Gospel, and Mark would have been an excellent source for recalling and
recording Peter's messages.

Bauckham's perspective, which cogently wrestles with the historical
data as found in Papias's preface, is a refreshing alternative to the mod-
els promoted by radical form critics. While reading the research of some
scholars one may get the impression that Mark authored his Gospel by
remembering what he could from a few sermons that he had heard from
Peter himself or from the rumors of others, as well as depending upon
a few other written sources (e.g., "Q"), or oral traditions from different
Christian communities. If Mark, however, regularly accompanied Peter
over a prolonged period of ministry (e.g., several months or a year), functioning as his translator and aiding him as he recounted his oral "gospel"
into another language, it would not be hard for Mark to have remembered
what Peter had communicated to the church(es) in Rome and elsewhere.[226]
Peter would also not be the first itinerant preacher who often repeated
his favorite stories and sermons, and the churches in Rome would not be
the first orally dependent audience who demanded encore performances
from important speakers. Such auditory repetitions would have certainly
enhanced Mark's ability to recall Peter's memorializations of Jesus' life and
teachings. Consequently, Bauckham's view that Mark interacted closely
with Peter to aid him with translating and communicating his "gospel" to
the church(es) in Rome fits well with Papias's testimony about the tradition he received concerning the origin of Mark's Gospel.

Bauckham also addressed other issues involving vocabulary found
in Papias's preface. Similarly to other scholars, he understood the term
"*chreia*" as a rhetorical term that should be interpreted to mean that Peter
adapted his message for the purpose of educating Christian communities
about Jesus rather than attempting to address their changing felt needs.
Bauckham explained this assertion by stating that "In the light of Papias's
use of rhetorical terms elsewhere, this interpretation of *pros tas chreias*
seems very likely correct, especially as we can see that it corresponds sufficiently to the short units of which Mark's narrative is composed for Papias to have regarded Mark as a collection of Peter's *chreiai* about Jesus."[227]

226. It should not be assumed that Rome was the only opportunity that John Mark
had to hear Peter's "gospel."

227. Bauckham, *The Eyewitnesses*, 215.

This view is dramatically at odds with some who believe Peter continually "adapted" his messages to meet the changing "needs" of his differing audiences. Instead, Bauckham recognized that *"chreia"* was a rhetorical reference to the technical "form" of Peter's teachings, which describes how his material was presented rather than a reference to the "evolution" of his gospel as he delivered it to various churches in the cultural contexts of different cities.[228]

Having addressed Papias's reference to the "χρείας" of Peter (i.e., the manner in which Peter presented his "material"), Bauckham turned to Mark's apparent lack of observable order (*taxis*, which in Greek is τάξις) in his Gospel. Regarding this apparent deficiency, he stated that "since he (Mark) was no more than a translator, he did not add to his material by investing it with artistic arrangement."[229] He continued to give an apt explanation regarding what first-century audiences generally expected with respect to acceptable literary styles for ancient biographies and histories, explaining that they valued data found in some form of orderly arrangement, which could have been either chronological or thematic. Recognizing this expectation, Bauckham argued that it was "because Mark was not himself an eyewitness of the life of Jesus that he was unable to supply the order that Peter had failed to give to his material."[230] The consequence of Mark's fidelity to Peter's testimonies, Bauckham explained, was that his Gospel lacked some aesthetic order.[231] This explains Papias's desire to compare and defend Mark's Gospel with other Gospels that were apparently more appreciated for their artistic and rhetorical prowess.[232] Bauckham spent the remaining portion of chapter 9 discussing Papias's explanation of the origins of the Gospels of Mark, Matthew, and John, and his defense of their authority, while also providing an analysis of literary or rhetorical criticism concerning them. He was convinced that Papias knew of the Gospel of John,[233] and contended that his comments about the Gospels of Mark and Matthew (as preserved by Eusebius) were his attempt to defend them as "histories" that contained eyewitness testimonies, while also

228. Schoedel held a similar position. Schoedel, *The Fragments*, 106–7.

229. Bauckham, *The Eyewitnesses*, 216.

230. Ibid., 221.

231. Ibid., 217.

232. Ibid., 218–21. It should be noted that while modern readers may either prefer the style of Mark's Gospel or see no problem with it at all; nevertheless, they should not presume their own literary or rhetorical tastes upon first and second-century audiences.

233. Ibid., 225.

explaining John's desire to compose another more rhetorically acceptable biography of the life and teachings of Jesus of Nazareth.

Bauckham's *Jesus and the Eyewitnesses* is a ground-breaking endeavor that will significantly influence many discussions and investigations focused on the development of the New Testament. While some of his theories are questionable, his research concerning the composition of ancient histories and the Gospels is both commendably and valuable. Consequently, his contribution with respect to origins of the Gospels and their credibility should not be ignored by any wishing to understand their purposes and integrity. He has also brought greater illumination upon Papias and his purpose(s); therefore, Bauckham's insights will contribute significantly to the discussions throughout this book.

Some Concluding Remarks

The amount of references to Papias in New Testament and patristic studies is immense, many of which appear in works where the average layman or disciplined researcher might not intuitively think to look. One such example is found in John R. W. Stott's small commentary, *The Epistles of John*, which is part of the Tyndale New Testament Commentaries series.[234] Although Stott's comments are brief, nevertheless they have merit and are worthy of consideration with respect to any study of Papias. Thus, it is a certainty that there are many other similar publications within which are countless other examples of salient discussions about Papias and his context. Nevertheless, to attempt to annotate and catalogue them all would render this book virtually unreadable. This being the case, I offer the sincerest of apologies to those that I have missed who otherwise should have been considered; and with this in mind I now turn to a brief biography of this great apostolic father.

---

234. Stott, *The Epistles of John*, 35–41.

3

The Life of Papias

Papias and His Ethnicity

The amount of data, as previously stated, providing certitude about Papias's life is minimal. For example, attestations concerning his place or date of birth, his ethnicity, and the extent of his education have not survived. Vernon Bartlet dated Papias's birth ca. 60 or earlier. He based his opinion on Irenaeus's reference to Papias as having been an "ancient man," a phrase which Irenaeus did not use to describe Polycarp. Regarding Papias's birth, he wrote, "In any case he seems to have been rather senior to Polycarp; for Irenaeus styles the former, as he never calls the latter (born c. A.D. 69 at least), 'a primitive man' (ἀρχαῖος ἀνήρ). Thus he may well have been born not later than 60, and possibly even earlier."[1] Similarly, Richard Bauckham dated Papias's birth ca. 50.[2] Irenaeus's reference to Papias as being very old is significant; however, it unfortunately is not precise. Thus, without greater specificity from Irenaeus or further corroboration from others, precision regarding the year of Papias's birth is not possible. Consequently, it seems reasonable to place Papias's birth around the same period as Polycarp's, which is ca. 70, although estimations for an earlier date cannot be ruled out entirely.

---

1. Bartlet, "Papias's Exposition," 17. Lightfoot also dated Papias's birth between 60–70. Lightfoot, *Essays*, 150. Munck also dated Papias's birth ca. 60. Munck, "Presbyters," 240.
2. Bauckham, *The Eyewitnesses*, 18.

J. B. Lightfoot believed that Papias was at least Phrygian and possibly even from Hierapolis since his name and various forms of it were apparently common Phrygian names, which have been found on inscriptions associated with Zeus and coins unearthed in the area. Consequently, he believed that the name "Papias" was the Phrygian "equivalent to the Greek Diogenes," which means "born of Zeus."[3] Being ethnically Phrygian at the turn of first century would have been an advantage for anyone ministering in Hierapolis. William Ramsay believed that pride in Phrygian nationality was particularly strong in Hierapolis as compared to other cities in the Lycus Valley.[4] He contended that the religious practices of the city confirmed his assertion, stating that "Greek became the sole language of the city, and a veneer of Greek civilization spread over it; but the veneer was much thinner than at Laodiceia or Apameia. Hierapolis maintained its importance through its religious position; and its remains and history bear witness to the strength of the religious feeling in it. The religion continued to be Lydo-Phrygian, and even Greek names for the gods were used less in Hierapolis than in many other cities."[5] If Papias was in fact from Hierapolis and of Phrygian ethnicity then he would have been well suited for ministry in that city.

"Papias," although not common, was also a Greek word that is translated as "janitor" or "keeper of the palace."[6] Phrygia was thoroughly Hellenized well before the end of the first century; therefore it is possible that Papias was of Greek descent, and as such he may have been given a rather uncommon Greek name. Given its nuance, however, it is hard to imagine that anyone might name their child "Papias," for what right-minded parent would name his or her son "janitor." If his name was given with the Greek connotation in mind then it seems more likely that it (if it was a Greek name at all) was the English equivalent of "Stewart," which when not used as a proper name means "servant." This possibility, however, seems unlikely. It is more reasonable to assume that if Papias was in fact Greek, or Roman for that matter, then his parents gave him this name with the Phrygian nuance in mind.

Hierapolis was located in southwest Asia Minor; therefore, if Papias was from Hierapolis or the Lycus valley then it is very likely that he

---

3. Lightfoot, *Colossians*, 48; and Lightfoot, *Essays*, 153. See also Körtner, *Papias*, 88; Rigg, "Papias on Mark," 162.

4. Ramsay, *Cities and Bishoprics of Phrygia*, vol. 1.1, 84.

5. Ibid., 88.

6. LSJ, s.v. "παπίας."

was of Gentile birth.[7] Archaeological evidence, however, indicates that Hierapolis also had a significant Jewish population; consequently, there is the possibility that Papias was also Jewish.[8] Paul's epistle to the Colossians confirms that the church in that city contained a certain percentage of Jewish members, for from its inception it struggled to maintain orthodoxy in the face of, among many other influences, a peculiar form of syncretistic Jewish spiritualism.[9] Consequently, as was the case with many churches in the middle of the first century, it appears that the churches in the Lycus Valley were originally comprised of a mixture of both Jewish and Gentile members. It is not unreasonable, therefore, to believe that such a mixture continued to some degree in these churches into the following generation.[10] If Papias was raised in one of these churches then he could have been of either Jewish or Gentile descent. Evidence of diasporic Jews receiving Gentile names can be found in Acts 6:5.[11] It is not inconceivable, therefore, that some Jews living in this region may have given their children Phrygian names. Consequently, certitude regarding Papias's ethnicity based upon his name is not well defended. If one were pressed to conjecture, however, the position that he was ethnically Phrygian and was raised in the Lycus Valley seems an attractive possibility. Regardless of the lack of concrete information about Papias's early life and ethnicity, the historical data confirms that he was appointed a bishop and that he ministered at Hierapolis.

7. On both the Hellenization and Christianization of Hierapolis see Ramsay, *Cities and Bishoprics of Phrygia*, vol. 1.2, 681–83.

8. "Hierapolis"; available from http://www.sacred-destinations.com/turkey/hierapolis-pamukkale.htm; Internet. For a discussion of potential size of the Jewish population in Phrygia see Polhill, *Paul*, 332.

9. Bruce, *Colossians*, 17–26; Polhill, *Paul*, 332–38.

10. For a discussion regarding Jewish-Christian relationships in the church from the end of the first century into the beginning of the second century see Holmes, *Apostolic Fathers*, 3rd ed., 8–14. Jewish or pro-Judaism influences were clearly present within the churches of Asia Minor into the early second century. For evidence of the tensions this caused the church during the period of Papias's ministry see Ignatius *To the Magnesians* 8–10 (LCL 24:248–51). For other evidence of Jewish–Christian tensions within the early church see *Didache* 8–10 (LCL 24:429–33); and *The Epistle of Barnabas* 4.6–9 (LCL 25:21–23).

11. Perumalil believed Papias to be a well educated bi-lingual Jew, see Perumalil, "Papias," 363.

PAPIAS AND HIS CITY

Christianity had a relatively early history in Hierapolis. The earliest reference of its association with the city is found in Paul's epistle to the Colossians. Paul's epistle to the Colossians is generally thought to have been written during his first imprisonment, which occurred at either Caesarea, Ephesus, or Rome around the late fifties or early sixties AD.[12] It appears that the gospel was first introduced to Hierapolis through the ministry of Epaphras of Colossae, an associate of the apostle Paul (Col 4:12–13). This evangelistic movement seems to have occurred as a result of Paul's Ephesian ministry, spreading from Ephesus approximately one hundred miles east into the Lycus valley (Acts 19:1–20). Taken together these biblical references place the birth of Christianity in this region during the mid to late 50s AD, having first spread to Colossae, and then later to Laodicea and Hierapolis. Paul implied, however, that he had never personally ministered in that part of the Phrygian region (Col 2–1).

The ruins of Hierapolis can be found in southwest Turkey on the north slope of the Lycus valley directly opposite the ancient city of Laodicea, being separated by six miles and the Maeander River.[13] Hierapolis is no longer inhabited and is presently known as "Pamukkale," which means "cotton castles." This name refers to the white cliffs that are formed by water flowing from hot springs into the valley below, leaving residual layers of white calcium carbonate to adorn the cliffs of the plateau where the ancient city was perched. These springs still flow today, and the effects of their deposits are stunning and can be seen for miles.[14] The city of Laodicea, with respect to its political and economical prominence, was considered of greater rank than that of Hierapolis, while both were more significant than the much smaller town of Colossae,[15] which lay approximately 10 to 12 miles southeast of Laodicea. The ruins of Colossae are found on both sides of the Lycus River, which is a tributary of the Maean-

12. Polhill, *Paul*, 332. Regarding the location of Paul's writing of Colossians, Bruce argued for Rome, but concerning the issue of the author's location he wrote, "The question is not of the first importance, as it makes little difference to the exegesis whether it was sent from Rome or Caesarea or Ephesus." Simpson and Bruce, *Ephesians and Colossians*, 164.

13. Polhill, *Paul*, 331.

14. For photos of the ruins of Hierapolis see "Hierapolis," available from http://www.ourfatherlutheran.net/biblehomelands/sevenchurches/hierapolis/hierapolis.htm; Internet. See also, "Hierapolis"; available from http://www.sacred-destinations.com/turkey/ hierapolis-pamukkale.htm; Internet.

15. Lightfoot, *Colossians*, 5.

der River. Archaeological evidence indicates that Hierapolis was a popular "resort" town in Asia Minor. It was generally thought that the city's hot springs held healing powers. These springs also proved profitable for the wool and carpet trade because they enabled the textile guilds to produce highly sought after purple textiles that were used to make wool clothing and carpets—the purple dye apparently deriving from the extract of the madder root.

Hierapolis means "holy city," and the city's name appears to have been well deserved because of its diverse religious associations.[16] Lightfoot wrote that Hierapolis had chosen "Apollo, the god alike of medicine and of festivity," to worship as its patron deity, although in Hierapolis he was "worshipped especially as 'Archegetes,' the Founder." Lightfoot recognized, however, that "older worship religious rites were borrowed also from other parts of the East."[17] This was confirmed by David Gill and Bruce Winter, who noted that Hierapolis was a "main cult center" of the eastern deity of Jupiter Dolichenus, explaining that "Jupiter Dolichenus was a form of the cult of Hadad, who was the consort of the Syrian deity Atergatis."[18] Co-opting Greek and Roman deities to represent the deities of local or regional cults may seem confusing for some, but such associations were a common practice for the patron cults of cities during the period of the Roman Empire. Regarding this co-opting Greek and Roman names for the gods of regional cults, Robyn Tracey wrote,

> It must be remembered that this was an old land . . . with a history of foreign domination, a history which must have been known, at least in part and orally, to the bulk of the population. Egyptians, Hittites, Assyrians, Persians, Greeks, all had at some stage held at least part of the region, by direct rule or through vassalage. Their perception, correct or otherwise, must have been that had it not been the Romans, it would have been the Parthians, or someone else. And Roman yoke was fairly light, particularly at first, with the retention of local dynasts and the limited "freedom" granted to the Greek cities not under their rule, combined with generally benign, if unenterprising governorship by the Romans themselves.
>
> Here the local religions posed no barrier to Roman rule. The gods, as complaisant as their devotees, amenably answered to

---

16. Ramsay, *Cities and Bishoprics of Phrygia*, vol. 1.1, 84.

17. Lightfoot, *Colossians*, 12–13.

18. Gill and Winter, "Acts and Roman Religion," 84.

whatever name the Roman rulers were pleased to call them by, just as they had previously accepted their new Greek names.[19]

Hierapolis is also the site of a cave once known as "Plutonium," which was believed to be sacred because it provided entrance to the underworld, thus leading to the "domain of the Roman god Pluto (the Greek Hades)."[20] The cave to this day emits poisonous gases that if inhaled are immediately fatal. Only the priests of the cult of Cybele were thought to be immune to its deadly vapors.[21] This immunity, however, could easily be received by anyone smart enough to hold his or her breath during their stay in the cave. Paul's epistle to the church at Colossae confirms that during the mid-first century AD the spiritual soil in the Lycus valley was fertile for religious diversity, and was accommodating to the syncretizing of different religious systems. It was in this environment that Epaphras first introduced the gospel, and approximately fifty years later it was to the church at Hierapolis that Papias was called to serve as bishop.

PAPIAS AND HIS COMPANIONS

The debate concerning Papias's companions is greatly contested. There is a Papian fragment from a contemporary of Papias who may have actually known him and those with whom he associated—Irenaeus of Lyons. The fragment is from Irenaeus's *Against Heresies* V.33.4, and has been preserved in Greek in Eusebius's *Ecclesiastical History* III.39.1; which reads, "And also these things Papias, the hearer of John, having been a companion of Polycarp, an ancient man, bears witness by writing in the fourth of his books . . ."[22] The period in which Irenaeus lived and his relationship with Polycarp is important and will be discussed later, but for the present it is necessary to evaluate the relative trust that other patristic authors placed upon Irenaeus's testimony regarding Papias's association with Polycarp.

---

19. Tracey, "Syria," 258. This is not to argue that Rome was tolerant of all religions, for clearly at times it was not. For a more recent discussion of theories regarding religious diversity in the Roman Empire see Bingham, "Early Christianity," 45–48.

20. "Hierapolis"; available from http://www.sacred-destinations.com/turkey/hierapolis-pamukkale.htm; Internet.

21. For greater explanation regarding the history and activities of the priests of the cult of Cybele (or Magna Mater), see Beard, North, Price, *Religions of Rome*, 1: 80, 96–98, 164–66, 263; and Smith, "Galli," 566–67.

22. Eusebius *Ecc. Hist.* III.39.1 (LCL153:291).

That Papias was a contemporary of Polycarp appears to be uncontested in patristic literature. The next attestation to Polycarp and Papias's relationship after the statement made by Irenaeus comes from Eusebius in his *Chronicle*, which has been preserved in Latin by Jerome and is roughly translated as: "The Apostle John (lived) all the way to Trajan's time, Irenaeus the honorable bishop wrote. After whom hearers of him became distinguished, they were bishop Papias of Hierapolis, and Polycarp of Smyrna, and Ignatius of Antioch."[23] More analysis of this fragment will follow, the present concern is Eusebius's confidence in the accuracy of the statement that Papias and Polycarp were contemporaries. Eusebius was so confident that they shared a common period in the church's history that he again affirmed that they were contemporaries in his *Ecclesiastical History*

23. Eusebius, *Die Chronik des Hieronymus*, 193–94. See also, Eusebii Pamphili, *Chronici Canones*, 275–76. Fotheringham's critical edition this passage in Latin reads as follows, "Johannem apostolum usque ad Traiani tempora Hireneus episcopus permansisse scribit, post quem auditores eius insignes fuerunt Papias Hierapolitanus episcopus et Polycarpus Zmyrnaeus et Ignatius Antiochenus." Holmes's citation of Eusebius's *Chronicle* from the critical editions of Schöne, Helms, and Fotheringham in his 1999 version of Lightfoot's *Apostolic Fathers* could lead to considerable confusion with respect to the singular or plural use of the word "bishop." (Holmes only cited Schöne in the 2007 edition of *Apostolic Fathers*. Holmes, *Apostolic Fathers*, 3rd ed., 733.) Regarding Jerome's preservation of Eusebius's *Chronicle*, Alden Mosshammer argued that Jerome's Latin text appears to be the more faithful translation of the *Chronicle* than the Armenian translation of Eusebius's chronology. For a more thorough discussion see Mosshammer, *The Chronicle of Eusebius*, 67–68. Helm's edition of Jerome's Latin text of Eusebius's *Chronicle* is slightly different than the Greek text provided by Holmes; see Holmes, *The Apostolic Fathers: Diglot Edition*, 562–63. This is because the Greek text provided by Holmes employs a quote found in Alfred Schöne's critical edition titled Eusebi, *Chronicorum canonum quae supersunt*, published as two volumes in 1866 and 1875. [For the Greek text provided by Holmes see also Eusebi, *Chronicorum Canonum*, 162.] The Greek text that Holmes employed is actually from Georgius Syncellus, a late ninth and early tenth-century Byzantine monk. Holmes's employment of this text gives the appearance that Holmes has provided a Papian fragment of Eusebius's *Chronicle* in the original Greek. To date there is no extant manuscript of this work from the hand of Eusebius. Holmes has actually employed Syncellus's quote or redaction of Eusebius's *Chronicle*. Mosshammer published a critical edition of Syncellus's *Ecloga Chronographica*. Mosshammer's edition followed the textual family "t" for this particular Papian fragment. In this fragment the word "bishops" (ἐπίσκοποι) is found in the plural, indicating that both Polycarp and Papias were both bishops who had been "hearers" of the apostle John. See Georgii Syncelli, *Ecloga Chronographica*, 424. Holmes's text has the word "bishop" in the singular, apparently following the younger Codex Parisinus, which is an eleventh century manuscript (see ibid., xviii and xxxvii). It is interesting that Syncellus stated that there were other sources that confirmed the *terminus a quo* of the apostle John's life and his possible relationships to Polycarp and Papias.

III.36.1–2, where he wrote, "At this time there flourished in Asia Polycarp, the companion of the Apostles, who had been appointed to the bishopric of the church in Smyrna by the eyewitnesses and ministers of the Lord. Distinguished men at the same time were Papias, who was himself bishop of the diocese of Hierapolis, and Ignatius."[24] It is clear from additional references to Papias in Eusebius's writings that he had depended heavily upon Irenaeus for identification of the period in which Papias lived. What is not clear is what other sources, if any, Eusebius also employed with respect to additional information about Papias.[25] Regardless of what may or may not have been his sources, he was at least confident that Irenaeus was an accurate witness of the time period of Polycarp's life, and thus felt no qualms about writing that Papias and Polycarp were contemporaries who not only lived during the same time period, but more importantly were of the same adult generation. Consequently, both Irenaeus and Eusebius believed that these two great Asiaic bishops were contemporaries in the truest sense of the word.[26]

Given that the surviving literary evidence from the early church affirming that Papias and Polycarp were contemporaries of the same adult generation it now becomes necessary to assess the credibility of Irenaeus's relationships to Polycarp, and consequently his ability to testify to Polycarp's relationship to Papias. It is largely recognized that at some point in his life Irenaeus knew Polycarp. It is his capacity, however, to accurately attest to the nature and extent of his relationship with Polycarp that at times is questioned. Some believe that Irenaeus was born in Smyrna, which was the city of Polycarp's bishopric, although the exact date and place of Irenaeus's birth is "uncertain."[27] Iain Mackenzie believed that even if Irenaeus was not actually born in Smyrna "he at least had his early upbringing there," and that it was during his time in Smyrna that he was

---

24. Eusebius *Ecc. Hist.* III.36.1–2 (LCL 153:280–81).

25. The possible existence of other sources will be discussed often in the body of this book as it examines other Papian fragments. Regarding the allusions to other such sources see *Chronicon Paschale* (PG 92:628); and Eusebius *Ecc. Hist.* IV.15.46 (LCL 153:359).

26. This is contrary to Richard Heard's assessment that Papias and Polycarp were "roughly contemporaries." Heard, "Papias' Quotations," 132. Bartlet and Lightfoot both speculated that Papias may have been older than Polycarp. Bartlet, "Papias," 2:311; Lightfoot, *Essays*, 150. Conversely, Bacon believed Papias to be younger than Polycarp, Bacon, *Studies*, 442, as well as his disciple, Bacon, "An Emendation," 183.

27. Osborn, *Irenaeus*, 2.

introduced to Polycarp.[28] Some date Irenaeus's birth as early as 98, while others date his birth as late as 147.[29] Concerning the great diversity of opinions regarding the date of Irenaeus's birth, Osborn has aptly stated, "The most probable date lies between 130 and 140. The early estimates ignore the late development of his writing. The late estimates probably make him too young for the episcopacy in 177, when he succeeded the ninety-year old Pothinus."[30]

Irenaeus at some point moved to Lyons, which is in present-day France, it is there that he later served as bishop during the last quarter of the second century. In his writings Irenaeus claimed to have personally interacted with Polycarp. As previously stated, some scholars question Irenaeus's ability to accurately recall his association with Polycarp. They speculate that Irenaeus may have only briefly met Polycarp at a very early age; consequently, they doubt his ability to legitimately testify to anything regarding Polycarp's teachings or those with whom he associated.[31] Irenaeus, however, felt quite secure in his ability to testify to Polycarp and his orthodoxy. An analysis of the vocabulary Irenaeus used to describe his stage of life in which he interacted with Polycarp indicates that not only did he have close contact with Polycarp, but also that their association occurred over a period of years, years that Irenaeus confessed were very influential for him.

The first personal testimony of Irenaeus to be addressed is found in his *Letter to Florinus*, which has been preserved by Eusebius. In this letter Irenaeus confronted Florinus's apostasy from the orthodox faith, a faith that Irenaeus argued was received from the apostles and faithfully transmitted through Polycarp and numerous others. Since both he and Florinus had personal contact with Polycarp and had received instruction from him, Irenaeus believed that he could legitimately identify what constituted orthodoxy and, consequently, Florinus's departure from it. Irenaeus, in

---

28. Mackenzie, *Irenaeus's Demonstration*, 36.

29. Osborn provided a survey of years offered by different scholars concerning Irenaeus's birth (Osborn, *Irenaeus*, 2). It is not in the purview of this chapter to debate at length the year of Irenaeus's birth, but only to discern the credibility of his opportunity to accurately testify about Polycarp and his associates.

30. Ibid.

31. Hall, *Papias*, 307–8. Perumalil provides a well documented discussion concerning scholars who doubt Irenaeus's ability to report accurately anything regarding the teachings and associations of Polycarp. Perumalil, "Papias and Irenaeus," 332–33, 335–37. Perumalil argued that Irenaeus was in his late teens when he associated with Polycarp (ibid., 336).

what appears to have been on open letter,[32] went to great lengths to describe his memories regarding both his and Florinus's relationship to the great bishop of Smyrna, stating that

> For while I was still a boy I knew you in lower Asia in Polycarp's house when you were a man of rank in the royal hall and endeavouring to stand well with him. I remember the events of those days more clearly than those which happened recently, for what we learned as children grows up with the soul and is united to it so that I can speak even of the place in which the blessed Polycarp sat and disputed, how he came in and went out, the character of his life, the appearance of his body, the discourses which he made to the people, how he reported his intercourse with John and with the others who had seen the Lord, how he remembered their words, and what were the things concerning the Lord which he had heard from them, and about their miracles, and about their teaching, and how Polycarp had received them from the eyewitnesses of the word of life, and reported all things in agreement with the Scriptures. I listened eagerly even then to these things through the mercy of God which was given me, and made notes of them not on paper but in my heart, and ever by the grace of God do I truly ruminate on them.[33]

It is important to note the term Irenaeus used to describe his stage of life in which his interactions with Polycarp occurred before discussing his personal testimony about his memories about Polycarp. Irenaeus stated that he was a παῖς (a boy) when he was exposed to Polycarp's relationship with Florinus. He also argued that it was his experience that memories "from childhood" (ἐκ παίδων) endured better than even many of his adult memories. The pertinent point is that Irenaeus's memories of Polycarp and those he associated with began during his "childhood." Regarding the quantity and quality of his memories, Irenaeus was quite adamant about them and their accuracy and legitimacy. Throughout his description of his relationship to Polycarp nowhere did Irenaeus state or imply that he was only "incidentally exposed" to Polycarp. Therefore, in his mind his knowledge about Polycarp was not vague or inconclusive, instead his interactions with Polycarp occurred over an extended period of time that was, to say the least, very impressionable for Irenaeus. That Polycarp influenced him with more than just his personality is observable from Irenaeus's confession that he had heard "discourses" (τὰς διαλέξεις) from Polycarp

32. Lewis, *Fourth Gospel*, 27.
33. Eusebius *Ecc. Hist.* V.20.4–7 (LCL 153:497–98).

rather than a single brief devotional. He also confessed to have had access to Polycarp's home, which was where he witnessed Florinus's association with the bishop. Lastly, Irenaeus stated that his relationship with Polycarp not only allowed him to listen to his mentor's instructions and discourses, but also to assess this apostolic father's character and manner of life.

Irenaeus employed a very interesting word to describe how he went about "making notes" of Polycarp and his activities with respect to his "memorializing" of him. He did not use a mundane Greek verb such as γράφω to state that he "wrote" or "inscribed" his memories of Polycarp on his heart. Instead he employed the verb ὑπομνηατίζομαι,[34] which was a rather technical word used to describe the "cataloguing" of large amounts of material.[35] Polybius used this word to describe the composition of histories.[36] It is also found in 1 Esdras 6:23 with respect to the writing of official government records. Lampe, concerning patristic literature, cited Eusebius as employing this word to refer to Hegesippus's collection of material about "the apostolic preaching," which he stated consumed "five books."[37] To be sure, the word can simply mean "to note down for remembrance," or "to make a memorandum." Liddell and Scott however, reveal that this word was predominantly used to refer to the act of writing "official diaries," "treatises," "annals," "dissertations," and "commentaries." Consequently, this verb was regularly used to describe the systematic cataloguing of large amounts of official records and important information. Such a nuance fits the context of Irenaeus's descriptions extremely well. That he had more than a single memory of Polycarp and his teachings is also clear from Irenaeus's use of the word αὐτὰ, which is the object of the participle ὑπομνηατίζόμενος. This participle's object is in the neuter plural because Irenaeus was not simply describing his memorializing of Polycarp—if that were true then the object of the participle would have been masculine since Irenaeus would have been only referring to the "man" that was Polycarp. Instead, Irenaeus was referring to more than just Polycarp, he was also referring to his teachings, his activities, his ministry, and his associations.

Irenaeus's language, when considered in its entirety, speaks of extensive memories that occurred over a prolonged period of time, and of

---

34. Eusebius *Ecc. Hist.* IV.8.2 (LCL 153:498–99).

35. LSJ, s.v. "ὑπομνηατίζομαι."

36. Polybius *Histories* 2.4.4, 5.35.5, Internet.

37. Lampe, *A Patristic Greek Lexicon*, s.v. "ὑπομνηατίζομαι." See also Eusebius *Ecc. Hist.* IV.8.2 (LCL 153:320).

accessibility that was more than incidental. Irenaeus's description is indicative of a student who idealized his teacher and mentor, rather than that of a mere child who possessed only a vague memory of the elderly bishop of Smyrna. Given his vocabulary, Osborne rightly observed that Polycarp was at the very least a "dominant influence" in Irenaeus's life.[38] B. H. Streeter asserted, however, that, "In the absence of any express statement to that effect, we are not entitled to infer that he (Irenaeus) was in any sense a personal pupil of Polycarp." Irenaeus's descriptions of his memories of Polycarp, however, strongly argue to the contrary against Streeter's conjecture.[39]

It should be observed with respect to Irenaeus's description of his memories that it was not his intent to merely brag about his relationship with the bishop of Smyrna. Instead, he was testifying against Florinus—a man who was his elder—in order to prove that Florinus's theological positions were incompatible with the doctrines they had received from Polycarp. It is important to note, therefore, that if Irenaeus's recollections were the least bit inaccurate then Florinus would have been in an excellent position to expose Irenaeus's inconsistencies, and as a result excuse him as misinformed; thus completely destroying Irenaeus's credibility. Irenaeus's assertions were not for personal promotion, rather they were provided as a foundation upon which he could defend orthodoxy; thus they were not made without significant risk.[40] Consequently, if for no other reason than this, accuracy was critical on Irenaeus's part. He was, therefore, constrained to employ the word "παῖς" as he described himself and his memory of Florinus's association with Polycarp. As will become evident, in any other context Irenaeus would not feel this same compulsion when describing his relationship to this apostolic father.

Just such a context is found in Eusebius's preservation of a fragment of Irenaeus's *Against Heresies*, in which he again briefly described his association with Polycarp. This description is found in *Ecclesiastical History* IV.14.3-4, which has also preserved Irenaeus's original Greek. The text in question reveals that Irenaeus wrote, "And Polycarp also was not only instructed by apostles and conversed with many who had seen the Lord, but was also appointed bishop by apostles in Asia in the church in Smyrna. We also saw him in our childhood, for he lived a long time and in extreme

---

38. Osborn, *Irenaeus*, 3.

39. Streeter, *The Four Gospels*, 443–44.

40. Lewis, *Fourth Gospel*, 27.

old age passed from life, a splendid and glorious martyr."[41] One might conclude by reading Kirsopp Lake's English translation of this fragment that there appears to be no appreciable difference in Irenaeus's vocabulary of his stage of life when describing his interactions with Polycarp. The Greek, however, reveals a distinct difference in Irenaeus's vocabulary that is not fully appreciated in Lake's translation. In *Against Heresies* Irenaeus did not employ the same word as he did in his *Letter to Florinus*. As argued above, a possible reason for this was that accuracy in his testimony regarding when he and Florinus had known Polycarp was crucial to protecting the credibility of Irenaeus's testimony. Irenaeus in *Against Heresies*, however, described his exposure to Polycarp as having occurred "in our first maturity" (τῇ πρώτῃ ἡμῶν ἡλικία).[42] The word Irenaeus employed in this text to describe the period of life in which he interacted with Polycarp was ἡλικία, which is often translated to describe the stage of life where one transitions from childhood to adulthood, or even of adulthood itself. This same word is used to describe Jesus' progression towards maturation at age twelve in Luke 2:52. The apostle Paul also used this word in Ephesians 4:13 to describe the level of maturity that all believers should strive to attain. Interestingly, it is also employed by Eusebius as he reported the approximate life stage of the martyr Germanicus, who although being very young was apparently old enough to stand trial and testify to his own faith in Christ, a stand that cost him his life.[43] Ironically, this word was even used in the ninth chapter of *The Martyrdom of Polycarp* to refer to Polycarp's age at eighty-six.[44]

One can see, therefore, that this term has a range of meanings that varies from "youth"[45] or "youthfulness," to the description of one who has reached "maturity" or even of old age as in the case of Polycarp. The important point for the current discussion is that in *Against Heresies* Irenaeus felt more freedom to describe his stage of life when he knew and interacted with Polycarp, a freedom he lacked when he was constrained to describe his common memories of Polycarp and Florinus. Consequently, in *Against Heresies* Irenaeus described his exposure to Polycarp as having occurred

41. Eusebius *Ecc. Hist.* IV.14.3–4 (LCL 153:336–37).

42. Translation mine. Irenaeus's employment of the first person plural pronoun is interesting. It is not clear if he had certain individuals in mind, or if he was referring to his entire generation in an attempt to explain how Polycarp's generation overlapped his own. Lake translated this phrase as "in our childhood."

43. Eusebius IV.15.5 (LCL 153:340–43).

44. *The Martyrdom of Polycarp* 9 (LCL 24: 378–79).

45. Grant, *Irenaeus*, 3.

later in life, and thus occurred during a period of greater maturity. The implication is that in Irenaeus's letter to Florinus we learn that his relationship with Polycarp began in his childhood, while in *Against Heresies* we discover that their association extended into the period that Irenaeus referred to as "our first maturity."[46] Such a period could range from childhood to early adolescence or to early adulthood, and thus would have involved a number of very influential years. Consequently, this extended period would make Irenaeus a more than credible witness of not only Polycarp's character and orthodoxy, but also of individuals that Polycarp considered to be his "companions." Irenaeus's description of his interactions with Polycarp, when taken in their entirety, makes Streeter's contention that Irenaeus's memories were "slight" because he was only exposed to Polycarp during "a short visit" indefensible.[47]

Concerning Polycarp's associates, Irenaeus stated frankly that Papias was a "companion" of Polycarp. The context of Irenaeus's statement is his defense of his millennial views, which he implied originated with the apostle John and were faithfully transmitted through Papias. Irenaeus's statement that Papias associated with Polycarp was only ancillary to his discussion concerning the validity of his theological position. Consequently, there is little evidence to consider his statement as anything but accurate. Taken at face value, therefore, any neutral reader would assume that Irenaeus was to some degree in a position to know that Polycarp and Papias were in fact "companions." Given Irenaeus's testimony regarding the extent of his association with Polycarp, however, it is reasonable to conclude that he was in fact well positioned to identify those with whom Polycarp associated. Consequently, the burden of proof weighs upon those

---

46. Translation mine.

47. Streeter, *The Four Gospels*, 444–45. Schoedel described Irenaeus's knowledge of Polycarp as "thin"; Schoedel, *The Fragments*, 90. If one were to grant Streeter's speculation that Irenaeus was exposed to Polycarp for only a "few months," it is still possible, given Irenaeus's descriptions of his firsthand memories, that he was completely accurate regarding Polycarp's relationship to Papias. Even if Irenaeus only witnessed a single brief encounter between Papias and Polycarp, he would still be an eyewitness to the nature of that interaction between these two eminent church leaders. Similarly, even if Irenaeus had never met Papias but had only heard Polycarp refer to Papias as his "companion," he again would be an eyewitness to Polycarp's attestation of his association with Papias. It is apparent, therefore, that Streeter inappropriately marginalized Irenaeus's testimony regarding Papias and his association with Polycarp. Holmes simply stated that Irenaeus "met Polycarp as a child" with no critical elaboration with respect to the extent of his description of their relationship. Holmes, *The Apostolic Fathers: Diglot Edition*, 202.

who would argue that Papias and Polycarp were not companions. In the absence of any such evidence, therefore, Irenaeus's contemporaneous witness that the two were "comrades" stands against all conjectures to the contrary.

Regarding the extent of the relationship between Polycarp and Papias, Irenaeus employed the word ἑταῖρος, which is generally translated as "companion." The word is less intimate than the Greek noun φίλος, which is often translated as "friend" (John 15:14). Although not as intimate as φίλος, ἑταῖρος clearly describes a relationship that is cordial and platonic. Even Eusebius, who had a less then positive evaluation of Papias, affirmed that he and Polycarp were fellow comrades and leaders of the Asiatic church during the transitional period from the first to the second century.

Papias's association with Polycarp is not the only relationship of Papias that is contested. Some scholars also doubt the accuracy of Irenaeus's statement that Papias was a "hearer of John," i.e., the apostle. The possibility of Papias's relationship with the apostle John and other apostles will be a constant theme within this book. It will be assumed for the current discussion that Papias was in fact a "hearer" and disciple of the last living apostle, who was the brother of James and a son of Zebedee, the one who leaned upon Jesus' chest at the Passover meal, and who composed the Fourth Gospel. Given Irenaeus's testimony of Papias and his associations, one can understand why Papias would be an important patristic figure for researching the origins of the apostolic writings and their coalescing into what is now recognized as the canonical New Testament.

PAPIAS AND HIS MINISTRY

The evolution of the church's offices during Papias's tenure as bishop (ἐπίσκοπος) is shrouded in mystery and greatly debated. Recognizing the nature of this debate, Alfred Plummer wrote, "The origin of the episcopate is, and is likely to remain, unknown. All the available evidence has been carefully collected, sifted, and estimated, and it is insufficient. Equally honest and equally capable critics infer different theories of the episcopate from it, and no solution of the problem can claim demonstration. We may hold, and perhaps be able to convince others, that one solution is more probable than another, but we cannot prove that it is the true one. All conclusions are tentative."[48] Keeping Plummer's observation in mind, it should be sufficient to acknowledge that at the time of Papias's service to his church(s) in

48. Plummer, "Bishop," 149.

Hierapolis, the church's understanding of the nature and authority of the office of bishop was to some degree in flux.[49] It is not the purpose of this book to research the entire scope of this debate. What it will do, however, is make observations about what Papias said concerning his own calling and experience as a bishop. It is hoped that these observations and the implications they produce will shed some light on the larger debate about the governance of the church during the second century. However, concerning any possible impact produced by this book, it will only venture as far as the data allows, and for the moment this limited coverage will have to suffice.

Patristic literature is unanimous that Papias served as a "bishop" at Hierapolis. The period in which he served was arguably one of the most precarious in the church's history. Christianity was viewed by many as a relatively new religion on the world's stage around the end of the first century, and as such it was constantly feeling pressures from within and from without. As stated earlier, during this period the church was regularly sorting out its understanding of its relationship to Judaism and its Jewish heritage. The apostolic generation had ended with the passing of the apostle John, and now there were few—if any—who could boast of actually knowing or seeing Jesus Christ in the flesh. Consequently, it was a period when the church experienced significant debate regarding the meaning of its message, its sacred writings, and its theology. Pre-gnostic influences, pagan religions, Judaism, and secular philosophies constantly pressed to influence the church's understanding of the traditions and doctrines it had received from its founder and his immediate followers. It was also a religion that on occasion was openly and brutally persecuted by the state, both regionally and universally. It was during this tenuous period that men such as Polycarp of Smyrna, Clement of Rome, Ignatius of Antioch, and Papias of Hierapolis were entrusted with the responsibility of protecting and guiding their respective flocks through the treacherous milieu of the Greco-Roman world at the commencement of the second century.

The picture, however, that some paint of Papias, his training, and of his ministry is that of a man with less than average intellectual acumen who in order to accumulate information about Jesus had to depend almost

49. The possibility that Papias may have had jurisdiction over more than one church within the district of Hierapolis is recognized. However, for the sake of simplicity, this book will discuss his oversight in the singular (that is as involving only a single congregation). This should not be assumed to mean that he was the only "elder" (πρεσβύτερος) or bishop (ἐπίσκοπος) in Hierapolis.

exclusively upon itinerant preachers, prophets, and missionaries[50] (some of whom probably had less than credible credentials) who happened to wander through Hierapolis and provided him with "spectacular stories" that to a more critical mind would have in all probability appeared to be more mythical than historical.[51] Ronald Higgins described Papias in this manner, "Papias now appears to me to be nothing more than an over-eager purveyor of half-baked harmonizations, who, in addition, never seems to have managed getting his facts right."[52] The historical data reviewed with a more critical approach, however, paints a somewhat different picture of Papias. Eusebius, while heavily depending upon Irenaeus, wrote that Polycarp and Papias "became famous" near or after the death of the apostle John.[53] The Greek word describing their relative fame is "γνωρίζω," which is literally translated as, "to make known" or "to reveal." Interestingly, while this verb in fragment 2 is plural, having both Polycarp and Papias as its subject, in fragment 4 it is in the singular and refers only to Papias. It is also noteworthy that both verbs are in the imperfect, which should probably be understood as an ingressive imperfect, meaning that they began to become known shortly after the death of John.[54] Regarding Papias, the salient question is, if he had ministered alone at some isolated post in Asia Minor then what would be the likelihood of him becoming "well known," so much so that he would be recognized as a peer with Polycarp, who arguably was the bishop of one of the most prominent Asiatic cities of that day?[55]

Concerning the elevation of Papias and Polycarp, in fragment 3 Eusebius wrote that by the time Polycarp was appointed to his bishopric at Smyrna that Papias was already becoming well known while serving in the

50. These individuals were also commonly referred to as "apostles," although they were not viewed as prestigious or authoritative as the original eleven apostles who had personally followed Jesus.

51. Burton, *Lectures*, 392–93.

52. Higgins, "Family Genealogy," 3

53. See the discussion of fragments 2 and 4 in chapter 4. It is not clear as to whether Eusebius estimated the popularity of this duo, or whether he possessed other literary sources that substantiated their rise to prominence. Given his dependence upon Irenaeus, the former seems to the more plausible conjecture. For the Greek texts of these fragments see Holmes, *Apostolic Fathers,* 3rd ed., 732.

54. Wallace, *The Basics*, 232–34.

55. C. Stewart Petrie correctly recognized that Hierapolis was "no remote outpost." Petrie, "Matthew,'" 15.

same capacity at Hierapolis.[56] One can only speculate as to why Papias had ascended to such prominence. Was it soon after the death of the apostle John that he published his *Exposition*; or were both he and Polycarp given the responsibility of reproducing and disseminating the Johannine writings, possibly even the last literary account of the life and teachings of Jesus originating from the hand of an eyewitness? Maybe it was Papias's own charisma as a preacher, prophet, or apologete that made him a rising "star" in the Lycus valley during the first quarter of the second century, or possibly both he and Polycarp were recognized by the Asiatic churches as the next generation of Christian leaders ordained to defend the apostolic traditions that they had personally received from those who had heard the very words of Jesus. Perumalil suggested that Papias's ordination to the bishopric was the reason for his rise to fame.[57] It does not seem likely, however, that Papias became famous in Asia Minor, as well as within the annals of the church's histories, simply because he became a bishop, for others had risen to this same responsibility, yet we know nothing about them. That is not to say that nothing was ever written by them or about them, but only that their status as bishops never ascended to the level of both Polycarp and Papias. One can only theorize about the reason(s) for Papias's ascension to prominence within the church of Asia Minor; nevertheless, the fact remains that the earliest historical data indicates that his rise to fame was no less spectacular than that of Polycarp. Consequently, notions that Papias possessed extremely limited exposure and involvement in the mainstream of the leadership of the orthodox church at the beginning of the second century is inconsistent with the historical data.

Regarding his testimony about his education and preparation for ministry, Papias was clearly emphatic with respect to its adequacy. When describing his education he stated, "I will not hesitate to set down for you, along with my interpretations, everything I carefully learned from the elders and carefully remembered, guaranteeing their truth."[58] Although

---

56. From this reference of Eusebius in *Ecc. Hist.* III.36.1–2, one could infer that Papias was indeed the senior of Polycarp. Such a conclusion, however, is merely a conjecture.

57. Perumalil, "Papias," 363.

58. Holmes, *Apostolic Fathers*, 3rd ed., 734. In Greek this sentence is "οὐκ ὀκνήσω δέ σοι καὶ ὅσα ποτὲ παρὰ τῶν πρεσβυτέρων καλῶς ἔμαθον καὶ καλῶς ἐμνημόνευσα συγκατατάξαι ταῖς ἑρμηνείαις διαβεβαιούμενος ὑπὲρ αὐτῶν ἀλήθειαν." A more literal translation would read: "And I will not hesitate also to set down the interpretations for you as much as at that time from the elders I well learned and I well remembered, (thus) guaranteeing on behalf of them (the) truth" or "guaranteeing on their behalf truth."

we do not know whether these words appeared at or near the beginning, or in the middle of Papias's preface, nevertheless, they illuminate Papias's opinion about his own training, as well as the purpose for his writings. His primary purpose for him *magnus opus* was to communicate the things he carefully learned and remembered from the elders along with their appropriate interpretations. It is important to note that neither the reflexive pronoun ἐμαυτου or the relative pronoun ἐμου appear in this text; therefore, one should not assume, as implied by Holmes's translation, that the interpretations that Papias promised to provide were *exclusively* his own. It is not out of the realm of possibility that some of the interpretations he recorded were from his sources (e.g., elders and/or apostles who were the Lord's disciples,[59] or were interpretations from the very lips of Jesus as testified to by his followers[60]). The antecedent of the intensive pronoun αὐτων is either "the elders" or "the interpretations," since both are plural.[61] This pronoun is primarily in the genitive because of the preposition ὑπὲρ. If the antecedent of this pronoun is "the elders," then Papias was guaranteeing by his own fidelity to their teachings the transmission to their traditions to his audience. If its antecedent was "the interpretations," then it seems he meant to guarantee their "truthfulness" (ἀλήθειαν). It is equally possible that by the clause "διαβεβαιούμενος ὑπὲρ αὐτων ἀλήθειαν" Papias intentionally nuanced his words with a double entendre in mind, meaning that he was guaranteeing both his fidelity to the elder's traditions and truthfulness of those traditions. Since the closest antecedent of the intensive pronoun is "the interpretations" it seems reasonable to assume that Papias at least meant to guarantee that they were consistent with what he perceived to be the truth.[62] The sentence, however, holds the possibility that both interpretations were intended. Regardless of which position one may take, there is little evidence to suggest that Papias only had in mind to guarantee his own personal interpretations of the traditions of the elders that he received from them and committed to memory. Papias stated, regarding his focus in preparing for ministry, that it was of first importance that he gain a correct mental grasp of meanings of the elders' instructions ("I learned well"), and afterwards, that he accurately retain those very same

59. For an example, see fragment 23, p. 248.

60. For an example, see fragment 1, p. 106.

61. The antecedent of the intensive pronoun cannot be Papias since a singular subject would demand a singular pronoun.

62. Günther Bornkamm understood the antecedent of the pronoun to be "the interpretations." He also assumed that these interpretations were specifically those of Papias and not "the elders." Bornkamm, "Elders," 6:676.

instructions ("I remembered well"). The result of this exacting education was that, in Papias's opinion, he was able to "guarantee their truth."[63]

Concerning Papias's description of his activities after this sentence, some understand his words as an explanation of how he went about "learning and remembering" the instructions and traditions of the elders. The argument being that Papias had to depend almost exclusively upon itinerant prophets and preachers, or other missionaries to pass through Hierapolis in order to provide him with sound bites and "stories" concerning the Lord and his oracles. If such a scenario was the case then Papias could hardly brag about "guaranteeing" the accuracy of any traditions (regardless of their apparent sources), or of the correctness of their interpretations. One might also wonder who would bother to subsidize such a questionable literary product that in reality would amount to nothing more than a collection of stories based upon nothing by hearsay.[64] An alternative theory would be to understand the rest of Papias's preface as explaining how, after having finished his training and, subsequently, having entered the ministry, he functioned as a bishop. In other words, once ordained to the bishopric and, consequently, receiving the responsibility of protecting the flock under his care, Papias made a habit of evaluating the "messages," "traditions," and/or "gospels" of those who had itinerated into his jurisdiction for the purpose of vetting them for officially sanctioned ministry during their stay in Hierapolis. Such a theory is entirely consistent with Paul's admonition to the Ephesian "bishops" regarding their responsibility to care for and protect the church entrusted to them (Acts 20.1–31). Paul's language in his farewell address to the leadership of the Ephesian church also indicates that at that time he saw no discernible distinction between the office of bishop or elder. Regarding the synonymous nature of these terms in Paul's thought, Beyer wrote, "The qualifications of presbyters here are like those of the bishops in 1 Tim 3:2ff. In fact, there is an alternation of the terms in Tt 1:7, where we suddenly have ἐπίσκοπος instead of πρεσβύτερος. This is another proof that the two terms originally referred to the same thing, namely, the guidance and representation of the congregation and the work of preaching and conducting worship."[65] This is not to suggest that during the period in which Papias ascended to his bishopric there still persisted no discernible difference between these two

---

63. Holmes, *Apostolic Fathers*, 3rd ed., 735.

64. The singular personal pronoun "σοι" (which is dative singular) in Papias's preface implies that he had a benefactor who subsidized the publication of *Exposition*.

65. Beyer, "ἐπίσκοπος," in *TDNT*, 2:617.

terms among the Asiatic churches. Some have argued that it was precisely during this time that the development of a "monarchial episcopate" arose within the church. Plummer contended that the evolution that elevated the office of bishop over the office of elder began in Asia Minor, stating that "it was established in Asia Minor before A.D. 100, and had become wide-spread in Christendom by 150."[66] Similarly, Leonhard Goppelt wrote, "The distinction made by the Pastorals between the elders and the bishops appeared in Asia Minor and probably led around the turn of the century to the monarchial episcopacy. The bishop became mainly the leader and representative of the church with the presbytery and a body of deacons subordinate to him."[67] This book does not attempt to thoroughly investigate the question of when and from where the monarchial episcopate arose; however, it does contend that when Papias was ordained to the bishopric he was entrusted with the responsibility of shepherding the flock within the district of Hierapolis; which meant caring for her needs, faithfully preaching the gospel, perpetuating the traditions he had received from the apostles,[68] and protecting her from the heresies of false teachers and false prophets. Given the spiritual climate at Hierapolis, such a mantle would demand that it not be entrusted to those who are intellectually weak and inept, but rather laid upon the shoulders of men who were well educated and capable of clearly articulating the orthodoxy of the Christian faith.

Eusebius's comments about Papias's intelligence, however, raises the question as to whether Papias did indeed possess the necessary skill sets needed to successfully carry out the responsibilities that ministry demands; for certainly the memorizing of "catechisms" does not guarantee that one is an adequately trained minister. The question remains, therefore, whether there is any possibility that Papias had access to formal education. Schoedel wrote regarding this question that Papias's location

---

66. Plummer, "Bishop," 150.

67. Goppelt, *Times*, 190.

68. K. Giles made the rather strange suggestion that in the first-century church "Christian elders" did not have a "teaching function." Giles, "Church Order," 222. Such an assumption ignores Paul's admonitions in Acts 20.28, as well as his clear instruction that elders and bishops must be able to teach (1 Tim 3:2; Titus 1:9). Regardless of Giles's misconceptions about the responsibilities of the office of elder in the early first-century church, he believed that by the beginning of the second century, the bishop was the "unquestionable leader of the Christian community in a given city" who "must be obeyed," and who was the primary minister of the Word (ibid., 225). Goppelt agreed that in Acts the terms "elder" and "bishop" referred to the "same office," but saw a difference between the two terms beginning to be understood by the time the Pastorals were written. Goppelt, *Times*, 189–90.

did not prohibit him from gaining access to formal training, stating that "Papias was bishop of Hierapolis in Phrygia, a city located near the meeting point of two important roads—that running from Antioch (in Syria) to Ephesus and that running from Attalia (in Pamphylia) to Smyrna. . . . It may also have been in Hierapolis that he picked up the rhetorical skills which he displays. For the cities of Asia Minor provided livelihoods for numerous rhetoricians in the period."[69]

This is not to argue that Papias is known to have obtained an education, only that he lived in a region that valued and afforded him the opportunity for training. Before the beginning of the Common Era, Asia Minor was known to possess one of the great libraries of the world at Pergamum. Literature was so important to the culture and economy of that region that when the Ptolemies of Egypt refused to export papyrus to Pergamum, King Eumenes II ordered the development of an alternative writing material, which led to the development of parchment. The secular elite, however, were not the only ones who valued education. The Ephesian church that spawned the Christian expansion into the Lycus Valley was aided by what could be viewed as the first known "Christian college" located at the School of Tyrannus, a school where the apostle Paul held daily lectures (Acts 19:8–10),[70] a program in which it would not be surprising that the headmaster required literacy as a prerequisite for graduation (1 Tim 4:13). Given the culture in which Papias lived and the Asiatic church's concern for orthodox instruction and training, it seems reasonable to assume that some formal training was expected of those who desired to ascend to the office of bishop. Additionally, that Papias went on to compose a work that consumed five volumes, implies that at some point in his life he achieved a respectable level of literacy and rhetorical training.[71]

Regardless of any possible education that Papias may have received, Eusebius felt confident he was incapable of benefiting from it, for with disrespect to Papias Eusebius wrote, "He certainly appears to be a man of very little intelligence, as one may say judging from his own words."[72] Apparently this was not always Eusebius's opinion of Papias, for fragment 4 indicates that earlier in his life he viewed Papias in a better light.[73] Scho-

69. Schoedel, *The Fragments*, 91.

70. For more information regarding this school see Bruce, *Acts*, 365–66; Polhill, *Acts*, 400–401.

71. Annand also referred to Papias as a "scholar." Annand, "Four Gospels," 50.

72. Holmes, *Apostolic Fathers*, 3rd ed., 739.

73. Schoedel believed that this complementary variant in fragment 4, p. 116, was

edel theorized that Eusebius's reference to Papias's "own words" was an allusion to a self deprecating statement possibly written by Papias, and thus provided the basis of Eusebius's derision of him.[74] Such statements, however, were common fare for ancient writers, and were usually given as an attempt at modesty rather than an accurate evaluation of the author's intelligence.[75] Eusebius was aware of these types of references; consequently it is doubtful that he was pointing to any such statement made by Papias, for him to have done so would have reflected poorly on his own intellectual stature rather than Papias's mental capacity. The context surrounding Eusebius's insult leads in a different direction. His reference to Papias's intelligence occurred as he assessed Papias's hermeneutical approach to "apostolic accounts" and his belief in a "material" millennial kingdom. Consequently, the context of Eusebius's statement implies that he believed Papias was intellectually inferior because of his chiliastic theology rather than any self-deprecating statement Papias may have made.

If this had been Eusebius's only statement about Papias, then today's scholars would probably believe him. But the fact that Eusebius himself admitted that Papias influenced "so many ecclesiastical writers after him"[76] argues that to some degree he was rational and persuasive rather than dense and a bore. Eusebius contended that it was Papias's antiquity that led so many askew in agreeing with his eschatology, but generally speaking, antiquity alone was no guarantor of a critical audience. To argue such implies that Irenaeus, Apollinaris, and others were mere lemmings, and such is demonstrably not the case. Eusebius, however, was not the only one to give an opinion of Papias. Agapius of Hierapolis called Papias "prominent."[77] Photius referred to him as a man of "apostolic character."[78] The author of a prologue to the Gospel of John labeled him "virtuous."[79] Anastasius of Sinai called him "famous,"[80] and although he may have taken his cue from Eusebius's references in fragment 2 or 4, he may also have

a later insertion. Schoedel, *The Fragments*, 104. See also Migne's editorial remarks. Eusebius *Historica* (PG 20:288). See also this book's discussion of fragment 4, p. 116, for a more thorough discussion on this textual variant.

74. Schoedel, *The Fragments*, 104.
75. For a more thorough explanation see Munck, "Presbyters," 225–26.
76. Holmes, *Apostolic Fathers*, 3rd ed., 739.
77. See fragment 24, p. 254.
78. See fragment 21, p. 242.
79. See fragment 27, p. 259.
80. See fragment 18, p. 236.

assessed Papias as a credible bishop and theologian based upon his evaluation of Papias's writings. Additionally, while Eusebius questioned Papias's intellect, he also wrote that Papias was a well known leader in the Asiatic church; and since there appears to be little evidence that the early church was in the habit of promoting drones, it seems reasonable to conclude that Eusebius's accusation that Papias was a simple-minded man was his own personal attack upon this apostolic father; an attack that Schoedel recognized as "unwarranted."[81]

Papias, after being trained and ordained to the bishopric at Hierapolis, probably began his ministry somewhere between 25 and 40 years of age.[82] His location provided the benefit of easy travel, and the time of his ascension to the bishopric was an important period for the church. Regarding Papias's situation, Bartlet wrote, "A man so situated, and with a passion for firsthand information as to Christ's teaching, had special chances of intercourse with such disciples of the first generation ('elders' he calls them) as visited or worked in Asia, so far as his youth or early manhood overlapped their later years."[83] At some point in his ministry, however, Papias must have come to the realization that the period of the apostolic generation had ended, which meant certain traditions he believed valuable were being tenuously preserved only through the medium of human memory. The tenuous nature of such material must have been one of the motivating factors that caused Papias to put to pen many traditions, interpretations, and the historical data that he thought too valuable to entrust to a future where orality and aurality were the only guarantors of their preservation. His research and labors produced his *magnum opus*, which he titled *An Exposition of the Oracles of the Lord*.[84] There is no evidence that *Exposition*

81. Schoedel, *The Fragments*, 104. Vardan Vardapet wrote that Eusebius labeled Papias a "heretic." See fragment 26, p. 258. There is no extant literary evidence supporting his claim. Consequently, it appears that in the same manner as Eusebius Vardapet was simply marginalizing Papias in spite of the historical evidence validating his orthodoxy.

82. This is based upon the assumption that Papias was born sometime between 60 to 75. If Papias actually knew some apostles and had actually survived until the middle of the second century, then he probably entered the ministry in his late twenties or early thirties.

83. Bartlet, "Papias," 2:309.

84. There is considerable debate on how to actually interpret the title of Papias's work. For a thorough analysis of its vocabulary see Lawlor, "Eusebius on Papias," 167–204. Consequently, throughout this book Papias's work will usually be referred to as *Exposition*. A more detailed analysis and interpretation of the title for his five-volume work will follow.

has survived the erosion of time. Adolf Harnack vainly searched for it. His efforts produced only a few potential references of it from the inventories of a few libraries in Europe, one in 1218, another in 1341, and possibly a third as late as 1534.[85] Theodor Zahn was of the opinion, however, that there are many unattributed Papian fragments embedded within patristic writings.[86] But, as stated earlier, attributing them to Papias is virtually impossible, and regrettably no complete manuscripts of his writings have survived. What exactly were Papias's purposes for his *Exposition*? If his title has any weight, then it would appear that he at least wanted to explain or clarify the meanings of some of the things that Jesus Christ actually said. Such a publication would be an important endeavor for his Greek-speaking congregation who sought to understand the teachings of their Aramaic-speaking Messiah. There is little doubt that after seventy years (the approximate time from Jesus' resurrection and ascension to Papias's ordination) a considerable reservoir of misinformation about Jesus and his teachings had developed. It was probably during this time that Papias began to be concerned that some of Jesus' meanings were being distorted by others who had attempted to translate Matthew's Aramaic Gospel into Greek; or by others who had "a great deal to say," or by those who misinterpreted Jesus' sayings (i.e., oral traditions) while promoting "someone else's commandments," or by teachers who relied upon "information from books" rather than "information from a living and abiding voice."[87] Concerning Papias's purpose for his *Exposition* and the importance it would have had for his second-century audience, Bartlet wrote,

> Although we are unable to conceive in detail the exact character of Papias' *Exposition of the Oracles of the Lord*, even our meagre[sic] knowledge of it, especially when taken in connexion[sic] with other Christian writings of the period, helps us not a little to realize the way in which our Gospels, and Gospels generally, were viewed and handled early in the 2nd century. Both it and the Oxyrhynchus Gospel teach us not

85. Harnack, *Geschichte der Altchristlichen Literatur bis Eusebius*, 69. Concerning confusion over whether these were the writings of Papias of Hierapolis and a medieval grammarian also named Papias see Lightfoot, *Essays*, 210–11.

86. By comparing a quote from Hippolytus with Irenaeus's quote of Papias (see fragment 1, p. 106), Zahn contended that their similarities proved (*beweist*) that Hippolytus had depended on Papias. Zahn, *Forschungen zur Geschichte des neutestamentlichen Kanons*, 6:128. For a thoughtful analysis of possible Papian fragments in patristic writings see Hill, "What Papias Said," 582–629.

87. Holmes, *Apostolic Fathers*, 3rd ed., 735.

only that Christ's sayings were the most prized part of the Gospel tradition, but also how strong were the tendencies at work making for change in their meaning and even wording. They were heard or read in environments of thought far other than those for which they were first spoken; and . . . their historical or original meaning was apt to be lost as soon as they passed beyond Palestine, and the fresh meanings or glosses put upon them tended insensibly to replace the Master's *ipsissima verba*. Here the instances afforded by the Oxyrhynchus Gospel of how in all good faith such a process of transformation took place, are most suggestive. They show how needful something like a standard exegesis, based on knowledge of the original historical sense, was becoming to the genuine transmission of Christ's own teaching, if it was not to be sublimated away in terms of Greek idealism and Oriental mysticism. Such a consummation was averted only by strenuous insistence on the part of the local Church leaders, that every care was to be taken to keep in touch with the historic meaning of the Lord's earthly teaching, as certified by Gospels historically known to be of Apostolic or quasi-Apostolic authorship, and expounded in the first instance by the aid of continuous local tradition going back to similar sources.[88]

That there was literature that painted conflicting pictures of Jesus' life during the last quarter of the first century is hardly questionable. Robert Stein, concerning the existence of such material, explained that Luke's reference to "many" narratives suggests that there were more literary accounts of the life and deeds of Jesus than just the Gospels of Mark and Matthew.[89] Luke's reference to these materials, therefore, tells us that even before Papias's birth attempts were being made to define the "historical Jesus." Some fifty or more years later, Papias's statements that some had attempted to translate Matthew's Aramaic Gospel "as best they could," while others who had "a great deal to say" supporting their positions through

88. Bartlet, "Papias," 2:312. It is questionable whether Bartlet should have placed so much value upon the Oxyrhynchus papyri. His argument was primarily about how gnostic writings show that gnostics both valued and distorted materials concerning Jesus. His comments have merit concerning the need of the orthodox church to preserve and clarify the historical meanings of Jesus' teachings.

89. Stein, *Synoptic Gospels*, 176–77. Richard J. Dillion thought that Luke's "many" only need to refer to Mark's Gospel and Q, see Dillion, "Preview Luke's Project," 207. Such a view, however, hardly respects the overwhelming evidence that "πολλοί" regularly refers to more than just "two." For a detailed discussion on Luke's prologue see Bock, *Luke* 1:1—9:50, 51–59.

"books" indicates that at the time when Papias commenced his ministry the debate was still raging, thus giving another impetus for his *Exposition*.

The preservation and exposition of certain sayings of Jesus, however, was not the only purpose for Papias's work. Both Eusebius (in fragment 5) and Philip of Side (in fragment 11) reported that Papias went to the effort to preserve accounts of post-Pentecost events. One such example was the consumption of poison by Barsabbas. Did Papias include this tradition because he believed it demonstrated the fulfillment of a prophetic oracle made by Jesus, or did he only include it for its value as a powerful apologetic of Jesus' supremacy? Without more material or contextual details from Papias one can only wonder. Another example of the importance that history played in Papias's work is his preservation of the "Elder's" tradition(s) concerning the origins of both the Gospels of Mark and Matthew.[90] The inclusion of these traditions clearly reveals that some material was included simply for their historical value rather than any spiritual benefit or theological insights they might produce.

As stated earlier, the question of when Papias wrote his *magnum opus* is one of considerable debate. Yarbrough made a strong case for dating Papias's *Exposition* as ca. 95–117.[91] Just as persuasively, however, Bauckham argued that whenever Papias wrote, he appears to have written about an earlier time in his life rather than about the period in which he was writing, which makes providing a date as to when Papias wrote his *Exposition* speculative at best. Nevertheless, Bauckham tentatively dated Papias as having written ca. 110.[92] His argument, however, also strengthens any position that Papias may have written later than 110. Lightfoot, while believing Papias wrote to contradict gnostic exegesis, dated Papias's writings as ca. 130 or later.[93] Schoedel, however, argued that there is little evidence

90. There is the question of whether Papias's Elder was the source of his tradition regarding Matthew's Aramaic Gospel. Eusebius's comments about the Gospel of Mark and the Aramaic Gospel of Matthew are divided by a transitional comment interjected by Eusebius; consequently, certitude about the Elder being Papias's source for both is not possible. Gundry contended little weight should be given to Eusebius's "editorial transition" between the traditions regarding these two Gospels; consequently, he believed that they both came from the same source, which was Papias's "Elder," who was in fact the apostle John. Gundry, *Older Is Better*, 58; Gundry, *Mark*, 1031.

91. Yarbrough, "The Date of Papias," 187–88.

92. Bauckham, *The Eyewitnesses*, 14.

93. Lightfoot, "Supernatural Religion," 150, 160–61. Bacon argued that Papias "probably" wrote "between AD 145 and 160." Bacon, "An Emendation," 176. Rigg believed that Papias wrote *Exposition* late in his life, and possibly as late as 160. Rigg, "Papias on Mark," 163, 173.

that Papias's wrote because of a gnostic threat.[94] The lack of evidence is primarily because there is little that survives from the hand of Papias. Little weight, therefore, can be placed upon the lack of evidence *not* found in the few meager quotes surviving from the hand of Papias.

Schoedel's position, however, appears to lead in the right direction. The fact that Papias influenced so many later bishops, apologists, and theologians during the second century, and yet none of them are known to cite him as an early anti-gnostic apologete or critic argues loudly for a pre 140 date for *Exposition*, even if such a conclusion is based upon an argument from silence. An example of the absence of Papias's engagement of gnostic thought can be observed in Irenaeus's employment of Papias.[95] In Fragment 1, which appears to be his only quote of Papias, Irenaeus did not quote Papias as providing any anti-gnostic arguments or proof texts. Ironically, Irenaeus never again appears to mention Papias and/or his arguments on any subject for that matter. Consequently, assuming that a major gnostic challenge to the church (if not full-blown formal Gnosticism) had developed by 140, the absence of any evidence from Irenaeus that Papias's provided a polemic against Gnosticism argues for Papias to have written before Gnosticism became a dominant threat to the church.[96] A reasonable conjecture, therefore, would be that Papias wrote no later than 130.[97]

If 130 is the *terminus ad quem* for Papias's *Exposition*, then what could be the *terminus a quo*? Eusebius indicated that Papias entered that ministry ca. 100. Again, the fact that his writings influenced so many that followed him would imply that he had achieved a certain level of theological maturity and rhetorical sophistication. Consequently, it appears that Bauckham's calculation (a view supported by several others) that Papias wrote ca. 110 seems a reasonable estimate for the earliest dating of Papias's work.[98] Consequently, given the apparent lack of any evidence that Papias

94. Schoedel, *The Fragments*, 91.

95. See fragment 1, p. 106.

96. Concerning the lack of a gnostic polemic in Papias's writings, Gundry aptly wrote, "The failure of Irenaeus and Eusebius to quote Papias against Gnosticism is best explained by Papias's having said nothing against Gnosticism because he wrote before it became a widespread threat, i.e., before A.D. 110." Gundry, *Older Is Better*, 50.

97. For a discussion of a time line of the growth of Gnosticism in the second century see Smith, *No Longer Jews*, 113–51. It is conceivable, however, that Papias had no intent of addressing the growing threat Gnosticism in his day.

98. Some have estimated Papias's birth at ca. 60. If true then he would have been approximately forty years of age in the year 100. Such an age could certainly produce a respectable amount of maturity. If Papias was somewhat of an intellectual prodigy

confronted a gnostic threat, it would appear that the better claim as to when Papias wrote would be nearer to 110 rather than to 130.[99]

It should be remembered, regardless of when or why Papias wrote, that the historical data indicates that Papias was preeminently a bishop. In other words, he was a full-time pastor. There is no evidence to suggest that he had any other career or profession to distract him. Instead, the evidence paints him as a dedicated shepherd of the Hieropolitan flock, as an educator of his congregation, as a preserver of the church's history, as one who was passionate about preserving the Lord's commandments, and as one who hungered to hear within those commandments the living and abiding voice of truth. Moreover, it was Papias's passion for the Lord's teachings, as handed down to him through the reminisces of Jesus' immediate followers, that apparently led to his death, a subject to which I now turn.

THE DEATH OF PAPIAS

While as there is virtually no information regarding the birth of Papias, there are some records describing his death. The historical record indicates that Papias suffered as a martyr. Many scholars are either unaware of these fragments, or they agree with Lightfoot's position that no credible historical evidence exists to suggest that Papias was a martyr. Unfortunately, Lightfoot's opinion on this matter is a good example of how a conjecture can sometimes evolve into an historical certitude. The earliest reference to Papias's death is found in the anonymous worked titled *Chronicon Paschale*, which is an early seventh-century Byzantine chronology of the world's history.[100] Lightfoot speculated that the author of the *CP* erred when he recorded that Papias was martyred in 163, arguing that "either he or his transcriber has substituted a well-known name, *Papias*, for a more obscure name, *Papylus*. If the last letters of the word were blurred or blotted in his copy of Eusebius, nothing would be more natural than such a change."[101]

(a possibility that few would entertain), then ca. 80 would be the earliest date for the composition of his work.

99. This should not be understood as arguing that is has been proven that Gnosticism or pre-Gnosticism could not have existed during the period in which Papias wrote. Moreover, the lack of evidence that Papias was confronted by Gnosticism proves very little given the small amount of extant Papian material.

100. *Chronicon Paschale* (PG 92:628).

101. Lightfoot, "Papias," 381–82. Schoedel accepted Lightfoot's conjecture without explanation; see Schoedel, "Papias," 237. See also Bartlet, "Papias's Exposition," 21; and

Lightfoot's conjecture regarding Papias's death was based on several major assumptions; the first is that the author of the *CP* depended solely upon Eusebius's *Ecclesiastical History* for his chronology; and secondly, that he misread the uncial script of Eusebius's *Ecclesiastical History*. The two names in uncial script would potentially appear as "ΠΑΠΙΑΣ" (Papias) and "ΠΑΠΥΛΟΣ" (Papulos). While an error caused by the visual similarities of the names is possible, it is not certain.[102] Regarding his initial assumption, Lightfoot confidently asserted that "there is no indication that the author of this chronicle used any other document in this part besides the History of Eusebius and the extant Martryology of Polycarp which Eusebius quotes."[103] Michael Whitby, however, in the introduction to his translation of the *CP* stated that its author employed several sources for his historiography, both sacred and secular.[104] Consequently, assertions that the author of the *CP* employed *only* Eusebius's *Ecclesiastical History* as he chronicled the history of the church and world during the first and second century are not well founded. Lastly, concerning Lightfoot's assumption that Papylus was a relatively unknown martyr, it is clearly anachronistic and, therefore, a poorly defended assertion to contend that because the martyrology titled *Acts of Carpus, Papylus, and Agathonicê* is "obscure" to today's audiences, then it must have been obscure to a medieval historian. Nevertheless, it was Lightfoot's position that the author of the *CP* replaced Papylus's name with the more popular name of Papias.[105]

There is no question that the author of the *CP* depended heavily upon Eusebius's work as he wrote. Both he and Eusebius, however, affirmed that additional literary accounts existed during the time of their writings detailing the martyrdoms that occurred during the reign of Marcus Aurelius, a point that Lightfoot seemed to give little weight or ignored

---

Bosio, *I Padri Apsotolici, Parte II*, 252. The name *Papylas* (as spelled in English) is found in Eusebius's *Ecc. Hist.* IV.15.48. While Lightfoot's conjecture is possible (if for no other reason than the fact that he could conceive of it), a legitimate question of this theory would be why the author of the *CP* did not find a more popular substitution for Papylus than Papias? Since the time of Eusebius, Papias's popularity had fallen on hard times, in large part because of Eusebius's distaste for him, but also because of Papias's chiliastic theology, which was not a dominant view in the east at the time when the *CP* was written.

102. Of course the exact spelling of the names would depend upon their case endings and their function in the sentences in which they were found.

103. Lightfoot, "Papias," 382.

104. *Chronicon Paschale 284–628*, xv.

105. The martyrology titled *Acts of Carpus, Papylus, and Agathonicê* will be discussed in greater detail below.

altogether. The reference to Papias's martyrdom in the *CP* reads as thus, "καὶ ἐν Περγάμῳ δὲ ἕτεροι ἐν οἷς ἧς καὶ Παπίας καὶ ἄλλοι πολλοὶ ὦν καὶ ἔγγραφα φέρονται τὰ μαρυτύρια."[106] Eusebius also testified to the existence of such sources, stating, "There are also extant memoirs of others also who suffered martyrdom in Pergamum, a city of Asia."[107] If there existed additional accounts detailing the martyrdoms that occurred during the reign of Marcus Aurelius then it is certainly possible and, therefore, reasonable to conclude that the author of the *CP* supplemented his work with these sources and was quite accurate when he recorded that Papias was a martyr, thus making no mistake at all.

This conclusion is even more credible given the fact that Lightfoot cited no Greek or Latin variants to support his conjecture. Ironically, the only textual evidence cited by Lightfoot argues against his position. Lightfoot mentioned in a footnote that the *Syriac Epitome* also indicates that Papias and Polycarp were martyred during the same period.[108] Lightfoot speculated, however, that "the martyrdom of Papias is combined with that of Polycarp in the *Syriac Epitome* of the *Chronicon* of Eusebius (p. 216, ed. Schöne). The source of the error is doubtless the same in both cases." A translation of the *Syriac Epitome* reads as follows: "At that time persecution in Asia occurred, Polycarp became a martyr, and Papias, of whose martyrdoms exist (written) in a book."[109] As is observable in this quote, the reader is again confronted by an author's statement that there existed another "book" that confirmed that Papias was martyred during the same persecutions under which Polycarp also suffered. Lightfoot contended that this reference to Papias's martyrdom was doubtlessly the result of the same source.

Lightfoot, unfortunately, never elaborated as to how the writer of the *Syriac Epitome* and the Byzantine author of the *CP* came to employ the same source (or a source containing the same error), or why neither attempted to review the document(s) detailing the accounts of these martyrdoms, or that neither discovered this apparent error when referencing Eusebius's well know *Ecclesiastical History*. Lightfoot's theory is solely based upon

---

106. Which is translated, "And in Pergamum also others, among them there was also Papias and many others, of whom also [the] writings bear the testimonies." *Chronicon Paschale*, (PG 92:627).

107. Eusebius *Ecc. Hist.* VI.15.48 (LCL 153:359).

108. Lightfoot, "Papias," 382.

109. Eusebi, *Chronicon*, 216. Translation mine. In Latin the text is as follows: "Cum persecutio in Asia esset, Polycarpos martyrium subiit et Papias, quorum martyria in libro (scripta) extant."

the supposed incompetence of not one but several authors or scribes who never discovered their apparent errors. He not only failed to supply textual variants that might lend support for his theory, but he systematically marginalized any evidence that contradicted his assertion.[110] Arguments from silence, as one can see, provide absolutely no opportunity for objective verification and can quickly spin into wild speculations, which regrettably for some is evidence enough to interpret such unfounded conjectures as historical "facts."[111] It should be at least acknowledged, however, that these witnesses to Papias's martyrdom are relatively late and can no longer direct the reader to other surviving documents for confirmation of the manner and date of Papias's death.

The last reference to Papias's martyrdom to be discussed comes from Photius, the great ninth-century patriarch of Constantinople. Photius only incidentally described Papias as a martyr in his work titled *Bibliotheca*. His reference to Papias reads as follows: "Παπίαν τὸν Ἱεραπόλες ἐπίσκπον καὶ μάρτυ"[112] It could easily be argued, since Photius was probably well educated,[113] that he relied upon the account of Papias martyrdom as found in the *CP*, and therefore, it is questionable whether he should be viewed as providing an independent witness. If in fact Papias was a martyr, then he apparently suffered his fate in the city of Pergamum.[114] Pergamum

110. Lightfoot discussed the question of Papias's martyrdom in the context of debating whether someone who died ca. 165 could have been old enough to have known the apostle John. Lightfoot concluded that since Papias was not a martyr then "The martyrdom of Papias, with its chronological perplexities (such as they are), disappears from history; and we may dismiss the argument of the author of 'Supernatural Religion,' that 'a writer who suffered martyrdom under Marcus Aurelius (c. A.D. 165) can scarcely have been a hearer of the Apostles.'" Lightfoot, "Papias," 382. This book will investigate the assertion of whether someone who died in the mid 160's could not have known the apostle John at a later point. Perumalil wrote that Papias died "in A.D. 125" or maybe as late as 130; however, he gave no evidence to support his claim. Perumalil, "Papias," 362.

111. It should be recognized that it is also possible that both Papias and Papylus suffered martyrdom at Pergamum.

112. Photius, *Bibliothèque*, 5:77. The clause in question is translated: ". . . Papias the bishop and martyr of Hierapolis." Holmes, *Apostolic Fathers,* 3rd ed., 755. The reference to Hierapolis should not be understood as where he was martyred, but rather that he was a martyr who was from the city of Hierapolis.

113. It would be reasonable to conclude that Photius, an archbishop of Constantinople in the eleventh century, had accessed a copy of the *CP* (a seventh-century work of a Byzantine author) from the imperial library at Constantinople.

114. In antiquity, the name "Pergamum" can either refer to a region once known as "the kingdom of Pergamum" or the city of Pergamum. References to Pergamum as

was approximately 200 miles northwest of Hierapolis. As is the case with Hierapolis, Pergamum had a very early history with Christianity, although it appears to have been considerably less tolerant of this relatively "new" faith. The church at Pergamum was one of the seven churches that received a letter that is embedded in the book of Revelation (Rev 2:12–17). This brief letter reveals that brutality towards those loyal to Jesus Christ had already begun to occur sometime before the end of the first century (Rev 2:13).[115]

Pergamum was one of the three leading cities of Asia during the first century. It had once served as the Roman capital of Asia, and as such it possessed the right to exercise capital punishment. Ephesus, however, replaced Pergamum as the capital city of Asia sometime during the reign of Augustus.[116] Pergamum was known to be one of the main centers in Asia Minor for the Imperial Cult. It is possible that either Antipas (a first-century Christian martyr mentioned in Rev 2:13) or Papias, or both, were open critics of this cult, and as a result they may have incurred the wrath of the state. Another possibility is that their ministries or preaching could have become a threat to the dominant temples in their respective cities. Such threats at times ignited flash mobs to anger and violence, an example of such is found in Acts 19:23–41 concerning the cultic vitality of the temple of Artemis in Ephesus.

Although Antipas appears to have been a citizen of Pergamum, Papias was not. Whether Papias possibly pursued martyrdom in the manner of Ignatius, or humbly accepted his fate like Polycarp, or whether he was martyred at the hands of a mob or by official state sanction is pure speculation. P. A. Brunt suggested that Christian martyrdoms were often the result of mob violence or the prejudice of regional or local officials, writing that

> It is clear that some martyrdoms occurred in every reign and that no emperor did more to protect the Christians than require prosecutions to be heard by due process of Law, forbidding pogroms and anonymous or calumnious[sic] charges. . . . Our extant records suggest that martyrdoms were generally

a kingdom generally only occur in the context of references to the political or geographical region that existed before the Roman Empire.

115. Pergamum was where the Christian Antipas was martyred.

116. Trebilco, "Asia," 304. The debate in the first and second century between Pergamum, Ephesus, and Smyrna as to which was the leading city in Asia Minor is legendary. For an insightful overview of this topic see Kampmann, "*Homonoia* Politics in Asia Minor," 373–93.

the result of popular agitation or of the personal animosity that individual pagans bore to individual Christians. But neither city magistrates nor governors were necessarily immune from vulgar prejudices, and governors enjoyed a wide discretion, which enabled them both to restrain persecution or to impose a sentence milder than the death penalty, and to exceed the limits of repression that Trajan had prescribed.[117]

If this assessment is accurate, then Papias may have been arrested simply because he was a leader of what many in his day considered to be a relatively new and despised illegal religion.

If Papias was arrested for being the leader of the Christians in Hierapolis and as such was accused and charged with a "capital offense," it would have been necessary to transport him to a city with the authority to carry out such a sentence. Ephesus of course was considerably closer to Hierapolis than Pergamum, and therefore would have been a more natural selection for the location of such a trial. Transporting Papias to Pergamum may have been necessary because of an appeal made by him to have his case heard by one someone possessing higher judicial authority than those hearing his case in Ephesus (e.g., the proconsul).[118] It is not likely, however, that such an appeal would have provided a venue for a more tolerant court. Pergamum in the book of the Revelation is referred to as the location of "Satan's throne" and the place where "Satan dwells" (Rev 2:13). Regarding this imagery of hostility by city of Pergamum toward Christianity, Adela Collins wrote, "On the symbolic level, then, the throne of Satan in the Book of Revelation represents a power opposing God and embodied in Roman imperial might. The message to Pergamom,[119] however, does not allow the interpreter to remain on this literary level. The text explicitly associates this image of Satan's throne with the city of Pergamum."[120] Pergamum was still a city of political influence and power within the

---

117. Brunt, "Marcus Aurelius," 500–501.

118. The *Acts of Carpus, Papylus, and Agathonicê* indicates that the trial of these martyrs was at Pergamum precisely because that was where the proconsul "was in residence." Musurillo, *The Acts*, 23. This Greek account indicates that Papylus was a citizen of Thyatira. It could be inferred from his discourse with the proconsul that he was a leader in the church in that city. If he was a bishop and was transported to Pergamum to stand trial for his rejection of polytheism and his loyalty to Christianity, then it is possible that he and Papias were victims of a scheme by the proconsul in Asia Minor to extinguish Christianity by depleting it of its leadership.

119. "Pergamom" is an alternative spelling for "Pergamum;" consequently, it should not be understood as a misspelling of the city's name throughout this book.

120. Collins, "Pergamom in Early Christian Literature," 167.

empire through the late first century and well into the second century, and one where intolerance of Christianity was common. It is also possible that Papias had journeyed to Pergamum on official church business, and while there he was accused of a capital offense (e.g., preaching against the Imperial Cult). As mentioned above, there are no extant records from the second century detailing the martyrdom of Papias; consequently, there are no descriptions of the manner of his execution. If he died as a martyr and if he was a Roman citizen then one could assume that he was beheaded, as was the case with the apostle Paul and Justin Martyr.[121] If, however, he was not a citizen of Rome, then it is not unreasonable to assume that he was martyred in one of the horrific fashions detailed by Eusebius in his accounts of the martyrdoms that occurred during the mid-second century.

Paul Keresztes believed, with respect to estimating the date of the martyrdom of Papias, that there were two waves of persecutions during the reign of Marcus Aurelius.[122] The first transpired early in Marcus's reign sometime between 161–168. This period of persecutions was apparently particularly intense from 166–168, while the second wave occurred ca. 177.[123] Keresztes speculated that during the first wave of persecutions the Roman Empire had suffered a series of revolts, natural disasters, and plagues, and that these ominous events created an atmosphere of fear that led to a universal edict calling for the offerings of sacrifices to appease the traditional gods of the Empire. Keresztes wrote regarding this period that

> We may be sure that Marcus Aurelius, in the serious circumstances of 166–168 AD, would not neglect this old republic practice. His historian gives a fair and suggestive indication of the character of these expiatory sacrifices. The *Vita* of Abercius (1–4) is more generous in giving details of the *religious festivities in Hierapolis*, following the edict of the joint chiefs of the Empire about the same time. This edict was clearly empire-wide and ordered the public performance of sacrifices, libations, and festivities to the gods. This edict, being promulgated by officials also *in Hierapolis*, was promptly complied with. The main centre of rituals, it appears, was the temple of Apollo, but there were

---

121. If Papias was a Roman citizen then his appeals would have carried more legal clout and, in a manner similar to Paul's case, would have required that he be transported in order to be heard by a higher court.

122. Keresztes, "Marcus Aurelius a Persecutor?" 327. Keresztes did not attempt to identify a possible year for Papias death, but only the periods that persecutions of Christians occurred under Marcus's reign.

123. Ibid., 332–34.

celebrations also to Heracles, Artemis, Aphrodite, and other gods. There are in Roman history several clear examples of similar *lectisternia*.[124]

Based upon his assessment of the situation within the empire from 166–168, Keresztes concluded that the Pergamum martyrdoms referred to by Eusebius (*Ecclesiastical History* IV.15.48) also occurred sometime within this same period, stating that "On the basis of our evidence in the *Vita* of Abercius, Orosius, the *Acts* of Justin and the Martyrdoms of Pergamum, we must assume the existence of a general edict by the joint Emperors, sometime during 161–168 AD, ordering sacrifices to placate the angry gods. This same evidence, when put within the context of Roman tradition and the events of the last few years of this same joint rule by Marcus Aurelius and Lucius Versus, further suggests that this empire-wide edict was issued some time during 166–168 AD."[125]

While Keresztes has made a compelling case that an "empire-wide edict" mandating sacrifices to appease the mythical gods of Rome occurred sometime between 166 and 168, he has not proven that all the martyrdoms that occurred in Asia Minor were executed during those three years, nor has he argued for such a conclusion. Certainly such an edict would grant license to hunt out Christian leaders for the purpose of appeasing the Roman gods and suppressing Christianity, but it should not be assumed that such an edict must have *initiated* animosity towards the adherents of this already illegal and despised religion. Persecutions and martyrdoms, as Brunt rightly recognized, occasionally occurred even before Marcus's edict. Consequently, there is nothing that demands that Papias and all the others who were martyred at Pergamum were all martyred together at the same time. It is possible that some Christian leaders were occasionally victims of local or regional persecutions from the mid 150s through the mid 160s, with the more draconian pogrom reaching a crescendo as the result of Marcus's edict, which was ordered ca. 166–68.

Whether Papias was martyred as early as 163 or as late as 166/167, a legitimate question remains, which is whether someone who died in either of those years could have possibly known the apostle John. It is this very question, not to mention textual and archaeological evidence about certain martyrdoms, that has led some to argue that Polycarp was martyred in 155 or 156.[126] Not wishing to marginalize the possibility of the earlier

124. Ibid., 330–31. Italics mine.

125. Ibid., 331.

126. C. H. Turner argued that Polycarp was martyred in 156. His evidence is far

dates, mathematically speaking it is certainly possible for someone who died in 166/67 to have been an adult during the final years of the apostle John's ministry and life. Irenaeus, who was the student of at least one apostolic father that actually studied under the apostle John (i.e., Polycarp), stated that the apostle John lived until "the times of Trajan."[127] Trajan's reign began in 98. Using Papias's contemporary Polycarp as a standard of measurement for Papias's approximate age, if Polycarp was in his mid-eighties in 166/67 (e.g., eighty-six years old) he would have been born ca. 80. That places Papias's age somewhere between eighteen to nineteen years old at the beginning of Trajan. As any high school teacher or college professor can attest, such an age is certainly old enough for one to become a competent student. If Papias was martyred in 163, as the author of the *CP* asserted, and was approximately eighty-six years of age at his death then he would have been born ca. 77/78, which would make him twenty to twenty-one at the beginning of Trajan's reign (98). Moreover, the longer the apostle John lived during the reign of Trajan, then the greater the possibility of both Papias and Polycarp to have known the last living apostle. Eusebius's *Chronicle* implies that the apostle John survived until the third year of Trajan's rule, ca. 100. This means that Papias would have known the apostle into his mid-twenties. There is no reasonable objection, therefore, that validates position that someone who died as late as 167 could not have known the apostle John.

There will be those who balk at the idea that anyone could have lived to such an age in a culture with virtually no advanced health care, and such an objection does have its merit. Some people, however, did live to advanced ages during the second century. Polycarp was spry and keen of intellect at age eighty-six, and would have lived longer had he not been executed. Pothinus, the bishop who preceded Irenaeus, lived to ninety years of age and would also have lived longer had he too not been martyred. Tracey cited an inscription in Syria which honors a priestess of Hadara for living to the ripe old age of one hundred.[128] Thus, even though people

---

too detailed to include in this book, however, a brief summary is worth noting. He conjectured that the possibility of a leap year coupled with the "high Sabbath" (the day of the week for Polycarp's martyrdom) being that of the feast of Purim as providing a compelling argument for the date of Polycarp's death as having been that of Saturday, February 22nd, 156. Turner put forth his theory to address some weaknesses of M. Waddington and Lightfoot's position that Polycarp was martyred in 155 rather than Eusebius's date of 167. Turner, *Polycarp's Martyrdom*, 4–25.

127. Irenaeus *Against Heresies* 2.22.5, 3.3.4 (ANF 1:392, 416).

128. Tracey, "Syria," 259 n. 84.

in any period do not generally live into their late eighties and nineties, it is not unheard of; nor is it reasonable to believe that some could not have survived to such ages in the first and second centuries. Consequently, there is no concrete historical data proving the contention that both Papias and Polycarp could not have known John the son of Zebedee as adults during the twilight years of his life.[129]

The fact that no account of Papias's death (if he was martyred) has survived with the martyrologies of those who also died at Pergamum does provide some with justification for doubting that he was in fact a martyr. However, there are only two extant manuscripts detailing the martyrdoms of some who suffered at Pergamum, an account which is titled, *Acts of Carpus, Papylus, and Agathonicê*.[130] The lack of a narrative for Papias's trial and subsequent martyrdom could be attributed to the possibility that his execution did not occur along with other Pergamum martyrdoms; and consequently the *commentarius* of his trial may not have been accessible to the author of *Acts of Carpus, Papylus, and Agathonicê*. It is also possible that the author found the account of Papias's death less suitable for his purposes, or that documents of Papias's death simply did not survive the sands of time. Nevertheless, it should not be assumed that the *Acts of Carpus, Papylus, and Agathonicê* provide the details for *all* the martyrdoms that occurred at Pergamum. The author of the CP informed his readers that "many others" were martyred in Pergamum. It hardly seems reasonable to conclude that an account detailing the deaths of only three martyrs deserves a description of "many others." Regarding the persecutions that arose under Marcus Aurelius's reign, Brunt argued that the persecutions in Asia were more severe precisely because that was where the church was the strongest.[131] Additionally, the historical data regarding the persecutions that occurred is Asia Minor during this period indicates that many others died for the faith in the mid-to-late second century. It is certainly possible, therefore, that Papias, a significant leader of Christianity in Hierapolis, did not survive this period of intense hostility. Consequently, the historical evidence does in fact reveal a socio-religious context during the mid-second century that was more than conducive for the possibility that Papias also became a victim of the brutality that was inflicted upon many

129. Rigg, "Papias on Mark," 173. The question of the theory that the apostle John was martyred with his brother James will be discussed later.

130. Bisbee, *Acts of the Martyrs*, 82. For an English translation see Musurillo, *The Acts*, xv–xvi, 22–37.

131. Brunt, "Marcus Aurelius," 515.

other faithful Christians. Regrettably, however, no early sources have survived that provide significant information detailing the manner of Papias's death. Consequently, certitude as to whether he was in fact a martyr is unachievable.

A CONCLUDING SUMMARY

As stated at the beginning in this chapter, few facts about the life of Papias can be verified with any credible degree of certitude. The whole of the historical record about him, however, makes certain conjectures reasonable, while other are more tentative. Keeping this in mind, a brief summary about his life, ministry, and death is here offered.

Papias was probably Phrygian by birth and was born somewhere in Asia Minor ca. 75–80. He became well known after ascending to the bishopric of Hierapolis ca. 105, and was quickly recognized as one of the more prominent Christian leaders of the Asiatic church. Irenaeus not only affirmed that Papias was of the generation that preceded him, but that he was also a "hearer" of the apostle John and a "companion" of Polycarp, who was also a student of the apostle John as well as the bishop of Smyrna. Consequently, both Papias and Polycarp are commonly referred to today as "apostolic fathers." Papias was sufficiently educated to have written sometime between 110 and 130 an influential five-volume work which he titled *An Exposition of the Oracles of the Lord*. No complete manuscript of this work has survived. In his writings he attempted to engage in historical analysis and rhetorical criticism of the apostolic traditions and the written events concerning Jesus and his teachings; however he was primarily concerned with providing explanations of their orthodox interpretations. His title indicates that he believed these "sayings" or "oracles" of Jesus were of divine origin.[132] Papias clearly valued apostolic testimony about the teachings and deeds of Jesus over the speculations of any who contradicted their witness. He was also an avowed chiliast and by the time of his writings he was aware of several books that are now part of the canonical New Testament.[133] His ministry appears to have endured several decades, but apparently did not survive a series of persecutions that occurred under the reign of Marcus Aurelius, during which he apparently died sometime in his eighties or possibly in his early nineties as a martyr in Pergamum ca.

132. This will be further elaborated upon in the next chapter.

133. The topic concerning which New Testament books Papias was aware of will be a major theme in the following chapter.

163. Regrettably certitude concerning the date and manner of his death is not possible. Having thus completed the biographical portion of this book, it is now time to turn more fully to Papias's witness to the writings of the New Testament as found in material that is commonly referred to as "The Fragments of Papias."

4

The Fragments of Papias

INTRODUCTION

THE PREVIOUS CHAPTERS HAVE shed some light on Papias's life, ministry, and culture; nevertheless, to a significant degree there is still very little that can be objectively known about him. Consequently, while they provide some helpful data, the best source for understanding Papias are his own words. Regrettably, however, very few of them have survived. Those interested in this patristic father or the origins of the New Testament, therefore, must look to the works of those who were either familiar with Papias or were familiar with his writings. A compilation of the fragments of Papias is not an original endeavor, nor are such collections hard to find.[1] Many of these collections, however, are selective with respect to which fragments they include. They are selective because their authors were either unaware of certain fragments, or because some fragments did not meet their specifications for what they believed constituted an actual Papian fragment. Consequently, some fragments containing important information about Papias are absent from several collections, even though they are helpful for learning more about Papias and his awareness of the apostolic writings. This book has assembled a collection of Papian fragments in order to provide a greater awareness of who Papias was, his knowledge of any New Testament writings, and his attitude towards them. It has attempted to do so chronologically, although a precise dating of certain fragments is

---

1. For the most recent compilation and comparison of lists of Papian fragments see Holmes, *Apostolic Fathers,* 3rd ed., 730–31.

not possible. Even though chronological precision with respect to all the Papian fragments is not entirely possible, this does not prohibit a profitable analysis of each individual fragment in order to ascertain Papias's knowledge and attitude towards the literary works that comprise the New Testament.

FRAGMENT 1

The blessing thus foretold undoubtedly belongs to the time of the kingdom, when the righteous will rise from the dead and reign, when creation, too, renewed and freed from bondage, will produce an abundance of food of all kinds from the dew of heaven and from the fertility of the earth, just as the elders, who saw John the disciple of the Lord, recalled having heard from him how the Lord used to teach about those times and say:

The days will come when vines will grow, each having ten thousand shoots, and on each shoot ten thousand branches, and on each branch ten thousand twigs, and on each twig ten thousand clusters, and in each cluster ten thousand grapes, and each grape when crushed will yield twenty-five measures of wine. And when one of the saints takes hold of a cluster, another cluster will cry out, "I am better, take me, bless the Lord through me." Similarly a grain of wheat will produce ten thousand heads, and every head will have ten thousand grains, and every grain ten pounds of fine flour, white and clean. And the other fruits, seeds, and grass will produce similar proportions, and all the animals feeding on these fruits produced by the soil will in turn become peaceful and harmonious toward one another, fully subject to man.

Papias, a man of the early period, who was a hearer of John and a companion of Polycarp, bears witness to these things in writing in the fourth of his books, for there are five books composed by him. And he goes on to say: *"These things are believable to those who believe.""And,"* he says, *"when Judas the traitor did not believe and asked, 'How, then, will such growth be accomplished by the Lord?'", the Lord said, 'Those who live until those times will see.'"*

Irenaeus of Lyons, *Against Heresies* 5.33.3–4
(written ca. 180–185)[2]

2. Holmes, *The Apostolic Fathers: Diglot Edition*, 579–81. In this edition this text is the fourteenth Papian fragment. Schoedel, Kleist, and Ehrman appropriately began

This particular fragment is preserved in a Latin translation of Irenaeus's *Against Heresies*. Irenaeus was a bishop in Lyons (in present-day France) during the last quarter of the second century, and was also one of the great apologists of that era.[3] He is the earliest author known to have quoted Papias; thus, his text with its reference to Papias is rightly positioned as the first Papian fragment. This text actually provides two fragments, Irenaeus attributed the first (which is contained in the middle paragraph) to a mysterious group that he referred to as "the elders."[4] The second is an actual Papian fragment, which is found in the last paragraph and has been italicized for precise identification. It is possible that Irenaeus relied upon Papias's *Exposition* as the literary source regarding teachings on the earth's millennial bountifulness; however, he stated that "the elders" were his source for that tradition.[5] Consequently, it is more probable that Irenaeus relied upon a different source for the fragment attributed to "the elders" and only employed Papias in order to corroborate it.[6] There is insufficient data, however, to determine whether Papias's source was actually oral or literary. Nevertheless, if one were pressed to conjecture, it would appear that this is but one example of Papias's preservation of oral material. This fragment provides no objective evidence that Papias knew any New Testament book. Charles Hill, however, appropriately acknowledged that this fragment has considerable resemblance to a passage found in *2 Baruch*.[8]

---

their lists with this fragment. Schoedel, *The Fragments*, 94–96; Kleist, *Papias*, 114–18; *Papias and Quadratus* (LCL 25:92–95).

3. See chapter 3 for more information regarding Irenaeus's relationship to Papias and other apostolic fathers.

4. For other examples of fragments attributed to this "anonymous" group see Holmes, *Apostolic Fathers*, 3rd ed., 769–73; Schoedel, *The Fragments*, 124–27.

5. Irenaeus generally referred to the "elders" as those who followed the Lord's disciples, and not those who had seen and heard the Lord (i.e. the apostles and their contemporaries). Chapman argued that this was also Papias's understanding of this term. Chapman, *John the Presbyter*. For a more comprehensive critique of Chapman's arguments see chapter 2.

6. Schoedel, *The Fragments*, 94–95; Körtner, *Papias*, 41–42. Lightfoot believed that a different literary work was the source for the fragment in the middle paragraph; however, he also provided a well reasoned theory that Irenaeus may have in fact relied upon Papias's *Exposition* as the source for the fragment. Lightfoot, *Essays*, 196–99.

7. Lightfoot speculated that Irenaeus's context implies that this fragment preserves a portion of Jesus' discourses during his last Passover regarding when he would again drink from the fruit of the vine, the inference being that Papias was aware of some or all of the canonical Gospels. Lightfoot, *Essays*, 158–59. His conjecture, while intriguing, is impossible to validate with certainty.

8. Hill, "Papias," 313–14. Hill considered these traditions as coming from "Jewish

There is not a lot of debate concerning the dating of *2 Baruch*. Both Tom Willett and A. F. J. Klijn believed the book to have been written sometime after the first fall of Jerusalem, which occurred in AD 70, but before AD 135.[9] *Second Baruch* 29.5b states, "The earth will also yield fruits ten thousandfold. And on one vine will be a thousand branches, and one branch will produce a thousand clusters, and one cluster will produce a thousand grapes, and one grape will produce a cor of wine. And those who are hungry will enjoy themselves and they will, moreover, see marvels every day."[10] A similar passage concerning the earth's fecundity during the Messiah's earthly reign is found in *1 Enoch* 10:18–19, which reads, "Then all the earth will be tilled in righteousness, and all of it will be planted with trees and filled with blessing; and all the trees of joy will be planted on it. They will plant vines on it, and every vine that will be planted on it will yield a thousand jugs of wine, and of every seed that is sown on it, each measure will yield a thousand measures, and each measure of olives will yield ten baths of oil."[11] George Nickelsburg and James VanderKam estimated that the portion of *1 Enoch* in which this passage is found originated in the "mid or late third century B.C.E."[12]

Hill speculated, however, that the passage provided by Irenaeus is inconsistent with the eschatology of the New Testament,[13] the inference being that neither Jesus nor his followers would have taught eschatology such as that found in this text from Irenaeus; consequently, it appears that Papias preserved what Jerome later labeled as "Jewish traditions of a millennium."[14] Hill's theory is tenuous at best; for it is a weak position

converts who carried over eschatological ideas of nationalistic apocalypses and perhaps from the synagogues," or from Gentiles who were engaged in "Jewish-Christian dialogue and debate." It was his position that these traditions were primarily Jewish in nature and, consequently, they do not appear to have originated with Jesus or his followers. Hill also conjectured that Papias included this tradition as he attempted to explain Jesus' meanings in Matt 26:27–29; ibid., 310. Rigg believed Papias confused themes found in Jewish literature with the teachings of Jesus; Rigg, "Papias on Mark," 165.

9. Willett, *2 Baruch and 4 Ezra*, 77–79. *Second Baruch*, trans. Klijn, 616–17.

10. *Second Baruch*, trans. Klijn, 630.

11. *1 Enoch*, trans. Nickelsburg and VanderKam, 30. Schoedel stated that Irenaeus's tradition was dependent upon "Jewish apocalyptic ideas," but believed that it was a later development of themes found in the passages of *2 Baruch* and *1 Enoch*. Schoedel, *The Fragments*, 94.

12. *1 Enoch*, trans. Nickelsburg and VanderKam, 3. E. Isaac also dated this portion of *1 Enoch* as "late pre-Maccabean." *1 Enoch*, trans. Isaac, 1:7.

13. Hill, "Papias," 313–14.

14. See fragment 8, p. 208.

to argue that the eschatological themes found in *2 Baruch*, *1 Enoch*, and the rest of the Pseudepigrapha would have been foreign to Jesus—a rabbi and itinerant preacher who ministered in Roman occupied Palestine after the end of the first quarter of the first century. Jesus would not have been ignorant of such millennial hopes while living in such a politically and religiously charged context. Consequently, it is not unreasonable to believe that he might have held such hopes or taught similar ideas concerning the millennial kingdom as described in *Against Heresies* 5.33.3–4. Regardless of what one might contend about Jesus' eschatology, that Papias addressed such millennial aspirations is evident and speaks to the possibility that he wrote during a period when "Jewish theologies" still had significant influence within the church, but before a time when deep anti-Jewish sentiment began to plague it.

Some have speculated that Papias's focus upon a physical kingdom of God implies a possible attempt to ward off Gnosticism.[15] His emphasis upon a literal millennial kingdom in which physical appetites are enjoyed could be construed as an anti-gnostic polemic. That the church wrestled with worldviews and philosophies that marginalized the physical realm while promoting the immaterial as "ideal" is evident in passages such as Acts 17:10–33; 1 Timothy 4:1–5; Colossians 2:20–23. Regarding the existence of streams of thought and religious practice that were consistent with Gnosticism and which the apostles taught were contrary to Christianity, Carl Smith wrote, "It must be admitted that numerous themes that later would be included in Gnosticism were being discussed and developed during the time when the NT books were being composed."[16] That Papias may have felt the need to address such ideologies is a reasonable conjecture. Does this mean that he was battling what some modern scholars recognize today as "full blown" Gnosticism? The data is insufficient to conclude with certitude that such was the case.[17] If one were forced to conjecture, then

15. Lightfoot, *Essays*, 160–61. Regarding Papias's possible interaction with Gnosticism see also Körtner, *Papias*, 167–72. Schoedel, however, saw little evidence of a gnostic threat in the writings of Papias. Schoedel, *The Fragments*, 95–96.

16. Smith, *No Longer Jews*, 152.

17. Smith argued that "gnostic dualism arose in the context of the disappointed messianism of the Jewish revolts in Judea and the Diaspora, and that its full expression did not develop until after the revolt in Cyrenaica and Egypt in 115–117 C.E." Ibid., 113. While some may view Smith's thesis as ambitious, he provided a helpful overview of the possible origins and development of Gnosticism that confronted the late second-century church, while also dealing with pre-gnosticism themes commonly found in the New Testament; ibid., 113–14. Lightfoot believed Papias to have written after 130 or even 140; Lightfoot, *Essays*, 151. If true, then the possibility that Papias

the lack of any late second-century apologist (e.g., Irenaeus) quoting arguments formulated by Papias to confront core gnostic tenets argues against Papias's awareness of a "gnostic" threat, or that any such polemic was a *significant* focus in his writings.[18] Charles M. Nielsen wrote that, "If Papias had had a Gnostic collection in mind, this would have been grist for the mills of Irenaeus and Eusebius, and it seems mostly likely that they would have been eager to mention the fact. But they tell us nothing."[19]

This fragment, however, reveals that Irenaeus understood Papias to have been both "a hearer"[20] of the apostle John and an associate of Polycarp, whom Irenaeus knew to be John's disciple. His reference to Papias as an "ancient man"[21] is interesting since generally speaking one does not refer to someone of their generation as "ancient" unless they themselves are viewed in a similar manner. Clearly, therefore, Irenaeus assigned Papias to a generation that preceded him. Historians estimate that Irenaeus was born between 125 to 140. Given his vocabulary and descriptions of Papias, it is reasonable to conclude that he believed Papias to have been born sometime during the first century. There have been some who found Irenaeus's description of Papias as "ancient" particularly significant since

---

might have confronted some form of Gnosticism increases with each passing year.

18. It is recognized that ancient authors, both Christian and pagan, were not as concerned with plagiarism as modern scholars; therefore, it should not be assumed that Papias's writings are only preserved in known Papian fragments. As Lightfoot wrote, "Literary property was not an idea recognized by early Christian writers. They were too much absorbed in their subject to concern themselves with their obligations to others. Plagiarism was not a crime, where they had all literary things in common." Lightfoot, *Essays*, 202. It is likely, therefore, that some Papian material is preserved or assumed without any reference to Papias at all. In such a literary context, it is certainly possible that Papias confronted some gnostic or pre-gnostic tenets. The lack of available data, therefore, proves very little. For example, if one found a bank statement of an account held by Bill Gates that indicated that he only had fifty dollars, it would not prove that Bill Gates was poor. The available data, however, does seem to suggest that pre-gnostic or "full blown" Gnosticism was not a major focus of Papias's writings. For a more thorough investigation of the tenets of Gnosticism see Jonas, *The Gnostic Religion*, 29–97; and Smith, *No Longer Jews*, 5–18.

19. Nielsen, "Papias," 532. This should not be construed as arguing that "full blown" Gnosticism could not have existed during the period in which Papias wrote. It is possible that Gnosticism existed at that time and that Papias, for whatever reason, was not interested in addressing it in *Exposition*.

20. In the Latin the phrase regarding Papias's relationship to John is *Haec autem et Papias Johannis auditor*. Eusebius preserved Irenaeus's Greek in his *Ecclesiastical History*, which refers to Papias as a ἀκουστής of John. Holmes, *Apostolic Fathers*, 3rd ed., 752.

21. *Fragments of Papias* 4 (ANF 1:154).

he is not known to have applied this description to Polycarp, who was approximately eighty-six years old when martyred.[22] Some have concluded, therefore, that Papias was probably older than Polycarp. Such a conclusion has its merits, it is, however, only a conjecture that is grounded upon silence; thus, it should not be pressed as a certainty. That Papias and Polycarp were simply members of the same adult generation seems to be the most defensible position with respect to the question of which one was older. Concerning the question of whether Irenaeus believed Papias to have known the apostle John, it is clear that he believed that Papias was at least his "hearer." Such a description, however, can also be construed as meaning that Papias was in fact a student of the apostle John.[23] As argued earlier, given Irenaeus's contemporaneous relationship to Polycarp, his exposure to Polycarp's teaching, his interactions with others of Polycarp's generation, and the period of time Irenaeus spent in Asia Minor, there seems little reason to doubt his veracity or the power of his memory with respect to Polycarp's association with Papias.

FRAGMENT 2

> Irenaeus and others record that John, the theologian and apostle, survived until the time of Trajan. After this Papias of Hierapolis and Polycarp, bishop of Smyrna, both of whom had heard him, became well known.
>
> Eusebius (ca. 260–340), *Chronicle*[24]

Eusebius affirmed in his *Chronicle* that in his day it was generally held that the apostle John survived until the third year of Trajan's reign, which began in 98. This fragment bears witness to the fact that Irenaeus was a major source for Eusebius's information concerning the life of the apostle

22. Polycarp *To the Philippians* 9.3 (LCL 24: 381).

23. Regarding the question of whether Irenaeus thought there was one or two "Johns," see Lewis, *Fourth Gospel*, 9–23. For an opposing view see Perumalil, "Papias and Irenaeus," 332–37.

24. Holmes, *The Apostolic Fathers: Diglot Edition*, 563. Holmes identified this fragment as from Eusebius and cited a work by the ninth-century chronographer George Synkellos as his source for Eusebius's text. Eusebi, *Chronicon*, 162. In an earlier edition of his *Apostolic Fathers*, Holmes also cited Jerome's Latin version of Eusebius's *Chronicle*, which Jerome translated ca. 374–379; see Eusebius, *Chronicle*, 193–94; Eusebii Pamphili, *Chronici*, 275–76; Hamell, *Handbook of Patrology*, 144. Eusebius composed his *Chronicle* before writing his *Ecclesiastical History*; consequently, it is placed here before other Papian fragments found in Eusebius's history of the church.

John. It also indicates that as Eusebius wrote his *Chronicle* he believed that Papias was a contemporary of Polycarp, and a hearer of the last living apostle. It was apparently soon after the death of John that both Papias and Polycarp rose to prominence as leaders in the Asiatic church. Jerome apparently indicated that Eusebius placed the death of the apostle John and the elevation of these two bishops as occurring ca. 103.[25] This fragment provides no quote or allusion to any New Testament writings. If accurate, however, this date for Papias's promotion to the bishopric makes it almost a certainty that he received traditions concerning some New Testament books originating from deep within the first century.[26]

Holmes listed this fragment as his first fragment, and as mentioned earlier, he provided a Greek text of it that he attributed to Eusebius.[27] Regrettably, no actual Greek manuscript of Eusebius's *Chronicle* is extant. As stated previously, Holmes's footnotes for this fragment indicate that he relied upon two different sources for this fragment, one of which was Jerome's Latin translation of Eusebius's *Chronicle*, while the other is from a Greek chronography authored by a late eighth-century and early ninth-century monk named George Syncellus.[28] Synkellos died sometime after 810. He was the "syncellus" or personal secretary of Tarasius the patriarch of Constantinople. Having obtained such an influential post in Constantinople indicates that he was a learned scholar in his own right. The Greek

25. Eusebii Pamphili, *Chronici*, 275–76.

26. This is based upon the assumption that Papias was at least in his mid to late twenties, or more reasonably, in his early thirties when he ascended to the bishopric at Hierapolis. Hill argued that Papias had received many traditions from an individual he knew as "the elder," consequently, these traditions were considerably older than Papias. Hill, "Papias," 313.

27. Holmes, *Apostolic Fathers*, 3rd ed., 733.

28. Eusebi, *Chronicon*, 162; Eusebii Pamphili, *Chronici*, 275–76. Holmes only cited the text from Schoene in the third edition (also spelled Schöne in some editions). Holmes, *Apostolic Fathers*, 3rd ed., 733. Hereafter, George Syncellus will simply be referred to as Synkellos. Theoretically, one could place this fragment as originating in the ninth century and attribute it to Synkellos. However, this would be an uncritical denial of Synkellos's and Jerome's actual source, which appears to be the reason why Holmes has attributed this fragment to Eusebius. For an English translation of Synkellos's chronography see Synkellos, *The Chronography* (Oxford: Oxford University Press, 2002). For the dating and value of Synkellos's chronography see Alder's and Tuffin's introductory remarks on pages xxix–xxxvi. Alder and Tuffin stated that Synkellos "depended heavily" on Eusebius's chronicle (see pages lx–lxi). Consequently, by comparing Jerome's Latin translation with Synkellos's Greek text concerning this reference to Papias it can be reasonably argued that Synkellos has either preserved Eusebius's original Greek or a text close to it.

fragment provided by Holmes appears to be a direct quote or close summary of Eusebius's *Chronicle*. There is a variant of the text concerning the word ἐπίσκοποι, but it produces no significant conflict between the meanings found in Synkellos's Greek text and Jerome's Latin translation of Eusebius's *Chronicle*.[29]

This early fragment written by Eusebius about Papias is conspicuously absent from the collections of Schoedel, Ehrman, and Kleist even though contains important data regarding Papias. It is important because it reveals a significant contradiction regarding Eusebius's opinion about Papias's relationship to the apostle John. This contradiction has been aptly addressed by Robert Grant, who concluded that as researchers survey Eusebius's treatment of Papias they will discover a transition within Eusebius that occurred over an extended period. It is a transition in which Eusebius's attitude towards Papias moved from one of relative respect to abject rejection.[30] Those who are quite familiar with Eusebius's *Ecclesiastical History* are aware that he wrote it over a period spanning more than a decade. He began his work in the midst of the Diocletian persecutions and finished it after Constantine's ascension. This period was certainly tumultuous and, given the turn of events that occurred during this time, one should not be surprised that Eusebius would undergo a significant degree of theological development.[31] While some may marginalize this fragment by not including it within their list of Papian fragments, it is an important witness to Papias's relationship to John the son of Zebedee. Given Eusebius's later attempt to distance Papias from the apostle John in his more well known work *Ecclesiastical History*, it is understandable that some might have missed this significant fragment. Eusebius's effort to marginalize Papias, however, was clearly prejudicial and unwarranted, and, as will become increasingly evident, his theories about Papias are contradicted by evidence embedded within the majority of other Papian fragments.

FRAGMENT 3

But so great a light of godliness shone upon the minds of Peter's listeners that they were not satisfied with a single hearing or with

29. A variant has ἐπίσκοποι in the singular, see Syncelli, *Ecloga Chronographica*, 424.

30. Grant, "Papias in Eusebius," 209–13.

31. See appendix 1 for a more thorough discussion of Eusebius's development as a theologian and his opinion of Papias.

the oral teaching of the divine proclamation. So, with all kinds of exhortations they begged Mark (whose Gospel is extant), since he was Peter's follower, to leave behind a written record of the teaching given to them verbally, and did not quit until they had persuaded the man, and thus they became the immediate cause of the Scripture called "The Gospel According to Mark." And they say that the apostle, aware of what had occurred because the Spirit had revealed it to him, was pleased with their zeal and sanctioned the writing for study in the churches. Clement (of Alexandria) quotes the story in the sixth book of *Hypotyposes*, and the bishop of Hierapolis, named Papias, corroborates him. He also says that Peter mentions Mark in his first epistle which, they say, he composed in Rome itself, as he himself indicates, referring to the city metaphorically as Babylon in these words: "She who is in Babylon, who is likewise chosen, sends you greetings, as does Mark, my son."[32]

Eusebius, *Ecclesiastical History* 2.15.[33]

The above fragment is not included in many collections of Papian material.[34] Nevertheless, it is included in this book because of Eusebius's assertion that Papias preserved a tradition regarding the origin of Mark's Gospel, which indicates that Papias was aware of its existence as well as the epistle of 1 Peter, an assertion that Eusebius reiterated in *Ecclesiastical History* III.39.17. It is here, however, that Eusebius preserved the tradition that 1 Peter was written when Peter was in Rome, while Mark's Gospel was composed during a period of Peter's absence from Rome—but while Peter was alive.[35] Eusebius cited more than one literary source to validate Peter's presence in Rome, the first being Clement of Alexandria—a late second-century author, and the other being Papias.[36] Based upon the witness of these two sources, Eusebius was quite confident that he possessed answers to several questions regarding the composition of Mark's Gospel. The first was that the Gospel of Mark—which Eusebius believed had

32. See 1 Pet 5.13.

33. Holmes, *The Apostolic Fathers: Diglot Edition*, 587.

34. This fragment is missing from the lists of Kürzinger, Kleist, Ehrman, and Schoedel.

35. For a discussion on Peter's possible presence in Rome see Wenham, *Redating*, 136–72.

36. A valid question regarding Clement of Alexandria's witness to this tradition is whether he provided an independent witness or did he rely upon Papias who wrote approximately fifty years earlier. Regrettably, neither of these sources is extant, and so it is not possible to answer this question conclusively.

survived to his own day, was informed primarily from the preaching of the apostle Peter. Secondly, that Mark had been a "follower" (i.e., a student or protégé) of Peter. If true, then Mark had heard Peter preach quite often; consequently, he was a reliable source capable of preserving the content of Peter's messages (i.e., his "gospel"). Eusebius's explanation of the final composition of the Gospel of Mark, however, provides a challenge to Bauckham's theory that Peter dictated his "Gospel" to Mark as Peter "was remembering" the teachings of Jesus and the events of his life.[37] Eusebius stated that his sources indicated that Mark composed his Gospel because of pressure from those who heard Peter's sermons and feared not having them in the form of a permanent record, and that Peter sanctioned Mark's composition at a later time.[38]

A legitimate question regarding Eusebius's understanding of the Gospel of Mark and the "original" composition of Mark's writings is: Was this compilation of Peter's sermons and reminiscences of Jesus by Peter's protégé *the* "Ur-Mark," or was it the canonical Gospel of Mark? Eusebius was of the opinion that Papias and Clement of Alexandria had referred to the canonical Gospel of Mark. Regarding the impetus for Mark to compose such a work, Eusebius wrote that Mark was virtually "harassed" by the congregations in Rome to compose a permanent record of Peter's memories of Jesus. Thus, the need or "*Sitz im Leben*" for Mark's Gospel did not arise from within himself or Peter, but from the desire of the church(es) in Rome to have an accurate record of Peter's reminiscences on the life, teachings, deeds, ministry, death, and resurrection of Jesus Christ. Eusebius was of the opinion, based upon his sources, that Mark's Gospel did not undergo serial redactions generated by unknown editors far removed from the apostles, nor did he understand that Mark's Gospel "evolved" over a prolonged period of time in order to meet ever changing and shifting theological or social concerns of some unknown audience. Instead it was composed to meet the felt need of believers in Rome to have a historical account that accurately described Jesus and his earthly ministry, and it was singularly guided not by his own reminiscences but those

---

37. Bauckham, *The Eyewitnesses*, 210–11. This challenge, however, does not detract from Bauckham's well argued thesis that Mark's Gospel was a history of the life and teachings of Jesus based upon the eyewitness testimony of Peter. For a more thorough discussion regarding Mark's responsibility as the preserver of Peter's testimony of Jesus see ibid., *The Eyewitnesses*, 155–82, 205–21.

 38. If accurate, and there appears little reason to doubt Eusebius's accuracy on this point, then this fragment provides a weighty challenge to the overly employed adage that first-century audiences placed little value on written testimony.

of the apostle Peter. And once completed, at some point in time before his martyrdom, Peter himself approved of its use in the churches at Rome.

Consequently, Eusebius was either ignorant of the possibility that Mark's Gospel may have undergone redactions,[39] or, and more likely, it meant little to him that Mark may have slightly edited Peter's reminiscences in order to create an acceptable and complete narrative of the life of Jesus for use in the church(es). For Eusebius, such a possibility would not have jeopardized the veracity and validity of Mark's effort to preserve Peter's eyewitness testimonies about the life and teachings of Jesus.[40] Regardless of what might be one's theory concerning the composition of the second Gospel of the New Testament, Eusebius was convinced that Papias was aware of Mark's original composition and that it was in fact the canonical Gospel of Mark.

Fragment 4

> At this time there flourished in Asia Polycarp, the disciple of the apostles, who had been appointed to the bishopric of the church in Smyrna by the eyewitnesses and ministers of the Lord. At this time Papias, who was himself bishop of the diocese of Hierapolis, *a man well skilled in all manner of learning, and well acquainted with the Scriptures*, became well known.

> Eusebius, *Ecclesiastical History* 3.36.1–2 [41]

Fragment 4 provides no new information regarding Papias's knowledge of any New Testament writings, nor does it reveal extensive historical data about the period of time in which he lived. It does, however, re-affirm Eusebius's belief that Papias was a contemporary of Polycarp, and that he served as a bishop during the same period in which Polycarp ministered,

---

39. This conjecture seems extremely unlikely given that Eusebius himself was an author who would have been quite familiar the normal practices involved in the publication of books.

40. It is not in the purview of the book to exhaustively investigate what may or may not have been the relationship of "Ur-Mark" and the Gospel of Mark. For an analysis of the possible sources of the Synoptic Gospels see Stein, *Synoptic Gospels*, 29–152; Carson and Moo, *An Introduction*, 77–133.

41. Holmes, *The Apostolic Fathers: Diglot Edition*, 563. This fragment was not included in the lists of Kleist and Ehrman. The text in italics has been added and it is a translation of a variant of the text that will be explained in greater detail during the discussion of this fragment.

and that these two bishops ascended to prominence at approximately the same time. There is an interesting textual variant concerning this fragment that has been included and italicized, which is also retained in Christian Frederick Cruses's translation of Eusebius's *Ecclesiastical History*.[42] Many translations of *Ecclesiastical History* do not contain this variant, however, because it potentially reveals a development in Eusebius's theology and, subsequently, and evolution in his attitude towards Papias, a brief discussion is in order.

Eusebius composed his *Ecclesiastical History* over a period of approximately a decade and a half, with his first edition being published ca. 311, and his last version being released in late 324 or early 325.[43] There are a couple of reasons for believing that the phrase "a man well skilled in all manner of learning, and well acquainted with the Scriptures," was originally composed by Eusebius. Robert Grant has argued, there is sufficient internal evidence within the cumulative writings of Eusebius to suggest that when he published the first edition (and possibly the second) of his *Ecclesiastical History* he regarded Papias as a respectable bishop.[44] However, by the final release of this work his eschatology had changed and he could no longer abide Papias's chiliasm. Regrettably for Papias his theology provided ammunition to Eusebius's opponents, both to those who were orthodox as well as to those who were heretical; consequently, in order to strengthen his own eschatological position Eusebius excised this complimentary reference to Papias from later editions of his history of the church. It appears that by marginalizing Papias Eusebius believed he could disassociate chiliasm from the earliest apostolic generation.[45]

A second possible conjecture explaining this variant, although less spectacular, is that the entire line may be the result of a copyist error commonly referred to as *parablepsis*. This possibility seems not entirely unrealistic when one considers that the variant, as found in Eduard Schwartz's and Theodor Mommsen's critical edition, is surrounded by lines that

---

42. Eusebius, *The Ecclesiastical History*, trans. Cruse, 120. This variant was also retained in Bright's Greek edition of Eusebius's history, see Eusebius, *Ecclesiastical History*, ed. Bright, 95. For a more detailed discussion regarding the textual history of Eusebius's *Ecclesiastical History* see Kirsopp Lake's introductory remarks in his translation of Eusebius *Ecc. Hist.* (LCL 153: xix–xxxiii); see also Lawlor, *Eusebiana*, 243–91.

43. Lawlor, *Eusebiana*, 291.

44. Grant, "Papias in Eusebius," 212–13.

45. For a discussion of chiliasm in the early church see Hoehner, "Evidence from Revelation 20," 237–44; Schaff, *History of the Church*, 2:613–20; Körtner, *Papias*, 194–96. Showers, *Difference*, 113–35.

average between fifty-one and fifty-two letters per line.[46] The variant in question contains a total of fifty letters. It is conceivable, therefore, that a scribe of an early rendition of Eusebius's history simply missed an entire line or two—depending on the original composition of the book (i.e., did each line contain twenty-five or fifty letters?). However, this seems to be the least defensible solution.

What makes this variant so difficult to analyze is that it is found in the best texts of both textual families of Eusebius's *Ecclesiastical History*. J.-P. Migne rejected it as an addition because he saw that it was inconsistent with Eusebius's derision of Papias in *Ecclesiastical History* III.39.13.[47] If this variant was not original to Eusebius's history, then it could only be a later insertion. If, however, it is a later addition, then one is left to wonder what would motivate or cause anyone to contaminate Eusebius's history with such a flagrant and inconsistent redaction, and why did this supposed scribe not also erase Eusebius's derogatory statement concerning Papias in III.39.13, if for no other reason than for the sake of harmony? One cannot argue that it was due to respect for the text, for clearly this potential rogue scribe had already displayed contempt for Eusebius's original version. Additionally, why would such a variant endure for so long and be so well attested? If the principle of preference for the harder reading is to have any influence, then it would argue for the variant being original.[48] Lastly, why did this copyist insert such an inconsistent statement about a bishop who was so clearly out of favor in the post-Constantinian church? It seems that such an absurd variant can only have endured if either it was original or that it was so early that it was perceived as original.

If this variant was original to Eusebius's earliest edition, it provides additional important information about Papias, such as that he had achieved an adequate education and that he was well versed in the Scripture (τῆς γραφῆς). This statement, however, was Eusebius's commentary regarding Papias's knowledge of the "Scriptures." Unfortunately Eusebius did not specify whether he had in mind one or both of the canons (i.e., the Old or New Testament). By viewing history from Eusebius's vantage point one could conclude that he was being anachronistic and was referring to both canons as "the Scriptures," but this is clearly conjecture; therefore, to continue speculating about Eusebius's exact meaning would be vanity. The safest position to hold, consequently, is to assume that Eusebius at least

---

46. Eusebius, *Die Kirchengeschichte*, 274.

47. Eusebius, *Historica* (PG 20: 288).

48. Metzger, *The Text*, 209.

had in mind the Old Testament, for it is clear that during the first century and a half of the church's existence the Old Testament was certainly viewed as Holy Scripture.

The possibility that the variant is a later insertion cannot be completely rejected. The question is, however, whether such a theory provides the best explanation for the existence of the variant. A better explanation is that Eusebius's compliment of Papias was removed by none other than Eusebius himself. However, as scribes continued to produce new manuscripts that relied upon Eusebius's first edition, his later redaction could not be completely erased from his history, and so scholars to this day are left to conjecture about this textual oddity in *Ecclesiastical History*.

FRAGMENT 5

Five books of Papias are in circulation, which are entitled "Expositions of the Sayings of the Lord." Irenaeus also mentions these as the only works written by him, saying something like this: "Papias, a man of the early period, who was a hearer of John and a companion of Polycarp, bears witness to these things in writing in the fourth of his books. For there are five books composed by him." (2) So says Irenaeus. Yet Papias himself, in the preface to his discourses, indicates that he was by no means a hearer or eyewitness of the holy apostles, but shows by the language he uses that he received the matters of the faith from those who had known them:

(3) I will not hesitate to set down for you, along with my own interpretations, everything I carefully learned from the elders and carefully remembered, guaranteeing their truth. For unlike most people I did not enjoy those who have a great deal to say, but those who teach the truth. Nor did I enjoy those who recall someone else's commandments, but those who remember the commandments given by the Lord to the faith and proceeding from the truth itself. (4) And if by chance someone who had been a follower of the elders should come my way, I inquired about the words of the elders—what Andrew or Peter said, or Philip, or Thomas or James, or John or Matthew, or any other of the Lord's disciples, and whatever Aristion and the elder John, the disciples of the Lord, were saying. For I did not think that information from books would profit me as much as information from a living and abiding voice.

(5) Here it is worth noting that he lists the name of John twice. The first he mentions in connection with Peter and James and Matthew and the rest of the apostles, clearly meaning the Evangelist, but he classes the other John with others outside the number of the apostles by changing the wording and putting Aristion before him, and he distinctly calls him "elder." (6) Moreover, by these remarks he confirms the truth of the story told by those who have said that there were two men in Asia who had the same name, and that there are two tombs in Ephesus, each of which even today is said to be John's. It is important to notice this, for it is probably the second, unless one prefers the first, who saw the Revelation that circulates under the name of John. (7) And Papias, of whom we are now speaking, acknowledges that he had received the words of the apostles from those who had followed them, but he says that he was himself a hearer of Aristion and John the elder. In any event he frequently mentions them by name and includes their traditions in his writings as well. Let these statements of ours not be wasted on the reader.

(8) It is worthwhile to add to the statements of Papias given above other sayings of his, in which he records some other remarkable things as well, which came down to him, as it were, from tradition. (9) That Philip the Apostle resided in Hierapolis with his daughters has already been stated, but now it must be pointed out that Papias, their contemporary, recalls that he heard an amazing story from Philip's daughters. For he reports that in his day a man rose from the dead, and again another amazing story involving Justus, who was surnamed Barsabbas: he drank a deadly poison and yet by the grace of the Lord suffered nothing unpleasant. . . .[49] (11) The same writer has recorded other accounts as having come to him from unwritten traditions, certain strange parables of the Lord and teachings of his and some other statements of a more mythical character. (12) Among other things he says that there will be a period of a thousand years after the resurrection of the dead when the Kingdom of Christ will be set up in material form on this earth. These ideas, I suppose, he got through a misunderstanding of the apostolic accounts, not realizing that the

49. Section 10 is omitted because it is not viewed as an actual Papian fragment, but rather as Eusebius's opinion that the Barsabbas mentioned by Papias was the same individual referred to in Acts 1.23. While it is reasonable to assume that Eusebius was correct, Ehrman appropriately recognized this section as Eusebian. Consequently, a detailed analysis of it is not included in this study. *The Fragments of Papias* (LCL 25:101).

things recorded in figurative language were spoken by them mystically. (13) For he certainly appears to be a man of very little intelligence, as one may say judging from his own words. Yet he was the reason that so many ecclesiastical writers after him held the same opinion, on the grounds that he was a man of the early period—like Irenaeus, for example, and anyone else who has expressed similar ideas.

(14) In his writing he also hands on other accounts of the sayings of the Lord belonging to Aristion, who has been mentioned above, and the traditions of the elder John, to which we refer those interested. For our present purpose we must add to his statements already quoted above a tradition concerning Mark, who wrote the Gospel, which has been set forth in these words:

(15) And the Elder used to say this: "Mark, having become Peter's interpreter, wrote down accurately everything he remembered, though not in order, of the things either said or done by Christ. For he neither heard the Lord nor followed him, but afterward, as I said, followed Peter, who adapted his teaching as needed but had no intention of giving an ordered account of the Lord's sayings. Consequently, Mark did nothing wrong in writing down some things as he remembered them, for he made it his one concern not to omit anything which he had heard, or to make any false statements in them."

Such, then, is the account given by Papias with respect to Mark. (16) But with respect to Matthew the following was said:

So Matthew composed the oracles in the Hebrew language and each person interpreted them as best he could.

(17) The same writer utilized testimonies from the first letter of John and, likewise, from that of Peter. And he has related another account about a woman accused of many sins before the Lord, which the Gospel According to the Hebrews contains. And these things we must take into account, in addition to what has already been stated.

I doubt the woman

Eusebius, *Ecclesiastical History* III.39[50]

The thirty-ninth chapter of Eusebius's *Ecclesiastical History* is by far the most well known and thoroughly discussed chapter in patristic literature with respect to information about Papias's life and writings. Munck has gone so far as to state that it is "the most important text dealing with

---

50. Holmes, *The Apostolic Fathers: Diglot Edition*, 563–69.

Papias."[51] Such a claim, however, generally marginalizes other fragments that in reality are just as important for understanding Papias and his purposes for writing *Exposition*. That his chapter is immensely important is without debate, however, it should not be uncritically held as always providing the most accurate information regarding Papias and his writings.[52]

Eusebius, in *Ecclesiastical History* III.39.1, corroborated Irenaeus's statement that Papias wrote a five-volume work which Eusebius stated was still in circulation in his day.[53] He is the first patristic author, however, to preserve the actual title of Papias's work, which he stated was λογίων κυριακῶν ἐξηγήσεως.[54] Schoedel recognized that it is common to find ἐξηγήσις in the titles of Greek works.[55] When found in Greek titles ἐξηγήσις is generally rendered into English as "exposition, explanation, or "interpretation."[56] Holmes translated ἐξηγήσεως, as *"Expositions" of the*

51. Munck, "Presbyters," 224; see also, Petrie, "Matthew," 15.

52. Exegeting particular portions or even words of this chapter has been the focus of many scholars, such as Munck, "Presbyters," 221–43; Lawlor, "Eusebius on Papias," 167–204; Matthew Black wrote an article on rhetorical vocabulary in Papias's preface. Black, "Rhetorical Terminology," 31–41. Mullins wrote an article that focused on the word ἔνια as found in Papias's preface. Mullins, "Papias," 216–24. More recently Armin Baum wrote an article on the clause "Mark, having become the interpreter of Peter." He contended that Mark did not receive data for his Gospel directly from Peter, but that Peter, being bi-lingual, wrote his sermons in Greek, from which Mark "interpreted" Peter's meanings, which he redacted into the Gospel bearing his name. Baum, "Der Presbyter des Papias," 23, 35.

53. Having already discussed Irenaeus's reference to Papias in the analysis of fragment 1, p. 106, this portion of this book will primarily focus upon Eusebius's comments and preservation of Papian material.

54. Holmes, *Apostolic Fathers*, 3rd ed., 732. English translations of Papias title usually reverse the word order of his Greek words; consequently the words in Papias's title will be discussed in the order in which they are generally found in English translations.

55. Schoedel, *The Fragments*, 96–97. An example can be found in LSJ notation on this word; see LSJ, s.v. "ἐξηγήσις." The work was from a pre-Socratic philosopher known as Zeno Eleacticus or "Zeno of Elea" (firth century BC). LSJ cited the title as "Ε* των Εμπεδοκλους," which in English is translated as *An Exposition of the "Sayings" of Empedocles*. It does not appear that LSJ provided the entire title; thus "Sayings" has been supplied in this title; nor does LSJ indicate whether ἐξηγήσις was nominative or genitive, or whether it is singular or plural. Zeno of Elea was a contemporary of Empedocles in the fifth century BC; therefore, it is possible that Zeno interacted with the writings of Empedocles. For an overview of the lives of these two early Greek philosophers see Barnes, *Early Greek Philosophy*, 150–201; and Burnet, *Early Greek Philosophy*, 202.

56. Lawlor argued that it is a misreading to keep ἐξηγήσεως in the genitive. He believed that it should be read in the nominative (ἐξηγήσις or ἐξηγήσεις; thus following the text "M"). Lawlor, "Eusebius on Papias," 167. See also Petrie, "Matthew," 16. His

Sayings of the Lord. However, the word ἐξηγήσεως is singular and should be translated literally in Papias's title as *"An Exposition" of the Oracles of the Lord.*[57] Although technically incorrect, translating this word in Papias's title as a plural rather than as a singular is understandable and not altogether inconsistent with the nature of Papias's work. That Papias's writings discussed and/or exposited multiple "oracles" of Jesus can hardly be contested. This feature seems to be the most recognized aspect of Papias's work among the patristic and medieval authors who mention it. Philip of Side simply referred to Papias writings as *Oracles of the Lord* (κυριακῶν λογίων),[58] as did George the Sinner.[59] Jerome, being the scholar that he was, provided Papias's entire title, which he translated into Latin as: *An Exposition of the Discourses of the Lord* (*Explanatio Sermonum Domini*).[60] Maximus the Confessor appears to have actually changed ἐξηγήσεως from the singular to the plural so that Papias's title would be read as *"Expositions" of the Lord* (τῶν κυριακῶν ἐξηγήσεων).[61] Apollinaris also changed Papias's title to *An Exposition of the "Sayings" of the Lord.*[62] In all these references to the title of Papias's writings, the implied common denominator is that Papias attempted to exposit multiple sayings of Jesus.

Translating ἐξηγήσεως as plural rather than singular, however, may inadvertently misrepresent Papias's intent for his work. Clearly he

---

theory is to be rejected since it is contrary to the witness of the majority of texts, being testified to by only one manuscript. Not only is this theory contrary to witness of manuscripts A, T, E, R, B, and D (for the manuscript evidence see Holmes, *Apostolic Fathers,* 3rd ed., 732), but it also ignores the references to Papias's title as preserved by Eusebius, Apollinaris, and Maximus. Holmes, *Apostolic Fathers,* 3rd ed., 732, 754.

57. Lightfoot, *Essays,* 142. For the most exhaustive discussion concerning the title of Papias's work see Lawlor, "Eusebius on Papias," 167–204. Hill also interpreted ἐξηγήσεως in the plural, although he was aware that it was singular. Hill, "Papias," 310, 313. Schoedel and many others correctly translate the word as singular. Schoedel, "Papias," in *ABD* 5:140; Bartlet, "Papias's Exposition," 15–16.

58. Holmes, *Apostolic Fathers,* 3rd ed., 742.

59. Ibid., 744.

60. Ibid., 746–47. For a discussion of the Latin translation and interpretation of ἐξηγήσεως see Lawlor, "Eusebius on Papias," 169–71. Körtner believed that Jerome misinterpreted Papias's title. Körtner, *Papias,* 156.

61. Holmes, *Apostolic Fathers,* 3rd ed., 752, 754. From Maximus's title it could be inferred that Maximus understood that some of the interpretations contained in Papias's *Exposition* came directly from Jesus. For examples of Jesus providing interpretations of his teachings see Matt 13:1–23, 34–50; 15:1–20.

62. Holmes, *Apostolic Fathers,* 3rd ed., 754. Apollinaris changed λογίων (oracles) to the more generic λογων (sayings, teachings, or books). He did, however, retain ἐξηγήσεως in the singular and genitive.

collected a series of traditions and "oracles" (i.e., divine sayings) from the lips of Jesus—both oral and written. The question is, however, why did he do so? Was it simply to preserve what he feared would inevitably be lost, or did he have a more theological purpose in mind? More specifically, did Papias collect sayings of Jesus in order to explain and interpret them thematically as a body of eschatological teachings, or was he simply bringing together completely unrelated "oracles" in order to preserve and "exposit" them individually. Without possessing a significant portion of his material it is impossible to know for certain his authorial intent. Exposing and/or interpreting the sayings of Jesus was certainly an important focus of his effort. Papias, however, was not simply known for being a collector, an expositor, or a member of the generation that followed the apostles. He was also "famous" for his belief in a material millennial kingdom on earth. He was so identified with chiliasm that he caught the ire of Eusebius, which inevitably lead to his fall from grace within the annals of the church's history—in spite of his great antiquity and "apostolic character."[63]

If some are inclined to see Papias as inept, then they will be unable to perceive him as capable of writing a literary composition containing cohesive theological thought with rhetorical style.[64] If, however, one is willing to consider the very real possibility that Papias was an educated pastor and leading theologian of the Asiatic church, then believing that he was capable of assembling a cohesive work is not so difficult. If such a perception is more accurate than the alternative, then it would mean that Papias's work emphasized the origins of the "oracles of the Lord," while also attempting to explain their meanings and significance with a special emphasis on eschatological themes found within them. If Papias approached his work in such a manner, then ἐξηγήσεως should be retained in the singular rather than the plural since interpreting ἐξηγήσεως in the plural might improperly suggest that Papias's work was fragmentary rather than cohesive.

Schoedel evaluated Papias's title as "clumsy," apparently because ἐξηγήσεως was in the genitive rather than in the nominative.[65] The genitive does not seem so irregular if one assumes before ἐξηγήσεως the preposi-

---

63. See fragment 21, p. 242.

64. See Higgins, "Family Genealogy," 3. See also Von Campenhausen's remarks; Von Campenhausen, *The Christian Bible*, 134–35.

65. Schoedel was not completely clear whether he thought *exēgēseōs* was clumsy because it was in the singular, or because it was in the genitive, or for both reasons. Regardless of his vagueness, he chose to follow Lawlor with respect to reading the last word of Papias's title in the nominative singular (i.e., *exēgēsis*). Schoedel, *The Fragments*, 96–97.

tion περί which often takes a genitive object.[66] In such a case Papias's title would be interpreted as *"Concerning" an Exposition of the Oracles of the Lord*. However, because περί is absent, Papias's title will be translated simply as *An "Exposition" of the Oracles of the Lord*.

The next word to be discussed in Papias's title is the adjective κυριακῶν,[67] which some have translated as "dominical."[68] This translation is a Middle English transliteration of the Latin word *dominicus*. When translated into English, κυριακῶν is generally rendered as "of the Lord," as in "the day *of the Lord*" or "the Lord's day." While translating κυριακῶν as "dominical" is technically acceptable, it is not a good English translation. A better example of an English translation can be found in 1 Corinthians 11.20 in which Paul stated, "When you meet together, it is not the Lord's supper (κυριακὸν δεῖπνον) that you eat." One does not generally translate the phrase κυριακὸν δεῖπνον as "the dominical supper," nor should they.[69] If one feels compelled to employ an adjective, then "divine" would seem a more appropriate word rather than using a Latin transliteration of the Greek adjective. In such a case, Papias's title would read as, *An Exposition of the Divine Oracles*. This, however, seems very generic, lacking the specific focus that Papias's writings clearly had, which was to provide explanations about the sayings of Jesus. Consequently, translating Papias's κυριακῶν as "of the Lord" or as "the Lord's" properly reflects Papias's intent, which the first-century church would have understood by his title. Translating Papias's title, therefore, as *An Exposition of the Oracles of the "Lord"* seems to be most appropriate for capturing the focus for his five-volume work.

PAPIAS'S AND THE LORD'S ORACLES

Just as there are discussions about how to interpret the previous two words, there is also a debate regarding the meaning and translation of λογίων. Bauckham, in a fashion similar to Hill, chose to transliterate the term λογίων into English, thus translating Papias's title as *Exposition of the*

66. Smyth explained the translation of περί with a genitive object in this manner, "Other relations: *about concerning* (Lat. *de*), the subject *about which* an act or thought centers." Smyth, *Grammar*, 383. This very construction can be found in sections 14, 15, and 16 of Eusebius's quotes of Papias. Holmes, *Apostolic Fathers*, 3rd ed., 738–41.

67. Lawlor, "Eusebius on Papias," 193–98.

68. Hill, "Papias," 310.

69. Ignatius, Papias's contemporary, used this adjective in his letter to the Magnesians. Ehrman translated the phrase containing it as "the Lord's day." Ignatius *To the Magnesians* 9 (LCL 24: 250–51).

Logia of the Lord.[70] He contended that "because the meaning of Greek *logia* here is disputed I have left it untranslated. It probably means something like 'accounts of what Jesus said and did.'"[71] Bauckham is certainly correct that in the context of Papias's title this word to some degree referred to the sayings and deeds of Jesus. His interpretation, however, fails to capitalize on the great richness λόγια would have had to Papias's audiences, both Christian, Jewish, and pagan.

The word λόγια when found in the Scriptures is generally translated as "oracles."[72] Some might contend that interpreting λόγια as oracles is too archaic and thus unhelpful for modern readers. If such a situation exists (and this assumption is quite questionable), it is only because in certain segments of post-modern society some expect vocabulary to be predominately neutral or secular.[73] This is because they assume that God is unknowable or at best impersonal. Such *a priori* theories assume too much; consequently, "oracles" is an exceptionally appropriate word for explaining what Papias meant. Moreover, those who translate this word in Papias's title as "sayings" leave their audiences with the impression that Papias was attempting to explain the teachings of the "mere mortal" known as Jesus of Nazareth. Although these sayings were from a very important religious figure, nevertheless they were only *human* words and *human* teachings. That is not what Papias meant, nor would that have been how his audience understood him regardless of one's religious persuasion, for in Papias's day all cultures were spiritual in their worldviews—none were "secular" as the word is commonly understood today. The first-century world in which the Asiatic church lived did not have the sensitivities of our post-modern world with respect to the activities of the gods; consequently, it is inappropriate for today's readers to presume their own sensitivities upon the meanings of a first-century author and his audience.

Regarding the possible range of meanings of λόγια and its synonyms, B. B. Warfield provided a comprehensive analysis of them in his book, *The Inspiration and Authority of the Bible*, in which he surveyed their usages in

---

70. Bauckham, *The Eyewitnesses*, 12.

71. For a thorough discussion on λόγια see Warfield, *Inspiration and Authority*, 351–407; Lawlor, "Eusebius on Papias," 189–93. Kürzinger appeared to translate λόγια and variations of it as found throughout Eusebius's handling of Papian material as diminutive, meaning "words" or "brief or concise reports" (*kurzen Berichte*). Kürzinger, *Papias*, 25. Black rightly criticized Kürzinger for failing to consider how λόγια was used in contexts dealing with divine utterances. Black, "Rhetorical Terminology," 32.

72. Rom 3:2, Heb 5:12, Acts 7:38, and 1 Pet 4:11.

73. Hunter, *Cultural Wars*, 135–70, 197–224.

pagan and sacred literature of both Greeks and Jews. Regarding the dominant nuance of λόγια and λόγιον in Greek literature, he concluded that

> A survey of this somewhat miscellaneous collection of pas-
> sages will certainly only strengthen the impression we derived
> from those in which λόγιον occur[s]—that in λόγιον we have a
> term expressive, in common usage at least, of the simple no-
> tion of a divine revelation, an oracle, and that independently
> of any accompanying implication of length or brevity, poetical
> or prose form, directness or indirectness of delivery. This is the
> meaning of λόγιον in the mass of profane Greek literature.[74]

Having discussed Greek usage of the word λόγια, Warfield reviewed
its use in the Septuagint, after which he concluded, "In all the forty-one instances of its usage . . . it is employed in its native and only current sense, of
'oracle,' a sacred utterance of the Divine Being."[75] Warfield also stated concerning Philo (a first-century Jewish philosopher) and his understanding
of λόγια that "the only real distinction between his usage of these words
and that of profane authors arises from the fact that to Philo nothing is an
oracle from heaven, a direct word of God, except what he found within the
sacred books of Israel."[76]

Gerhard Kittel also research the use of the phrase τὰ λόγια in Greek
literature, and with respect to its "pre-Christian" usage, he defined this
term as "'Saying,' 'pronouncement,' esp. 'saying which may be traced back
to the deity.'" However, within biblical literature λόγια began to take on a
more specific meaning. Concerning its use in the Septuagint, Kittel simply
stated that "in the LXX λόγιον is used for the Word of God."[77] The great
question is when did λόγια begin to be applied to the words of Jesus. Kittel recognized that in Romans 3:2 this term continued to have the same
nuance as found in the Old Testament, stating that "R. 3:2 deals with the
λόγια τοῦ θεοῦ imparted to the Jews. It is obvious that the reference is to
the OT promises. Literally, τὰ λόγια τοῦ θεοῦ is simply a reference to God's
speaking."[78] He suggested, therefore, that given this meaning it should not
be surprising that apostles such as Paul understood that God had spoken

---

74. Warfield, *Inspiration and Authority*, 365–66. For a discussion about "oracles"
of Apollo associated with the city of Hierapolis see Parke, *The Oracles of Apollo*,
153–57, 180–83.

75. Warfield, *Inspiration and Authority*, 369.

76. Ibid., 374.

77. Kittel, "λόγιον," in *TDNT*, 4:137.

78. Ibid., 4:138.

in Jesus and that he was still speaking during the period in which Paul was ministering. Concerning this development of τὰ λόγια in the New Testament, Kittel concluded,

> In sum, there are two lines of NT usage. The first is a continuation of the ancient use for an individual divine saying, Ac. 7:38: the oracles delivered to Moses at Sinai; 1 Pt. 4:11: the words and statements spoken by the charismatic. The second refers, not to a saying, but to the divine action fulfilled as the salvation history of the old and new covenant, to the oracle of God, or to what God says to the world. R. 3:2: Individual oracles, biblical sayings and promises are undoubtedly given to the Jew, but there is also given to him the whole event of salvation history in which God spoke (Hb. 1:1) up to what took place in Jesus Christ. Cf. esp. Hb 5:12: . . . they are again to immerse themselves, and to be instructed, in the event of revelation which has taken place in Jesus, the λόγια τοῦ θεοῦ which have taken place in Him, and which do, of course, include His words and sayings.[79]

This development certainly has immense implications with respect to how patristic writers would have viewed the words of Jesus and the narratives that contained them (i.e., the canonical Gospels).

While not occurring with great frequency, the phrase τὰ λόγια τοῦ κυρίου and the concepts associated with it do appear in the writings of those who immediately followed the apostolic generation. Lawlor recognized that in *1 Clement* the word λόγια appeared only four times and "always with reference to the Old Testament;" thus he concluded that "whether intentionally or not, . . . Clement regarded the word λόγια as specially applicable to words of God in the Old Testament."[80] While it is undeniable that the apostolic fathers would have understood λόγια to refer to the Old Testament, it appears that sometime during the beginning of the second century, as implied by Papias's title, this phrase also began to be applied to the words and deeds of Jesus. An example of this is found in Polycarp's letter to the Philippians, which seems to have been written ca. 110.[81] In

---

79. Ibid., 4:139.

80. Lawlor, "Eusebius on Papias," 191.

81. Ehrman's dating of this epistle is not entirely critical. He relied completely upon P. N. Harrison's theory, the result being that he believed that material in this letter can be dated anywhere between 110 to 150. See his introductory remarks in Polycarp *To the Philippians* (LCL 24: 326–29). Schoedel's explanation of the dating of this letter is more objective. He relied upon Eusebius, who dated Ignatius's death as occurring in the eleventh year of Trajan's reign (ca. 109–110), which began 98. Polycarp, *To*

chapter 7, Polycarp employed the phrase τὰ λόγια τοῦ κυρίου within the context of allusions and quotes found within the New Testament,

> For anyone who does not confess that Jesus Christ has come in the flesh is an antichrist (1 John 4.2–3); and whoever does not confess that witness of the cross is a devil (1 John 3.8); and whoever distorts the words (*oracles*) of the Lord for his own passions, saying that there is neither resurrection nor judgment—this one is the first born of Satan. 2. And so, let us leave behind the idle speculation of the multitudes and false teachings and turn to the word that was delivered to us from the beginning, being alert in prayer and persistent in fasting. Through our entreaties let us ask the God who sees all things not to bring us into temptation (Matthew 6.13), just as the Lord said, "For the spirit is willing but the flesh is weak." (Matthew 26.41).[82]

It is certainly possible that when Polycarp wrote the phrase "the oracles of the Lord" (τὰ λόγια τοῦ κυρίου) he was thinking of Old Testament passages. The question, however, is whether that is the most reasonable explanation of what he meant. As Ehrman observed in his footnotes regarding this quote (as well as throughout his translation of the entire epistle), Polycarp was certainly aware of the Gospel of Matthew, as well as other New Testament writings. Polycarp's warning was directed toward those who would distort "the oracles of the Lord" by denying the resurrection and the last judgment. The Gospel of Matthew records some of Jesus' teachings concerning the resurrection of the dead (Matt 22.29–32), as well as the final future judgment (Matt 5.21–22; 11.20–24). Consequently,

---

the Philippians, trans. Schoedel, 5:4. Polycarp's letter in chapter nine acknowledges that Ignatius had suffered but without specifics, while in chap. 13 Polycarp requested more detailed information concerning Ignatius's sufferings. Consequently, this letter appears to have been written around the time of Ignatius's martyrdom, for certainly in the following years details about Ignatius's martyrdom would have become well known among the Asiatic churches. Therefore, Polycarp's letter can hardly have been written later than 115. Holmes, *The Apostolic Fathers: Diglot Edition*, 204.

82. Polycarp *Letter to the Philippians* 7 (LCL 24: 343). Italics mine. Ehrman's footnotes citing biblical references have been inserted within the block quote. Körtner argued that this phrase in Polycarp's letter is to be distinguished from the phrase Λογίων κυριακῶν found in Papias's title because in Papias's title "the Lord" is the object and not the subject. Körtner, *Papias*, 156. Consequently, Körtner believed that Papias was expositing oracles that were about the Lord rather than expositing oracles from the Lord. However, fragments 1 and 23 argue against his theory, for in each of them Papias's discussion was about what the Lord said instead of being a discussion about the Lord. Körtner believed, however, that although the term λόγια was not identical to the Gospels, it did refer to materials (Stoffe) found within them (ibid.).

while it is possible that Polycarp was thinking about the Old Testament when he wrote the phrase τὰ λόγια τοῦ κυρίου, his immediate context, however, indicates that it is more probable that he was referring to divine words uttered by Jesus as found in Matthew's Gospel.

Another important witness to the development of the term λόγια as a reference to the words of Jesus is found in the very writings of Papias as he discussed the origins of the Gospels of Matthew and Mark. Papias in both cases employed λόγια as he described their composition. Papias's comments about Mark's Gospel are actually a quote from his source, "the elder." His statements about Matthew's Gospel, however, may or may not be from this same individual.[83] Consequently, Papias did not invent the idea that the Gospel narratives contained divine oracles, but, as will become evident, he received this "tradition" from his source and mentor, the apostle John. Papias described Mark's Gospel as τῶν κυριακῶν ποιούμενος λογίων,[84] with respect to Matthew's composition, however, he simply referred to it as τὰ λόγια.[85] Kittel, therefore, believed that for Papias the phrase τὰ λόγια spoke of both the teachings and deeds of Jesus as found in the Gospel narratives.[86]

It is recognized that the term τὰ λόγια when found in other contexts will occasionally have different nuances or meanings. The salient question, however, is what is the context in which this term is found within Papias's title and writings? Rigg believed that the entire debate over how to translate λόγια in Papias's title has generated "an endless and futile discussion."[87] The significance of the difference in meanings and the context in which it is found in *Exposition* is certainly worthy of the exacting debate. If one is willing to acknowledge that Papias was an orthodox Christian and a trained bishop who was a student of a follower of Jesus, and who was aware of several apostolic writings, and who valued apostolic traditions over all other teachings, then one should have little doubt that when Papias employed the term λόγια with reference to the words of Jesus that he meant that those words, whether confirmed through oral traditions or found in the written narratives deriving directly from Jesus' immediate followers, were in fact the utterances of God. Consequently, they were by definition and nature "oracles," and as such they were to be received, preserved, and

83. This issue will be investigated with greater depth later.

84. Literally translated: "The making of Lord's oracles."

85. Holmes, *Apostolic Fathers*, 3rd ed., 738–40.

86. Kittel, "λόγιον," in *TDNT*, 4:140–41.

87. Rigg, "Papias on Mark," 163.

correctly understood above all other forms of human speech, rhetoric, and philosophy. To ignore this understanding of λόγια as found in Papias's title in order to avoid "disputes" is to unjustifiably surrender a central theological emphasis of not only Papias but also of the apostolic leadership that preceded him. For, as previously noted, this was not a conclusion that originated from Papias, but a "tradition" that he has received from his mentor and teacher, the apostle John. Therefore, in spite of the many other possible options, it seems that the most appropriate translation of Papias's title is *An Exposition of the "Oracles" of the Lord.*[88]

EUSEBIUS REJECTS IRENAEUS'S CLAIM

Having provided the title of Papias's writings, Eusebius immediately attempted to challenge Irenaeus's claim that Papias was an associate of the apostle John.[89] The evidence he cites, however, does not validate his position. Concerning this attempt by Eusebius, C. Stewart Petrie stated that

> Eusebius then quotes Papias, using Papias's own words allegedly to refute Irenaeus. But the quotation which he now brings forward to support his assertion against Irenaeus does not provide the support he claims. Instead, he would appear to have made a somewhat hasty assertion based on a careless reading of what Papias says. In face of his own quotation from Papias, his assertion is inaccurate and therefore misleading. . . . Consequently, there is nothing to justify the careless confidence with which Eusebius contradicts Irenaeus. It is fair to assume that, if Eusebius had been able to produce a more positive declaration from Papias, he certainly would have done so. But this was apparently the best he could do. Yet Irenaeus . . . had described Papias as a "hearer of John and a companion of Polycarp". Eusebius offers no valid reasons for contradicting him: he has merely indulged in a little unconvincing special pleading.[90]

88. While understanding "oracles" as utterances from the lips of Jesus (and thus understanding this word as a subjective genitive), translating Papias's title in this fashion also respects the possibility that at times Papias may have also discussed traditions about Jesus. Körtner, *Papias*, 154–63. As mentioned earlier, throughout this book Papias's five-volume work will simply be referred to as *Exposition*.

89. Having already discussed Irenaeus's statement about Papias in chapter 3, and in the analysis of fragment 1, p. 106, as well as in appendix 1, the current discussion concerning the Papian fragments in Eusebius's thirty-ninth chapter will focus primarily upon the statements Eusebius made about Papias, and any additional information Eusebius may have provided about his writings.

90. Petrie, "Matthew," 16, 18.

Eusebius's quote of Papias does, however, provide additional information about Papias's *Exposition*. By writing κατὰ τὸ προοίμιον τῶν αυτοῦ λόγων, Eusebius provided an important observation about *Exposition*.[91] Holmes translated the clause τῶν αυτοῦ λόγων as "his discourses," the clear inference being that Papias did not merely "collect" sayings of or about Jesus. Concerning his effort, Hill wrote, "One essential thing should be kept in mind: Papias was above all a collector of traditions, and some traditions will necessarily be more trustworthy than others."[92] There is little doubt that an important purpose of Papias's work was to preserve material he valued, especially material that in his day was exclusively oral. Papias, however, did not receive his fame for simply being a collector. He was also famous for being a theologian, and as stated previously, it was his eschatology for which he was most noted. Keeping in mind, therefore, that Eusebius was to some degree familiar with Papias's work, his description implies that Papias interacted with the material he preserved. While he did collect traditions, both oral and written, he collected them for the purpose of "expositing" them, i.e., clarifying their meanings. Consequently, it appears that he was much more than just a collector of oral traditions and amazing stories, he was a pastor–theologian who was concerned with educating his audience about the oracles of the Lord and their correct interpretations, interpretations that he had received from the elders, as well as those he had discovered for himself.

Eusebius was rather emphatic (οὐδαμῶς) that in his opinion Papias had made no confession to the effect that he had personally known any of the apostles.[93] His convictions, unfortunately, were based upon the thinnest of exegetical evidence. It should be noted that Eusebius never argued that Papias could not have known any of the apostles, for he confirmed that Papias had met others who had known the apostles. As discussed previously, if Papias knew others who had known apostles, then it is certainly possible that Papias was old enough to have known the apostles as well. Moreover, nothing in Eusebius's discussion about Papias indicates that he believed Papias was too young to have known an apostle. Eusebius's treatment of Papias in fact reveals that he understood him to be a contemporary

91. Holmes, *Apostolic Fathers*, 3rd ed., 734–35.

92. Hill, "Papias," 309.

93. Eusebius wrote concerning Papias's relationship to the apostolic generation that "So says Irenaeus. Yet Papias himself, in the preface to his discourses, indicates that he was by no means a hearer or eyewitness of the holy apostles, but shows by the language he uses he received the matters of the faith from those who had known them." Holmes, *Apostolic Fathers*, 3rd ed., 735. See also Perumalil, "Papias and Irenaeus," 335.

of Polycarp, whom Eusebius clearly believed to be a disciple of the apostle John, as well as other apostles.[94] As Munck has stated, "Eusebius did not doubt that Papias belonged to the earliest Christian period."[95] Regarding those that Papias knew, Eusebius only argued that he had never personally met any of the apostles—most importantly that he had not met the apostle John. He never argued that he could have not met one of the apostles of Jesus Christ. He rested his entire case that Papias had confessed or implied that he had not known any apostles on the mere fact that Papias wrote the name "John" twice, and a perceived significance in Papias's change in word order. It should be noted that Eusebius clearly understood the John in the first group to be an honored member of the apostolic colloquium, maintaining that "here it is worth noting that he lists the name of John twice. The first he mentions in connection with Peter and James and Matthew and the rest of the apostles, clearly meaning the Evangelist. . . ."[96] Eusebius's statement that this first John was from among "the rest of the apostles" indicates that he believed him to be an apostle, and that by referring to this John as "the Evangelist" he made it clear that he understood this particular John to be the author of the Fourth Gospel. The second John, however, in Eusebius's opinion was a different John because Papias mentioned him "after" the apostolic tribe.

The evidence that Eusebius provided for creating two Johns cannot bear the considerable weight that he demanded of it. Some scholars have attempted to explain the significance of Eusebius's insistence on recognizing two Johns by explaining Papias's use of the present tense verb λέγουσιν, which they argue indicates that Papias was referring to activities that were occurring during the actual time in which he was writing (thus possibly providing evidence for a pre-100 dating of *Exposition*).[97] Other scholars have interpreted this verb as a historic present, meaning that Papias was speaking about an earlier period in his ministry as if it were in real time.[98]

---

94. See the discussion on fragment 2 of this book, p. 111, and Eusebius *Ecc. Hist.* III.36.1; V.20.6–7; V.24.16 (LCL 153: 281, 497–99, 511).

95. Munck, "Presbyters," 226.

96. Holmes, *Apostolic Fathers*, 3rd ed., 735.

97. Perumalil, "Papias and Irenaeus," 334–45.

98. Bauckham, *The Eyewitnesses*, 14–30. Lightfoot identified the verb as an historical present; however, he contended that it was provided only for the sake of variety. Lightfoot, *Essays*, 150; see also Schoedel, *The Fragments*, 99. Munck interpreted this verb to mean that both Aristion and John were still living. Munck, "Presbyters," 230–31. Gundry provided an insightful discussion on the use of the historical present. Gundry, *Matthew*, 1028–31.

Additionally, Eusebius argued that since Papias had identified the second John as "the elder" then the second John could not have been an apostle. It will become evident while analyzing Papias's statements that Eusebius unjustifiably separated the apostle John from the rest of the apostles by placing such weight upon Papias's second mentioning of a John. It should be sufficient for the moment to acknowledge that at times it appears that Papias was speaking about an earlier period in his life in real time, a period in which he referred to apostolic instructions that he had received from others (thus he employed the aorist εἶπεν), as well as a period in which he received personal tutelage from the last living tradition-bearing apostle (thus, λέγουσιν is understood as an historical present).

Lastly, Eusebius claimed that his exegetical discovery "proved" that Papias was aware of two Johns that either lived in Ephesus at the same time, or possibly lived in Ephesus at approximately the same time. Consequently, Eusebius believed he had solved Dionysius of Alexandria's great mystery concerning the two tombs of the apostle John.[99] Briefly stated, it was Dionysius's contention that the tradition-bearers of the apostle John's tomb(s) had somehow missed another very influential John of Ephesus who in reality occupies a tomb that is thought to be occupied by the more famous apostle John.[100] Knowing Dionysius's speculations concerning the debate surrounding which tomb the apostle John occupied and the identity of the author of the book of Revelation, Eusebius contended that Papias's preface *proved* the existence of two Johns. The fact remains, however, that Papias's preface does not even contain the words apostle, Ephesus, or tombs; consequently, it cannot prove Eusebius's contention.[101]

PAPIAS AND THE TRUTH

It becomes necessary at this point to attempt to let Papias speak for himself. One cannot be certain about where Eusebius's quote of Papias actually occurred in Papias's preface. However, if Luke's prefaces in his Gospel and the book of Acts can be employed as templates, it can be reasonably assumed that Eusebius drew this quote near the beginning of the preface of Papias's five-volume work, for in this quote Papias appeared to be addressing his

99. Eusebius *Ecclesiastical History* VII.25.12–16 (LCL 265:201–3).

100. Later references to a "John of Ephesus" should not be understood as references to the apostle John.

101. See appendix 1 of this book for a much more comprehensive discussion of this issue.

benefactor.[102] Papias boldly stated that he purposed to provide everything that he had careful learned and careful remembered from the elders, as well as interpretations concerning their instructions. Eusebius preserved Papias's Greek preface as stating, Οὐκ ὀκνήσω δέ σοι καὶ ὅσα ποτὲ παρὰ τῶν πρεσβυτέρων καλῶς ἔμαθον καὶ καλῶς ἐμνημόνευσα συγκατατάξαι ταῖς ἑρμηνείαις διαβεβαιούμενος ὑπὲρ αὐτῶν ἀλήθειαν.[103] A literal translation of this sentence is "And I will not hesitate also to set down the interpretations for you as much as at that time from the elders I well learned and I well remembered, (thus) guaranteeing on behalf of them (the) truth."[104] As recognized earlier, it is a mistake to assume that Papias intended to provide exclusively his own interpretations concerning the traditions he received from the elders, for nowhere does he demonstrably make such a claim.[105] Instead, his foremost concern was to set down in an orderly fashion the traditions he had well learned from his sources—the elders. This is not to argue that Papias did not provide any of his own insights. He was a pastor, and as most know all to well, pastors are often more than willing to volunteer their own theological insights. Nevertheless, by translating Papias's preface to state "along with my own interpretations," Holmes has made an interpretation that the text does not support.[106]

102. Lightfoot, *Essays*, 143. This is assumed by the clause Οὐκ ὀκνήσω δέ σοι. It was not uncommon in ancient literature for authors to address their sponsors. It is also possible, although less likely, that Papias may have been addressing an adversary.

103. Holmes, *Apostolic Fathers*, 3rd ed., 734.

104. The last clause could also be rendered as "guaranteeing on their behalf truth."

105. Kleist suggested that Papias's work was a type of "running commentary" in which some of the "explanations" he set down were from his "presbyters." Kleist, *Papias*, 105–6.

106. Lake translated this portion of Papias's preface as "And I shall not hesitate to append to the interpretations all that I ever learnt well from the presbyters and remembered well." His translation correctly leaves the infinitive συγκατατάξαι indefinite. Eusebius *Ecc. Hist.* III.39.3 (LCL 153:290–91). See also Rigg, "Papias on Mark," 165. There is a question of whether the text should read συγκατατάξαι or συγτάξαι. Holmes, *Apostolic Fathers*, 3rd ed., 734. The manuscript evidence is equally divided. Both Lake and Holmes preferred συγκατατάξαι. This infinitive is somewhat difficult to translate. Lake's "to append" is not very satisfying since it appears that Papias intended to do more than simply add interpretations. He intended to provide them in an orderly arrangement (τάξις) along with the things he had learned from the elders. Holmes's "along with" seems to be a good translation for the prefix συγκατα of τάξαι. Consequently, a possible translation for this infinitive as, "within an orderly arrangement." Walls translated this word as "setting down alongside." Walls, "Papias," 138. Τάξις appears to be a cognate of τάσσω, which is interpreted as "to arrange." LSJ cited the use of a "συγκατατάσσω," which was interpreted as "to arrange or draw up together." LSJ, s.v. "συγκατα*σβέννυμι." Therefore, Holmes translation "to arrange" is preferred, although it should be understood as indefinite.

Regarding these traditions, Papias confessed that he had "learned them well," meaning he had correctly grasped their meanings and significance; and that he had "remembered them well," indicating that he had faithfully and accurately committed them to memory. Consequently, Papias felt he could guarantee his benefactor accuracy concerning the material and interpretations he provided.[107] The clause from which Papias's guarantee is taken is διαβεβαιούμενους ὑπὲρ αὐτῶν ἀλήθειαν. The word "ἀλήθειαν," being anarthrous, can be understood as being either definite or indefinite. It is translated with a variety of meanings ranging from: *truth, truthfulness, dependability, uprightness* (with respect to thought or deed), or *reality*. The question is, did Papias mean to guarantee the dependability or truthfulness of his work as an accurate transmission of the traditions of his sources who were "the elders," or was he guaranteeing that his work communicated "truth" that was the product of their traditions. While some scholars might demand a determinative decision as to which of these two possibilities Papias intended, ancient audiences were often amused by such word plays that afforded them the opportunity of discovering deeper and more important meanings rather than appreciating a meaning that was obvious to everyone. Consequently, Papias may have meant to imply both meanings, rather than pitting one against the other. The clause, therefore, is translated, "as a result, guaranteeing on their behalf truth."[108]

---

107. Lightfoot, *Essays*, 147.

108. Research in Greek literature, philosophy, and rhetoric is vast and diverse. Concerning proper and acceptable styles, what was acceptable among philosophers was not acceptable at times for rhetoricians. Schenkeveld, "Philosophical Prose," 196–264. Galen Rowe provided a survey of rhetorical devices that he categorized as "tropes." While discussing rhetorical devices that create a change in meaning he wrote, "As in the case of trope, where a word or brief phrase is changed from its proper meaning into another meaning in order to achieve a certain effect, so this category designates thought figures in which one thought may be expressed through another, dissimilar thought." Rowe, "Style," 150. Among Rowe's categories, the trope that possibly could best fit Papias's use of ἀλήθεια is "Emphasis" (ibid., 127). This should not be understood as arguing that Papias was an accomplished philosopher or rhetorician, only that it is possible that while writing he attempted to employ a style that would effectively engage his audience. R. Dean Anderson noted that rhetoricians such as Cicero and Quintilian associated "word-play" with "wit;" however, word-play was "*not* the figure of choice when dealing with important (or) serious subjects." Anderson, *Ancient Rhetorical Theory*, 285. It is equally as possible that on this point Papias was simply imprecise.

PAPIAS'S ELDERS

The greatest debate concerning this sentence by far focuses on the question of who exactly were Papias's instructors and sources, or more precisely, who was Papias referring to when he spoke of "the elders." As mentioned previously, Eusebius was convinced that Papias had not personally known any of the apostles. It was his position that Papias had "received the matters of the faith from those who had known them," i.e., from followers and/or acquaintances of the apostles. Consequently, he believed that Papias's knowledge about Jesus was completely based upon third hand information, while his information about Jesus' immediate followers was solely based upon secondhand information.[109] Maintaining, however, that Papias was completely isolated from reliable eyewitness testimony that was available to others is an artificial constraint.

It should be noted that the period in which both Irenaeus and Eusebius placed Papias makes it a certainty that he had in fact received third hand information about Jesus, as well as secondhand information about Jesus' immediate followers. However, because Eusebius identified Papias as a contemporary of Polycarp, and because Irenaeus referred to him as Polycarp's associate or companion, it is just as possible that Papias received some of his information about Jesus from a few of his immediate followers (secondhand) who had heard him and who had witnessed his ministry and miracles (firsthand). While some, such as Eusebius and Hall, have attempted to remove Papias as far from the apostolic generation as possible, the historical evidence indicates that he lived within a matrix of time that afforded him access to information about Jesus from a variety of sources, some of which were supremely credible (eyewitnesses), as well as those who were not as credible but perceived as trustworthy (secondhand), and lest we forget, from those that he found to be completely non-credible (third-hand and/or unconfirmable hearsay). Given this era, his tenacious demand to hear only the words of the apostles and disciples of the Lord is certainly understandable.

The question still remains, however, who were Papias's "elders"? In order to answer this question, which originates in section 2, it is necessary to exegete section 4 of Eusebius's thirty-ninth chapter. Doing so provides some clarity in ascertaining who these travelers were that Papias examined and what if any was their relationship to the elders. It is the position of

109. Bacon held that Papias "was not even a hearer of the 'disciples of the apostles.'" Bacon, "Syriac Translator," 8.

this book, as stated earlier, that section 4 does not describe how Papias received his information that he claimed to have both learned and remembered well.[110] Instead, Papias was describing how he carried out his responsibility as the bishop at Hierapolis with respect to protecting his congregation from those whose teachings and doctrines were contrary to apostolic instruction, and, therefore, were by definition contrary to the truth. Papias stated in this section that if he came in contact with anyone who had claimed to have associated with the elders he would "inquire" about the "words of the elders." Regarding these travelers, Bauckham noted that "The usual translation is 'anyone who had been a follower of,' but this is potentially misleading, especially in contemporary English. The meaning of the verb *parakoloutheō* is not so much 'come after' as 'go closely with, attend.' Moreover, the rendering of *parēkolouthēkōs* by the English noun 'follower' suggests that the person was no longer in the relationship of disciple to the elders, whereas all that is meant is that the person had been present at their teaching (and might well be again)."[111]

One should not conclude, consequently, that Papias assumed to know anything about these travelers other then what they claimed for themselves. Such an assumption adequately explains Papias's need to examine

110. This should not be understood to suggest that Papias never learned anything new about Jesus or about the traditions of the elders from some who came to Hierapolis. For certainly if a recognized disciple of Jesus, or a well known companion of Peter or Paul, came to Hierapolis, then there is little doubt that Papias would have received their fellowship and sought out new information. However, this does not appear to be the situation that Papias was describing in section 4.

111. Bauckham, *The Eyewitnesses*, 15. This verb (παρηκολουθηκώς) is a perfect participle and should probably be understood as an aoristic or dramatic historic perfect. Wallace defined this use of the perfect as "The aorist/dramatic perfect is used as a simple past tense without concern for present consequences. In this respect, it shares a kinship with the historic present. This use is informed by the *contextual* intrusions (narrative). The key to detecting a dramatic perfect is the absence of any notion of existing results." Wallace, *The Basics*, 249. This is precisely what we see in Papias's use; he employed this verb in a narrative describing his own experience with no reference to any existing results. Bauckham translated it as "had been in attendance" (also see page 15). Petrie compared the definition of this word as found in Liddell and Scott to that found in Arndt-Gingrich, and decided that the debate over its exact meaning was "inconclusive," and then chose to translate it as "closely associated." Petrie, "Matthew," 16–17 n. 4. If the possibilities of understanding the exact nature of the relationship between these travelers and the elders is truly "inconclusive," then translating this participle as "having attended" or as "having associated with" rather than "*closely* associated" seems sufficient since such translations provide no bias with respect to the extent of the possible relationship that travelers may have had with Papias's elders.

them. Having met these hitherto unknown travelers,[112] Papias stated that it was his habit to examine them.[113] The word ἀνακρίνω is generally translated as *to question* (as in a general question), *examine; conduct an examination* (as is judicial hearings; an indication of an investigation); *to judge, to call to account, to discern.*[114] The great debate concerning Papias's meaning on this point is, was he simply attempting to gain new information or was he attempting to discern a traveler's orthodoxy. Regardless of how one answers this question, it should be recognized that Papias's greatest concern was for the preservation of orthodoxy, for he doggedly wanted to know nothing other than the words of those who were the immediate followers of Jesus. Concerning Papias's commitment to apostolic words, A. C. Perumalil wrote that Papias "did not place [his] trust in the words of the other sub-apostolic elders who were the followers of the apostolic men. For this reason he always compared their teachings with those of the apostles."[115] Papias's practice of comparing an itinerant's words with apostolic teachings implies that Papias already possessed the words of the apostles, and that he was attempting to ascertain whether or not these travelers actually knew the apostolic teachings, and whether they were faithfully transmitting them and their meanings. Papias himself stated that he was unimpressed with the sermons, lectures, or musings of others; instead he desired to hear only the words and teachings that were truly apostolic in origin and meaning.

There is a great exegetical debate concerning the syntactical relationship of the clause τοὺς τῶν πρεσβυτέρων ἀνέκρινον λόγους and the clause that immediately follows, which is τί Ἀνδρέας ἢ τί Πέτρος εἶπεν ἢ τί Φίλιππος ἢ τί Θωμᾶς ἢ Ἰάκωβος ἢ τί Ἰωάννης ἢ Ματθαῖος ἢ τις ἕτερος τῶν τοῦ κυρίου μαθητῶν. The interrogative pronoun τί plays an important part for understanding their relationship. In the preceding clause "τοὺς λόγους" is in the accusative because it is the object of the verb ἀνέκρινον; thus, the

---

112. These "travelers" were clearly unfamiliar to Papias, for why else would he have felt the need to "examine" them if in fact he already knew them.

113. The verb "ἀνέκρινον" is the imperfect of ἀνακρίνω. This word describes Papias's investigative activities. It is understood as a customary imperfect, although it could also be understood as an ingressive imperfect, which would be translated "I began to examine them." For uses of the imperfect tense see Wallace, *The Basics*, 232–38. Bacon contended that Papias's investigations occurred during his "boyhood." Bacon, "An Emendation," 176. It hardly seems likely that it would have been appropriate for a child to perform such examinations upon his elders.

114. BAGD, s.v. "ἀνακρίνω."

115. Perumalil, "Papias and Irenaeus," 334.

literal translation is "I was examining the words of the elders." The interrogative pronoun τί is also accusative; however, it is singular. The reason for the switch from the plural to the singular is obvious, Papias wanted to be very clear concerning specifically whose teachings he valued (i.e., those of the apostles) as he interrogated any itinerants preachers/prophets that ventured into his jurisdiction. There are two choices that are generally promoted for explaining the syntactical relation between these two accusatives. Gundry argued that the two accusatives are appositional, meaning that the second accusative refers to the same thing as the previous accusative. In other words, the second accusative is a simple restatement of that which was previously mentioned.[116] Wallace explained the function of the appositional accusative in this manner, "The accusative case can be an appositive to another substantive in the same case. An appositional construction involves two adjacent substantives that refer to the same person or thing and have the same syntactical relation to the rest of the clause. The first accusative substantive can belong to any accusative category, and the second is merely a clarification of whom or what is mentioned. Thus, the appositive 'piggy-backs' on the first accusative's use, as it were. *It is a common use of the accusative.*"[117] In reality, the entire second clause is appositional to the first clause, being correctly connected by both τοὺς λόγους and the accusative interrogative pronoun τί.

Bauckham and others, however, offer a different explanation of their syntactical relationship that provides an alternative interpretation. Bauckham argued concerning these accusatives that "Papias' words are ambiguous only because he takes it for granted that the words of the elders in which he would be interested are those which transmit traditions." Thus, he translated Papias's preface as stating, "he inquired about the words of the elders, [that is] what [according to the elders] Andrew and Peter had said."[118] He later explained his theory stating that "Some scholars, including apparently Eusebius himself, have understood categories (2) and (3), the elders and the Lord's disciples, as one and the same, but in that case it is hard to understand why Papias uses the word 'elders' so emphatically and does not simply label this group 'the Lord's disciples.' It is much more

---

116. Gundry, *Mark*, 1029.

117. Wallace, *The Basics*, 89. Italics mine. Schoedel denied that these clauses were appositional. Schoedel, "Papias," 250. He did not, however, explain or provide an alternative syntactical relationship.

118. Bauckham, "Papias and Polycrates," 60.

satisfactory to read the text in the sense indicated *by the words I have added in square brackets* in the translation just given."[119]

Papias's meanings, however, are not vague; moreover, as previously stated, appositional accusatives are a very common grammatical construction in Greek literature. Bauckham's translation is more satisfying to him and others primarily because it changes Papias's text to support a particular interpretive position. Such a translation understands the accusative τί as either an accusative of "general reference," or as syntactically unconnected with the previous clause.[120] Consequently, some feel justified in translating Papias's text in a way that completely ignores normal Greek grammar, while simultaneously supplying words for its perceived lack of clarity in order to provide for themselves a more "satisfactory" interpretation.

Generally speaking, while it is hardly defendable to ignore a more reasonable and acceptable syntactical explanation in order to justify one's interpretation of a text, there are times when identifying an accusative as one of general reference offers the best solution to understanding the syntactical relationship between two substantives. The question remains, however, as to whether this particular syntactical explanation is appropriate while attempting to interpret Papias's statement. Smyth wrote concerning different contexts where it is appropriate to identify accusatives as being instances of general reference that "To verbs denoting a state, and to adjectives, an accusative to denote a thing in respect to which the verb or adjective is limited."[121] Clearly this does not fit this context since Papias's clauses involve neither a verb nor an adjective that demands an accusative. Secondly, Smyth next wrote, "a. Of the parts of a body. . . . The accusative of the part in apposition to the whole." This again does not fit Papias's context since Papias was discussing his examination, and not part of something that belonged to a greater "whole." The third category that Smyth recognized was "b. of qualities and attributes (nature, size, name, birth, number, etc.)." This category obviously does not apply since Papias was

119. Bauckham, *The Eyewitnesses*, 16–17. Italics mine.

120. Gundry, *Mark*, 1029. Chapman argued that instead of seeing these accusatives as "co-ordinating, . . . it is possible to subordinate it (τί) to λόγους, thus making 'what Andrew and Peter said' the subject of the Presbyters' discourses: 'I used to inquire the words of the Presbyters, what (they said) Peter and Andrew said.'" Chapman, *John the Presbyter*, 10. Chapman, however, did not provide a corroborating example of an accusative being used in such a manner to substantiate his theory.

121. Smyth, *Grammar*, 360. The definitions of the accusative of general reference that follow are also taken from Smyth's discussion in his Greek grammar found on pages 360–61.

not "investigating" certain qualities, attributes, or sizes of anything. Smyth also provided a fourth category, which was "c. Of the sphere in general. Often of indefinite relations." Some may feel that this possibly fits Papias's context, but in reality it does not since Papias was certainly not searching for an indefinite connection between the travelers' words and those of the apostles; instead, he was seeking precision and adherence of their words with the words of his apostolic sources. Smyth also addressed a few additional rare options, none of which fits Papias's context. He did, however, point out that "for the accusative of respect the instrumental dative is also employed." Actually, during the time in which the New Testament was being written, the accusative of general reference had all but disappeared and was replaced by instrumental datives.[122] Wallace explained the accusative of respect or general reference in this manner,

> The accusative substantive restricts the reference of the verbal action. It indicates with reference to what the verbal action is represented as true. An author will use this accusative to qualify a statement that would otherwise typically not be true. This accusative could thus be called a frame of reference accusative or limiting accusative. *This is not common in Koine Greek.*
>
> Before the accusative substantive you can usually supply the words with reference to or concerning. Because this usage is rare in the NT, *it should be employed as a last resort—that is, only after other categories are exhausted.*[123]

This is not to argue that there is no such thing as an accusative of general reference, but only that by the beginning of the second century this grammatical device was a rather rare event in Greek literature. It should, therefore, only be relied upon as a last resort when attempting to explain the relationship between two accusatives. It is to argue, however, that it should definitely not be employed when there is another more reasonable explanation for identifying the syntactical relationship between two accusatives.

Some scholars embrace translations such as Bauckham's because they insist that Papias understood and employed the term "elders" in the same manner as Irenaeus, who often used the term to refer to those who had been disciples of apostles, while not including the apostles. This theory, as previously mentioned, was made popular by John Chapman, who is often cited in defense of this approach. Such an approach, as argued earlier, is

---

122. Wallace, *Beyond the Basics*, 203–4.

123. Wallace, *The Basics*, 91. Italics mine.

clearly anachronistic.[124] Irenaeus became the bishop of Lyons at the beginning of the last quarter of the second century, while Papias ascended to his bishopric ca. 105. The period between the ministries of these two was unquestionably one of considerable growth and development with respect to the vocabulary and practice of the church. Nowhere is this more true than concerning the office of "elder" (i.e., a church elder, pastor, and/or keeper of apostolic traditions), for it was during this critical period that the church witnessed the rise of the monarchical episcopacy. Moreover, concerning use of the term "presbyter" by Papias, Clement, and Irenaeus, Munck confessed that "Irenaeus on the other hand uses the word most loosely of the three. It [the term presbyter] means both a written and oral source, and it is not clear to what generation they are to be assigned."[125] Consequently, given the variety of meanings that Irenaeus employed by the term πρεσβύτερος, one should not assume that when Papias used this word he had in mind a specific meaning from Irenaeus's multiple uses, and that Irenaeus's usage of this term demands the exclusion of any possibility that Papias's used it to refer to the apostles. It follows, therefore, that the most reasonable explanation of the syntactical relationship between the accusative λόγους in the clause "τοὺς τῶν πρεσβυτέρων ἀνέκρινον λόγους" and the accusative τί in the clause "τί Ἀνδρέας ἢ τί Πέτρος εἶπεν, . . ." is that they are appositional. Consequently, Gundry's comments on this subject are well defended

> Second, taking that the two designations as synonymous conforms to the natural understanding of Papias's text. For if they are not synonymous, Papias jumps backward from

---

124. What is so troubling about this approach is that it continually surfaces in literature concerning Papias in spite of the fact that even Chapman recognized Irenaeus's use of the word elder was at times both unnatural and untrustworthy. Moreover, Chapman himself admitted that for Irenaeus the term "elder" was synonymous with the term "apostle," stating, "Who were the Presbyters? Undoubtedly the simplest way to translate (πρεσβυτέρων in Papias's clause) is this: 'I inquired the word of the Presbyters, that is to say, what Andrew or Peter said,' etc., thus identifying the Apostles enumerated with the Presbyters whose words are asked for. *At first sight this even appears to be the only possible meaning.*" Italics mine. And again, Chapman, quoting Lightfoot, wrote, "What classes of persons he intends to include under the designation of 'elders' he makes clear by the names which follow. The category would include not only Apostles like Andrew and Peter, but also other personal disciples of Christ, such as Aristion and the second John. In other words, the term with him (i.e., Irenaeus) is a synonyme for the Fathers of the Church in the first generation." Chapman, *John the Presbyter*, 9–10, quoting Lightfoot, *Essays*, 145.

125. Munck, "Presbyters," 235.

second-generation elders to first-generation disciples without any warning only to turn around and use "elder" and "Lord's disciple" for one and the same man. This use of "elder" and "Lord's disciple" for John shows that we are not to regard the repeated τί as an accusative of general reference (the accusative of "last resort"), meaning "the words of the elders *concerning* what Andrew or Peter had said," but as an appositive: "the words of the elders, i.e., what Andrew or Peter had said." This use also shows that the expressions do not stand in apposition to each other because the later elders repeated what earlier disciples had said; rather, what the Lord's disciples had said is identical with the words of the elders because the elders *were* the disciples Andrew, Peter, and the rest.[126]

It should be sufficient, therefore, to acknowledge that the elders (τῶν πρεσβυτέρων) who had taught Papias included specific apostles. And, as it is obvious from Papias's statement, it is precisely this colloquium of apostolic elders that Papias was most passionate about learning from, and whose teachings he was most passionate about preserving.

Since the most natural understanding of the relationship between the two accusatives in question is to view them as appositional, one should understand Papias's inquiry of these itinerants as attempts to ascertain their fidelity to the teachings of the apostolic elders rather than a simple request to share with him all that they claimed to have heard from any elder. As stated earlier, Papias's investigative practices tacitly implies what he had previously confessed, which is that he had already learned and memorized during an earlier period in his life the instructions of the elders. The question is, however, to which "elders" was Papias most committed. In order that no one might be confused about this issue, Papias specifically identified the individuals whose words he wished to hear; they were Andrew, Peter, Philip, Thomas, James, John, and Matthew (i.e., the eyewitnesses of Jesus' ministry, as well as his handpicked future leaders for his church).

Eusebius understood all of these elders as members of the apostolic consortium. There is some question as to whether James was James the son of Zebedee or James the brother of Jesus. James of Zebedee died sometime between 41–44 (Acts 12:1–2); afterward James the brother of Jesus also became recognized as the leading elder of the church in Jerusalem (Acts 15:12–21; 1 Cor 15:7; Gal 1:19, 2:8–9). Although it is unclear as to which James Papias was referring to, it should be noted that both were viewed by

126. Gundry, *Mark*, 1029.

the early church as apostles.[127] Papias could not have heard either James of Zebedee or James the brother of Jesus, who is believed to have died ca. 62.[128] Consequently, regardless of which James Papias referred to, he could not have learned anything from them via firsthand instruction, but instead would have depended upon others to transmit to him any traditions that were attributed to them. It is difficult, therefore, to be definitive about which James Papias had in mind without additional material from him. Many scholars lean towards the James who was a son of Zebedee.[129] This James seems to have the better claim since he was one of the original apostles who had followed Jesus throughout his ministry.

There is also some question concerning which Philip Papias had in mind. Here, however, an apostolic connection between Papias and the apostle Philip is more defendable. Eusebius stated that the apostle Philip, who had at least three daughters, settled in Hierapolis, which was the jurisdiction of Papias's bishopric. Some, however, contend that Papias actually associated with Philip the evangelist and not the apostle Philip.[130] Eusebius, however, was quite confident that the apostle Philip had relocated to Hierapolis. Concerning which Philip Eusebius believed Papias to have known, Christopher R. Matthews wrote, "The most natural reading of *Hist. eccl.* 3.39.9 equates the Philip mentioned there with the Philip in 3.39.4. No cogent reason exists, therefore, to doubt that Papias presumed the apostolic identity of the Philip mentioned in 3.39.9."[131] Consequently, while there is some question with respect to which "James" Papias referred to, his reference to the apostle Philip is not as vulnerable to speculation.[132]

Papias's selectivity concerning whose words were worthy of preservation has tremendous implications for understanding the theological development of the first and second-century church. Papias made it clear that he was only interested in instruction that originated from known

127. Paul called James (who was the half brother of Jesus) an apostle in Gal 1:19.

128. For historical references to James's death see Josephus, *Antiquities of the Jews*, 4:140; and Eusebius *Ecc. Hist.* II.23.1–25 (LCL 153: 169–79). For a discussion concerning the historicity of the narratives concerning the death of James, Weiss, and Knopf, *Earliest Christianity*, 2:707–12.

129. Deeks believed that Papias was referring to James of Zebedee simply because Papias's list of apostles included James's brother John. Deeks, "Papias Revisited," 297. Munck also believed that when Papias referred to James and Philip he had the apostles in mind. Munck, "Presbyters," 231.

130. Körtner, *Papias*, 145–46.

131. Matthews, *Philip*, 33.

132. For a more thorough discussion see appendix 2.

apostles, for it was this very specific band of witnesses that were for him the official guarantors of words, deeds, and meanings of the Lord Jesus Christ. They were truly "elders" in the sense that they were trustworthy disseminators of traditions that were the foundation of the church. What we have, therefore, in Papias's selectivity is the very genesis of what is recognized today as apostolic orthodoxy. Matthews's comments upon Papias's list of apostolic elders who transmitted the orthodox traditions of the early church are insightful,

> The passage is often interpreted to mean that the words of certain apostles, identified by Papias as "disciples of the Lord," were transmitted orally to Papias by the followers of certain "presbyters" or students of the apostles. These presbyters are not identified as office-holders but representatives of the older Christian generation. In spite of the popularity of this view, however, it is more likely that the "presbyters" are to be equated with the individually named personal disciples of Jesus in Papias' prologue. . . . For at an early period "presbyters," in the sense of authorities of an earlier day, can hardly be distinguished from apostles and other personal disciples of Jesus. Eusebius' statement that Papias "received the words of the apostles from their followers" (*Hist. eccl.* 3.39.7; cf. 3.39.2), is not explicitly confirmed by Papias' own words. . . . Consequently when Papias mentions his direct contact with the presbyters (*Hist. eccl.* 3.39.3), . . . it is natural to assume that he is referring either to some of the nine presbyters named, or at least to men of the same category. In Papias, then, a presbyter is not the second link in a chain of tradition arranged in terms of generations (e.g., apostles, presbyters, followers of the presbyters), but a figure from the early period belonging to the category of persons who guarantee the authentic transmission of tradition.[133]

Papias's reference to these apostles was not because they were "old men," although compared to him and his generation they certainly were. Instead, he referred to them as elders because they were "*the*" recognized providers and keepers of the church traditions and dogma.[134] Their au-

---

133. Matthews, *Philip*, 20–21. In the quote above, Matthews also quotes Munck. For Munck's quote see Munck, "Presbyters," 239.

134. While there has been considerable debate about the possible meanings of the term πρεσβύτερος, there are very few that would argue that it could not mean "members of the older generation who are regarded as mediators of the authentic tradition and reliable teachers." Bornkamm, "πρεσβύτερος," in *TDNT*, 6: 676. See also Kümmel, *Introduction*, 172. Even some, who do not believe that Papias's second reference to this

thority as eyewitnesses and followers of Jesus was highly valued by those who wanted to know details about the "historical" Jesus. This is not to say that their authority was never challenged, for the data indicates that the fledgling church constantly felt challenges from within and from without. The epistles of 2 and 3 John provide confirmation of such challenges. Nevertheless, as Papias's practices and concerns reveal, for those who desired only to receive accurate information about Jesus (i.e., about his ministry and his teachings), the credibility of his immediate followers was unmatched.[135] The context and syntactical relationship of Papias's words, therefore, indicate that his "elders" were none other than the followers of Jesus who today are known as the apostles, and as such they were the standard bearers and guarantors of officially recognized traditions of the church.[136]

PAPIAS'S HIGHEST CONCERN

Having answered the question of who were Papias's elders, along with their function and authority within the church, it is now necessary to return to Papias's words in section 3 concerning his distaste for open speculations. Papias stated that "for unlike most people I did not enjoy those who have a great deal to say, but those who teach the truth."[137] Unlike Papias's earlier reference, this reference to truth is definite.[138] Papias did not suffer long philosophical speculations and prolonged dialogues that were common fare of rabbinic schools and Greek philosophers. He instead valued those who gave clear and relevant instruction that originated from "the Truth." Additionally, in order to prevent any possible confusion concerning which instructions Papias was referring to, he precisely identified the "commandments" that he had in mind. "Nor did I enjoy those who recall someone else's commandments,[139] but those who remember the commandments

John should be understood as meaning that he was a recognized tradition bearer of the church, do acknowledge this meaning was applied to Papias's initial list of apostles. Deeks, "Papias Revisited," 296.

135. Metzger, *The Text*, 51.

136. Lightfoot argued that the designation of the second John as "the elder" was a reference to his "official title, designating a member of the order of the presbyterate." Lightfoot, *Essays*, 146.

137. Holmes, *Apostolic Fathers*, 3rd ed., 735.

138. The word Papias employed was τάληθη~, which is a crasis of τά and ἀληθής.

139. Munck translated this phrase as "strange commandments." Munck, "Presbyters," 224. Ehrman translated it as "the commandments of strangers." *Papias and*

given by the Lord to the faith and proceeding from the truth itself."[140] Consequently, Papias did not value diversity of thought when it came to matters of the apostolic faith. All other philosophers and teachers were to be discarded when compared to the "commandments" that the Lord had transmitted to his followers. Such a passion reveals a common conviction that Papias held with Polycarp, who in a similar fashion wrote, "And so, let us leave behind the idle speculation of the multitudes and the false teachings and turn to the word that was delivered to us from the beginning."[141] Charles M. Nielsen in a rather strained fashion conjectured that Papias's comment about those who "recall someone else's commandments" was a back-handed reference to some who preferred Pauline doctrines over those originating from the Lord.[142] However, as the analysis of fragment 23 will make clear, there is data that severely undermines Nielsen's theory; consequently, Papias's reference to the commandments of others is more likely an allusion to the philosophies of those whose teachings were outside the boundaries of apostolic traditions. Papias's reference to what "the many" preferred to hear and Polycarp's reference to the "idle speculations of the multitude," implies that the intellectual culture in which the Asiatic church ministered was one that appreciated speculations and conjectures concerning the nature of truth. These two orthodox bishops, however, did not give themselves to the preferences of the crowds, nor did they waste their time by devoting themselves to philosophical shadow boxing. Instead, they chose to stand fast to the truth as it had been received from the Lord himself, and rejected any late comers who attempted to alter its content or question its veracity. They were in the truest sense "apostolic men."

What Papias highly valued were those who remembered and accurately communicated the commandments of Jesus. Papias's statement in Greek is "ἀλλὰ τοῖς τὰς παρὰ τοῦ κυρίου τῇ πίστει δεδομένας," which is literally translated as "But those (remembering) the things having been

---

Quadratus (LCL 25:99). Holmes's translation is appropriate since the phrase "τὰς ἀλλοτρίας ἐντολὰς" does not suggest a subversive or mysterious source, but rather a source that Papias did not prefer since it did not adhere to apostolic traditions.

140. Holmes, *Apostolic Fathers*, 3rd ed., 735. It should be noted what Papias did not "enjoy" was "the many things" being spoken and not necessarily those who were speaking. In other words, τὰ πολλα is in the accusative and is the object of the verb ἔχαιρον (I was enjoying). Literally translated, the clause should read, "For I was not enjoying the many things by the ones speaking. . . ."

141. Polycarp *To the Philippians* 7.2 (LCL 24:343).

142. Nielsen, "Papias," 530–35.

given by the Lord to the faith."[143] His statement makes it clear that he believed there was a body of teachings that Jesus entrusted to his immediate followers for the purpose of educating those who would believe upon him. Papias understood that this body of doctrine comprised the heart of the true Christian faith, and that adherence to it was non-negotiable.[144] His statements do not support the theoretical conjectures in the vein of Edward H. Hall and Walter Bauer, who conceived of a struggling church that was searching for something worthy of believing.[145] Instead, these statements reveal that after the passing of the last apostle there were men like Polycarp and Papias who were committed to preserving the foundational truths and commandments that Jesus delivered to his immediate followers. Jesus himself had commissioned his followers to proselytize others (Matt 10:27; 28:18–20; Luke 24:44–48), and he did so with the expectation that they would safe-guard his teachings by faithfully and accurately disseminating them into the hearts and minds of converts in the following generations (Mark 8:38; John 15:7; 2 John 9).[146]

Having identified the traditions that he valued and the origin from which they came, Papias made an additional compelling comment. He stated that the truth contained in the faith was not a stagnant pool of dogma, but that it was "coming from the truth itself."[147] The antecedent of παραγινομένας is "the things" (or commandments) that the Lord had given to the faith since τὰς δεδομένας and παραγινομένας are both accusative and feminine plural. Holmes translated the present participle παραγινομένας as "proceeding," while Petrie awkwardly translated it as "reaching us."[148] The word is generally translated as "coming," "being present," or "being near." Papias was explaining that the commandments that the apostles had received had come directly from Jesus who was in fact the essence and

143. Holmes, *Apostolic Fathers*, 3rd ed., 734. The antecedent for the article τοῖς is "the ones remembering," while τὰς δεδομένας refers to the "commandments" of Jesus in contrast to the commandments of others.

144. Papias's reference to "faith" is articular and, therefore, definite. Consequently, Papias believed that Jesus had given doctrine to "The Faith," and not just teachings to encourage "faith" for the purpose of promoting virtuous living.

145. Walter Bauer argued that "east of Phrygian Hierapolis we could hardly discern any traces of orthodoxy. Christianity and heresy were essentially synonymous there." Bauer, *Orthodoxy and Heresy*, 229.

146. See also Matt 28:18–20; John 8:31 and 14:23.

147. The clause in Greek is "καὶ ἀπ αὐτῆς παραγινομένας τῆς ἀληθείας." Holmes, *Apostolic Fathers*, 3rd ed., 734–35.

148. Petrie, "Matthew," 16. Ehrman translated this word as "proceed." *Papias and Quadratus* (LCL 25:99).

source of all truth.[149] The notion that Jesus is in his essence "the Truth" is a significant theme throughout the Johannine writings.[150] John Polhill stated concerning its significance in the Johannine writings that "'Truth' is an important word in Johannine literature, referring to the revelation of God in Jesus Christ. It is often a virtual synonym for Jesus (John 1:14, 17; John 14:6; 1 John 5:20)."[151] Such a view of Jesus as the "Truth" makes Papias's strict adherence to apostolic doctrines even more understandable, knowing that as he faithfully defended the instructions of the apostles he was actually preserving the teachings of Jesus who was in fact the fountainhead of truth. More than anything else, for Papias fidelity to apostolic doctrines was about worship, evangelism, and faithfulness to Christ, for by his fidelity to their traditions Papias believed that he was faithfully transmitting the very meanings of Jesus, who was the embodiment of truth itself.[152]

Although much of section 4 has been addressed previously, there are still a few important points worthy of discussion. This section, as argued earlier, is not Papias's explanation of how he gathered all of his traditions but rather of how he functioned as the bishop of Hierapolis when confronted with itinerant preachers and prophets who claimed to have heard recognized "elders" (i.e., bearers of official traditions and church dogma). His cautious examination of these itinerants is completely consistent with the apostle Paul's commissioning of the elders and bishops of the Ephesian church, which was a commission that possessed the responsibility of feeding and protecting the flock entrusted to their care (Acts 20:17–38). Papias was able to determine the veracity of the claims of these travelers by examining the accuracy of their teachings with those of known apostles and disciples of Jesus (μαθηταί) who Papias labeled as "elders."[153] Papias

149. Schoedel translated τῆς ἀληθείας as "the Truth." Although he failed to elaborate upon what he meant, it is assumed that he believed Papias was referring to Jesus. Schoedel, *The Fragments*, 99; see also Lightfoot, *Essays*, 143. For a biblical reference to Jesus as "the Truth" see John 1:14; 14:6. Such a conclusion is reasonable given Papias's association with the apostle John, and the fact that a major theme within John's writings was to identify Jesus as "the truth"; see Bauckham, *The Eyewitnesses*, 21.

150. John 1:17; 14:6; 17:19; 18:37; 1 John 2:21; 3:19; 2 John 2–4; 3 John 3–4, 8.

151. Polhill, "2 John and 3 John," 30.

152. Given his knowledge of Matthew's Hebraic Gospel, there is little doubt that Papias was aware that Jesus spoke in Aramaic. However, through his association with the apostle John and other disciples of Jesus, Papias was confident that although the other apostolic Gospels were not written in Jesus' native language, they accurately communicated Jesus' meanings.

153. It should not be assumed, as with the case of Aristion, that everyone who

was confident in his ability to examine these itinerants because he had been well educated by recognized elders of the church; therefore he was qualified to interrogate any visitors of Hierapolis claiming to have a special word from the Lord or from his immediate followers. Acceptable church dogma and tradition for Papias did not "originate" from just anyone; instead, it had to come from recognized and trustworthy sources. Papias was extremely conservative with respect to sources that he considered to be trustworthy; more specifically he wanted to know only the words of the apostles Andrew, Peter, Philip, Thomas, James, John, Matthew, or any others who had personally followed Jesus.

Bauckham argued that "not too much weight should be placed on the particular names in Papias's list of seven disciples."[154] He believed that there was more symbolism in Papias's restricting his list to seven names rather than the identity of those who Papias listed. Whether or not Papias meant to stress the number seven is debatable, but to ignore the weightiness of the individuals named by Papias is ridiculous.[155] These seven were certainly viewed by the earliest Christians as foundational leaders of the church to whom special honor was due.[156] Their significance as founders of the church and originators of her traditions, therefore, can hardly be overestimated. Similarly ignoring the significance of the apostles named by Papias, David D. Deeks argued that "we must therefore conclude that Papias belonged to a congregation that wished not to be part of the emerging early catholicism."[157] Contrary to Deeks's speculative theory, Papias's insistence on preserving and promoting apostolic traditions would place him squarely within the mainstream of the emerging catholic church. Papias was not attempting to distance himself and the church at Hierapolis from the universal church; instead, he was attempting to influence the universal church and its future by demanding that she remain faithful to the commandments she had received from the Lord through his immediate followers.

Papias's list makes it clear that he wished to hear the traditions associated with the apostles (i.e., the immediate followers of Jesus), and that he

---

followed Jesus was elevated to the status of "elder."

154. Bauckham, *The Eyewitnesses*, 20.

155. Several have commented upon the Johannine nature of Papias's list of apostles. See Bauckham, *The Eyewitnesses*, 20–21, 418; Hengel, *The Question*, 16–19. One should no more lightly esteem those listed by Papias as those listed in the eleventh chapter of Hebrews.

156. See Eph 2:20; 3:5; 4:11; 2 Pet 3:2; Rev 21:14.

157. Deeks, "Papias Revisited: Part II," 324.

was unwilling that any of their traditions should perish. The interrogative pronoun (τί) used by Papias is singular, specifically meaning that he wanted to hear from those that he was examining the traditions associated with each individual apostle he named.[158] He also employed the aorist of λέγω (εἶπεν), indicating that he wanted to know what each individual apostle had said in the past, implying that in most cases they were no longer able to speak, probably because most of them had died.[159] An implication of Papias's statement is that their traditions were fixed and no longer subject to expansions.

Papias made two important shifts in his vocabulary while explaining his practice of examining these travelers, both of which are found in the clause "ἅ τε Ἀριστίων καὶ ὁ πρεσβύτερος Ἰωάννης, οἱ τοῦ μαθηταί, λέγουσιν." The first important shift in vocabulary is Papias's transition to the relative pronoun ἅ, which is neuter, accusative, and plural. By using an accusative relative pronoun Papias indicated that his subject matter was still appositional to his previous subject; therefore, it was syntactically related to the words of the individual elders, which were the focus of Papias's examinations.[160] He indicated by employing a neuter pronoun that his focus was still upon the traditions of the apostolic elders, and not the itinerant preachers or prophets who happened to meander into Hierapolis. Papias was not focused on who he was interrogating as much as what they confessed were the traditions of the apostles. Lastly, by employing a plural pronoun instead of a singular, Papias indicated with respect to the period of which he was speaking that the leadership of the church had begun to compile the traditions of each individual apostle into a collective body of official church traditions, which Papias himself had learned and remembered well by personally hearing the orations of Jesus' followers, one of which was Aristion and another being the elder John who was one of the twelve apostles and a son of Zebedee. This personal instruction is indicated by Papias's second important change in vocabulary, which was

158. Munck argued there was "no significance" to be found in the repetition of τί. Munck, "Presbyters," 224.

159. Kleist, Papias, 110. Perumalil, "Papias," 363.

160. Munck discussed the syntactical relationship of this relative pronoun (which he recognized as appositional to the preceding interrogative clause) but failed to acknowledge Papias's shift from singular interrogative pronouns to a plural relative pronoun, as well as the implications of such a shift. See Munck, "Presbyters," 237 n. 42. Munck also disagreed with Lawlor, who argued the text as it stands at this point is "awkward"; thus, it appears that Eusebius omitted "a portion of the text." Lawlor, "Eusebius on Papias," 210. This suggestion is not only purely speculative, but Eusebius's quote of Papias makes perfect sense without the need of any textual emendation.

his use of the verb λέγουσιν in the present tense, meaning that there was a period in his life when he observed this coalescing of apostolic traditions into a cumulative body of official church dogma.[161] And it was this body of traditions that Papias demanded these itinerants to recite in order to prove their fidelity to the truth that was received from the source of all truth, the Lord Jesus Christ.

A Distinction between John and Aristion

Papias also made a distinction between Aristion and John. First, Papias stated that they both were disciples of the Lord in the same sense as the apostles he had previously listed were disciples of Jesus, meaning both had followed Jesus during his ministry, and that both had heard him teach.[162] Both, however, did not share the same official rank within the church. John was an elder, Aristion was not. Information about Aristion is rare. Some have suggested that he may be the source of "the spurious ending of Mark (vss. 9–20)," which an Armenian manuscript attributes to an "Ariston."[163] Whether the reference in this manuscript accurately identifies the true source of this "tradition," or whether these two names refer to the same individual is questionable. What is not in doubt is that Papias provided the majority of what is knowable about Aristion. Some have suggested that Aristion did in fact attain to the officer of elder.[164] There is, however,

161. The Greek verb λέγουσιν is interpreted as a historical present, thus enabling Papias to speak of an earlier period in his ministry in real time. The significance of Papias's syntax will be discussed more fully below. About the coalescing of recognized apostolic traditions in a single body of church dogma, Von Campenhausen ironically argued that Papias's influence upon this process was destabilizing rather than being an attempt on his part to protect the orthodox traditions that he had received. Von Campenhausen, *The Christian Bible*, 134–35. His assertion, however, is unwarranted.

162. Hill believed that it is "unclear" whether Aristion and Eusebius's John the elder had "personally" known Jesus. Hill, "Papias," 310. His skepticism is unwarranted. Some have suggested that Aristion and the elder John were not disciples of the Lord, but students of the disciples of the Lord. Abbott, "The 'Elders' of Papias," 333ff.; Bacon, "An Emendation, 176–83; Bacon, "Syriac Translator," 1–23. Bacon and Abbot support their positions by conjectural emendations of the text or by relying upon terminology found in the writings of Irenaeus and applying it to Papias. Their arguments have little substance, being predominately built upon conjectures.

163. Bacon, "An Emendation," 177.

164. Deeks, "Papias Revisited," 297. Even though Deeks observed that Papias had not labeled Aristion as an elder, he later argued that Aristion did in fact have "presbyteral authority," (see page 300 n. 8). Munck also argued that Aristion was a presbyter. Munck, "Presbyters," 239–40.

no historical reference to him as ever obtaining such a status. Why he may have not achieved this rank is a matter of speculation. Maybe he was divorced. Such a marital status would have severely restricted one's ministry. Maybe he felt called to be an itinerant preacher or prophet and was unwilling to settle in any specific jurisdiction. Maybe Aristion had only followed Jesus for a relatively short period of time, and as a result he may not have been viewed by others as worthy of the title of "elder." Regardless of what conjectures one may put forth, Papias did not identify him as an elder; therefore, one should not assume that he was. That is not to say that Papias did not perceive him as a credible eyewitness of Jesus' ministry, for he clearly identified him as a disciple of Jesus and was interested in what he had to say. In the limited material available from Papias, however, there is no suggestion that he recognized Aristion as one possessing the official rank of elder within the Asiatic church.[165]

THE ELDER JOHN AND PAPIAS

At this point it becomes necessary to discuss Papias's reference to a John he referred to as "ὁ πρεσβύτερος Ἰωάννης" (i.e., the elder John).[166] Some have argued that, unlike his previous two uses of the word πρεσβύτερος, at this point Papias used the word πρεσβύτερος as "strictly a comparative adjective meaning 'older' (e.g., Lk 15.25, 1 Ti 5.1–2); in practice it often lost its comparative sense and came to mean 'an old man' (e.g., Ac 2.17)."[167]

165. Deeks insisted that "presbyter and disciple of the Lord" were synonymous. Deeks, "Papias Revisited," 297.

166. It is noted that πρεσβύτερος is in the first attributive position. It is, therefore, correctly translated as "the elder John." Wallace, citing Roberston, stated that in such cases "the adjective receives greater emphasis than the substantives." Wallace, *The Basics*, 135. Robertson, *A Grammar*, 776. Consequently, Papias was emphasizing John's rank as a tradition bearer. An adjective in the attributive position does not demand that it be preceded by an article. An anarthrous adjective in the first attributed position is common in Koine Greek, although not as common as the "article-adjective-noun" construction. Wallace, *The Basics*, 138. See also Black, *Read New Testament Greek*, 41–42. It is possible that the article indicates that the adjective πρεσβύτερος was being used as a substantive rather than a comparative adjective (Wallace, *The Basics*, 130–31). This again would mean that Papias was emphasizing the office John held (i.e., that of an elder) and not his age. This is consistent with the context of Papias's statements, which is clearly focused upon sanctioned leaders who were recognized as official bearers of the church's traditions. However, because Papias employed an article with his second reference to one named John, the article is, therefore, simply understood as anaphoric.

167. Deeks, "Papias Revisited," 296. See also Bauckham, *The Eyewitnesses*, 422.

As stated previously, the presence of the article ὁ with the second reference to John (which is the only name listed twice in this quote from Papias) indicates that the article is anaphoric; meaning it identifies this later mentioning of a John as a reference to same John previously mentioned.

Deeks speculated that although the article could be understood as anaphoric it was not, arguing that "while the existence of an anaphoric article cannot be ruled out, it is wrong to conclude that every definite article preceding a proper noun is necessarily anaphoric."[168] It was his position that the use of an article with a proper name was "largely a matter of the author's whim."[169] While it may be true that in certain circumstances an author may for some unknown reason employ an article with a previously unmentioned proper name; such cases, however, are generally the exception and not the rule. Moreover, as one surveys Papias's use of proper names and articles, it is demonstrably observable that he followed normal Greek grammatical rules and not some perceived whim. The only time Papias employed an article with a proper name was with his second reference of John. He did not employ an article with any of the seven apostolic names, nor did he employ it with Aristion's name. He only used an article with his second mentioning of John.[170]

Munck understood the reference to "the elder John" as distinguishing this John, who was an office bearer in the church, from the apostle John. Munck, "Presbyters," 238. See also Hill, "Papias," 310. Petrie in some sense combined the usage of "elder" to be both speaking of one who was old, but also as a reference to one who is worthy and held "prestige and authority." He argued, however, it did not refer to an office in "any official sense." He also gave a good explanation of how the Jewish usage of this word influenced the church's usage. Petrie, "Matthew," 18–19. For a more thorough explanation of how the church's Jewish roots influenced its usage of this word see Giles, "Church Order," 219–26. A great problem with viewing Papias's usage of this word as referring as only a comparative adjective is that by approximately AD 50 the word "elder" with respect to the church's leadership referred to one who held an official position of leadership that afforded him the authority to make binding decisions upon the church at large (see Acts 15:1–22). Also, Paul's qualification for an elder in 1 Tim 31ff. and Titus 1:5ff. does not intend that an elder must be "elderly" (that is "old"). In fact, Paul expected an elder to manage his household well and have believing "children," implying that an elder could still be of child-bearing age or at least have "children" under his management. Paul's instructions for appointing elders emphasized spiritually mature leadership, not only leaders who were "old."

168. Deeks, "Papias Revisited," 297.

169. Ibid. Deeks quoted J. W. Wenham for support of his position. See Wenham, *New Testament Greek*, 36.

170. An interestingly observation is Eusebius's own employed an anaphoric article with Aristion's name when he mentioned him after his quote of Papias, indicating that he was speaking about the previously mentioned Aristion; see Eusebius *Ecc. Hist.*

Deeks also doubted the article attached to John was titular in meaning; however, he provided no defense for this claim.[171] Smyth listed "Titles of official persons" as a class of substantives that are often anarthrous.[172] Consequently, even if Papias was identifying John as one who possessed an official title or position it would not require that he employ an article. In other words, the use of an article is not necessary to identify one who possessed an official title, although at times it can. Additionally, if Papias was referring to a different elder John instead of the apostle John then he almost assuredly would *not* have employed an article if for no other reason than to avoid any confusion concerning whether or not he was speaking about the John that he had just previously mentioned. This makes contextual sense since Papias had identified the previous seven apostles as "elders"; therefore, by his employment of the article he identified the second elder John as the same elder John that he had previously mentioned group of elders, the John who was in fact an influential member of the apostolic colloquium.

Lastly, Papias's association of Aristion with John and his explanation of how John functioned almost assuredly makes it clear that Papias was not using the term πρεσβύτερος as only a comparative adjective. If John was a personal disciple of the Lord who lived long enough to witness Trajan's ascension to the throne, then without question he was an older gentleman. Tradition places the apostle John's death around the fourth or fifth year of Trajan's reign (ca. 103).[173] If the apostle John was born ca. AD 7 it would mean that he was approximately ninety-six years old at his death, and about ten years younger than Jesus.[174] Papias also identified Aristion as a disciple of the Lord. It is assumed, therefore, that Aristion was a disciple of Jesus in a similar sense that the seven apostles listed by Papias were, meaning that although he was not selected by Jesus to be an apostle, he had personally followed Jesus—possibly as one of the seventy mentioned in Luke 10:1–17 or as one of the one-hundred and twenty mentioned in Acts 1:15. Having followed Jesus and then having survived long enough for Papias to have heard him recite his eyewitness testimony

---

III.39.4–5 (LCL 153: 292).

171. Deeks, "Papias Revisited," 297.

172. Smyth, *Grammar*, 290.

173. Eusebius, *Chronicle*, 193, and Eusebii Pamphili, *Chronici*, 275. The following dates are provided as estimates. It is recognized that there is considerable debate regarding them. They are provided, however, for the sake of discussion.

174. It is assumed that Jesus was born relatively close to Herod the Great's death, which occurred ca. 4 BC.

of Jesus means that like the apostle John he also was a man of considerable age. The question is, however, how old could he have been? If the apostle John was approximately ten years younger than Jesus, it would make him approximately twenty-four years old when Jesus died.[175] The question then becomes, how old could Aristion have been and still be considered a credible disciple of Jesus.[176] If Aristion was fifteen or sixteen years old when he started following Jesus, and if he only followed Jesus during his last year of ministry, he would have been approximately sixteen or seventeen when Jesus was crucified.[177] That would mean that Aristion was approximately seventy-six years old in AD 90, while "the elder" John would have been approximately eighty-three. The point of this exercise is that Aristion, having been a personal disciple of Jesus, was also of considerable age, and by employing even a most conservative estimation of his age he still would have been viewed as a peer of the apostle John. What would be the sense, therefore, in emphasizing John's antiquity while ignoring the antiquity of Aristion? Consequently, while Aristion was certainly Papias's "elder," Papias did not refer to him as such because it would have confused his readers by implying that Aristion had attained to the same position as the apostle John, which was that of an elder and official bearer church traditions and dogma, which was a position Aristion apparently never achieved.

THE COALESCING OF APOSTOLIC TRADITIONS

Some have argued, as previously noted, that the reference to John as "the elder" was a term of endearment. Such a claim, however, ignores the entire focus of Papias's statements. It should not be forgotten that the context of Papias's statements is his utmost concern was for the accurate preservation of the apostolic traditions. Moreover, Papias emphasized these two disciples of the Lord specifically because they both were able to confirm

175. Assuming Jesus was crucified ca. 30 (see Carson and Moo, *Introduction*, 126). If Jesus was crucified in 33 then John would have been approximately twenty-six years old. The exact date of Jesus' crucifixion is greatly debated. However, it is not in the purview of this book to prove the year of Jesus' crucifixion. Consequently, these dates are provided only for the sake of estimating the approximate ages of the apostle John and Aristion.

176. For the sake of discussion it will be assumed that Aristion was younger than John, although this is not a certainty.

177. This approximates Aristion's birth ca. 14. This year is merely suggested as the latest one could have been born and still be viewed as a respectable follower of Jesus.

the traditions associated with the seven original disciples of the Lord mentioned by Papias. Therefore, the weight of the data indicates that Papias was not emphasizing the fact that John was old or was a "dear old friend," but that the Asiatic church recognized him as the last surviving authoritative tradition-bearing elder from among the founding leaders of the church. His reason for mentioning John twice was that, unlike the other elders, John was still alive and able to confirm the combined teachings of the apostles, teachings that he agreed with and was still promoting at some point in Papias's own lifetime. It was his "traditions" that Papias had personally learned and remembered well. Papias was well positioned, consequently, to examine the teachings of itinerant preachers and prophets who had arrived at Hierapolis and were attempting to influence the church in his jurisdiction. Knowing what was at stake, Papias was not of the habit of abdicating his "pulpit" to just anyone who claimed to have associated with apostles or elders. Instead, he sought to ascertain their "orthodoxy," that is their faithful conformity to the commandments that Jesus had actually taught to his immediate followers, who in turn faithfully transmitted them to approved men who were committed to preserving Jesus' words and meanings. Papias was not some hapless part-time pastor who thirsted to be entertained by anything and everything from the lips of anyone who happened to wander through Hierapolis seeking an audience. Instead, he was a bishop ordained by the apostle John to shepherd and protect the flock at Hierapolis by preserving the teachings and commandments of the Lord as he had received them from John. He was unquestionably in the truest sense of the term an apostolic man.

The second important shift, which has been briefly discussed, is Papias's change from the aorist tense when referring to what the seven apostolic elders had said in the past to the present tense in order to discuss what Aristion and the elder John were still communicating (λέγουσιν).[178] This shift is significant because it reveals that there was a period of time in which John and Aristion were ministering and articulating the combined traditions of the apostolic leadership of the first-century church.[179] Moreover, this shift in tense can also be understood as Papias's claim that during this period he heard the very teachings of the apostle John. The question

178. The aorist is understood as simple past tense, indicating that they had spoken. For other theories of the relevance of this shift and what is commonly referred to as a "historical present," see the discussion associated with footnote 98 on page 133.

179. Although not the position of this book, it is recognized that this present tense verb could indicate that Papias was referring to the state of affairs in the church as he wrote. See Perumalil, "Papias and Irenaeus," 334; and Perumalil, "Papias," 363.

concerning his statement is whether he in fact made such a claim. Petrie has argued,

> Here Papias sets out three sources on which he had depended for information or confirmation: (1) what he himself had learnt from the elders; (2) what he had learnt from followers of the elders as to (a) what the elders had said in the past—implying, in view of what follows, that some were no longer accessible, owing to death or for other reasons; and (b) what two disciples of the Lord were (still) saying—these being still accessible to some followers, *but not to Papias himself.* On the question which Eusebius has raised, and on the answer which he insists the passage "makes plain," Papias is neutral: Papias says neither that he was "a hearer and eye-witness" of the apostles nor that he was not. He simply does not, in the passage quoted, mention the matter.[180]

Petrie's contention that Eusebius's quote of Papias implies that Papias was "neutral" or did not "mention" that he had heard the apostle John is an overstatement. What Papias did not write that may have satisfied Petrie was "and whatever Aristion and the elder John say, which I myself have heard." Papias did, however, openly confess that he had "carefully learned and carefully remembered (teachings) *from the elders,*" after which he named the elders whose words he considered worthy of preservation and conformity, all of whom were apostles. Among these apostolic elders that he valued most was the elder John, who has been identified as the apostle John.[181] Petrie's position only makes sense if one ignores Papias's earlier confession to have learned from multiple elders, or if one rejects the possibility that the elder John was also the apostle John. Petrie argued, however, that Papias's initial mentioning of a list of the elders included the apostle John, writing that, "Those 'ancient worthies' who had spoken were seven of the Twelve."[182] Ironically, Petrie also referred to Eusebius's John the elder as an "elusive mythical figure," while later stating that Papias in fact had been a hearer of the apostle John.[183] Therefore, while Papias may

---

180. Petrie, "Matthew," 17. Italics mine.

181. Petrie himself saw the article before the second mentioning of John's name as anaphoric; thereby indicating that Papias was speaking of the previously mentioned John. Petrie, "Matthew," 21.

182. Ibid., 19. Petrie understood the word elder to mean "ancient worthies."

183. Ibid., 20, 24. Bauckham argued that Papias had not only not heard the apostle John, but had also not personally heard Eusebius's John the elder, but had learned what they had to say from their followers. Bauckham, *The Eyewitnesses*, 19. Given

not have been clear enough to satisfy Petrie; nevertheless, he was in no sense "neutral" about whether he had learned from any apostles, the apostle John being the most likely candidate under whom he had studied.[184]

THE LIVING AND ABIDING VOICE

Recognizing that Papias was speaking about a time in which the apostle John was still teaching, he also made a statement consistent with the common preference in Greek intellectual culture for oral discourse, a comment that some have taken to an extreme. Papias stated that given a choice he preferred to listen to a speaker rather than reading books about the speaker's subject. His exact words were "For I did not think that information from books would profit me as much as information from a living and abiding voice."[185] Loveday Alexander wrote a well defended article that identifies the term "living voice" as a common proverb that referred to the preference for oral dialogue over written instruction in both rabbinical schools and Hellenistic culture. Alexander, however, also explained that Greek culture was not monolithic in its distaste for written texts, and that in different contexts literature was more appreciated than in others. Jaap Mansfeld corroborated this point, stating that "the expression 'the living voice' strongly or less strongly contrasted with the written word, may mean somewhat different things at different times."[186] Concerning Papias's use, Alexander concluded that "Papias was not intellectual and has no links with Platonism. . . . But again it should be noted that Papias' concern in his preface is with teaching and with the passing on and preservation of authentic tradition, not with instruction in manual skills—so that once again the school tradition seems to provide the most helpful cultural background."[187] The fact that Papias did not have a thoroughly Platonic view of the written text is clear from Papias's own words, for he did not say that he "could not learn from books," but rather that he did not expect to learn "as much from books" as from the living and abiding

---

Bauckham's position, one could certainly question whether Papias had any right to confidently assert that he had accurately learned anything that the apostle John had said or taught.

184. Hill asserted that it was unclear whether Papias had heard the apostle John. Hill, "Papias," 310.

185. Holmes, *Apostolic Fathers,* 3rd ed., 735.

186. Mansfeld, "Galen, Papias," 320.

187. Alexander, "The Living Voice," 243.

voice. Unlike Hellenistic religions, however, Judaism was thoroughly text based and had a high value for the written word (Josh 1:6–9; Pss 1 and 119).[188] Consequently, since Christianity originated from Judaism it also had a great appreciation for the written word (Matt 5:17–20; 1 Cor 4:6; 1 Tim 4:13; 2 Tim 3:14–17). It is extremely unlikely, therefore, that Papias was thoroughly Greek in his view of the written word. Alexander recognized this possibility, writing that "both Papias and Clement may reflect tensions within a Christianity which was about to enter its own 'scholastic' phase. The second century sees the church in the process of defining its own canon of 'prescribed texts' from which all future Christian teaching would be derived."[189]

Bauckham took a slightly different understanding of Papias's statement concerning his preference for a living voice over books. He adeptly argued that Papias preferred a living voice to books because he valued eyewitness testimony as a historian. Papias was concerned about preserving the testimonies of reliable firsthand witnesses. Bauckham argued that Papias did not suffer from some form of book phobia, which is obvious by the fact that he wrote on a subject that consumed five volumes. He was simply explaining that during the earlier years of his ministry, he valued listening to and learning from eyewitnesses rather than reading about what they saw and heard in books. As Bauckham explained,

> So we may see Papias's Prologue as claiming that he followed the best practice of historians: he made careful inquiries, collected the testimonies of eyewitnesses, set them down in a series of notes, and finally arranged his material artistically to form a work of literature. His preference for the testimony of eyewitnesses, obtained at second or third hand, is therefore that of the historian, for whom, if direct autopsy was not available (i.e., the historian himself was not present at the events), indirect autopsy was more or less essential.
>
> What is most important for our purpose is that, when Papias speaks of "a living and surviving voice," he is not speaking metaphorically of the "voice" of oral tradition, as many scholars have supposed. He speaks quite literally of the voice of an informant—someone who has personal memories of the word and deeds of Jesus and who is still alive. In fact, even if

---

188. This should not be understood as arguing that Judaism in its many forms was exclusively a text-based religion, but only that it was not exclusively an oral-based religion. Instead it was quite comfortable with its sacred texts.

189. Ibid., 245.

the suggestion that he alludes specifically to historiographic practices is rejected, his must be his meaning. As we have seen, the saying about the superiority of the "living voice" to books refers not to oral tradition as superior to books, but to direct instruction of an instructor, informant, or orator as superior to written sources.[190]

Bauckham's and Alexander's points are well defended, and the truth about Papias's preference for firsthand instruction and/or eyewitness testimony is probably adequately explained in the positions of both scholars. Consequently, Papias should no longer be employed as supporting the theory that during his day the church only preferred and depended upon the charismatic preaching of itinerant prophets.[191] She of course listened to their messages, but did she disdain the written word, such as the Scriptures and the apostolic writings—absolutely not! This is not to argue that all gladly or submissively received written correspondence from the apostles.[192] However, most did, and in their personal absence the apostles viewed their epistles as inherently authoritative, as did the majority in the audiences to which they wrote.[193]

There is one additional point to be made regarding Papias's phrase "a living and abiding voice."[194] Alexander believed the presence of the word "abiding" to be an "odd" addition of Papias to this well recognized proverb, stating that it was probably an "echo of 1 Pet 1:23 (or some similar phrase current in the Christian rhetoric of second-century Asia Minor)."[195] The concept of remaining or abiding is an important theme throughout the New Testament, but is nowhere more important than in the Johannine writings. Of the approximately 110 times μένω occurs in the New Testament, over a third of its occurrences appear in John's writings. The majority of its usages in the remaining two-thirds are generally generic, meaning that it was used to refer to someone "remaining" someplace. There are a few occurrences, however, where the term possesses a relational/spiritual aspect of one's union with God, the gospel, or of God's

190. Bauckham, *The Eyewitnesses*, 27.

191. Holmes, *Apostolic Fathers*, 3rd ed., 723.

192. 2 Cor 10:10; 3 John 9.

193. 1 Cor 4:6; 14:38; Gal 1:8–9; 2 Tim 4:1–2; 1 John 5:13.

194. In Greek, the phrase is "παρὰ ζώσης φωνῆς καὶ μενούσης." The Greek verb for "abiding" is μένω, which occurs in the New Testament a little over 110 times. Metzger, *Lexical Aids*, 12.

195. Alexander, "The Living Voice," 225.

enduring presence or his word.[196] The apostle John, in contrast, employed this word approximately forty times, 75 percent of which spoke directly to one's spiritual union with God, Jesus, his teachings, the Holy Spirit, or of existing in darkness and sin. Two specific references have special relevance to Papias's preface. Concerning the importance of remaining faithful to Jesus' teachings, the apostle John reported that Jesus said, "If you remain in me and my words remain in you, ask whatever you wish, and it will be given to you," and again, "If you obey my commandments, you will remain in my love, just as I have obeyed my Father's commands and remain in his love."[197] Moreover, with respect to fidelity to the teachings of Jesus, in 2 John 9 the apostle John rather forcefully wrote that "anyone who runs ahead and does not continue (μένων) in the teaching of Christ does not have God; whoever continues in the teaching has both the Father and the Son." It would appear, therefore, that Papias's reference to the "living and abiding voice" should be understood to mean that early in Papias's ministry he made a special effort to hear the "living" (i.e., still alive, or surviving) and "abiding" (i.e., faithful to the words of Jesus) voices of eyewitnesses of Jesus' teachings and deeds.[198]

Papias's reference to certain "books" is most interesting. Lightfoot suggested the possibility that Papias was referring to the "twenty-four" volume work by Basilides, which is possible but may be too late if Papias wrote his work in 110 or shortly thereafter.[199] It has been suggested that Basilides flourished during the reign of Hadrian (117–138). This should not be understood to mean that there was not other literature about the teachings and deeds of Jesus in existence before Papias wrote. Luke's prologue implies that narratives other than the canonical Gospels existed during the last quarter of the first century. Stein wrote concerning the amount of this material that "[i]f we take seriously the 'many' of

196. See 1 Pet 1:23, and possibly Gal 2:5.

197. John 15:7 and 10.

198. Holmes observed that "abiding" could possibly be interpreted as "surviving." Holmes, *Apostolic Fathers*, 3rd ed., 735. While μένω can be translated as "to survive," this would be rather redundant since one who is living would be by definition "surviving." Given the presence of ζώσης and the significance of the concept of "abiding" in Johannine literature, there is good reason for understanding Papias's employment of μένω as a reference to remaining faithful to Jesus and his teachings rather than a reference to one's enduring life. Bauckham also translated μένω as "surviving." He recognized that it may have been an allusion to John 21:22. He did not, however, discuss the more significant nuance of this word with respect to faithfulness to Jesus and his teachings found throughout the Gospel of John. Bauckham, *The Eyewitnesses*, 21–22.

199. Lightfoot, *Essays*, 161. See also Hill, "Papias," 312.

Luke 1:1 ('In as much as *many* have undertaken to compile a narrative of the things which have been accomplished among us' [italics added]), this would indicate that when Luke wrote his Gospel there existed more written material than just Mark and Q (or simply Matthew, according to the Griesbach hypothesis)."[200] It is reasonable, therefore, to assume that towards the end of the first century different narratives about the life and teachings of Jesus were available throughout Asia Minor. And while we do not know how much of this material existed during Papias's education and ministry, we do know that for a period in Papias's life personal disciples of Jesus were living, and if given a choice, he desired to listen and interact with them rather than to read what others had written about Jesus. Papias's statement, therefore, about his preference for first person instruction from eyewitnesses of Jesus' life and ministry should not be understood as a categorical rejection of all written material.

Given the above grammatical analysis of Eusebius's quote of Papias's preface, a translation is here offered:

> For I will not hesitate for you to set down along with the interpretations what so ever at that time I carefully learned and I carefully remembered from the elders, thus guaranteeing on their behalf truth. For I was not of the habit of enjoying the many things that people were saying—although the crowds generally did, but rather the truth being presented by teachers. Neither the other commandments being remembered by some, but the things [or commandments] being remembered by others which were given from the Lord to the faith, and coming from the truth itself. And if perchance someone who associated with the elders arrived, I was of the habit of investigating the words of the elders, what Andrew or what Peter said, or what Philip or what Thomas, or James or what John or Matthew or what was said by any other of the disciples of the Lord, and which Aristion and the elder John, the disciples of the Lord, were still saying. For I was not thinking I would benefit so much by the things from books, as much as by the things from a living and abiding voice.[201]

200. Stein, *Synoptic Gospels*, 176–77.

201. A more literal translation would be "I will not hesitate for you to set down along with the interpretations whatsoever at that time I carefully learned and I carefully remembered from the elders, (thus) guaranteeing on their behalf truth. For I was not enjoying the many things by the ones speaking—even as the many, but the truth by the ones teaching. Neither the other commandments by the ones remembering, but by those (remembering) the things [or commandments] having been given from

The above translation takes some liberties in order to provide a more readable version of Papias's preface while attempting to not unjustifiably distort Papias's meanings. As this translation reveals, Papias's main concern was not with the itinerant ministers per se, but with the content of their messages and fidelity of those messages to apostolic traditions.

EUSEBIUS'S COMMENTARY ON PAPIAS

Eusebius's exegesis and commentary on the first quote of Papias's preface begins in section 5. It is in this passage that Eusebius clearly stated his opinion that Papias's first reference to a "John" was to the apostle John. This is obvious since Eusebius called that John "the Evangelist," which also indicates that he believed the apostle John authored the Fourth Gospel. He stated, however, that Papias's second mentioning of a John was not a reference to the apostle. He supported his position with four points, the first being that Papias changed his wording. What he could have possibly meant by referring to Papias's change in wording is not clear. He could have been referring to Papias's transition from the aorist to the present tense of the verb λέγω, or his change from the singular interrogative τί to the plural relative pronoun ἅ. Such arguments seem to assume that the apostle John was not alive during Papias's lifetime. Earlier in *Ecclesiastical History*, however, Eusebius stated that Polycarp was a hearer of the apostle John and a companion of Papias; consequently, he contradicted himself by stating that there was a period of time during Papias's life when he could have heard the apostle John. His argument, therefore, does not prove his position since it is undermined by his own admissions.

Eusebius's second reason seems to be that since Papias placed Aristion's name ahead of the name of John then his second reference to a John could not have been to the apostle since such an ordering would have been a *faux pas* that no one would have dared to commit. Such an

---

the Lord to the faith, and coming from the truth itself. And if perhaps having arrived one having associated with the elders, I was examining the words of the elders, what Andrew or what Peter said, or what Philip or what Thomas, or James or what John or Matthew or any other of the disciples of the Lord, (and) which Aristion and the elder John, the disciples of the Lord, say. For I was not thinking I would benefit so much (by) the things from books, as much as the things from a living and abiding voice." The words in parenthesis are added to provide a smoother translation, while words in brackets provide an alternate reading. The above translations are provided with the hope of avoiding the dramatic liberties that can be observed in other translations. For an example of such a translation see Kleist, "Rereading the Papias," 11–12, 16–17.

argument carries little weight, and one only need to inspect Papias's own listing of apostles for evidence supporting this assertion. Andrew is mentioned before Peter in Papias's list of the seven apostles, while Thomas (the doubter) is listed before James, John, and Matthew. Few scholars would suggest that Andrew was more prestigious than Peter, or that Thomas was more respected than the sons of thunder or an author of a Gospel.[202] Consequently, Eusebius's second argument is without merit. Eusebius's third argument was that Papias had distinctly called the second John "elder." Concerning the confusion surrounding Papias's use of the term "elder," Polhill explained,

> This is based on a passage from Papias (early second century) that Eusebius quotes and understands to be speaking of two Johns in Ephesus, the apostle and the Elder John. The quote is somewhat obscure and seems to apply the term elder to the apostles as well as the other John. *In itself the term elder is quite general and could apply to the apostles as well as some other church leader.* The term was used by Jews for their leaders (Acts 4.5). It was taken over by the Christians in their church organization (Acts 11:30; 1 Tim 5:17; Titus 1:5). Peter called himself a "fellow elder" (1 Pet 5:1). The term comes from the Greek word meaning old and carries a tone of veneration. It well fits the figure of the apostle John, whom Eusebius depicts as returning from his exile on Patmos to Ephesus after the death of the Emperor Domitian.[203]

Since Papias employed term "elder" to all seven apostles (a list which included the apostle John) Eusebius's third argument is considerably weak; thus, it is not well defended.

The first half of section 6 contains Eusebius's fourth and last argument, which is that Papias's preface "confirms" the story that there were two men in the whole of "Asia" that had the same name (i.e., John), and that they both must have been buried in Ephesus, thus the confusion over which tomb the apostle John occupies. There is little doubt that there was

202. One might suggest that in Papias's initial list he mentioned only apostles. Aristion and Eusebius's John the elder were not apostles; therefore, Papias would not have been concerned about mentioning Aristion before any apostle. It was Eusebius's conjecture, however, that prestige would have determined any ordering of names (even among apostles), which is demonstrably not the case. Secondly, it should be recognized that Papias also called Aristion a disciple of the Lord in the same manner as the other apostles. Consequently, although he was not an apostle, he was a prestigious Christian.

203. Polhill, "2 John and 3 John," 30. Italics mine.

more than one man named John in Asia. It does not follow, however, that because there was more than one person in Asia named John then Papias's words conclusively proves that in Ephesus a different John was buried in a tomb thought to be occupied by the apostle John.[204] As Schoedel has aptly stated, "The existence of two such tombs proves nothing."[205] Consequently, Eusebius's contention that Papias referred to two Johns is based upon the poorest of exegesis and the slimmest of historical data.

Having explained his theory about how many Johns Papias mentioned, Eusebius made an additional suggestion that reveals his motivation for discovering a second John, which was to separate the honored apostle John from the debate concerning the book of Revelation. Eusebius, apparently following the lead of Dionysius of Alexandria, believed that his second John was the author of the book of Revelation.[206] He recognized, however, that his theory was not a certainty and conceded that others attributed this book to the apostle John.[207] Ironically, Eusebius has the distinction of placing the book of Revelation on both his list of "recognized" (ὁμολογοθμένοις) and "spurious" (νόθοις) books used among the churches of his day, which reveals that even in his day there was a considerable portion of the church that viewed the book of Revelation as both sacred and/or of apostolic origin.[208] Consequently, while Eusebius was convinced by his own theories about the book of Revelation and the existence of a second John, he also admitted that there were others who disagreed with his positions.

The initial portion of section 7 should be understood as Eusebius's conclusion about those he believed Papias had heard based upon his own exegesis of Papias's preface in sections 5 and 6, as well as his reading of *Exposition*.[209] It is his commentary on Papias's sources, and he has supported

204. This issue is addressed extensively in appendix 1.

205. Schoedel, *The Fragments*, 102.

206. Eusebius was quite familiar with Dionysius's theory on the authorship of the book of Revelation. See Eusebius *Ecc. Hist.* VII.25.1–27 (LCL 265:197–209). See also Munck, "Presbyters," 224–25.

207. "εἰ μή τις ἐθέλοι τὸν πρῶτον." Holmes, *Apostolic Fathers*, 3rd ed., 736.

208. Eusebius *Ecc. Hist.* III.25.1–4 (LCL 153:256). Dionysius himself, while not believing the book of Revelation was written by the apostle John, still contended it was sacred and part of the canon; see ibid., *Ecc. Hist.* VII.25.4–5 (LCL 265: 197–98).

209. Holmes's translation is here provided: "And Papias, of whom we are now speaking, acknowledges that he had received the words of the apostles from those who had followed them, but he says that the was himself a hearer of Aristion and John the elder." Holmes, *Apostolic Fathers*, 3rd ed., 735–37.

it with insufficient data. If Eusebius had possessed stronger evidence proving his conjecture about Papias's non-relationship with the apostle John or any other apostle, one can be assured that he would have employed it in order to further buttress his poorly defended position, but as Petrie suggested, this was "the best he could do."[210] Consequently, Papias should not be understood as having stated that he received all of his information about the teachings of Jesus from the followers of the apostles, but that he received some of his traditions from actual disciples of Jesus, which ironically is an admission that Eusebius also affirmed. Eusebius wrote, "but he (Papias) says that he was himself a hearer of Aristion and John the Elder." This admission by Eusebius damages his own theory about the improbability of Papias's association with any of the apostles of Jesus, for Eusebius's quote of Papias identifies that both were personal followers of Jesus. Eusebius, consequently, tacitly admitted that Papias was educated during a period that afforded him the opportunity to interact with eyewitnesses of Jesus' life and ministry. Consequently, it was never his theory that Papias *did not live during a period in which he could have heard the apostle John*, but only that *he never heard John or any other apostle*, a theory for which he never provided a convincing argument for its defense.

Eusebius in the last portion of section 7 stated that both Aristion and John the elder were significant sources for Papias's material, writing that "he frequently mentions them by name and includes their traditions in his writings as well." The word Eusebius used for "traditions" was παραδόσεις, which is also the word used to describe authoritative traditions of Judaism that were preserved by the scribes and Pharisees (Mark 7:5–13). These traditions were given to the Jewish community to provide direction for the proper practice of Judaism. This same word was used by Paul to describe traditions that were delivered to the church in Corinth, traditions that Paul commended the Corinthian Christians for observing, and which he also expected them to faithfully retain (1 Cor 11:2). Consequently, this word refers to, among other things, authoritative practices and beliefs that were handed down to the church from its recognized leaders with the expectation that they would be preserved and obeyed. Such an admission by Eusebius lends further support to the position that John was described as an "elder" not because he was old, but primarily because he was someone who possessed the authority of overseeing the transmission of orthodox Christian practices and beliefs, which were called "traditions" during the period in which Paul and Papias were active in ministry. Eusebius contended that

210. Petrie, "Matthew," 16.

Aristion and John were not incidental sources for Papias's *magnum opus*, but rather that Papias mentioned them frequently (πολλάκις); therefore, their importance to his work was significant to say the least.

PAPIAS AND PHILIP

The word παράδοσεις was not only used to describe orthodox practices and beliefs. Eusebius also employed this word with reference to historical events performed by the founding leaders of Christianity as sections 8 through 10 reveal.[211] He described some of these events reported by Papias as "remarkable things" (παράδοξά τινα), which he stated that Papias indicated that the sources for these "events" were the daughters of the apostle Philip, who had also settled in Hierapolis. Some, who have no problem believing that there could be two Johns buried in Ephesus, have conjectured that it is unlikely that there were two Philips (both of whom had devoted Christian daughters) who were buried in Hierapolis.[212] While some suggest that Eusebius erred in stating that Papias had known the apostle Philip's daughters, it is clear that Eusebius was convinced that Hierapolis was the apostle Philip's final resting place.[213] Eusebius indicated concerning Philip's daughters that Papias had received[214] at least one and possibly two "amazing accounts" from them, the first concerning the resurrection of a man from the dead.[215] Matthews conjectured from Eusebius's

211. Holmes translated sections 8 through 10 as "It is worthwhile to add to the statements of Papias given above other sayings of his, in which he records some other remarkable things as well, which came done to him, as it were, from tradition. That Philip the Apostle resided in Hierapolis with his daughters has already been stated, but now it must be pointed out that Papias, their contemporary, recalls that he heard an amazing story from Philip's daughters. For he reports that in his day a man rose from the dead, and again another amazing story involving Justus, who was surnamed Barsabbas: he drank a deadly poison and yet by the grace of the Lord suffered nothing unpleasant." Holmes, *Apostolic Fathers*, 3rd ed., 737.

212. Schoedel, *The Fragments*, 103. For a more detailed discussion of this issue see appendix 2. Lightfoot, having previously thought that Papias had only known Philip the evangelist later changed his position and argued that he also knew the apostle Philip; see Lightfoot, *Essays*, 149; ibid., *Colossians*, 45–46.

213. Lawlor and Oulton, *Eusebius*, 2:116–18.

214. The Greek word is παρειληφέναι, which is a perfect active infinite of παραλάμβανω. Given Papias's context this word is properly translated as "to receive."

215. Holmes translated the Greek word διήγησιν as "story." Holmes, *Apostolic Fathers*, 3rd ed., 737. See also Schoedel, *The Fragments*, 103; and *Papias and Quadratus* (LCL 25:101). One could infer from his translation that the truthfulness of the event

reference concerning the source of this report that Philip's daughters "appear not as prophetesses but as mediators of 'apostolic tradition' on a par with Papias' other authorities."[216] Matthews has clearly projected more than Eusebius's commentary would suggest. First, he has failed to distinguish the difference between transmitting acceptable beliefs and practices for the church and the reporting of historical events. Secondly, he unjustifiably extrapolated that since the daughters of Philip reported a couple of accounts then they must have attained to the status of mediating other "apostolic traditions," or had risen to the status of an "elder." Simply because Philip's daughters were perceived as credible witnesses for reporting historic events does not mean that they would be granted the same authority and responsibility possessed by the church's recognized leaders for transmitting orthodox doctrines or discerning correct practices for the first-century church. Lastly, corroboration of Matthews's conjecture is not found elsewhere within the annuals of the church's history. His position is, therefore, built largely upon an argument of silence.

It is noteworthy that as Eusebius discussed Papias's association with Philip's family he stated that he was "their contemporary."[217] Eusebius's exact words were, "ὡς δὲ κατὰ τοὺς αὐτοὺς ὁ Παπίας γενόμενος," which is interpreted to state that Papias had been with or among the apostle Philip's family (κατὰ τοὺς αὐτοὺς).[218] The significance of this observation is that the pronoun is masculine, meaning that Papias had been with both the apostle Philip and his daughters. If Eusebius meant to state that Papias had only been with Philip's daughters then he would have employed a feminine pronoun (e.g., τάς αὐτάς). Consequently, Eusebius unwittingly contradicted himself by stating that Papias had not only received these accounts from Philip's daughters but that he had also been with their father, the apostle Philip.[219] Once again, not only did Eusebius place Papias

___

or its accuracy was in doubt. This Greek word is used with reference to narratives or historical reports; therefore, "story" hardly seems the most appropriate translation. Just because Eusebius understood this account as "amazing" does not imply that he doubted its truthfulness or accuracy. He reported many other amazing accounts throughout his *Ecclesiastical History*, accounts that he clearly believed were true.

216. Matthews, *Philip*, 27.

217. Holmes, *Apostolic Fathers*, 3rd ed., 737; Schoedel, *The Fragments*, 103; *Papias and Quadratus* (LCL 25:101).

218. A literal translation is "And that Papias having been among them."

219. Lawlor and Oulton, *Eusebius*, 2:114–15. Schoedel, while recognizing Eusebius's contradiction, argued that the clause κατὰ τοὺς αὐτοὺς should probably be understood as a euphemism for "*chronous*" or "time." However, he provided no substantive support for his position. Schoedel, *The Fragments*, 103.

within the lifetime of the apostles, but he also unwittingly placed Papias within direct earshot of at least one living apostle.

Eusebius reported that the first account that Papias received from the daughters of Philip concerned the raising of a man from the dead, about which Eusebius provided no specific details. Philip of Side also confirmed that accounts of people who were raised from the dead could be found in *Exposition*. Philip, however, provided more details concerning some of these events, which will be discussed in greater detail during the analysis of fragment 11.[220] Literally interpreted, Eusebius wrote that Papias had received one report from Philip's daughters about a man who had been raised from the dead. Immediately following this report, however, Eusebius also wrote about another account concerning Barsabbas's immunity to drinking "deadly poison." He connected these two reports with the conjunctional clause "and again another" (καὶ αὖ πάλιν ἕτερον), thus implying that the apostle's daughters were Papias's source for the second report as well. Philip of Side also understood the report concerning Barsabbas to have come from the daughters of Philip; therefore, it is reasonable to assume that Papias had received more than a single "amazing account" from Philip's daughters.

PAPIAS AND MARK 16:9–20

Given the lack of context and surviving material from Papias's hand, his purpose for including these reports is uncertain. His accounts of people being raised from the dead may have been provided as corroboration for sayings of Jesus such as those found in Matthew 10:8, Luke 7:22, John 11:25 and 14:12.[221] The report about Barsabbas is quite interesting when compared with the much debated traditional ending of the Gospel of Mark.[222] Given Papias's knowledge of Mark's Gospel, the question arises

220. While Eusebius stated that Papias recorded that a man had been raised from the dead, Philip discussed the raising of a woman and others, as well as the longevity of some of their lives. One could infer from such details that the author of fragment 11, p. 215, also had access to a manuscript of Papias's *Exposition*.

221. They may have also been recorded simply for their historical value.

222. It is the author's position that Mark 16:9–20 is an addition to the Gospel, and that Mark's original ending was lost. For a discussion of the text critical analysis of the endings of the Gospel of Mark see Metzger, *A Textual Commentary*, 102–7. For a discussion on the major views regarding Mark's ending see Gundry, *Mark*, 1009–21. This author also assumes a pre-AD 70 composition of the Gospel of Mark. For theories on the dating of Mark's Gospel see Carson and Moo, *Introduction*, 177–82. Bacon

regarding the relationship of Papias's report about Barsabbas safely drinking poison and the promise of protection while doing so found in Mark 16:18.[223] The earliest patristic references to Mark 16:9–20 are found in Irenaeus's *Against Heresies* III.10.5–6 and Tatian's *Diatessaron* LIII–LV, both of which were written during the last half of the second century, which is several decades after Papias's *Exposition*.[224] Concerning Papias's report about Barsabbas, the issues are: Was Papias aware of Mark 16:9–20, and if not, did his writings influence its composition, or is it merely coincidental that Mark 16:18 promises safety from drinking poison and that Papias preserved a report detailing just such an event. The fact that Irenaeus had a significant connection to the Asiatic church makes it unlikely that the connection between Papias and Mark 16:18 is merely coincidental.

If Papias knew of Mark 16:9–20, then he may have included the account about Barsabbas as an example of the fulfillment of what he believed to be an oracle of the Lord. The inclusion of such an event would lend support to the theory that providing explanations and fulfillments of the sayings of Jesus was an important purpose for Papias's five-volume work, as implied by his title.[225] If Papias was unaware of what is currently viewed as the traditional ending of Mark, then it appears that preserving important historical accounts ("traditions" as Eusebius called them) in the life of the early church was one of the purposes for Papias's *Exposition*. Consequently, including such miraculous post-Pentecost accounts about the early church's activities may also reveal an apologetic purpose for Papias's writings. If Papias was unaware of Mark 16:9–20, then one could infer that

believed that an Armenian manuscript containing Mark 16:9–20 under the "formal title" of "From the Presbyter Ariston" was actually a reference to Papias's source Aristion. Bacon, "An Emendation," 177. He judicially questioned, however, whether these verses could have come from an actual disciple of Jesus. While the idea is provocative, little weight can be placed on the theory that Mark 16:9–20 was originally from the hand of Papias's Aristion.

223. Eusebius identified Barsabbas as one of the possible apostolic replacements for Judas in Acts 1:23. Eusebius *Ecc. Hist.* III.39.9–10 (LCL 153:295). As stated earlier, this section is understood as Eusebius's personal explanation of specific identity of the Barsabbas's that Papias had written about, and while Eusebius was in all probability accurate in his assessment, his theory, nonetheless, will not be dealt with as an actual Papian fragment.

224. Irenaeus *Against Heresies* III.10.5–6 (ANF 1:425–26); Tatian *Diatessaron* LIII–LV (ANF 9:125–29).

225. Other possible examples of fulfillments of Jesus' oracles are Luke 10:19 and the ability to drink poison without harm, or Matt 10:8 and the ability of Jesus' followers to raise the dead.

his writings to some degree influenced the author(s) of this particular ending of the Gospel of Mark; however, this is all only conjecture.[226] Certainty, therefore, about why Papias included the report about Barsabbas as well as other fantastic accounts, and their relationship to the ending of Mark's Gospel is simply unattainable without further material from *Exposition*. While not ruling out other possibilities, it seems reasonable to assume that Papias intentionally preserved some select events that occurred during the first century of the church's existence if for no other reason than for their historical value.[227]

PAPIAS AND ORAL TRADITIONS

Eusebius also provided important details about Papias's *Exposition* in sections 11 and 12. While one should not accept Eusebius's comments about Papias's writings without critical assessment, his comments are nevertheless important. In section 11 Eusebius wrote that Papias recorded other unwritten traditions,[228] which should be understood as referring to other reports in addition to the accounts about Barsabbas and those who were raised from the dead. One of the features about Papias's writings that struck Eusebius was that Papias had preserved traditions that were oral, that is, until he decided to record them in *Exposition*. Eusebius stated that some of these traditions involved strange parables (ξένας παραβολὰς) of the "Savior,"[229] as well as his teachings (καὶ διδασκαλίας αὐτοῦ). What Eusebius meant by strange parables is open to speculation, although Irenaeus's Papian fragment (fragment 1) could certainly be an adequate example of a parable that Eusebius may have thought strange, given his distaste for millennial theology. Eusebius, however, may have had something else in mind; consequently, one should not lean too heavily upon Irenaeus's quote of Papias as an example since chiliasm was not a rare approach to eschatology in Eusebius's day.

While Eusebius's comments about Papias's preservation of "strange parables" are interesting, his additional comment about Jesus' teachings

---

226. Metzger believed that Mark 16:9–20 was composed sometime during the "first half of the second century." Metzger, *A Textual Commentary*, 105.

227. Rigg, "Papias on Mark," 165.

228. "ἄλλα . . . ἐκ παραδόσεως ἀγράφου."

229. The Greek word that Holmes translated as "Lord" is actually σωτῆρος, which is more appropriately translated as "savior." For the correct translation see *Papias and Quadratus* (LCL 25:101).

(διδασκαλίας) may be more insightful. His comment reveals that *Exposition* was not exclusively devoted to preserving "stories" that to a more critical mind were too spectacular to accept as real. Papias apparently also discussed lessons or "oracles" that were believed to have originated from the Lord, which, when compared to parables, were more straightforward and didactic in nature. Given the difference between preserving the teachings of Jesus and the reporting of events, and Jesus' propensity to teach, one should assume that this instructional material would have also included some "interpretations" or explanations that Papias believed originated from the lips of Jesus. Consequently, as argued earlier, it is a poor assumption to conclude that the "interpretations" contained in Papias's writings were exclusively his own. What is valuable about Eusebius's observations, assuming he was fairly familiar with *Exposition*, is that they support the position that Papias's work was predominately devoted to "explaining" the meanings of Jesus' teachings from sources that were both oral and written.

Eusebius also stated that Papias included material that Eusebius believed was mythical in nature (μυθικώτερα). Unlike his previous comments, however, he was clearer about what he actually meant, contending that among these "mythical" materials was the idea that there will be a resurrection for the dead, which will be followed by the Lord Jesus Christ establishing a physical millennial kingdom on earth. His summary of Papias's eschatology is clearly an outline of what is commonly referred to today as premillennialism. The only reference in the New Testament for this specific chain of events is found in Revelation 20:1–6.[230] While one might be tempted to conclude from this statement that Papias knew of the book of Revelation, it should be noted that Eusebius provided no additional evidence from Papias's *Exposition* to support this conclusion. Given his aversion to chiliasm and the book of Revelation, it is understandable that Eusebius would not feel compelled to elaborate further upon any sources supporting Papias's eschatology. Consequently, one can only infer from Eusebius's statement that Papias was aware of the book of Revelation since, objectively speaking, his statement proves nothing about any such knowledge. Eusebius's comment, however, does indicate that Papias had an interest in preserving eschatological traditions that he perceived as important; consequently, his work possessed among other things a theological component. Papias was not simply a collector of fantastic stories.[231] Papias

---

230. While there is no direct reference to Jesus reigning with resurrected saints *on the earth* in Rev 20:1–6, the following verses (Rev 20:7–9) reveal that the kingdom mentioned in verses 4–6 had been established upon the earth.

231. Burton, *Lectures*, 392–93.

was also to a certain degree both a theologian and historian. Perumalil speculated that Papias wrote the "first known commentary on the words" of Jesus.[232] While it is questionable whether Papias did in fact compose the *first* commentary on the teachings of Jesus,[233] based upon Papias's title and these comments by Eusebius (as well as comments and quotes in other Papian fragments), it seems reasonable to conclude that *Exposition* was to some degree a type of commentary.

Eusebius's admission about the nature of Papias's *Exposition* in the last portion of section 12 is very compelling. Having surveyed Papias's writings, he concluded that Papias had misunderstood *apostolic accounts* (τὰς ἀποστολικὰς . . . διηγήσεις) with respect to any teaching on a millennium.[234] The relevance of Eusebius's observation is that even though he disagreed with Papias's interpretation of his sources, he recognized them as "apostolic" in nature. In other words, he described the material that Papias interacted with as generally from or about the apostles. Papias, as will become evident later on, was aware of Mark's Gospel, and other canonical Gospels, as well as other material about the life of Jesus; therefore, it is not hard to conceive that Eusebius would generalize Papias's *Exposition* as dealing with "apostolic accounts." Eusebius, however, was of the opinion that Papias had misunderstood his material because he approached it with a flawed hermeneutic, for immediately afterward he stated that "having

232. Perumalil, "Papias," 363.

233. Perumalil was not clear about whether he thought Papias's *Exposition* was the first known commentary on the words of Jesus for the first-century church or for modern historians.

234. Holmes, in the third edition of *The Apostolic Fathers*, corrected δηγήσεις to διηγήσεις, which is translated as "an account, a historical record, a narrative." See the fragment from *Ecc. Hist.* III.39.12 in Holmes, *The Apostolic Fathers: Diglot Edition*, 566, and compare it with Holmes, *Apostolic Fathers*, 3rd ed., 738. Apparently Kleist incorrectly translated this word as "interpretations." Kleist, *Papias*, 117. Kleist's translation of the last half of section 12 takes considerable liberties. Eusebius's comment is rather difficult to translate. It seems, consequently, that the most appropriate translation is, "Which things I was thinking to suppose (as) being misconstrued apostolic accounts." This translation understands the infinitive ὑπολαβεῖν as complementary of the verb ἡγοῦμαι, which has Eusebius as its subject. For alternate readings see Holmes, *Apostolic Fathers*, 3rd ed., 739. Lake's translation of the participle παρεκδεξάμενον as "perverse" could be construed as being polemical; consequently, "misconstrued" is preferred. Eusebius *Ecc. Hist.* III.39.12 (LCL 153:294–95). Ehrman chose not to translate the last portion of section 12 through 13. He rightfully saw it as Eusebius's comments on Papias's writing and his intelligence; therefore, this entire section is not considered a Papian fragment. *Papias and Quadratus* (LCL 25:101–3). However, his commentary about Papias's writings does provide valuable insights from Eusebius about the nature of Papias's work; consequently, they are important.

not perceived the things by example *to them* (or *by them*) had been mystically spoken."[235] It is not clear whether Eusebius was referring to teachings spoken *by* the apostles or teachings spoken *to* the apostles. Nevertheless, he believed that Papias had interacted with material that Eusebius recognized to be "apostolic" in nature.

EUSEBIUS'S LOW ESTIMATION OF PAPIAS

Holmes translated the last portion of section 12 as "These ideas, I suppose, he got through a misunderstanding of the apostolic accounts, not realizing that *the things recorded* in figurative language were spoken by them mystically."[236] The actual Greek word in this sentence for the phrase "the things recorded" is the Greek article τὰ, the antecedent of which is "the apostolic accounts." Holmes has accurately interpreted this important referent in Eusebius's characterization of Papias's *Exposition*, indicating that in his opinion Papias had interacted with "recorded" materials that Eusebius understood to be apostolic. The salient point concerning Eusebius's observations about *Exposition* is that it was not solely dedicated to preserving oral material, but that it also interacted with literary material that he described as apostolic. Thus, Eusebius never described Papias's writings as given exclusively to oral traditions. He instead indicated that Papias's work interacted with both types of material, some that were oral and some that were written. What bothered Eusebius most about Papias, however, was not his subject matter or the "vehicle" of his material, but his approach to it, which in his estimation employed a predominately "non-Alexandrian" hermeneutic.[237] Consequently, he evaluated Papias as a man of low intel-

235. This clause in Greek is "τὰ ἐν ὑποδείγμασι πρὸς αὐτῶν μυστικῶς εἰρημένα μὴ συνεωρακότα." The translation of this clause is provided by the author. For the text see Holmes, *Apostolic Fathers*, 3rd ed., 738. The preposition πρὸς before the genitive pronoun αὐτῶν is difficult to interpret since the construction is rare. Schoedel interpreted the clause as meaning things spoken "by them" Schoedel, *The Fragments*, 104. Similarly, see also Lake in Eusebius *Ecc. Hist.* III.39.12 (LCL 153:297); and Holmes, *Apostolic Fathers*, 3rd ed., 739.

236. Holmes, *Apostolic Fathers*, 3rd ed., 738–39. Italics mine. The entire Greek text is "ἃ καὶ ἡγοῦμαι τὰς ἀποστολικὰς παρεκδεξάμενον διηγήσεις ὑπολαβεῖν, τὰ ἐν ὑποδείγμασι πρὸς αὐτῶν μυστικῶς εἰρημένα μὴ συνεωρακότα."

237. Some scholars question whether there ever truly existed a sharp distinction between an "Antiochene" approach to interpreting the Scriptures and that of the "Alexandrian school." For an introduction to differing hermeneutical approaches found in early church see Froehlich, *Biblical Interpretation*, 8–23. What is apparent, however, is Eusebius's distain for Papias's hermeneutical approach to certain "apostolic accounts."

lectual acumen, stating that "surely he appears as a man possessing an extremely small mind, as to say being proved from his words."[238]

Eusebius's insult is clearly pejorative, and although his derisive comment would not be tolerated in current academic discourse, one should not dismiss Eusebius's comment as valueless. He may have made his assessment about Papias solely because of his hermeneutical approach and eschatology, but he may also have made it because of the vocabulary and literary style that Papias employed. The context in which this insult is found seems to indicate that it was Papias's approach to his material, as well as his eschatology, that stirred Eusebius's ire. The possibility remains, however, that Eusebius may have also provided a legitimate assessment of Papias's literary ability, for no other Papian fragment contradicts or affirms Eusebius's evaluation of Papias's writing ability. Nevertheless, the pool of Papian fragments is so small it is not possible for modern historians, rhetoricians, grammarians, and literary critics to evaluate Eusebius's critique with any degree of certitude.[239] However, since Eusebius was so transparent in his contempt for Papias, one could safely conclude that it was his disdain for Papias and his eschatology that to a significant degree motivated him to marginalize Papias and promote his own theological biases.[240]

Eusebius, however, in the last half of section 13 recognized that regardless of Papias's literary style or possible lack thereof, he influenced many of the church's "leaders" after him, men that Eusebius could not similarly impugn.[241] Eusebius, as discussed earlier, blamed their willingness

---

Eusebius *Ecc. Hist.* III.39.12 (LCL 153: 297).

238. Translation mine. For the Greek text see Holmes, *Apostolic Fathers*, 3rd ed., 738. Schoedel questioned if Eusebius was using Papias's own self-effacing comments against him. Schoedel, *The Fragments*, 104. It seems unlikely that Eusebius would have based his entire evaluation on this type of common authorial statement. Eusebius himself made a similar attempt at humility, see Eusebius *Ecc. Hist.* I.1.3–4 (LCL 153:9). Consequently, it seems more reasonable to assume that Eusebius's critique was based upon his exposure to the whole of Papias's *Exposition* rather than a simple introductory remark by its author.

239. Kürzinger's work notwithstanding.

240. See appendix 1 for a more thorough discussion on this issue.

241. "καὶ τοῖς μετ' αὐτὸν πλείστοις ὅσοις τῶν ἐκκλησιαστικῶν . . . ," Holmes, *Apostolic Fathers*, 3rd ed., 738. This clause may be translated as "And after him many devout ecclesiastical (leaders) . . ." Holmes and others have labeled those influenced by Papias as ecclesiastical "writers," see Holmes, *Apostolic Fathers*, 3rd ed., 739. Schoedel more appropriately translated ἐκκλησιαστικῶν as "churchmen." Schoedel, *The Fragments*, 104.

to follow Papias's chiliasm on his great antiquity.[242] His statement that Papias influenced many (πλείστοις) others is a tacit admission concerning Papias's intelligence and literary capacity. Eusebius's admission argues that Papias was not so incompetent that he was incapable of significantly influence future leaders of the church in the generations that followed.[243] Eusebius pointed to Irenaeus as being a prime example of one who had regrettably fallen into Papias's error, writing also that "as is any other who has declared similar thinking."[244] It was unthinkable for Eusebius that any independent critical thinker might come to believe in the millennium. He instead labeled Papias as the fountainhead of this theological error, which he contended was the product of Papias's meager intelligence and faulty hermeneutic. Munck has appropriately observed concerning Eusebius's entire treatment of Papias that "this mention of Papias' work in Eusebius' History is, as can be seen, entirely one-sided."[245] Eusebius's value as a church historian can hardly be overstated; however, his lack of objectivity and balance when discussing those with whom he disagreed is an indelible blight upon his legacy.

ARISTION'S CONTRIBUTIONS TO PAPIAS

Eusebius returned in section 14 to discussing the impact that Aristion and the elder John had upon Papias's *Exposition*. He initially stated that embedded in Papias's writings were narrative accounts (διηγήσεις) provided by Aristion.[246] Based upon Eusebius's vocabulary one should not presume that he meant that Aristion had only provided Papias with oral material. In the first verse of the Third Gospel, Luke also spoke of others who had compiled written accounts (διήγησιν) concerning the life of Jesus. It is not unthinkable, therefore, to believe that Aristion, who Papias stated was a

242. The Greek phrase is: "τὴν ἀρχαιότητα τἀνδρὸς προβεβλημένοις," which is translated as "the ones having put forth" or "relied upon the antiquity of the man." Holmes, *Apostolic Fathers*, 3rd ed., 738.

243. Mansfeld conjectured that Papias had achieved a "solid pagan education." Mansfeld, "Galen, Papias," 328.

244. Translation mine. "καὶ ἔι τις ἄλλος τὰ ὅμοια φρονῶν ἀναπέφηνεν." For the Greek text see Holmes, *Apostolic Fathers*, 3rd ed., 738.

245. Munck, "Presbyters," 226. Perumalil believed Eusebius's insult was the product of a moment of "excitement" over Papias's chiliastic views. Perumalil, "Papias and Irenaeus," 335. Eusebius, however, was more calculating than he was petulant.

246. "δὲ τῇ ἑαυτοῦ γραφῇ παγαδίδωσιν Ἀριστίωνος . . . τῶν τοῦ κυρίου λόγων διηγήσεις" Holmes, *Apostolic Fathers*, 3rd ed., 738.

disciple of Jesus in the same manner as the original twelve apostles,[247] had recorded notes on the things he heard Jesus say or the things he saw him accomplish. Whether these notes became source material for any of the four canonical Gospels is purely speculative.[248] The salient point is that one should not assume that Aristion had only provided oral material for Papias's *Exposition*.

Eusebius characterized Aristion's material as "accounts" or "narratives," while he referred to the material provided by the elder John as "traditions" (παραδόσεις). There is significance in this distinction. "Traditions" in first-century Jewish and Christian communities bore the weight of authoritative practice and belief (Acts 15:6–30; 1 Cor 11:2), while "accounts" spoke of narratives and historical events (Luke 1:1). It is intriguing that Eusebius characterized material from "the elder" John as "traditions," while Aristion, who apparently was not an elder but was an eyewitness of the life of Jesus, only provided "accounts" about Jesus. Once again, this distinction in the descriptions of these materials lends weight to the argument that Papias's reference to John as "the elder" was not simply a reference to him as being "the Old Man John,"[249] but to his official title, which spoke to his recognized authority for protecting and transmitting official church dogma and practices.

This is not to say that in the eyes of Papias Aristion's narratives were not viewed as valuable, for clearly they were since they preserved "sayings" of Jesus. Any such accounts to the early church would have been highly valued. Eusebius, however, did not refer to them as "oracles" but simply as "words" (λόγων). A possible reason for this could be that by the time Eusebius wrote, all the words of Jesus were viewed as canonical since they were believed to be the words of God, whether they were prophetic, didactic, or simply conversational. We can only assume that since Papias included them in his exposition of the Lord's *oracles*, (i.e., the divine utterances of Jesus) they were viewed as authoritative; consequently, they were important to Papias's authorial purposes.

247. He did not, however, share their status as "apostles."

248. As stated in the introduction, this book will not explore the subject of "Q" material.

249. Kleist, *Papias*, 111.

PAPIAS, THE ELDER, AND THE GOSPEL OF MARK

Eusebius, in the last half of section 14 through section 15, left the subject of Papias's many references to the materials provided by Aristion and the elder John in order to focus upon a "tradition" preserved by Papias that was of the utmost importance to Eusebius since it spoke about the origin and source of the Gospel of Mark. Eusebius provided in this section an actual quote of Papias containing information from the source he referred to as "the Elder." It was Eusebius's position that this individual was his infamous "John the elder" and not the apostle John. Since Eusebius's case for this person was based upon the weakest of exegesis and the thinnest of evidence it is concluded that this "elder" was in fact the John who was a follower of Jesus and a son of Zebedee. Eusebius referred to this quote as "a tradition" (παράδοσιν), implying that he viewed this information from John as an issue of official church belief and not simply an opinion or hearsay. An important question concerning Eusebius's characterization of this quote is whether Papias or the apostle John also referred to it as a "tradition." Eusebius's reference to this quote as a "tradition" is currently the only evidence available for answering this question; therefore, one cannot be certain as to how Papias or the apostle John viewed and/or labeled this explanation of the origin of Mark's Gospel.

Section 15 may be the most discussed patristic quote concerning the origin of Mark's composition on the life and teachings of Jesus Christ.[250] Regardless of all that has been speculated about this quote, Eusebius, having been familiar with *Exposition*, was of the opinion that it referred to the canonical Gospel of Mark.[251] Holmes's translation states that Mark had become Peter's "interpreter" (ἑρμηνευτής).[252] Lawlor understood this term to mean that Mark was Peter's "translator" as he preached in his native Aramaic tongue to Greek audiences.[253] A lot has been made about the pos-

---

250. Rigg, "Papias on Mark," 161.

251. Eusebius *Ecc. Hist.* II.15.1; III.34.6; III.39.14 (LCL 153:143, 251, 297). See also fragment 3, p. 114.

252. Holmes, *Apostolic Fathers*, 3rd ed., 738–39.

253. Lawlor, "Eusebius on Papias," 200. Schoedel also translated ἑρμηνευτής as "translator." Schoedel, *The Fragments*, 106, as did Ehrman. *Papias and Quadratus* (LCL 25:103). Bauckham believed that since Peter probably spoke Greek that Papias meant Mark had translated Peter's Greek oral messages into Greek literature. Bauckham, *The Eyewitnesses*, 205–7. In the Greek this sentence is: "Μάρκος μέν ἑρμηνευτής Πέτρου γενόμενος, ὅσα ἐμνημόνευσεν, ἀκριβῶς ἔγραψεν." Holmes, *Apostolic Fathers*, 3rd ed., 738. This clause is literally translated as, "Mark, indeed having been the translator (or interpreter) of Peter, whatsoever he remembered he wrote accurately." The initial clause

sible range of meanings for this word. The two main possibilities seem to be either "interpreter" or "translator." Whether one or the other is the correct interpretation depends upon the context. Some scholars have at times pitted one against the other when dealing with this issue.[254] However, given the context of this quotation and the dynamic of Mark's relationship with the apostle Peter, both meanings may apply, for the biblical record (1 Pet 5:13) and the church's history state that the two were closely associated. Concerning their relationship, Eusebius, depending upon this quote and the traditions of Papias, Irenaeus, and others, recorded that Mark was Peter's "follower" (ἀκόλουθον), meaning his association with Peter was not incidental, but rather that Peter was Mark's mentor.[255] Mark, consequently, had ample opportunity to hear Peter's preaching, as well as his personal recollections (both formally and informally), about the things accomplished and taught by Jesus. Therefore, since it is highly probable that he repeatedly aided Peter in translating his messages into Greek (whether they were Peter's oral messages or his written narratives), as his personal disciple one could be assured that Mark often discussed with Peter his precise meanings so that he could accurately translate Peter's messages for his Greek audiences. Given the dynamic of their relationship, it is not unrea-

---

(ἑρμηνευτὴς Πέτρου γενόμενος) appears to speak of a period prior to the composition of Mark's Gospel, although this is certainly debatable. See Baum, "Der Presbyter des Papias," 22–23. Baum argued that Mark "interpreted" Peter's sermons that Peter had preserved in Greek (page 35). However, Baum too narrowly restricted the temporal aspect between aorist participles, as well as too narrowly defined the range of nuances that are implied by the word "ἑρμηνευτής." For a more thorough range of meanings of this word see LSJ, s.v. "ἑρμηνεία." It is the position of this author to interpret this clause as antecedent to the action of the verb, with the aorist participle also having a causal force. This would mean that before Mark composed his Gospel he had functioned as Peter's translator and/or his interpreter. This fits the context well since it is not uncommon for one who functions as a translator for an audience to have to make interpretive decisions concerning the exact meaning of the speaker. Whether one takes Bauckham's or Baum's view, or an alternative, the witness of Papias and Eusebius is that Mark was a close associate of Peter and familiar with his messages.

254. Baum, "Der Presbyter des Papias," 22–25, 35.

255. See also fragment 3, p. 114. Rigg, relying upon Zahn, believed Mark may not have associated with Peter for an "entire year." Rigg, "Papias on Mark," 168. Regardless what some scholars may conjecture about the length of their relationship, Irenaeus stated that Mark was Peter's "disciple," see Eusebius *Ecc. Hist.* V.5.3 (LCL 153: 455); while Clement of Alexandria also confirmed that Mark had been a follower of Peter; ibid., VI.14.6 (LCL 265: 49). Consequently, there is no evidence to imply that Mark was only incidentally associated with the apostle Peter. Given that the earliest records of the church state that Peter mentored Mark, if one is inclined to assume anything, it should be that Mark was a close associate of this leading apostle.

sonable to believe that over time Mark not only became an excellent witness and "translator" of Peter's sermons, but also an excellent "interpreter" of his exact meanings. The context of Papias's quote, therefore, allows for ἑρμηνευτής to be translated as either "interpreter" or "translator" without demanding that one interpretation exclude the other. Nevertheless, given Papias's use of this word elsewhere in his preface and the fact that one must chose one or the other, "translator" is hereby preferred.

Papias also stated that the elder (i.e., the apostle John) commented that Mark accurately recorded the data he remembered from Peter's reminiscences. The significance of this sentence and its historical value should not be overlooked. Papias stated that Mark had accurately recorded what he learned from the apostle Peter, who was unquestionably one of Jesus' foremost disciples. Mark was not, therefore, "creating" or molding a message, nor was he developing his own "macro" theology for his audience, but rather he remembered and recorded via Peter's reminiscences Peter's own the eyewitness testimonials of the deeds and teachings of his mentor, Jesus Christ. This severely undermines several of the tenets that radical form critics employ to formulate their conclusions concerning the origins of Gospel narratives. Stein wrote concerning to the practices of these critics and the origins of the canonical Gospels that "For some form critics, however, a *non sequitur* often takes place that assumes that the *Sitz im Leben* that preserved and molded the gospel traditions also gave them their birth. As a result, the needs of the early church are seen not only as the preserver but also as the creator of the traditions. The tradition was not only *to* the church and *for* the church but also *from* the church. . . . Upon closer examination, there seems to be little objective evidence to support such a view."[256]

Papias's quote of the apostle John testifies that the canonical Gospel of Mark was not the culmination of messages developed by separate Christian communities created to meet their specific felt needs, which later evolved through serial redactions into a single literary composition. Instead, it is the product of a translator who was a dedicated student of the apostle Peter who often interacted with him with respect to his messages and their exact meanings. As Mansfeld stated, "So, according to Papias, Peter's oral teaching in Hebrew (or Aramaic) is available in Mark's accurate Greek translation in writing."[257] As a result of Mark's relationship with Peter, and because of the hunger of Christians in a particular city (Rome?),

---

256. Stein, *Synoptic Gospels*, 185.
257. Mansfeld, "Galen, Papias," 326.

Mark acquiesced to their request and composed his Gospel so that they would have an accurate permanent record of the life and teachings of Jesus. Consequently, Papias testified concerning this initial clause that he heard the apostle John say that Mark, who had been Peter's translator, accurately wrote down what he remembered Peter to have communicated during his ministry abroad.

THE TAXING QUESTION OF MARK'S ORDER

While Papias's source was confident about the origin of Mark's Gospel, he admitted that there were questions regarding its arrangement.[258] He confessed that Mark accurately wrote the things he remembered, although not with "τάξει."[259] As with most words found in Papias's preface, what exactly he meant by this word has been greatly discussed. Rigg was of the opinion that τάξει should be amended to τάχυς, meaning that Mark

258. It should be noted that this description of Mark's Gospel comes from the apostle John through Papias. More precisely, unless one is inclined to completely discount this record, this witness is not of Papias's own invention. It is also highly likely that Papias was in complete agreement with this tradition, or why else would he have submitted it in defense of Mark's effort? Bauckham had doubts about Papias's statements, writing, "To be sure, we cannot easily suppose that Papias quotes the words of the Elder *verbatim*. After all he does not report what the Elder said on a specific occasion, but what the Elder 'used to say on this topic. . . .' We cannot tell how far he has attributed to the Elder his own glosses on what the Elder said." Bauckham, *The Eyewitnesses*, 204. Kleist actually translated τάξει as "verbatim." Kleist, *Papias*, 115, 207–8. In a previous article he translated this word as "completeness." Kleist, "Rereading Papias," 14–16. Rigg believed that Papias's "old age" had undermined his ability to read his "rough notes" or to communicate effectively with his amanuensis. Rigg, "Papias on Mark," 172. Schoedel theorized that the literary style of Papias's preface and his quote of John are the same, which meant that Papias had "reworked" what he had received from the Elder. Consequently, it is impossible "to distinguish between Papias and his source." Schoedel, *The Fragments*, 106. Such suspicions are unwarranted. Papias claimed he had *remembered well* the things he learned from his instructors, i.e., the "elders." One may also infer from what Papias wrote that this tradition concerning the source of Mark's Gospel was something the apostle John was in the habit of stating (ἔλεγε being translated as a habitual imperfect, which is consistent with Bauckham's reading). Consequently, while Papias may not have quoted the apostle John "verbatim," there is no reason to believe that he did not accurately record the precise meaning of the apostle John. Lastly, Papias would not be the first student whose personal writing style in some ways mimicked the mentor that he so respectfully admired.

259. The actual clause in Greek is "ἀκριβῶς ἔγραψεν, οὐ μέντοι τάξει." Holmes, *Apostolic Fathers*, 3rd ed., 738. Schoedel translated τάξει as "order." Schoedel, *The Fragments*, 106.

accurately wrote what he remembered, although not "hastily."[260] Textual evidence supporting Rigg's theory does not exist; therefore, his position is based upon an argument from silence. He also failed to explain the presence and emphasis of other cognates of τάξει found elsewhere in Papias's writings.[261] F. H. Colson argued that in Papias's context τάξει does not refer to a lack of chronology in Mark's Gospel, but its apparent lack of good rhetorical orderliness.[262] Arthur Wright in response to Colson contended that because Mark's Gospel has rhetorically acceptable style Papias must have been addressing Mark's poor chronology.[263] Alistair Stewart-Sykes understood Papias's reference to τάξει to mean *any* formal "arrangement" whether rhetorical or chronological; consequently, the apostle John stated that Mark had not employed any particular style at all.[264] The positions of Colson, Wright, and Stewart-Sykes are all well defended, and any one of them may be more accurate than the others.

The problem with these interpretations is that we lack the specific context from which the charge(s) against Mark's writings were fired. We only know the vocabulary of the criticism, and not the actual critics. Moreover, when dealing with this question, the issue itself becomes confusing because some modern scholars at times project their own appreciation for Mark's work into the fray that surrounded his Gospel during the late first century. For example, Wright felt that "Mark's Gospel in my opinion is by no means badly arranged."[265] Similarly, Rigg asserted that "Mark's account of the Gospel has order. In my opinion, it discovers a magnificently orderly account."[266] The fact of the matter is that one does not know who criticized Mark's Gospel and why it failed to meet their expectation(s); consequently, feelings of modern scholars about Mark's effort are of no real benefit to understanding criticisms originating from the first century. Additionally, it is not even clear that these first-century critics were entirely reasonable. The fact that so many appreciated this Gospel (both in this century and the first) may suggest that these critics were either educational elitist or possibly others who were simply antagonistic toward Peter's message.

---

260. Rigg, "Papias on Mark," 161, 171.

261. See section 3 and second half of section 15 of Eusebius *Ecc. Hist.* III.39.

262. Colson, "Τάξει," 63; as did Kürzinger. Kürzinger, *Papias*, 49.

263. Wright, "Τάξει in Papias," 299.

264. Stewart-Sykes, "Τάξει Again," 490.

265. Wright, "Τάξει in Papias," 299.

266. Rigg, "Papias on Mark," 170.

Consequently, there may have been little chance that Mark could have written anything that would have met with their approval.

It is also possible that Mark composed his Gospel without giving any real thought of satisfying the literary critics of his day, or of any who would eventually arise in the centuries to follow. The historical record explaining the origin of his Gospel suggests that it was composed for the church's encouragement and not for the satisfaction of literary elitists. In other words, Mark's Gospel was an "in-house" narrative for the common worshiper; it was not composed with a concern for a broader audience, such as the general public.[267] However, as Mark's Gospel began to be exposed to the public at large there were naturally those who marginalized it for its perceived deficiencies, or possibly for its poor chronology,[268] while others for its apparent lack of good rhetorical style, or maybe all of the above. Mark may have received such poor reviews because what he valued (i.e., faithfulness to Peter's eyewitness testimonies and sermons) was not greatly appreciated by rhetoricians or literary critics. Conversely, the things they may have highly valued (e.g., a birth narrative and an explanation of Jesus' education and training) were conspicuously absent in his Gospel. Wolfram Kinzig wrote concerning the criticism of outsiders towards early Christian literature that

> Christianity, although an off-shoot of Palestinian Judaism, began to flourish in a Greek-speaking environment in which a thorough knowledge of the rules of classical rhetoric formed part of a good education. . . . [T]he early Christians, driven by a missionary zeal quite unknown in antiquity, were soon confronted with the problem as to how to communicate their religious message to a target audience educated according to the standards and norms of Greek *paideia*. The style of the writings in which this message was contained formed part of this problem. As soon as cultured pagans became aware of the new sect trying to seek converts from among their midst they pointed out, not without some malice, that the writings on which the Christians based their claim for religious superiority were written in the simple and unrefined Greek of provincial fisherman, peasants and tax collectors and did not conform to the rules of what was generally recognized as polished style. This was not, however, a problem which the Greek-speaking Christians

267. Stewart-Sykes suggested that these criticisms may have come from within the church. Stewart-Sykes, "Τάξει Again," 488.

268. Colson provides a helpful list of things that may have been expected of ancient histories and/or biographies. Colson, "Τάξει," 67.

were only confronted with from outside. The more Christian- ity climbed the social ladder, the more its propagandists, most of whom had by now themselves received a classical education, became aware of the rhetorical shortcomings of the gospel mes- sage. Many authors admitted the linguistic and stylistic flaws . . . but argued that in order to make converts the new religion had to use a simple style comprehensible to everybody. In ad- dition they insisted that at the heart of the Christian message lay truth, not stylistic beauty, and that it was precisely this truth in all its simplicity that gave the Christian message its power of persuasion.[269]

Consequently, while there are good reasons to research the possibilities of what Mark's critics may have meant, certitude about the actual criticisms leveled against his Gospel or their validity is impossible. What one can be certain about in general is that by the late first century the Gospel of Mark came under fire for its lack of a "proper" arrangement.[270] In response to these criticisms, he was defended by the apostle John and Papias on the grounds that his Gospel was not composed in order to satisfy the particu- lar requirements of these critics; instead, it was written as a simple record of the life and teachings of Jesus Christ from the eyewitness reminiscences of one of his most devoted followers, the apostle Peter. This testimony from Papias is consistent with other accounts concerning the origin of the Second Gospel, accounts that indicate it was written for the benefit of the church rather than for rhetorical or philosophical elitists. Consequently, τάξει is translated as "arrangement," which seems to respect the spectrum of this word's possible meanings.

Papias's source stated that Mark's composition contained accounts "of the things either said or done by Christ."[271] This description of the contents of Mark's Gospel indicates that his work was not simply a compilation of loose notes about the teachings of Jesus, but an account that included both his teachings and his activities. So while Mark had not composed what some would view as a properly arranged literary work, he did attempt to give a comprehensive narrative of Jesus' ministry. It is at this point that the apostle John explained the reason for the limitations of Mark's efforts. He

269. Kinzig, "The Greek Christian Writers," 634–35.

270. Bauckham preferred "orderly" or "coherent arrangement." Bauckham, *The Eyewitnesses*, 220–21.

271. Holmes, *Apostolic Fathers*, 3rd ed., 739. There is a textual question concerning whether the text should read "Christ" or "Lord." For the manuscript evidence see ibid., 738. The textual support for both is equally divided.

was limited because he had personally never heard or followed the Lord; consequently, he was in no position to elaborate upon the activities and teachings of Jesus. He instead relied almost exclusively upon eyewitness testimonials from the apostle Peter. Such a statement suggests that Mark was not considered the creator of Petrine theology as found in the Second Gospel, but rather he was Peter's translator, who felt compelled to faithfully record Peter's meanings.

The incidental statement made by the apostle John that Mark had "neither heard the Lord nor followed him" is significant since it is would be the boldest of deceptions to say that Peter was the source of the Second Gospel if Mark was known to have been more than its simple translator and editor. If the apostle John, or Eusebius's "John the elder," or the late first-century church had known that Mark was the driving force behind the theological content contained in his Gospel then what possible purpose could such a statement serve? Was it the scheme of the late first-century church to attribute to Peter what it rightfully knew to be from the hand of Mark? Moreover, if Mark's Gospel suffered from a lack of credibility then what possible remedy could be produced by such an ill conceived statement that only further distanced Mark from Jesus? If one were to conspire on how to make Mark's effort less credible, then one could have hardly invented a more damning statement then the one made by the apostle John and Papias. It would have been far easier to produce a more reasonable and acceptable deception, such as simply stating that Mark himself had in fact been a distant follower of Jesus. But that is not what Papias documented for his audience.

Regardless of the perceived deficiencies reported by Papias concerning the origin of Mark's Gospel, it is clear that the primary concern of the early church was for an honest explanation of the origin and source of the Gospel according to Mark, nothing more and nothing less. Consequently, Papias recorded that the apostle John believed that Mark had faithfully recorded the heart and body of the gospel message that he received from his mentor, the apostle Peter. Additionally, as will become increasingly evident, he also believed that Mark had exerted little influence upon the collective body of Peter's reminiscences.[272] Mark refrained from inappropriately influencing the body and central thesis of Peter's messages precisely because he had not followed Jesus. Bauckham wrote concerning Mark's fidelity to Peter that "It was because Mark was not himself an eyewitness of the history of Jesus that he was unable to supply the order that Peter had failed to give to his material. . . . Mark should not be criticized

---

272. Contrary to Kümmel's conjectures. Kümmel, *Introduction*, 64–68.

for having confined himself to translating and recording Peter's teaching as accurately and completely as possible. He was right not to attempt an ordering of the material that, not being an eyewitness himself, he could not have achieved satisfactorily."[273] Regrettably, it was his faithfulness to his mentor and his caution to not contaminate Peter's testimonials that, for some critics of Papias's day, inevitably detracted from Mark's effort because, in their "educated" opinion, it resulted in a less than acceptable literary product.

THE NATURE OF *CHREIAI*

Having addressed the literary purpose and style of Mark's Gospel, Papias's source explained Peter's use of Jesus' words, stating that Peter "adapted his teachings as needed."[274] Bauckham appropriately recognized the possible inference that such a translation could produce, writing that "read in this way, Papias's words might be thought in surprising agreement with the approach to the study of the Gospels known as form criticism."[275] Given the research on chreia in the last fifty years, however, translating this word to read "as needed" or "as 'according to needs'" has now been largely abandoned."[276] Bauckham also recognized concerning its range of meanings that "it is worth pointing out that the term chreia evidently covered quite a wide range of types of content. On the basis of Theon's examples, it is possible to classify chreiai as brief narratives containing only actions, as brief narratives containing only sayings, and mixed types containing both actions and sayings."[277]

273. Bauckham, *The Eyewitnesses*, 221. See pages 202–39 for a more a thorough explanation of Mark's fidelity to Peter's message and its impact upon the Second Gospel.

274. Holmes, *Apostolic Fathers*, 3rd ed., 738–39. The Greek clause is ὅς πρὸς τὰς χρείας ἐποιεῖτο τὰς διδασκαλίας. It is noted that ἐποιεῖτο is the imperfect of ποιέω, and is interpreted as a customary or habitual imperfect.

275. Bauckham, *The Eyewitnesses*, 214.

276. Ibid., 215. R. O. P. Taylor is considered to be responsible for bringing to the fore the critical research concerning the meaning of chreia in Hellenistic rhetorical contexts. Taylor, *Groundwork*, 75–90. Concerning chreia Kürzinger confidently asserted that "auf jeden Fall bestätigen die Untersuchungen, daß χρεία ein in der hellenistischen Rhetorik viel gebrauchter Terminus technicus ist." Kürzinger, *Papias*, 52. His discussion addressed many of the same examples put forth by Taylor. Schoedel's transliteration/translation of chreia as "*chria*-form" is not very helpful. Schoedel, *The Fragments*, 107. Kleist without explanation apparently translated chreia as "the Lord's ministry." Kleist, *Papias*, 118.

277. Bauckham, *The Eyewitnesses*, 215–16.

A book by Ronald F. Hock and Edward N. O'Neil, titled *The Chreia in Ancient Rhetoric*, is also extremely helpful for gaining a better understanding of what Papias may have meant by this term. Hock defined a chreia as "a saying or action that is expressed concisely, attributed to a character, and regarded as useful for living."[278] He noted, in a fashion similar to Bauckham, that there were many different types and subsets of chreiai, and that they were often employed in many different formal educational contexts as well as for rhetorical training. He explained that at "times *chreiai* depict philosophers in typical situations, such as chiding students, attacking vices, responding to critics, debating with one another, and reflecting on the philosophical life."[279] One could argue that such a description aptly fits many of the pericopes about Jesus in the Gospel of Mark.[280] Hock actually provided Luke 19:45–46 as an example of a chreia, which he translated as, "Jesus, on entering the Temple, began to evict the sellers and said to them: 'It is written, My house shall be a house of prayer, but you have made it a cave for brigands.'"[281] When compared to the apostle John's description of Peter's preaching practice, Hock's example is helpful for gaining a clearer understanding of Peter's homiletical practices. It appears that Peter was not in the habit of giving sermons "according to the needs" of his audiences, but rather his teachings were provided as "concise reminiscences" of the words and actions of Jesus.[282] More specifically, Peter's homiletical focus was not so much upon the varied contexts of his many different audiences, but rather upon proclaiming and explaining the teachings and deeds of Jesus.[283] Such an approach to Jesus' words is akin to what many evangelicals commonly refer to as "expository preaching." The obviously difference, however, is that instead of Peter teaching about the sayings

278. Hock, "General Introduction," 26. By the word "character" Hock was not arguing that the individual or event being described was fictional. Hock suggested that a difference between "reminiscences" and "chreiai" is that of "length," with reminiscences being longer. Hock briefly described *chreia* as "a concise and praiseworthy reminiscence about some character," see ibid., 9.

279. Ibid., 4.

280. Taylor, *Groundwork*, 81.

281. Hock, "General Introduction," 24.

282. Lake translated this chreia as "as necessity demanded." Eusebius *Ecc. Hist.* III.25.15 (LCL 153:297). Ehrman translated it as "for the needs at hand." *Papias and Quadratus* (LCL 25:103). Neither translations seems accurate since they raise more questions than they answer.

283. Black suggested that given the context of Papias's statement about Mark, that chreia and λόγια were "virtually synonymous expressions." Black, "Rhetorical Terminology," 34.

and deeds of Jesus from a pericope found in the Gospel narratives, he exclusively proclaimed the supremacy of Jesus as Savior and Lord of the world from his personal eyewitness memories of what Jesus actually said and did. The salient point, therefore, concerning Papias's witness to Peter's approach to preaching is that it was his concern to explain the teachings and deeds of Jesus rather than worrying about meeting the felt needs of his audiences.[284] And it was this bedrock of chreiai or "praiseworthy reminiscences" of the apostle Peter from which the Gospel of Mark was mined.

Papias's source went on to say that initially it was not Peter's intention to coalesce his many sermons into one comprehensive and orderly arrangement (σύνταξιν). Why he never thought of it one can only speculate. The historical record concerning the genesis of Mark's Gospel also indicates that it was not the brainchild of Mark. Instead, this idea originated with members of a church in Rome,[285] who realized that Peter's absence had or would leave them without a trustworthy record of the Lord's activities and "oracles" (λογίων).[286] Upon realizing this potentially precarious situation they drafted Mark into service in order to meet their pressing need for a permanent record of the personal reminiscences from the apostle Peter on the life and teachings of Jesus Christ.

MARK'S INFLUENCE UPON THE SECOND GOSPEL

Given this situation, Papias's source defended Mark from any wrong doing, primarily because Mark, having been Peter's "follower" and "interpreter," was supremely qualified to compose just such a literary narrative. Moreover, because of Mark's respect for his mentor and his value for historical integrity, he accurately coalesced Peter's accounts of the words and

284. Taylor explained that in order for chreias to be effective it was important to "establish the prestige of the person, in order to give authority to the words of the example." He believed this is exactly what one observed in the preface to Mark's Gospel, chapter 1:1–11. Taylor, *Groundwork*, 81.

285. See fragment 3, p. 114.

286. There is a textual variant that witnesses to "λόγων," which is translated as "sayings," which is the translation Holmes provided. Holmes, *Apostolic Fathers*, 3rd ed., 740–41; as did Ehrman. *Papias and Quadratus* (LCL 25:103). The majority of texts, however, witness to λογίων as being original. Lake correctly translated this word as "oracles." Eusebius *Ecc. Hist.* III.39.15 (LCL 153: 297); as did Schoedel. Schoedel, *The Fragments*, 107. Bauckham translated this entire clause as "short reports of what the Lord said and did." He believed this best paralleled the preceding phrase "the things either said or done by the Lord." Bauckham, *The Eyewitnesses*, 214. The structure of these clauses, however, gives no indication that there was any attempt at parallelism.

deeds of Jesus into what he considered to be a suitable narrative given his self-imposed limitations. Try as he might, however, it was impossible for Mark to completely erase his fingerprint from this composition, for Papias's source stated that Mark "did nothing wrong in writing down some things as he remembered them."[287] Terence Y. Mullins wrote an article on the history of how this clause has been interpreted and what Papias meant by the word "some" (ἔνια).[288] Mullins correctly observed that ἔνια "cannot indicate an extended narrative the size of the Second Gospel," but that it must refer to a smaller portion of a larger whole.[289] Consequently, Mullins offered that Mark wrote only a few things from his memory with respect to Peter's accounts, but the majority of what he wrote was from material written by Peter that Mark had translated, explaining that "the construction of the opening sentence permits the interpretation that Mark first translated Peter's written reminiscences and then added to them what he remembered from Peter's oral teaching."[290] This is very similar to Bauckham's theory, the major difference being that Bauckham believed that the majority of Mark's Gospel came from Mark recording Peter's dictations, while afterwards Mark added a few additional things that he remembered from Peter messages.[291] The interpretations of Mullins and Bauckham are certainly possible, and both rightly observed that the mentioning of "some things" referred to Mark's input (regardless of what it may or may not have been) and not that of Peter's.[292] As to the exact extent of Mark's influence upon Peter's material, Papias's source was very specific, stating that it was Mark's greatest concern not to leave out (παραλιπεῖν) any essential material or falsify (i.e., redact with the purpose of altering inherent meanings) anything which he had received from Peter.[293] Consequently, the

287. Holmes, *Apostolic Fathers,* 3rd ed., 741. Papias's defense of Mark's effort hardly suggests Zahn's inference that Papias was "dissatisfied with the information supplied by the Gospel literature already in existence." Zahn, *Introduction,* 2:441. That Papias was interested in correctly interpreting such literature can hardly be doubted, that is not to say, however, that he viewed it as insufficient or flawed.

288. Mullins, "Papias," 216–24.

289. Ibid., 219.

290. Ibid., 224, see also page 222. Schoedel believed "some" referred to some "oracles" from Jesus since Mark's Gospel, as compared to Matthew's, contained fewer of them. Schoedel, *The Fragments,* 108.

291. For a detailed explanation see Bauckham, *The Eyewitnesses,* 210–21.

292. Contrary to Zahn's interpretation which argued that "some" referred to Peter's input upon the Second Gospel. Zahn, *Introduction,* 2:440.

293. The text reads, "ἑνὸς γὰρ ἐποιήσατο πρόνοιαν," which is translated as "He made (his) one concern." Holmes, *Apostolic Fathers,* 3rd ed., 740–41.

testimony of Papias and his source was that Mark did not feel the liberty to consider the material he preserved his own; therefore, he was careful not to inappropriately influence its content or meaning. He simply desired to be a window through which Peter's reminiscences may pass.

If Papias's preservation of the apostle John's testimony about Mark's influence upon the composition of his Gospel is accurate, then what did he mean by the term "some things"? If Mark drew from a reservoir of Peter's sermons, testimonials, and reminiscences in order to produce a narrative of the life and teachings of Jesus that was a comprehensive literary record, then certainly to some degree Mark functioned as an editor. As such he would have assembled Peter's accounts in some type of order, which he appears to have done; first following the basic chronology of Jesus' life, while at times appearing to assemble materials thematically.[294] Such editorial work would necessarily involve transitional statements, which are commonly referred to as Markan seams and summary statements.[295] Whether Mark significantly influenced his Gospel is a debate that is largely driven from perspective. Papias's source believed that Mark's influence was minimal; many scholars today, however, believe Mark's input was systemic and significant. Regardless of one's perspective, Papias's source believed that Mark had only provided "some things" from his memory. Since his source had previously stated that Mark accurately wrote down everything he remembered Peter to have communicated, one can infer from this second statement that as Mark arranged his materials he was careful that his editorial decisions did not substantively change what he remembered of Peter messages on the life of Jesus. At times, however, the placement of certain materials within his Gospel was by necessity Mark's own decisions. This reading is consistent with Papias's source who also asserted that Mark had accurately written everything he remembered from Peter, although not in order (τάξει, i.e., a strict chronology or "proper" arrangement), which Mark could not do because Peter had not provided an order for him. Consequently, some of the placement of events and teachings of Jesus in the Second Gospel was of Mark's design, and because this was the extent of Mark's input he was free from any charge of omission or deception.[296]

294. For an example of a possible Markan thematic arrangement see the collection of Jesus' parables in Mark 4.1–33.

295. For a more thorough treatment of Mark's editorial influence upon his Gospel see Stein, *Synoptic Gospels*, 76–94, 262–72.

296. Kleist suggested a similar theory concerning the meaning of what "some things" referred to, but he failed to elaborate more thoroughly upon it since it was not completely compatible with the theory he held; see Kleist, "Rereading Papias," 9–10.

Regardless of what Papias's source believed, from the late first century until today there is great debate surrounding Mark's success in minimizing his influence upon the Second Gospel. The apostle John, however, was unimpressed with this controversy and held that Mark was "sinless" (οὐδεν ἥμαρτε) in the matter.[297]

Regrettably, section 15 contains the entirety of Eusebius's Papian fragment about the origin of the Gospel of Mark from the lips of Papias's elder. Some conclude that this elder was Eusebius's "John the elder," since Eusebius stated that Papias claimed to not only have heard him, but also frequently mentioned him as his source for many of the traditions Papias preserved.[298] In all probability, however, this elder was not Eusebius's mythical John of Ephesus but the apostle John. Consequently, Papias recorded John's testimony that the Gospel of Mark was born out a desire to preserve the reminiscences and messages of the apostle Peter. Other records preserved by Eusebius indicated that Mark was pressed into this service by a specific community of believers who resided in Rome.[299] It was this community's desire to have an accurate record of Peter's testimonials of Jesus so that they might know with certitude the accomplishments and teachings of their savior. In order to secure such a literary narrative they pressed into service one who had the ability and humility to accurately record what he remembered from Peter's repetitive proclamations concerning his eyewitness accountings of Jesus' deeds and message concerning the kingdom of God. These were messages that Mark had translated and interpreted into fluent Greek as Peter preached the gospel of Jesus Christ to Greek audiences in Asia Minor, and inevitably in the heart of the Empire itself.

MATTHEW'S INITIAL GOSPEL

Having explained Papias's witness to the origin and composition of the Gospel of Mark, Eusebius next turned his attention to Papias's preservation of the early church's tradition concerning the initial Gospel of Matthew.[300] It should be noted that Eusebius separated Papias's comments about the

297. Holmes, *Apostolic Fathers,* 3rd ed., 740.

298. See section 7.

299. Eusebius *Ecc. Hist.* II.14–15 (LCL 153:141–45).

300. Matthew's Hebraic Gospel is referred to as his "initial" composition or Gospel narrative because to date there is no proof that he did not also compose the canonical Gospel of Matthew.

Gospels of Mark and Matthew with his own transitional statement. Given the μέν construction introducing the statements describing the works of these two authors it seems reasonable to conclude that these traditions were found in close proximity to one another. Moreover, since they discuss the origins of the oracles (τὰ λόγια) of the Lord it seems safe to assume that they were found relatively early in Papias's five-volume work.[301] This is not to conjecture that the chronology of these two statements reflects the order in which these two Gospels were composed. Consequently, one should not assume that Mark's Greek Gospel was written before Matthew's initial composition.[302]

Papias's source made only two important comments concerning Matthew's early literary effort. First, he claimed that Matthew's initial work was written in Aramaic or Hebrew (Ἑβραΐς διαλέκτῳ); and secondly, Matthew composed his narrative in an orderly arrangement (συνετάξατο).[303] As Schoedel aptly wrote concerning the format of Matthew's composition, "Matthew put together the *logia* in a systematic and (to Papias) more

301. About the relationship of these two traditions Black wrote, "We cannot, therefore, be certain that the two statements were juxtaposed in this way by anyone other than Eusebius, nor can we assume (as many have done) that both are 'traditions' of 'the elder.'" Black, "Rhetorical Terminology," 32. Eusebius, however, deserves more credit than Black has given him. Even if the two fragments were books apart, Eusebius appears to have appropriately joined them thematically. Consequently, there is reasonable evidence to believe they came from the same source. Black is correct, however, that there is a possibility that they came from different sources.

302. While it is possible that Mark's Greek Gospel was written before Matthew's Hebraic Gospel, it seems more probable that Matthew wrote his Hebraic work first. However, without further data from the first century, certitude is not possible, for Eusebius's chronology may preserve the actual order in which the two Gospels were composed. However, Eusebius preserved a fragment from Origen's commentary on Matthew that indicated that Matthew's Hebraic Gospel was written before the Greek Gospels of Mark, Luke, and John. Origin as quoted by Eusebius, indicating that ". . . as having learnt by tradition concerning the four Gospels, which alone are unquestionable in the Church of God under heaven, that first was written that according to Matthew, who was once a taxcollector (*sic*) but afterwards an apostle of Jesus Christ, who published it for those who from Judaism came to believe, composed as it was in the Hebrew Language. Secondly, that according to Mark, who wrote it in accordance with Peter's instructions. . . ." Origen, however, made no reference to the canonical Greek Gospel of Matthew. Eusebius *Ecc. Hist.* VI.25.4 (LCL 265:75).

303. There is a textual variant with συνετάξατο, but being the majority witness it is preferred. Holmes, *Apostolic Fathers*, 3rd ed., 740. This verb is the aorist of συντάσσω, which is translated to mean "to put in order" or "to arrange, organize." This word is commonly interpreted to mean "to compose or compile a narrative or book" when used in the context of literary works; see LSJ, s.v. "συντάσσω."

satisfying way.["304] Schoedel also contended, with respect to Matthew's initial Gospel, that Papias was not referring to "a collection of OT oracles or a collection of sayings of Jesus like 'Q.'"[305] Trusting the testimony of his source, Papias also described the entirety of Matthew's Hebraic composition as "the oracles" (τὰ λόγια). This term, as suggested earlier, should be interpreted as referring to divine proclamations. It is assumed that by discussing these two works together, and because Mark and Matthew are most famous for composing Gospels, that Eusebius understood Matthew's *The Oracles* to be a Gospel narrative, and very possibly the actual title of Matthew's initial composition on the life and teachings of Jesus. If it was not Matthew's title for the work, then it must have been a title given by the first generation church, which implies much concerning their opinion of the work's value and importance.

Some contend that Matthew's initial Gospel was described as such simply because it contained many Old Testament quotes concerning Jesus' fulfillment of messianic promises. It is not likely that this description or title was given to this composition only because it contained Old Testament passages.[306] Since this work to some degree addressed the life and teachings of Jesus, it is probable that it also contained reminiscences of the sayings of Jesus. Consequently, the term oracles would also naturally apply to words uttered by Jesus. More importantly, because this composition was written in Aramaic it also would have been viewed as containing the actual words spoken by Jesus, that is his *ipsissima verba*. Such a work would have been highly valued by the Jerusalem church and Jewish believers. One might also infer from such a title, if it was in fact the title that he provided, that Matthew was actually affirming the divinity of Jesus, and thus, emphasizing the significance of his teachings. Certitude about this inference, however, is not possible without more Papian material.

The burning question for many scholars is what has happened to Matthew's Hebraic Gospel? Schoedel doubted it ever existed, arguing that Papias only meant "to underscore the reliability of his (major?) written

304. Schoedel, *The Fragments*, 110.

305. Ibid., 109. For a more thorough discussion of Matthew's Hebraic composition being associated with Q see Black, "Rhetorical Terminology," 34–38.

306. This is also a common assumption. Given that Matthew's canonical Gospel contains many Old Testament passages that the author believed were fulfilled by Jesus (Matt 1:22; 2:15, 17, 23; 4:14; 8:17; 12:17; 13:35; 21:4; 26:54, 56; 27:9), and the fact that the early church understood that the oracles of God were contained in the Old Testament, it is reasonable to concluded that Matthew's Hebraic composition, which Papias referred to as *The Oracles*, also contained some Old Testament passages.

sources by showing that they were based one way or the other on the language actually spoken by Jesus."[307] Papias's vocabulary and his distinction between Matthew's Hebraic Gospel and Mark's Greek Gospel makes his suggestion unlikely. Kürzinger believed that Matthew wrote his composition in a Jewish rhetorical style rather than in the Aramaic language.[308] Gundry, arriving at the same conclusion, argued that "'A Hebrew dialect,' then, does not imply that Matthew wrote in the Aramaic language. In other connections we should expect the conjunction of 'Hebrew' and 'dialect' to form a linguistic reference. But the stylistic contrast between Mark and Matthew cancels such an expectation here. . . . In describing Matthew, then, 'a Hebrew dialect' means a Hebrew way of presenting Jesus' messiahship . . . the contrast between Mark and Matthew has to do with literary style, not with linguistic form."[309]

This position is extremely attractive, for if true it would answer many questions concerning what is commonly referred to as the "Synoptic problem." This theory, however, is unpersuasive for many scholars. Schoedel, responding to particular assertion, observed that "it is true that the rhetoricians use (dialect) to mean 'style.' But the adjectives that go with it are terms like 'exalted,' 'poetic,' and 'one's own.'"[310] Thus, when the term διαλέκτῳ is used in connection with an ethnic form of speech it is translated as "language" and not style; consequently, very few accept Kürzinger's position.

Jerome at one time believed that Matthew's Hebraic Gospel existed in his day, for in *Illustrious Men* he wrote, "Matthew, also called Levi, apostle and aforetimes publican, composed a gospel of Christ at first published in Judea in Hebrew for the sake of those of the circumcision who believed, but this was afterwards translated in Greek though by what author is

---

307. Schoedel, *The Fragments*, 109–10.

308. Kürzinger wrote, "Und von diesen her kennt Papias wohl vor allem die Ἑβραΐς διαλέκτῳ, d.h. die dem Judentum eigentümlichen Stilund Darstellungsformen mit ihren besonderen Mitteln der Komposition und Gliederung . . . den Papias also vom griechischen AT her kennen mußte, erkennt er in der literarischen Art des Mt-Ev wieder." Kürzinger, *Papias*, 22. See pages 20–24 and 33–36 for a thorough discussion on this issue. Kürzinger's work is an insightful explanation of the rhetorical language employed by Papias. Among other things, his research provides support for the theory that Papias had achieved some formal level of Hellenistic education. Kürzinger's weakness, however, was his propensity to interpret everything Papias wrote through the lens of rhetorical criticism. Consequently, his arguments concerning the phase Ἑβραΐς διαλέκτῳ seems forced and unnatural.

309. Gundry, *Matthew*, 619–20.

310. Schoedel, *The Fragments*, 110.

uncertain. The Hebrew itself has been preserved until the present day in the library at Caesarea which Pamphilus so diligently gathered."[311] Timothy C. G. Thornton, however, has made a good case for the suggestion that Jerome was mistaken in his identification of this Aramaic work with Matthew's initial Gospel, which Jerome had only heard about as he wrote *Illustrious Men*. Jerome realized his mistake once he had the opportunity to actually interact with a manuscript of the Gospel in question. Thornton observed that later in his life Jerome attempted to distance himself from his earlier assertion, explaining, "Moreover he does not now himself claim that his Aramaic Gospel is the original Gospel written by Matthew but only asserts that 'most people' call it the original Gospel of Matthew."[312] Jerome's possible confusion about Matthew's Hebraic Gospel surviving to his day has little bearing on whether Matthew ever actually wrote a Gospel in Aramaic. The witness of Papias, who probably wrote early in the second century (ca. 110), is that it was tradition of the first-century church that the apostle John testified to the existence of a Hebraic Gospel that originated from the hand of the apostle Matthew.

While many modern scholars may be saddened at the loss of such a valuable composition, its existence may have caused far more problems for the first-century church. Eusebius's Papian fragment also preserves a cryptic statement from Papias's source stating that as Matthew's Hebraic Gospel was disseminated, "each person translated them as best as he could."[313] Such attempts at translation would certainly involve interpretive decisions by the translator. One can only imagine what meanings were spawned from Matthew's Hebraic Gospel by someone's faulty understanding of the Aramaic language. Augustine, writing near the end of the fourth century, bemoaned the fact that too many budding interpreters had attempted to translate biblical Greek texts into Latin.[314] It does not take much effort to imagine that what was true about the diversity of Latin translations in

311. Jerome *Illustrious Men* 3 (NPNF2 3:362).

312. Thornton, "Jerome and the 'Hebrew Gospel,'" 120

313. The actual Greek sentence is "ἡρμήνευσε δ' αὐτὰ ὡς ἦν δυνατὸς ἕκαστος." Holmes, *Apostolic Fathers*, 3rd ed., 740.

314. Augustine, *Teaching Christianity*, trans. Hill, 136. Just before this statement Augustine mentioned that there were only a few recognized translations of the Scriptures from Hebrew to Greek. Edmund Hill believed that Augustine was referring to Greek translations of the Hebrew Old Testament (see footnote 34 on page 163). Ironically, after his statement about these numerous Latin translations Augustine contended that "this state of affairs has been more of a help than a hindrance." Although recognizing Augustine's brilliance, his assessment seems overly optimistic.

Augustine's day was equally as true about interpretations from those who attempted to translate Matthew's Hebraic Gospel into Greek during the late first century, and Luke's preface seems to confirm this probability.[315] As Holmes has argued, "For all the confusion and uncertainty he engenders, Papias nevertheless clearly and forcefully reminds us that the written Gospels represent only a fraction of the material concerning the life and sayings of Jesus in circulation in the last half of the first and first half of the second centuries."[316] It may be that a diversity of faulty interpretations produced by poor translations of Matthew's Hebraic Gospel provided part of Papias's motivation to write his five-volume work, a work in which he attempted to exposit accurately the divine utterances of Jesus found in the canonical Gospels, as well as to explain other divine utterances that circulated in oral traditions.[317] These two brief statements comprise the whole of Eusebius's Papian fragment describing Matthew's Hebraic Gospel composition. While some are thankful for Eusebius's effort, most would prefer to have additional material, since this fragment produces an important question concerning the relationship between Matthew's Hebraic work and the canonical Gospel that also bears his name.[318] Regrettably, there is little evidence available today to answer this perplexing question. Regardless of how some may answer that question, the witness of Papias is that

315. Luke 1:1–2 states that "many (πολλοί) have undertaken to draw up an account of the things that have been fulfilled among us, just as they were handed down to us by those who from the first were eyewitnesses and servants of the word."

316. Holmes, *Apostolic Fathers*, 3rd ed., 723. Holmes also stated that "(2) even after gospels were written, oral tradition continued to circulate and to influence the written text." Such a statement implies that oral traditions influenced later redactions of the canonical Gospels, which is something that Papias and the apostle John "*clearly and forcefully*" did not suggest, nor is there weighty evidence to suggest this occurred with regularity concerning any literature of the New Testament. Instead, the apostle John's statements, springing the first century, suggest that he viewed Mark's Gospel as a finished composition originating exclusively from Mark's memory of Peter's reminiscences. A composition that he was careful to insure contained no significant omissions or falsifications. Neither Papias nor the apostle John suggested that after Mark completed his Gospel that it underwent repeated redactions based upon oral traditions. Such conjectures find no defense in the statements of Papias or the apostle John, and to suggest so is to promote a gross inaccuracy.

317. Kleist believed that Papias was "not satisfied with any of the Gospels" of his day, which lead him to seek out more complete material. Kleist, *Papias*, 111. A more comprehensive investigation of the Papian fragments suggests, however, that he was satisfied with the existing material, and that his purpose was to corroborate and explain that material more clearly.

318. The answer to this question goes well beyond the scope of this book.

Matthew composed in Aramaic a narrative about Jesus that Papias's source (most probably the apostle John) simply referred to as *The Oracles.*[319]

PAPIAS'S KNOWLEDGE OF CERTAIN EPISTLES

While Eusebius's Papian fragment about Matthew's Hebraic Gospel produces many questions about whether Papias knew the canonical Gospel of Matthew, Eusebius's next statement in section 17 about Papias's use of other canonical apostolic writings produces more certainty. Eusebius stated that Papias employed testimonies (μαρτυρίαις) from 1 John and 1 Peter. Eusebius wrote in *Ecclesiastical History* II.15.2 that Papias actually quoted 1 Peter 5:13 as proof that the author of the Gospel of Mark associated with Peter and that both were present in Rome when Peter composed his first epistle.[320] Possible confirmation that Papias quoted 1 John may be found in a fragment from Maximus the Confessor that stated that believers in the early church were called "children," which is a common term of endearment found in the Johannine epistles.[321] Eusebius, however, provided no examples of Papias's use of 1 John, which Eusebius believed to be an authentic Johannine epistle.[322] Eusebius's lack of Papian quotes of 1 John is understandable given his desire to disassociate the apostle John from Papias. If Eusebius was correct, however, about his admission that Papias employed passages of 1 John, and there appears to be little reason to doubt him, Eusebius via Papias's testimony may have provided the earliest reference to the canonical epistle of 1 John.[323] The fact that Papias quoted 1 John implies that he appreciated John's content in that epistle and that he felt it was beneficial for his authorial purposes for his *Exposition.* Since Eusebius did not provide an example of how Papias employed material from 1 John, one can only speculate as to what purpose John's material may have functioned in *Exposition.*[324] Regardless of such speculations,

---

319. Lightfoot believed that the canonical Gospel of Matthew already existed by the time Papias wrote his five volume work. Lightfoot, *Essays*, 169. His suggestion is certainly warranted, as Ehrman has aptly observed that Polycarp was also familiar with Matthew's canonical Greek Gospel. Polycarp, *To the Philippians* (LCL 24:329).

320. See the discussion on fragment 3, p. 114.

321. See the discussion on fragment 14, p. 230.

322. Eusebius *Ecc. Hist.* III.24.17 (LCL 153:255).

323. This depends upon one's dating of Papias's *Exposition* and Polycarp's letter to the Philippians.

324. Since Eusebius referred to Papias's quotes from 1 John as "testimonies" a reasonable conjecture would be that Papias may have employed passages such as 1 John 1:1–4; 2:25; 3:5, 7–8, 23; 4:21; 5:9–12.

Eusebius was confident that Papias had employed material from 1 John and 1 Peter. Consequently, Eusebius has provided sufficient evidence that these two epistles existed and were in circulation by the beginning of the second century.

PAPIAS AND THE PERICOPE ADULTERAE

Eusebius's last statement about material in *Exposition* concerned the *pericope adulterae*. Holmes placed John 7:53—8:11 as the fourth Papian fragment; however, he rightly questioned what version of this account Papias knew. Concerning the inclusion of this account he wrote,

> Fragment 4 is unique to Lightfoot's collection and calls for special comment. Lightfoot included the story of Jesus and the woman taken in adultery among the items attributed to Papias. He did so on the strength of the similarity of the wording in fragment 3 (a "woman accused of many sins") and the unusual form of the story as found in certain manuscripts of the New Testament, especially Codex Bezae Cantabrigiensis, the earliest (fifth c.) New Testament manuscript to contain the account.
>
> It is unlikely, however, that Papias knew the story in precisely this form, inasmuch as it now appears that there were at least two independent stories about Jesus and a sinful women in circulation among Christians in the first two centuries of the church, so that the traditional form found in many New Testament manuscripts may well represent a conflation of two independent shorter, earlier versions of the incident.[325]

Some of Holmes's suggestions concerning this pericope are certainly insightful. However, while recognizing that several versions of this account are known to scholars, Holmes suggested that the account that Papias may have been familiar with was the version found in the Syrian "paraphrase" of the Greek *Didascalia*, which he stated was written "near the beginning of the third century."[326] One is left to wonder that if this Syrian translation is a "paraphrase" of a Greek source then how anyone could assume it to be the version that Papias knew. Paraphrases by definition take liberties with their sources, and the fact that the account is from a Syrian translation of a Greek text creates additional complexities to this issue. Agapius of Hierapolis confirmed that Papias was aware of this pericope, and that

325. Holmes, *Apostolic Fathers*, 3rd ed., 724–25.
326. Ibid., 725–26.

Papias confirmed its association with the Fourth Gospel.[327] Holmes, however, in an earlier edition of *The Apostolic Fathers* conjectured that Agapius was anachronistic while assuming that Papias knew the tradition of this account that apparently Agapius also had in his version of the Fourth Gospel.[328] Agapius, however, who was probably familiar with *Exposition*, stated that Papias claimed this pericope could be found in the canonical Gospel of John. Lightfoot's theory about how this could have occurred is compelling. He suggested that

> Have we not here one of those illustrious anecdotes which Papias derived from the report of the elders, and to which he "did not scruple to give a place along with his interpretations" of our Lord's sayings? Its introduction as an illustration of the words of John viii. 15 would thus be an exact parallel to the treatment of the saying in Matthew xxvi. 29. A reader or transcriber of St. John, familiar with Papias, would copy it down in the margin, either from Papias himself or from the Gospel of Hebrew; and hence it would gain currency. The *Codex Bezae*, the oldest Greek manuscript by two or three centuries which contains this narrative, is remarkable for its additions. May we not suspect that others besides this pericope . . . were derived from this exegetical work of Papias?[329]

Consequently, given Lightfoot's insightful theory, it is just as possible that Papias received this pericope as an oral tradition from the lips of the apostle John, and because of its apostolic origin he inserted it into his personal manuscript of the Fourth Gospel. Regrettably, the consequence of his action may have created what has become one of the more thorny text critical problems for today's New Testament scholars. This theory, however, because of its speculative nature is impossible to corroborate.

Unfortunately, Eusebius was not helpful in providing better answers to the questions surrounding the *pericope adulterae*, for his only comment was that Papias included a version of it in his *magnum opus*, and that this event was also found in *The Gospel according to the Hebrews*.[330] What is

327. For a more thorough discussion on this matter see fragment 24, p. 254.

328. Holmes, *The Apostolic Fathers: Diglot Edition*, 559.

329. Lightfoot, *Essays*, 204–5.

330. One can assume that while the pericope found in the *Gospel according to the Hebrews* was essentially the same account, it is likely that it was a somewhat different version of the pericope. Lightfoot, *Essays*, 152. For a thorough discussion on the *adulterae* pericope see Burge, "The Woman Caught in Adultery," 141–48; Cadbury, "Lukan Authorship," 237–45; Wallace, "Adulteress Reconsidered," 290–96; and Lightfoot, *Essays*, 203–5.

most compelling about Eusebius's observations is that he did not associate *The Gospel according to the Hebrews* with Matthew's Hebraic Gospel. As noted above, Jerome stated that a Gospel written in Hebrew could be found in the library at Caesarea. It seems reasonable, therefore, to assume that Eusebius was aware of this Gospel since he was quite familiar with the library of Caesarea and because he knew some of the accounts contained in *The Gospel according to the Hebrews*; he did not, however, at this very natural point associate that Gospel with the Aramaic Gospel written by the apostle Matthew.[331]

A Summary of Eusebius's Data on Papias

The church and historians are immensely indebted to Eusebius for his efforts to preserve the history of the early church. It is obvious, however, that as he handled his material some individuals fared better than others, which is not unusual in the writings of histories, both past and present, whether sacred or secular. And while Papias did not fare well in Eusebius's biased opinion, Eusebius did leave us with important information about him, information that has been corroborated by others. Eusebius described Papias and his influence in the following manner.

Papias was bishop in Hierapolis of Asia Minor during the same period and of the same stature as his friend Polycarp. He was an author, historian, theologian, and preserver of some oral traditions, as well as a commentator/expositor of others that were written. He was concerned with truth, as well as the truth about what Jesus actually did and taught. He was an inquirer and a critical evaluator of both the public discourses and of the literature of his day. He had also personally heard those who followed Jesus during his ministry in Palestine; consequently, he preserved some of their reminiscences of the things that Jesus taught. Eusebius also claimed that Papias was aware of an Aramaic Gospel of Matthew, as well as the canonical Gospel of Mark, and the epistles of 1 Peter and 1 John. Papias's hermeneutical approach was apparently more Antiochene than Alexandrian. His tradition regarding Mark's Gospel credits Peter as its dominant source, as well as suggesting that it was not a narrative that suffered serial redactions over a prolonged period of time, but rather it was the literary product originating exclusively from the hand of Mark. Papias was also aware of a version of the *pericope adulterae*. Based upon what he

331. It would have been natural to make the suggestion that this account was found in Matthew's Hebraic Gospel since he had just discussed it in the preceding lines.

understood Jesus to have taught his immediate disciples, Papias personally believed that Jesus would physically return and establish his Millennial kingdom on earth.

Eusebius, while believing that Papias was intellectually deficient, also noted that in the generations that followed he significantly influenced many prominent church leaders. He stated in *Ecclesiastical History* that Papias had not interacted with the apostle John; however, his arguments lack sufficient evidence to support his biased assertions. Moreover, his earlier writings actually contradict what he wrote later in life. Regardless of Eusebius's prejudicial attitude towards Papias, he has provided enough data about Papias to indicate he was an intriguing figure and rising leader of the Asiatic church at the beginning of the second century. One can only hope that somewhere in a secluded monastic library lies a manuscript of Papias's *magnum opus* that someday may yet be discovered; thus, answering many questions while also removing many speculations concerning Papias and his writings. Until such a day arrives, we are constrained to analyze these few fragments that concern him and what he wrote.

Fragment 6

From Apollinarius: Judas did not die by hanging but lived on, having been cut down before he choked to death. Indeed, the Acts of the Apostles makes this clear: "Falling headlong, he burst open in the middle and his intestines spilled out." Papias, the disciple of John, recounts this more clearly in the fourth book of the *Exposition of the Sayings* as follows:

Judas was a terrible, walking example of ungodliness in the world, his flesh so bloated that he was not able to pass through a place where a wagon passes easily, not even his bloated head by itself. For his eyelids, they say, were so swollen that he could not see the light at all, and his eyes could not be seen, even by a doctor using an optical instrument, so far had they sunk below the outer surface. His genitals appeared more loathsome and larger than anyone's, and when he relieved himself there passed through it pus and worms from every part of his body, much to his shame. After much agony and punishment, they say, he finally died in his own place, and because of the stench the area is deserted and uninhabitable even now, in fact, to this day no one can pass that place unless they hold their nose, so great was the discharge from his body and so far did it spread over the ground.

Apollinaris of Laodicaea (fourth c.);
reconstructed from fragments compiled by various editors[332]

Holmes, as is evident, attributed fragment 6 to Apollinaris of Laodicaea, who was a bishop in Syria in the fourth century. This Apollinaris was also known as "Apollinaris the Younger" since he was the son of "Apollinaris the Elder."[333] The younger Apollinaris is at times confused with the late second-century Apollinaris, who was a bishop of Hierapolis (also known as Apollinarius Claudius).[334] While the dating of this fragment is important for other reasons, whether it is from Apollinaris of the second century or Apollinaris of the fourth century has little bearing upon its actual content, the exactness of which is greatly debated and not entirely clear. It is also not hard to believe that both Apollinaris's were to some degree exposed and/or familiar with Papias's writings. Apollinaris of Hierapolis was a bishop in the same city where Papias ministered approximately fifty years earlier, while Apollinaris of Laodicaea was a bishop in Syria in the late fourth century, which allows ample time for manuscripts of *Exposition* to have circulated to that particular region of the Christian Empire.

Martin Routh documented that this fragment is actually a compilation of several fragments, a couple of which were from the writings of Theophylact,[335] who was the archbishop of Archrida around the turn of the twelfth century.[336] Regarding the correct reading of this fragment, A. Cleveland Coxe argued that it should read as: "Judas walked about in this world a sad example of impiety; for his body having swollen to such an extent that he could not pass where a chariot could pass easily, he was crushed by the chariot, so that his bowels gushed out."[337] Coxe theorized that Theophylact had embellished what Papias had written as he found it

---

332. Holmes, *The Apostolic Fathers: Diglot Edition*, 582–85.

333. Younger, "Apollinaris the Elder," 33–34. There is some confusion with respect to how to spell Apollinaris's name, for an apt explanation of this issue see Schaff, *History of the Church*, 3:709 n. 1.

334. Salmon, "Apollinaris," 33. Schoedel and Kürzinger acknowledged the possibility that this fragment may have originated with Apollinaris of Hierapolis. Kürzinger, *Papias*, 104–5; Schoedel, *The Fragments*, 111. If this fragment is indeed from Apollinaris of Hierapolis, then it should be listed as the second fragment.

335. Routh, *Reliquiæ Sacræ*, 1:25–27.

336. Schaff, *History of the Church*, 4:643–45.

337. *The Fragments of Papias* (ANF 1:153).

in Apollinaris's writings. The fact that this fragment was assimilated from a collection of quotes from Theophylact as he interacted with Apollinaris's quotes of Papias makes it difficult to regard either of the above conjectures as accurate reflections of what Papias actually wrote. Whatever Papias may have written, it appears that he preserved a tradition of Judas's death that shares affinities with the account of his death as found in Acts.[338]

Schoedel's discussion upon this fragment can hardly be improved.[339] He observed that because of the grotesque embellishments of Judas's physical features in this fragment some perceive the gnostic tenet that rejected all things physical. Schoedel, however, has sufficiently documented that such descriptions were a common literary device for emphasizing the demise of the wicked. These descriptions in ancient literature were a provocative way of communicating that God's righteous justice inevitably falls upon the ungodly (e.g., Acts 12:20–23).[340]

If there is a significant weakness in Schoedel's discussion, it is that he fully accepted the fragment above as entirely from the hand of Papias. The most that can be confidently asserted from this fragment is that it concerns data that was found in the fourth book of his *Exposition*, and that Papias perceived that Judas died as the epitome of impiety. In reality, however, one cannot even be certain of the context in which Papias provided his tradition(s) regarding Judas, or that he even knew of the book of Acts, for the reference to Acts 1:18 was from Apollinaris and not Papias. However, because of this fragment's affinities with the account of Judas's death as found in Acts it seems reasonable to conclude that Papias was aware of Luke's history of the early church. But certitude about his potential knowledge of Acts is not possible from this fragment alone since it was Apollinaris who employed a quote from Papias to validate his interpretation of Luke's account. Schoedel speculated that it may have been Papias's purpose to harmonize Matthew's account of Judas's apparent suicide (Matt 27:10) with that of Luke's description of Judas's dismal end (Acts 1:18–19).[341] Nonetheless, no one can be sure that Papias had any intent to harmonize his tradition about Judas's death with those preserved by Luke or Matthew. Vernon Bartlet argued that if anyone seems to have

---

338. For a brief discussion concerning the account of Judas's death in Acts and the Gospel of Matthew see Polhill, *Acts*, 92–93.

339. Schoedel, *The Fragments*, 111–13.

340. Ibid., 112. See also Polhill, *Acts*, 284–85; Bruce, *Acts*, 241–42.

341. Schoedel, *The Fragments*, 111.

been motivated to harmonize the Scriptures it was Apollinaris, explaining that

> Yet Papias, I think, can really be cleared of the grosser form of such developments which all scholars hitherto have believed that he shared, on the strength of a comment of Acts 1.18 of Apollinarius. . . . [His redactions of Papias] are proper to the special "harmonizing" interest which Apollinarius's *scholion* as a whole exhibits, but which need not have been present to the earlier writer's mind at all. For Apollinarius's account related to the two conflicting narratives in Matthew and Acts, not to any *logion* of the Lord's, which alone we are entitled to make the basis of Papias's comment.[342]

Bartlet overstated his case by implying that Papias was only interested in expositions of the sayings of Jesus, for *Exposition* clearly contained more than just discussions about the teachings of Jesus.[343] Nevertheless, his observation that one cannot be certain that Papias even intended to harmonize traditions of Jesus is well defended. In conclusion, there is little agreement on the exact content and meaning of this fragment, let alone its original context. Was it Papias's intent to harmonize his tradition of Judas's death with the traditions about him found in the Gospel of Matthew and Acts, or was it the intent of Apollinaris? Without further Papian material certitude is not possible. Consequently, while data found in this fragment is interesting, it is one of the least credible Papian fragments.

Fragment 7

> The other two of which the first is "The elder to the elect lady and her children" and the other "The elder unto Gaius the beloved whom I love in truth," are said to be the work of John the presbyterian to the memory of whom another sepulcher is shown at Ephesus to the present day, though some think that there are two memorials of this same John the evangelist. We shall treat of this matter in its turn when we come to Papias his disciple.

Jerome Lives of Illustrious Men 9 (ca. AD 393)[344]

342. Bartlet, "Papias's Exposition," 37–38.

343. See the analysis of fragment 5, p. 119.

344. Jerome *Illustrious Men* 9 (NPNF2 3:364–65). This fragment is absent from the lists of Holmes, Schoedel, Kleist, Körtner, Kürzinger, and Ehrman. While one might

This Papian fragment begins a long list of patristic and medieval writers who although they understood Eusebius's exegesis of Papias's preface, and may have even agreed with him in part, they still categorically rejected his opinion that Papias did not know the apostle John. This particular fragment is found in Jerome's treatment of the apostle John in *Illustrious Men*. It provides no demonstrable evidence that Papias was aware of New Testament. Its context is Jerome's discussion of the authorship of 2 and 3 John. While discussing their authorship Jerome simply referred to Papias as "his disciple," the antecedent of the pronoun being "John the Evangelist." Jerome in this fragment also addressed the possibility of the existence of Eusebius's "John the elder." It is significant that Jerome did not include this John in his encyclopedia of canonical authors. The omission of one who may have written 2 and 3 John is striking given Jerome's stated purpose for *Illustrious Men*, which he detailed in his preface, "You have urged me, Dexter, to follow the example of Tranquillus in giving a systematic account of ecclesiastical writers, and do for our writers what he did for the illustrious men of letters among the Gentiles, namely, to briefly set before you *all those who have published any memorable writing on the Holy Scriptures*, from the time of our Lord's passion until the fourteenth year of Emperor Theodosius."[345]

Having stated his purpose, Jerome composed a catalogue of those who were believed to be the authors of all the canonical books of the New Testament.[346] A chapter devoted to Eusebius's "John the elder" is conspicuously absent from Jerome's list of canonical authors. Being the scholar that

understand its absence (the argument being that it provides no new data regarding Papias), this fragment is significant because it testifies to the position that Papias was in fact a disciple of the apostle John. Hereafter, this work will be referred to as *Illustrious Men*. Jerome also mentioned Papias in his summary of Mark in *Illustrious Men*. If this Papian fragment were to be included in this book it might be listed as fragment "3b" since Jerome appears to have drawn his data about Papias from Eusebius. Alternatively, it might also have been included as fragment "7a" since technically it would have been Jerome's first reference to Papias in *Illustrious Men*. Since his reference to Papias in his treatment of Mark only duplicates what Eusebius had previously written it will not be included as an independent fragment. Jerome reverently admitted in his preface dependence upon Eusebius for much of his information about the authors from the church's earliest period; ibid., 3:359. He also wrote admirably of Eusebius in his summary of Eusebius in chapter 81 of *Illustrious Men* (see page 378). Jerome's rejection of Eusebius's opinion regarding Papias's relationship to the apostle John is compelling given his respect for Eusebius.

345. Ibid., 3:359. Italics mine.

346. Jerome discussed the debate concerning the authorship of Hebrews in his treatment of the apostle Paul. Ibid., 363.

he was, Jerome felt compelled to acknowledge the debate surrounding the authorship of the last two Johannine epistles. He put little credibility, however, in the theory that Eusebius's "John" was truly the author of the epistle of 2 and 3 John, for in his letter to Paulinus he openly affirmed that all three epistles were written by the apostle John.[347] Regarding Papias's relationship to the apostle John, the next three fragments will make it transparently clear that Jerome believed Papias was indeed a hearer of the apostle John.

FRAGMENT 8

Papias, a hearer of John and bishop of Hierapolis, wrote only five books, which he entitled *An Exposition of the Discourses of the Lord*. In them, when he asserts in his preface that he is not following diverse conjectures but has the apostles as his authorities, he says:

I used to inquire about what Andrew or Peter had said, or Philip or Thomas or James or John or Matthew, or any other of the Lord's disciples, and what Aristion and John the elder, disciples of the Lord, were saying. For books to read are not as useful to me as the living voice sounding out clearly up to the present day in persons of their authorities.

From this it is clear that in the list of names itself there is one John who is placed among the apostles, and another, John the Elder, whom he lists after Aristion. We have mentioned this fact because of the statement made above,[348] which we have recorded on the authority of a considerable number of people, that the two later epistles of John are not the work of the Apostle but the Elder. He (Papias) is the one who is said to have promulgated the Jewish traditions of a millennium, and he is followed by Irenaeus, Apollinarius, and others, who say that after the resurrection the Lord will reign in the flesh with the saints.

Jerome (ca. 342–420), *Famous Men* 18[349]

347. Jerome *Letter 53: To Paulinus* (NPNF2 6:102).

348. See Jerome's comment in his chapter on Mark in Jerome *Illustrious Men 7* (NPNF2 3:364–65). *Illustrious Men* was written ca. 393.

349. Holmes, *The Apostolic Fathers: Diglot Edition*, 575. This fragment and other Papian fragments found in the writings of Jerome are absent from Kleist's list.

Jerome briefly addressed the life of Papias as promised in his previous treatment of the apostle John.[350] If one will compare the above fragment to fragment 5 as preserved by Eusebius one will note that Jerome has either redacted Papias and/or Eusebius, or he has relied upon his memory, which was slightly faulty but retaining Papias's basic content.[351] An investigation of Jerome's practice of translating quotations reveals that there were occasions when he was not as accurate as he could have been. At times, not only did he paraphrase his sources, but he also habitually reported as fact what was clearly only a conjecture. J. N. D. Kelly wrote regarding this predilection of Jerome,

> For example, while Jerome rightly leaned heavily on Eusebius in the earlier part [of *Famous Men*], he used him quite uncritically, never questioning his reliability or bothering to correct his mistakes even when he might have done so. Several times, through sheer carelessness, he misunderstood him or mistranslated him. Even worse, he attempted to conceal his dependence, taking up his master's statements or opinions and shamelessly reporting them as if they were his own. And when he ventured (as he frequently did) to supplement or improve on the information he found in his source, more often than not his additions and alterations either were untrustworthy or show him representing as firm facts what Eusebius had more prudently reported to be rumours or possibilities.[352]

This very weakness is evident in Jerome's treatment of Papias, for in the above fragment Jerome failed to explain the conjectural nature of the theory that the latter two Johannine epistles were composed by Eusebius's "John the elder." While this is a weakness of Jerome, Eusebius, to his own credit, was more careful with his speculation regarding the last two Johannine epistles.[353] Jerome's comment seems rather odd given his other statements concerning the authorship of the Johannine epistles. It should be

---

350. If one reads Jerome's treatment of the apostle John in *Illustrious Men*, it is clear that he believed Eusebius's "John the elder" was a historical figure. Concerning this second "John," Jerome acknowledged the debate as to whether or not he was the author of the "later epistles" of John. Regarding the other books attributed to the apostle John, however, it was his opinion that both the book of Revelation and the Gospel of John were composed by the apostle John who was a son of Zebedee and one of the twelve who followed Jesus. Jerome *Illustrious Men* 9 (NPNF2 3:364–65).

351. Compare with Eusebius's quote of Papias in Holmes, *Apostolic Fathers*, 3rd ed., 735.

352. Kelly, *Jerome*, 177.

353. Eusebius *Ecc. Hist.* III.24.3 (LCL 153:256–57).

noted, however, that he was not providing his own conviction, but rather the reports of others.

What is most compelling for the purpose of this book, however, is that in this fragment Jerome again referred to Papias as a "hearer" of John. As one surveys all the Papian fragments composed by Jerome (especially fragment 10, which was written several years later), it is clear that Jerome understood Papias to have been a hearer of John the "evangelist." This is significant since Jerome was of the opinion that this John was both one of the original twelve apostles of Jesus as well as the individual who authored the Gospel of John. Consequently, given Jerome's predilection for depending heavily upon Eusebius, especially in matters of the church's earliest history, one can only assume that Jerome had been confronted by insurmountable evidence that Eusebius was in fact wrong in his assertion that Papias had not known the apostle John.

Jerome also confirmed that Papias had authored a five-volume work.[354] One could infer from his statement that a major emphasis of Papias's work was that Jesus taught[355] there would be a literal Millennial kingdom on earth, which is consistent with what can be observed from other Papian fragments. Jerome, however, characterized these accounts as "the Jewish tradition of a millennium." It appears that he is referring to traditions similar to the one found in fragment 1 regarding the bountiful character of Jesus' millennial kingdom. Jerome, however, considered them to be more Jewish than Christian.[356] He placed Papias after Clement, Ignatius, and Polycarp, and before Quadratus in *Illustrious Men*. His placement, consequently, decidedly reveals that he believed Papias to have been a member of the generation commonly referred to as the apostolic fathers.

Jerome's interpretation of Papias also helps one to understand the type of "oral traditions" that Papias would not tolerate, which were teachings that generated "diverse conjectures" (*varias opiniones*). Instead, he understood Papias to have valued only those discourses that he knew to have originated from or to have been consistent with the known traditions of the apostles. One should not assume that Jerome depended entirely on Eusebius for his information regarding Papias, or that he did not have

---

354. Richardson's translation of Jerome's treatment of Papias implies that Jerome believed that Papias wrote an additional work titled, *Second Coming of Our Lord or Millennium*; see Jerome *Illustrious Men* 18 (NPNF2 3:367). This appears to be more than the Latin should bear; therefore, Holmes's translation, which is cited above, is preferred.

355. As testified to by a group that Papias cryptically referred to as "the elders."

356. For further discussion of this issue see fragment 1, p. 106.

access to Papias's *Exposition*, for the analysis of the next fragment indicates that Papias's *magnum opus* was still extant in Jerome's day, and that it was still in demand in some parts of the empire. It should also be recognized that Jerome's statement regarding the last two Johannine epistles was not drawn from Papias, but from the conjectures of "others." Regrettably, Jerome failed to acknowledge who these others were, as well as the bases for their theories.[357] Nevertheless, whatever may have been of Jerome's view concerning the authorship of these two epistles he still viewed them as authoritative and included them in his Latin edition of the canonical New Testament.

FRAGMENT 9

> Moreover, the rumor, reaching you—that the books of Josephus and the writings of saints Papias and Polycarp have been translated by me—is false; I have neither the leisure nor the strength to translate work such as those into another language with corresponding elegance.

> Jerome, *To Lucinus* (Letter 71.5)[358]

Jerome sent *Letter 71* to a wealthy Spaniard named Lucinus with several scribes as they returned to Hispania from Palestine. He wrote this letter near the end of the fourth century (ca. 398).[359] Lucinus had originally sent these scribes for the purpose of making copies of certain works that Jerome had translated into Latin. Jerome used the opportunity of their return to write a letter expressing his thankfulness to Lucinus for supporting his work, and to encourage him unto greater devotion to the Lord. He also urged his friend and benefactor to make a pilgrimage and join him in the Holy Land. He only mentioned Papias in this letter because Lucinus was under the impression that he had translated Papias's *Exposition* along with other important works. This fragment provides no information concerning Papias's knowledge of any apostolic writings.

---

357. Jerome might have concluded this from his readings of Eusebius, but to date I have not found a clear statement from Eusebius that his "John the Elder" authored the last two Johannine epistles. For a more thorough discussion of Eusebius's treatment of Papias see appendix 1, and Grant, "Papias in Eusebius," 209–13.

358. Holmes, *The Apostolic Fathers: Diglot Edition*, 576–77.

359. Jerome *Letter 71: To Lucinus* (NPNF2 6:152).

One could conclude, however, from Jerome's statement that he viewed Papias's work as possessing a measure of literary eloquence, although it could be argued that he was simply attempting to provide a satisfactory explanation for why he would not translate the works desired by Lucinus. Clearly Jerome was competent enough to translate literature from Greek to Latin. The question seems to be, however, whether he wanted or had time to translate these works while giving proper attention to preserving the original meanings and nuances of their authors.[360] One cannot know with certainty why Jerome declined this opportunity. It is clear, however, that he had not translated Papias's five-volume work, nor was he inclined to do so.

This fragment also reveals two interesting points concerning *Exposition*. The first is that it was still extant by the beginning of the fifth century AD, for if it was no longer available then Jerome could not have obtained a copy and he would have simply explained that the work no longer existed, and that would have been the end of the matter with regard to Papias's writings. The second is that in Jerome's day there was still some interest, if not a demand, for *Exposition*. Lucinus was "a wealthy" Spaniard who lived in Hispania, which was in the south-western end of the Roman Empire in present day Portugal and Spain.[361] As mentioned previously, Lucinus had heard a rumor that Jerome had translated Papias's writings; consequently, he was hoping to secure a copy for himself. The rumor, however, was false. Regardless of its truthfulness, his request reveals that, in spite of Eusebius's disparaging remarks, some believed that Papias's *Exposition* still held some value for the church.

FRAGMENT 10

> The growth of this heresy is described for us by Irenaeus, bishop of the church of Lyons, a man of the apostolic times, who was a disciple of Papias the hearer of the evangelist John.
>
> Jerome, *To Theodora*, Letter 75.3[362]

---

360. To understand Jerome's approach to translation see Jerome *Letter 57: To Pammachius* (NPNF2 6:112–19); see also Fremantle's introductory comments on pages xxxii–xxxiii.

361. Blázquez, "Hispania and Palestine," 165.

362. Jerome *Letter 75: To Theodora* (NPNF2 6:156).

This Papian fragment is embedded in Jerome's letter to Theodora, the purpose of which was to express his sympathy to her on the passing of her husband Lucinus, and to encourage her to remain loyal to the true faith while rejecting all forms of Gnosticism. The immediate context of this Papian fragment is Jerome's explanation of the origins of Gnosticism and its perversion of the true faith, a faith that Jerome argued could be traced back to the apostles themselves through the apostolic fathers. This fragment reveals several important characteristics of patristic and medieval authors. The first is that at times they were not as precise as today's scholars would like them to have been in their identification of the initial generations of the early church. This is seen in Jerome's reference to Irenaeus as "a man of the apostolic times." A modern reader might understand this to mean that Jerome believed Irenaeus was a contemporary of the apostles or at least one who lived during the generation that succeeded the apostles. Irenaeus, by his own admission, lived toward the end of the generation of the apostolic fathers and not during the lifetime of the apostles, which is what the reader should understand as Jerome's meaning. Since Irenaeus knew at least one "apostolic father" who had received the orthodox faith directly from an apostle (i.e., Polycarp, who was a disciple of the apostle John), then Jerome's description of Irenaeus as one who lived during the "apostolic times" was not entirely inappropriate. This description, however, can be easily misinterpreted by modern readers.

Jerome also referred to Irenaeus as a "disciple of Papias." Regrettably, however, Irenaeus left no statement to confirm this relationship, nor has any other patristic author corroborated that Irenaeus had personally sat under the tutelage of Papias. There are, however, references to Irenaeus as having followed and propagated the millennial doctrines of Papias.[363] Since Irenaeus was known to have promoted eschatology consistent with that of Papias, it would not be inappropriate to refer to him as his student, even if he had not personally known Papias. That is not to say that Irenaeus did not know or was not a student of Papias, but only that to date there is no corroborating evidence of this relationship. Regarding Jerome's opinion about Papias's relationship to the apostle John, it is apparent that he believed Papias was a "hearer" of John the evangelist, whom Jerome understood to be the apostle who authored the Fourth Gospel.

---

363. See Eusebius *Ecc. Hist.* III.39.11–13 (LCL 153:295–97), and also Jerome's comment about Irenaeus above in Papian, see fragment 7, p. 206.

A SUMMARY OF JEROME'S VIEW OF PAPIAS

Before moving on to other fragments, it might be helpful at this point to summarize Jerome's knowledge of Papias, his associates, and his witness to the New Testament. Fragments 7 through 10 provide no objective evidence that Papias was aware of the New Testament. Jerome, however, in sharp contrast to Eusebius's opinion repeatedly associated Papias with the apostle John, calling him John's "disciple" in fragment 7, and his "hearer" in fragments 8 and 10. Jerome believed that Eusebius had correctly exegeted Papias's preface; thereby providing for him evidence that there was a "John the Elder" who was not the apostle John and who may have written the last two Johannine epistles. It is highly questionable, however, that Jerome actually believed Eusebius's John was indeed their author.[364] Regarding his understanding of Eusebius's exegesis of Papias's preface, it should be noted that Greek was not Jerome's native tongue; consequently, out of respect for Eusebius he may have deferred too quickly to Eusebius's conjectures concerning a second John. Moreover, as previously discussed, there is significant warrant to reject Eusebius's exegesis of Papias's preface with respect to the mythical John the elder.

Ironically, although Jerome believed in the existence of Eusebius's inferior John, he rejected Eusebius's theory that Papias did not know the apostle John. Instead, he continually associated Papias with the last living apostle. For Jerome to have repetitively done so clearly implies that he possessed compelling evidence that justified his rejection of Eusebius's conjecture concerning Papias's relationship to the apostle John. Where would he have found such evidence? He may have found it in the writings of Irenaeus or in those of Papias. Regardless, he disagreed with one of his most important and respected sources for the church's early history. Jerome, however, never fully explained his break from Eusebius regarding Papias's relationship to the apostle John; therefore, understanding his rejection of Eusebius's opinion about their relationship with certitude is not possible.

Jerome also corroborated much of what has already been discussed regarding Papias's life and ministry, which is that he was a bishop of the church at Hierapolis during the same period in which Polycarp, Ignatius, Clement, and Quadratus were ministering. Jerome affirmed that Papias believed his doctrines to have originated from the apostles. Moreover, he affirmed that during a particular period of Papias's life he was able to listen

---

364. Contra Bruce's assertion on this issue, see Bruce, *The Canon*, 227.

to orthodoxy being verbally proclaimed by those whom Papias viewed as trustworthy authorities, which he preferred, as opposed to reading various speculations about the "gospel" or the significance of Jesus' life and teachings. Regarding the preservation of oral traditions, Jerome confirmed that Papias wrote a five-volume work titled, *An Exposition of the Discourses of the Lord*,[365] in which, among other possible themes, he understood Papias to have propagated "Jewish traditions" about a literal Millennial kingdom on earth from which Jesus would reign universally as lord and king.[366] Jerome believed this work had a significant impact upon the eschatology of Irenaeus, as well as others. In conclusion, Jerome believed Papias to have been an associate of the apostle John and an important member of the colloquium known today as the apostolic fathers.

FRAGMENT 11

Papias, bishop of Hierapolis, who was a disciple of John the Theologian[367] and companion of Polycarp, wrote five books on the sayings[368] of the Lord. In them he made a list of apostles and after Peter and John, Philip and Thomas and Matthew, he included among disciples of the Lord Aristion and another John, who he also called "the Elder." So, some think that this John is the author of the two short catholic epistles which circulate under the name of John, because the men of the earliest period accept only the first epistle. And some have mistakenly thought that the Apocalypse was also his. And Papias is also in error regarding the millennium, and so is Irenaeus, who follows him.

Papias says in his second book that John the Theologian and James his brother were killed by the Jews. The aforesaid Papias recorded, on authority of the daughters of Philip, that Barsabbas, who was also called Justus, drank the poison of a snake in the name of Christ when put to the test by the unbelievers and was protected from all harm. He also records other amazing things,

365. Holmes, *The Apostolic Fathers: Diglot Edition*, 574–75.

366. Ibid.

367. In literature from this period, "John the Theologian" is commonly recognized as a reference to the apostle John. With regard to this title, it is not taken from a direct quote from Papias, as some have inferred from this statement (see Harris, *Background to John*, Internet), but rather it is Philip's reference to the apostle John.

368. The vocabulary of this fragment (κυριακῶν λογίων) indicates that the writer was either referring to Papias's actual title or a dominant characteristic of *Exposition*; therefore, the phrase "sayings of the Lord" is better translated as "oracles of the Lord."

in particular one about Manaim's mother, who was raised from the dead. As for those who were raised from the dead by Christ, he states that they survived until the time of Hadrian.

Philip of Side (fifth c.); *Church History*.[369]

This fragment is at times disparaged by some scholars; nevertheless, some of these criticisms cannot be justly defended. Philip of Side was from Pamphylia and was ordained as a deacon by John Chrysostom at Constantinople during the first half of the fifth century. He was also a church historian who fancied himself a master of many other subjects. He was an assiduous author, and between 434–439 he wrote a massive thirty-six volume work that he titled, *Church History*.[370] Regrettably, like so many other patristic works, Philip's writings are not extant, save a few fragments, one of which contains his summary comments about Papias's *Exposition*. It should be noted initially that his summary contains no direct quote from Papias. This, however, should not overly detract from the value of Philip's statements about Papias's work. As previously discussed, he may have not been a great historian, and he may have depended too heavily upon Eusebius, nevertheless, he had read excerpts of Papias's *Exposition* for himself. Evidence for this assertion is supported by the observation that he provided additional data from Papias's work, data that to date has not been found in any other patristic literature concerning the writings of Papias. It appears, therefore, that Philip had personally read excerpts from *Exposition*, and as a result he is an important source for information concerning Papias and his writings.

It is recognized that for some this is a precarious position. To argue, however, that Philip or his epitomizer[371] was completely untrustworthy is to err on the side of blind skepticism since Philip's *Church History* is no longer extant. Consequently, we are no longer able to evaluate him as a

369. Holmes, *The Apostolic Fathers: Diglot Edition*, 570–73.

370. Culpepper, *John*, 170–71.

371. This is a common reference to the writer who preserved Philip's summary of Papias's writings. In reality, it is not certain whether this fragment is completely from the hand of Philip or his epitomizer, or whether the epitomizer has credited some of his own conclusions to the more famous Philip of Side. Schoedel dated the manuscript containing this fragment as from the eighth century. Schoedel, *The Fragments*, 118. Since it appears that this epitomizer has to some degree recorded some material that could be found in Philip's writings, this fragment is placed here. As will become evident, however, there is some question of whether all the material in this fragment came from Philip.

historian for ourselves. We must, therefore, be more critical when evaluating what we can observe from Philip's hand, instead of basing our critiques upon the generalization of others. An example of blind generalization is seen in Schoedel's comments about Philip. He argued that Philip was "untrustworthy," apparently basing his opinion of Philip upon an evaluation made by the ninth-century patriarch Photius of Constantinople. More specifically, because of Photius's critique Schoedel called Philip a "bungler" who "cannot be trusted."[372] Photius's review of Philip was certainly stinging and uncomplimentary, but he criticized Philip for being verbose, pedantic, diffuse, disorganized, and boring; he did not, however, criticize him for being grossly inaccurate while detailing the church's history.[373] Socrates of Constantinople,[374] who was Philip's contemporary, gave a similar although less biting critique of Philip's *Church History*, which may provide insight as to why Photius evaluated Philip so poorly. Socrates wrote that Philip had unnecessarily mixed astronomy, math, music, and geography with his treatment of the church's history. Socrates contended that these other topics were irrelevant for those who wished to learn about Philip's main subject, which was the history of the church.[375] While Philip

372. Schoedel, *The Fragments*, 120.

373. Photius, *Bibliothèque*, 1:20–21.

374. Also known as Socrates Scholasticus.

375. Socrates *Ecclesiastical History* (NPNF2 2:168). It is also noted that Socrates did criticize Philip for his chronology in *Church History*. However, this same charge has been appropriately leveled against Eusebius. Arthur McGiffert wrote in his introduction concerning Eusebius's chronology that "In the third place, severe censure must be placed upon our author for his carelessness and inaccuracy in matters of chronology. We should expect that one who had produced the most extensive chronological work that had ever been given to the world, would be thoroughly at home in the province, but in truth his chronology is the most defective feature of his work. . . . In fact, the critical spirit which actuates him in dealing with many other matters seems to leave him entirely when he is concerned with chronology; and instead of proceeding with the care and circumspection of an historian, he accepts what he finds with the unquestioning faith of a child. There is no case in which he can be convicted of disingenuousness, but at times his obtuseness is almost beyond belief. An identity of names, or a resemblance between events recorded by different authors, will often be enough to lead him all unconsciously by himself into the most absurd and contradictory conclusions." Eusebius *The Church History of Eusebius* (NPNF2 1:50–51). An example of Eusebius's carelessness with his chronology is his suggestion that Pionius died around the time of Polycarp's martyrdom. He dated Polycarp's death either late in the reign of Antonius (d. 161) or sometime during Marcus's reign (d. 180). In *Chronicle* Eusebius dated Polycarp's death ca. 166/167. However, Pionius was martyred during Decius's reign (249–51), approximately eighty to ninety years later. See Eusebius *Ecc. Hist.* IV.14.10–15.1, VI.15.47. Concerning Philip, however, Socrates did not criticize him

may have overextended himself by dealing with subjects well beyond his expertise, no one, including Socrates or Photius, criticized Philip's grasp of the church's history.

Keeping in mind the discussion above, evaluating Philip should be exercised on the basis of what remains from his writings and not solely from the opinions of others. By surveying fragment 11 one can observe that Philip referred to specific individuals and events that he asserted were contained in Papias's work, some of which appeared in the second volume of *Exposition*. Whether one thinks that Philip misunderstood or inappropriately exegeted Papias is an issue worthy of debate, but the fact remains that Philip provided what amounts to be the equivalent of a footnote in a style commonly found in patristic literature when he directed his readers to the second book of Papias's five-volume work.[376] An example of this "style" of footnoting is easily observable by Eusebius's simply reference to Papias's preface.[377]

One of Philip's conclusions was that Eusebius had incorrectly speculated that Papias was not an associate of the apostle John. This is clear from Philip's description of Papias as "a hearer" of that last living apostle.[378] Philip, however, agreed with Eusebius about much of the uncontested information concerning Papias found throughout patristic literature, which was that he was a bishop of Hierapolis, that he was an associate and contemporary of Polycarp, and that he wrote a five-volume work about the life and teachings of Jesus. Ironically, Philip also acknowledged the existence of Eusebius's John "the Elder," as well as the debates regarding what New Testament books he may have written. Likewise, he corroborated Eusebius's observation that a portion of Papias's five-volume work was also

---

for his accuracy with respect to specific events in the church's history.

376. The reference to this particular volume, as well as the details provided, implies that *Exposition* was still extant at the time this fragment was composed.

377. See fragment 5, p. 119.

378. This is in contrast to the translation maintained by Holmes, which described Papias as a "disciple" of the apostle John. Holmes, *Apostolic Fathers*, 3rd ed., 742–43. Philip did not call Papias a "μαθητής" (i.e., "disciple") of John. The term Philip employed is "ἀκουστής," which referred to someone who had actually heard the voice of another (i.e., Papias had actually heard the voice of the apostle John). Consequently, Philip's vocabulary suggests direct contact between the apostle John and Papias. The problem with Holmes's translation is that one could consider his/herself a "disciple" of Jesus without ever having actually listened to his teachings in person. Holmes provided no explanation for providing such an egregious translation.

devoted to preserving "amazing accounts" (such as the one provided by the daughters of the apostle Philip about Barsabbas).[379]

Philip of Side, however, discussed some of these events in greater detail, such as the type of poison Barsabbas drank, which was snake venom. He also provided the reason for this perilous behavior, stating that Barsabbas had been put to the test by unbelievers, but having sipped the deadly nectar in the "name of Christ" he was spared from any fatal effects.[380] Moreover, while Eusebius only referred to an unnamed man who had been raised from the dead, Philip specifically referred to the mother of an individual named "Manaim" who had also been raised from the dead. When compared with Eusebius's summary of Papias's writings, it is apparent that Philip or his epitomizer has provided an independent witness to some of the contents found in *Exposition*.[381]

Schoedel, however, was unimpressed with this data, arguing that it is "hardly impressive enough to prove independent acquaintance with Papias; they may represent contamination from other legendary materials."[382] While it is legitimate to question if the epitomizer correctly quoted or understood Philip's summary of Papias, arguing that either he or Philip mixed up their sources, or that Philip conjoined Papian material with other "legendary material" is a less than satisfactory conjecture since it is impossible to confirm or disprove. Eusebius himself observed that Papias's work contained this very type of material (i.e., "legendary" material), which he referred to as "amazing."[383] One should not be surprised, therefore, that Philip also confirmed this material was contained in Papias's *Exposition*. It seems more reasonable, consequently, to argue for Philip or the epitomizer as possessing firsthand exposure to Papias's writings since the mere argument that legendary materials existed is no proof against the possibility that Papias was not in fact the one who had preserved them.

---

379. Eusebius *Ecc. Hist.* III.39.9 (LCL 153:294–95). For a discussion regarding which "Philip" Eusebius believed Papias had known see the discussion concerning fragment 5, p. 119, and appendix 2 of this book.

380. There is some question as to whether Papias received this account from Philip's daughters. The author of this fragment indicated that he believed the daughters of Philip were also the authority for the tradition about Barsabbas.

381. Even Schoedel referred to this data as "fresh material." Schoedel, *The Fragments*, 118.

382. Ibid., 5:119.

383. Holmes, *Apostolic Fathers*, 3rd ed., 743.

One of the more debated topics regarding Philip's summary of *Exposition* is his assertion that in the second volume Papias allegedly wrote that John the Theologian and James his brother were "*killed* by the Jews."[384] Countless articles have been written on the accuracy of this statement.[385] The question of if and when the apostle John was martyred is important because if he was martyred during or around the same time as his brother James (ca. 44), then it would be virtually impossible for Papias to have been a disciple of the apostle John. Thus, a brief investigation into the date and cause of his death is in order.

It should be noted from the outset that as with several other Papian fragments this fragment provides no direct quote from Papias by which to validate the claims made by Philip or his epitomizer. Nevertheless, because of Philip's knowledge of Eusebius's *Ecclesiastical History* it is reasonable to conclude that he was also aware of Eusebius's assertion that the apostle John had lived a long life. It seems demonstrably clear that he also knew of Eusebius's exegesis of Papias's preface; nevertheless, he still believed that Papias was a contemporary of Polycarp and a disciple of the apostle John, while also concluding that John had joined his brother James in suffering a martyr's fate at the hands of the Jews. Regrettably, without possessing the exact quote from Papias's second book, one is left to wonder what exactly was the basis for such a conclusion. A few scholars in the past have attempted to use the early death of the apostle John to explain how he could not have written some of the literature traditionally attributed to him.[386] However, as A. M. Hunter has adeptly concluded, "Those who accept the early martyrdom of the Apostle (John) show quite a monumental preference for inferior evidence."[387]

It may be a misguided focus to speculate about the date of the apostle John's death if the author's emphasis was not on *when* he died but on *who* was responsible for his death. In reality, the assertion in this fragment does not demand that the two brothers were martyred at the same time, but only that the Jews were responsible for both of their deaths. It is entirely possible, therefore, that Papias's emphasis or Philip's deduction from Papias's second volume focused upon those that were responsible for the deaths of

---

384. "Ἰουδαίων ἀνῃρέθησαν," Holmes, *Apostolic Fathers,* 3rd ed., 742.

385. For a discussion regarding the traditions about the death of the apostle John see Culpepper, *John,* 171–74.

386. Badham, "The Martyrdom of St. John," 733–35; and idem, "The Martyrdom of John the Apostle," 739; and Bernard, *Studia Sacra,* 260–61.

387. Hunter, "Johannine Studies," 222.

the sons of Zebedee rather than when they died.[388] Moreover, there is no concrete evidence dictating that the two "Sons of Thunder" died at or near the same time. As Hill aptly observed concerning the question of when the apostle John died, "Despite recurring speculation, this last item, even if not spurious, does not imply that John's death was early."[389]

Regardless of what may have been observable in the second book of Papias's *Exposition* concerning the death of the apostle John, there is still the question of whether the apostle John was in fact a martyr. Tertullian wrote that John was baptized in boiling oil that would have proven fatal except for the grace of God. Some believed, consequently, that he had earned the title of martyr.[390] Origen labeled John a martyr because of his banishment to Patmos.[391] Neither Origen or Tertullian, however, made any mention of John as having been "killed" by the Jews (ὑπὸ Ἰουδαίων ἀνηρέθησαν) as Philip claimed Papias asserted. Given the subject matter of Eusebius's *Ecclesiastical History* and his respect for those who suffered martyrdom (such as Polycarp, Germanicus), as well as his prejudicial attitude towards the Jews, it is hardly believable that if Papias had ostensibly recorded that the Jews were involved in the martyrdom of John, whether directly or indirectly, that Eusebius would not have referred to such an event in greater detail. Even if Papias had not recorded such an event, it seems hard to believe that it would not have been preserved by the churches in Asia Minor, let alone by the churches of Ephesus. Eusebius, however, made no reference to such an event while detailing the twilight years of the last surviving apostle.[392]

Eusebius did, however, twice record Polycrates's reference to the apostle John as having been a "martyr" (see *Ecc. Hist.* III.31.3, V.24.3). His second quote of Polycrates strongly implies that both he and Polycrates believed the apostle John had justifiably earned this honorable title. J. H. Bernard suggested that during the period in which Polycrates wrote the

388. Hengel recognized that there is no need to assume that the sons of Zebedee died as a result of the same event or around the same time. Hengel, *The Question*, 159.

389. Hill, "Papias," 310.

390. Tertullian *Against Heresies* I.36 (ANF 3:260).

391. Origen *Commentary on Matthew* 16.6 (PG 13:1385).

392. See Eusebius *Ecc. Hist.* III.23.14 (LCL: 153: 240–43). It is recognized that by the late second century the term "martyr" had developed the technical definition of one who had given their life as a witness to the gospel of Jesus Christ. See Strathmann, "μάρτυς," in *TDNT*, 4:505–6. However, the earliest patristic authors who wrote less than 100 years after the apostle John's death testified that he was an exception to this "technical" meaning of μάρτυς.

term "μάρτυς" was in flux and that at times it was applied to some who had endured sufferings for the sake of Christ but had not died for his name.[393] If Bernard's theory is accurate, then it is easy to see how later readers might mistakenly believe that the apostle John suffered a violent death because of Polycrates's reference to him as a "martyr and teacher" among other known martyrs such as Polycarp of Smyrna, Thraseas of Eumenaea, and Sagaris of Laodicaea. Polycrates did not, however, apply this same label to Melito of Sardis, who by all accounts was a great "witness" to the Christian faith, but was apparently not one whose death was the direct result of his allegiance to Christ.

Bernard also cited Revelation 1.9 as a possible reason for Polycrates to have referred to John as a "μάρτυς."[394] The author identified himself in this passage by writing, "I, John . . . was on the island of Patmos on account of the word of God and the testimony of Jesus," (i.e., τὴν μαρτυρίαν Ἰησοῦ). If Bernard's theory is correct, then Polycrates referred to the apostle John as a "martyr" in deference to the apostle's self designation rather than being concerned whether he had not actually technically fulfilled the qualification for ultimately receiving the title of "martyr."

Eusebius, however, never elaborated upon what he believed Polycrates meant when he referred to the apostle John as a martyr. Regarding Eusebius's silence on this matter, R. Alan Culpepper mused,

> Questions still remain. A fragment attributed to the second book of Papias contains a report of the martyrdom of John. Did Eusebius know all five books of Papias? If so, why does Eusebius not mention John's martyrdom? Did he interpret the report in such a way that it did not conflict with the tradition of John's long life and residence in Ephesus? Or did he suppress the report in favor of the tradition that the apostle wrote the Fourth Gospel? The latter is difficult to accept since Eusebius assumes the five books of Papias are still available and does not hesitate to challenge Irenaeus on the link between Papias and John.[395]

Contrary to Martin Hengel's conjecture that Eusebius "suppressed" important data concerning the apostle John's death, Culpepper rightly

393. Bernard, *Studia Sacra*, 265. Concerning the apostle John, Tertullian's reference to his suffering because of his testimony to Christ and the gospel could explain why some awarded him the title of martyr in the late second century; see Tertullian *Against Heresies* I.36 (ANF 3: 260).

394. Bernard, *Studia Sacra*, 266.

395. Culpepper, *John*, 155.

concluded that it is not likely that Eusebius inappropriately "neglected" any data regarding John's death.[396] Culpepper speculated, however, that it is conceivable that Eusebius had not read "all" of Papias's five-volume work, and as a result missed some important information concerning John's martyrdom. This, however, seems highly unlikely, especially given Eusebius's anti-Semitic bent, for if in fact the Jews had martyred the apostle John directly or indirectly (as with the death of John's brother James), then it seems extremely improbable that Eusebius would have been ignorant of such a tradition.

Nevertheless, it is possible that Eusebius may have missed some important data found in Papias's writings detailing John's death when he first released *Ecclesiastical History*.[397] Remembering, however, that the time between the first and last releases of *Ecclesiastical History* was well over a decade, it seems reasonable to conclude that during the intervening years someone would have pointed out this glaring omission to Eusebius if Papias had clearly described Jewish responsibility or participation in the apostle John's martyrdom. Eusebius, however, was familiar with Papias's writings, not to mention other traditions about John's final days, and the fact that he did not preserve any such account strongly suggests that an account proving that the "Jews" were directly or indirectly responsible for the death of John was never there to be observed. And while Eusebius clearly held some prejudice attitudes towards Papias, he was not above citing him when it came to providing valuable confirmatory data concerning the church's founding leaders and its earliest writings, such as Mark composition of his Gospel from the reminiscences of the apostle Peter, or that Matthew initially composed a Gospel in Aramaic. Even if he was so prejudicial towards Papias that he could no longer bear referring to him in *Ecclesiastical History*, Eusebius certainly would have, given his anti-Semitic thesis, anonymously preserved any tradition involving Jewish responsibility for John's martyrdom rather than to allow such damning information to fade from the annals of history.[398]

So how could such an accusation have been made? Culpepper documented several examples in patristic literature where some writers

---

396. Hengel, *The Question*, 21.

397. Hengel also speculated that one cannot be sure of how familiar Eusebius was with the entirety of Papias's writings. Ibid., 21.

398. Moreover, Bernard argued that it would be "highly improbable" that Irenaeus, who was a disciple of Polycarp, would have never heard about the apparent martyrdom of the apostle John, or that he would have mistaken Eusebius's "John the Elder" for the apostle John, who he reported lived until Trajan's reign. Bernard, *Studia Sacra*, 263.

honored apostolic figures in ways that could confuse modern readers. For example, the Calendar of Carthage commemorated the deaths of John the Baptist and James the apostle on the same day, which was December 27th. One could see how a reader could inadvertently conclude that it was John the apostle who was martyred instead of John the Baptist. The Syrian martyrology, which dates to a time just prior to the writing of Philip's *Church History*, is more direct and "commemorates . . . the martyrdom of the 'apostles John and James at Jerusalem' on December 27."[399] A comprehensive discussion on the fragment 11 was put forth by Bernard, who argued that Philip's claim regarding what Papias wrote was the result of a misunderstanding. Bernard wrote, "I call it a misinterpretation, for it is difficult to suppose that a statement by Papias to the effect that John had suffered martyrdom could have been completely ignored by Eusebius and the ecclesiastical writers of his day."[400] Bernard provided several examples of how someone could carelessly misinterpret such a text, many of them similar to those that have already been suggested.[401]

There are other conjectures that may explain this incorrect assertion about what Papias wrote. One intriguing possibility is that Philip incorrectly exegeted Papias in a fashion similar to Eusebius. Another is that Philip leaped upon an event that Papias mentioned that occurred late in the apostle's life near his death, an event that he interpreted as meeting the qualifications of martyrdom.[402] A reason why other church historians missed this observation was that this event was so obscure that connecting it to John's death was not reasonable; consequently, they ignored it because for them his conclusion seemed unwarranted. Alternatively, the same conjecture(s) could be leveled against Papias. In other words, it was Papias who concluded that the Jews were responsible for the death of the apostle John because of a specific event that occurred late in the John's life. While Eusebius and other historians rejected this accusation as unwarranted, Philip the Side and, as will be seen later, George the Sinner affirmed Papias's conclusion.[403] This, however, seems to be the weakest of

399. Culpepper, *John*, 172. See also, Hengel, *The Question*, 157–59. For a more thorough discussion see Bernard, *Studia Sacra*, 274–84.

400. Ibid., 269.

401. Ibid., 270–75. Lightfoot recommended a different possibility, suggesting that this mistake was the result of lacunae. Lightfoot, *Essays*, 212.

402. This is assuming that Philip was the source of this mistake; however, the source of this mistake is uncertain.

403. Hengel believed that the only reason we know of a tradition of John's martyrdom is because of Philip's preservation of this Papian tradition. Hengel, *The Question*,

possibilities. The most reasonable solution to this mystery is that either Philip or his epitomizer simply misunderstood Papias and/or another earlier church writer concerning the death of the apostle John (Polycrates?).

Given all the available data, there appears little objective evidence that the apostle John was "killed" by the Jews as Philip or his epitomizer claimed Papias to have maintained. Moreover, there is no extant account of the apostle John having been executed directly or indirectly by the hands of the Jews. Bernard's position that Philip or someone else simply misunderstood the writings of Papias has considerable merit. As a result of this confusion, Bernard argued that "I submit, therefore, that the idea that Papias is an authority for the 'red martyrdom' of John the son of Zebedee must be dismissed. In the light of the universal belief of the Church, it would be very difficult to suppose that Papias gave currency to any such idea."[404] Consequently, it should be doubted that Papias ever suggested that the apostle John died a martyr's death; moreover, it is likely that the apostle John engaged fruitful ministry while outliving the rest of the apostles.

It must also be recognized, however, that the possibility still exists (however slim it may be) that the apostle John was martyred in the twilight years of his life, for during the persecutions of the church being aged was no shield against violence from those who hated devoted Christians. Examples of such violence are evident in the martyrdoms of Polycarp and Photinus. Regrettably, however, certitude about what Papias actually wrote or meant was lost when Philip failed to provide the exact text that justified his assertion, which itself speaks against the strength of this claim. While this too is an argument from silence, at times such arguments are indeed very loud. Why such a claim was made is anyone's guess. Bernard and others have suggested that there was apologetic capital to be garnered by harmonizing the fates of James and John with the prophecy concerning them in Matthew 20:22–23 and Mark 10:38–39.[405] This too, however, is only speculation since the relevance of these texts with respect to the supposed martyrdom of the apostle John was never suggested or explained by the author of this fragment.

---

21. However, even if Philip or George the Sinner had not made this reference to the death of the apostle John his "martyrdom" would still be debated because of Eusebius's preservation of Polycrates's reference to the apostle John as a "martyr."

404. Bernard, *Studia Sacra*, 274–75.

405. Ibid., 270.

A second often debated aspect about this fragment concerns the reference to how long certain individuals survived after being revived from the dead by the miraculous power of Jesus Christ. By emphasizing the reference to Hadrian, who reigned from 117–138, some have argued that Papias must have written his *Exposition* around or after 140. As previously discussed, neither Papias, nor Quadratus for that matter, made any direct reference to Hadrian's "reign." Instead, their references were to Hadrian's lifetime; consequently, since we do not have Papias's exact quote one cannot be certain about the exact date or period of Papias's reference. It can be reasonably assumed, however, that Papias referred to the period of Hadrian's adulthood rather than only the period of his reign.[406] Theoretically, this means that Papias could have written his *magnum opus* sometime between 100 until just before his death, which has been estimated as late as 167. Such a wide span seems to be overly cautious; consequently, sometime between 110 to 140 seems to be a more reasonable conjecture, although still being only an estimate.[407]

In conclusion, fragment 11 is intriguing because its author demonstrates both familiarity with Papias's writings as well as with what others have written about him. Regrettably, however, there is also evidence suggesting that he was not always careful with his materials. Contrary to Eusebius, however, he believed that Papias was in fact a disciple of the apostle John. Not surprisingly, he was also aware of Eusebius's theory concerning a second John. Since the primary focus of his work was the history of the church, it is certain that he was aware of Eusebius's record, as well as the traditions of others, concerning the longevity of the apostle John's life. Nevertheless, similarly to John's brother James, he believed that the Jews were in some way responsible for the death of apostle John. Consequently, one would assume that the author of this fragment believed that the apostle John was martyred later in life, rather than earlier as some have asserted. This author contended that corroboration for his assertion could be found in the second book of *Exposition*. While some believe that Papias is the source for this tradition, nevertheless, it appears that it is the author of fragment 11 who has made an error, either being mislead by other sources or by his own misreading of Papias. Without possessing the second volume of *Exposition*, however, one cannot be certain that a

---

406. Hadrian was born ca. 76.

407. It is also possible that Papias wrote *Exposition* several years before AD 110. However, the best estimation of when he wrote appears to be ca. 110 or shortly thereafter.

mistake has been made or the possible source(s) for this error. Regardless of what one might conjecture about certain issues contained in this fragment, it provides no demonstrable proof that Papias was aware of any writings contained in the canonical the New Testament.

FRAGMENT 12

> Regarding, however, the divine inspiration of the book [i.e., the
> Revelation of John] we think it superfluous to speak at length,
> since the blessed Gregory (I mean the Theologian) and Cyril,
> and men of an older generation as well, namely Papias, Irenaeus,
> Methodius, and Hippolytus, bear witness to its genuineness.

Andrew of Caesarea (563–637), *Preface to the Apocalypse*[408]

Very little is known about Andrew of Caesarea other than he was a late fifth-century bishop in Cappadocia and that he wrote one of the first Greek commentaries on the book of Revelation.[409] His commentary is one of the earliest to preserve a Greek text of Revelation, which makes it valuable for text critical issues. As one might expect, Andrew addressed the authority and genuineness of the book of Revelation in his preface, where he also contended that it was divinely inspired. One reason for his confidence in its authority and inspiration was his conviction that it was authored by the apostle John.[410] Andrew defended the validity of this position by naming past church leaders and scholars who he contended shared his opinion. One of whom was Papias, who is the earliest member of Andrew's patristic list.

There is some question regarding the others that he claimed affirmed the book's authority and genuineness. The first mentioned by Andrew is the well-known Gregory of Nazianzus, who is also referred to as "Gregory the Great," who is also a well known member of the triad commonly referred to as "The Cappadocian Fathers." Ironically, Gregory did not include the book of Revelation in his canonical list.[411] He did, however, cite it in some of his other writings, in which he referred to it as "Scripture," and as coming from

408. Holmes, *The Apostolic Fathers: Diglot Edition*, 576–77.

409. Norris, "Andrew of Caesarea," 52. Manlio Simonetti dated Andrew in the late sixth century. Simonetti, "Andrew of Caesarea," 38.

410. Andrew of Caesarea, *The Apocalypse of John the Theologian* (PG 106: 224, 418).

411. Bruce, *The Canon*, 211–13.

the hand of "the evangelist John."[412] Simonetti wrote that Andrew's commentary "is rich in often extensive citations from earlier authors, esp. . . . Gregory of Nazianzen [sic]."[413] Andrew's familiarity with Gregory's writings might explain his confidence concerning Gregory's view of the book of Revelation.

Regarding Andrew's reference to Cyril, in the *Patrologia Graeca* a Latin text is also included with the Greek text of Andrew's commentary. This Latin text identifies Cyril as from "*Alexandrinum*," even though this identification is absent in the Greek. Assuming this Cyril to be Cyril of Alexandria makes sense since Cyril of Jerusalem did not include Revelation in his New Testament canonical list.[414] Cyril of Alexandria was a contemporary of Andrew, and being the patriarch of Alexandria he was one of the leading scholars of his day.[415]

Andrew also stated that some leaders from the earliest generations of the church had recognized the authenticity of the book of Revelation. One from the patristic generation who affirmed the apostolic origin of Revelation was Irenaeus. Concerning Revelation he wrote that it had been written by a John whom he identified as "the Lord's disciple,"[416] and since evidence indicates that he knew of only one John who had authored writings contained in the New Testament it is assumed that this John was one of the sons of Zebedee.[417] Andrew also mentioned Hippolytus, who was a late second-century and early third-century bishop and martyr. F. F. Bruce wrote regarding Hippolytus that he was "the last significant figure in the Roman church to write in Greek," and that he "was the greatest scholar of his age in the west."[418] Faithful to his purpose of *Illustrious Men*, Jerome provided a list of

---

412. Gregory, *Canon and Text*, 275.

413. Simonetti, "Andrew of Caesarea," 38.

414. Bruce, *The Canon*, 210–13.

415. For a thorough discussion of Cyril's life and ministry see McGuckin, "Cyril of Alexandria," 205–36.

416. Irenaeus, *On the Detection and Refutation*, 175. The relevant Latin text reads, "*significavit Joannes Domini discipulus in Apocalypsi*," which Grant translated as, "John the Lord's disciple spoke yet more clearly . . . ." Grant's translation, therefore, is superior to that of Rambaut and Roberts, which reads: "In a still clearer light has John, in the Apocalypse, indicated to the Lord's disciples. . . ." See Irenaeus *Against Heresies* V.26.1 (ANF 1: 554). For the Latin text see Irenaeus *Contra Haereses* (PG 7:1192).

417. For a more thorough analysis of how many "Johns" Irenaeus may have known see the review of Lewis's book titled *Fourth Gospel: Its Extent, Meaning, and Value* in chapter 2 of this book.

418. Bruce, *The Canon*, 177–78. For a more thorough discussion of Hippolytus's life see Schaff, *History of the Church*, 2:757–74.

Hippolytus's writings, among them being a work titled, *On the Apocalypse.*[419] It is probable that this work was the source of Andrew's information regarding Hippolytus's opinion on the origin of the book of Revelation. Regrettably, this work is only extant in a few fragments.

Methodius is the most mysterious of the patristic figures listed by Andrew. He appears to have been a bishop of the mid to late third and early fourth century who may have been martyred in 311 or as late as 320.[420] Jerome also included him in *Illustrious Men*, stating that he was a bishop of Olympus in Lycia.[421] As with Hippolytus, Jerome provided a list of books attributed to Methodius, one of which was titled, *On the Resurrection*, which may have dealt with the origin and authority of Revelation, but this is not a certainty. When viewed chronologically, Andrew's list of bishops, scholars, and martyrs spans the church's history from the early second century up to Andrew's own day. It is clear, however, that he believed that Papias not only knew of the book of Revelation, but also that he indicated it had indeed originated from the hand of the apostle John. This particular fragment, however, contains no direct quote from Papias regarding the book of Revelation.

FRAGMENT 13

But Papias says, word for word:

> "Some of them"—obviously meaning those which once were holy—"he assigned to rule over the orderly arrangement of the earth, and commissioned them to rule well." And next he says: "But as it turned out, their administration came to nothing. And the great dragon, the ancient serpent, who is called the Devil and Satan, was cast out; the deceiver of the whole world was cast down to the earth along with his angels."
>
> Andrew of Caesarea, *On the Apocalypse*, chap. 34, serm. 12[422]

It seems that Holmes, following Lightfoot, has misattributed the length of this Papian fragment. Its context is Andrew's commentary on Revelation 12:7–8, in which one would expect the exposition of verses 7–8 to be followed by his analysis of the next passages, which would be introduced by the

---

419. Jerome *Illustrious Men* 61 (NPNF2 3:375).

420. Methodius, *A Treatise on Chastity*, 3–5.

421. Jerome *Illustrious Men* 83 (NPNF23:378–79).

422. Holmes, *The Apostolic Fathers: Diglot Edition*, 576–79.

text of Revelation 12:9, which seems to be the case. It appears, therefore, that Papias's quote should end at the word "nothing." The sentence that immediately follows, which is "And the great dragon, the ancient serpent, who is called the Devil and Satan, was cast out; the deceiver of the whole world was cast down to the earth along with his angels," is the text of Revelation 12:9; consequently, it should be recognized as the introductory verse for Andrew's expository comments in the following section.[423] While Andrew relied on Papias to elaborate about Satan's pre-fall commission, this fragment alone provides no objective evidence that Papias was aware of the book of Revelation; instead, it only associates a text in Papias's writings regarding Satan's fall with a passage on this same theme found in Revelation. This association, however, when taken with consideration of the preceding fragment, provides greater support for the assertion that Papias was indeed aware of the book of Revelation.

FRAGMENT 14

> They used to call those who practiced a godly innocence "children," as Papias shows in the first book of the *Expositions of the Lord*, and also Clement of Alexandria in his *Pedagogue*.
>
> Maximus the Confessor (ca. 580–662), *Scholia on Dionysius the Areopagite, On the Ecclesiastical Hierarchy*, chap. 2[424]

This fragment is from the great Byzantine scholar Maximus the Confessor, also known as Maximus the Theologian and Maximus of Constantinople.[425] Andrew Louth wrote that little is verifiable with respect to Maximus's early years. He was born ca. 580 and apparently received a quality education and served with distinction in the court of Emperor Heraclius.[426] He renounced his civic post at some point in his thirties and became a monk. By all accounts he was a competent theologian and philosopher. He is best known as a defender of orthodoxy against the Monothelite heresy. Like so many

---

423. The text as it is laid out in the *PG* makes this clear. Andrew of Caesarea, *The Apocalypse of John the Theologian* 12:7–8 (PG: 106:325–27). Schoedel and Ehrman also end this Papian fragment before the quote of Rev 12:9. Schoedel, *The Fragments*, 113; *Papias and Quadratus* (LCL 25:111).

424. Holmes, *The Apostolic Fathers: Diglot Edition*, 580–81.

425. Louth, *Maximus*, 3–18. See also Schaff, *History of the Church*, 4:622–26.

426. Louth, *Denys*, 4–5, 199.

before him, his defense of orthodoxy came at a great price. He was tried and condemned as a heretic, and exiled to Lazica, but not before the mutilation of the weapons he so forcefully used to defend the faith, which were his tongue and right hand. He died as a result of his wounds while in exile on August 16, 662, at the approximate age of eighty-one. He is, consequently, justifiably recognized as a martyr. Almost twenty years after his death, his position that Christ had both a divine and a human will was vindicated at the Sixth Ecumenical Council at Constantinople in 680.[427]

Maximus provided two Papian fragments, both found in his commentary on Pseudo-Dionysius's book titled, *Ecclesiastical Hierarchy*.[428] The above fragment provides no objective proof that Papias was aware of any New Testament writings since Maximus was not quoting Papias but only speculating about the possible source of Pseudo-Dionysius's reference to believers as "children." One could infer, however, from Maximus's musing that he was personally familiar with Papias's writings since he referred to specific content that could be found in the "first book" of *Exposition*. Maximus discovered from Papias's initial volume that in the first century believers were called "children." That orthodox believers were affectionately referred to as

427. Louth, *Maximus*, 18.

428. For a discussion of the identity of the author of *Ecclesiastical Hierarchy* and his theological and philosophical perspectives see Louth, *Denys*, 1–31; for an analysis of his influence on Maximus see pages 113–16 and Louth, *Maximus*, 28–32. Louth speculated that "Denys," as he called him, wrote sometime at the end of the first century and the beginning of the second century (page 17). If, however, Maximus was correct in his conjecture that Denys had relied upon Papias for information then there are two implications regarding Maximus's understanding of the composition of *Ecclesiastical Hierarchy*. The first would be that Maximus was aware that the writings of Denys were not truly composed by Dionysius the Areopagite of Acts 17:34; for it hardly seems reasonable to believe that a civic leader (presumably in his forties) in Athens during the time of Paul's visit would have been familiar with Papias's *Exposition* and then afterwards composed *Ecclesiastical Hierarchy*. (If Denys were forty years old in 49, approximately when Paul left Athens and came to Corinth, then Denys would have been around ninety-one years old at the turn of the century, and over 100 years old in 110—the proposed date of Papias's composition of *Exposition*.) The second implication would be that the author of *Ecclesiastical Hierarchy* probably wrote after Papias had written his *Exposition*. This implies that the author wrote *Ecclesiastical Hierarchy* not at the end of the first century, but more probably no earlier than late in the first quarter of the second century. But, again, this conjecture is based upon the accuracy of Maximus's speculation. There are others who argue that the writings of Pseudo-Dionysius originated in the late fifth to early sixth century. See Dionysius the Pseudo-Areopagite, *The Ecclesiastical Hierarchy*, 1–15. For the dating of Paul's address to the Areopagus in Athens see Bruce, *New Testament History*, 295–317; and Polhill, *Acts*, 365–83.

such is especially observable in the Johannine epistles, in which the author of all three epistles often referred to his audience as "children."[429] Certainly Papias, being the prominent bishop in Asia Minor and an associate of the apostle John, would have been familiar with this term of endearment for the members of the church at Ephesus and its surrounding region. If one were to balk at such a theory, then the fact that Eusebius corroborated that Papias employed "testimonies" from 1 John argues that Papias was familiar with this epistle, an epistle in which its author addressed his readers as "children" thirteen times.[430] Nevertheless, while interesting, this fragment provides little evidence regarding Papias's awareness of the writings of the New Testament.

FRAGMENT 15

> When he says these things he is hinting, I think, at Papias, who was then bishop of Hierapolis in Asia and flourishing in the days of the holy Evangelist John. For this Papias, in the fourth book of his *Expositions of the Lord*, mentioned food among the sources of enjoyment in the resurrection. Later on Apollinarius believed this doctrine, which some refer to as the millennium. . . . and Irenaeus of Lyons says the same thing in the fifth book of his *Against Heresies* and cites in support of his statement the above-mentioned Papias.
>
> Maximus the Confessor, *Scholia on Dionysius the Areopagite,*
> *On the Ecclesiastical Hierarchy*, chap. 7[431]

One can clearly observe from this fragment that Maximus believed Papias was an adult and actively ministered during the lifetime of the apostle John. His identification of John as "the Evangelist" indicates that Maximus was referring to the author of the Fourth Gospel. He did not, however, explicitly refer to Papias as John's "hearer" or disciple. Maximus also asserted that both Apollinaris, possibly the late second-century bishop of

---

429. The apostle John is viewed as the author of all three Johannine epistles. For a greater discussion concerning this question see Joslin, "An Introduction to 1 John," 4–26; Polhill, "2 John and 3 John," 29–38; Hiebert, *The Epistles of John*, 275–83; and Stott, *The Epistles of John*, 13–41.

430. See 1 John 2:1, 12, 13, 18, 28; 3:2, 7, 10, 18; 4:4; 5:2, 21. In the other Johannine epistle, see also 2 John 1, 4, 13; and 3 John 4.

431. Holmes, *The Apostolic Fathers: Diglot Edition*, 582–83.

Hierapolis,[432] and Irenaeus held to an eschatology that affirmed a literal millennial kingdom where physical appetites could be enjoyed. This is confirmed from Irenaeus's own writings.[433] By relying only upon this fragment one cannot conclude that Maximus was intimately familiar with Papias's five-volume work, for all the data he mentioned in this fragment can also be found in Irenaeus's reference to Papias in the fifth volume of *Against Heresies*. Some may assume from this fragment that Papias was familiar with the book of Revelation; however, at best this is an inference. Taken in conjunction with the previous fragment, however, it is reasonable to conclude that Maximus was to some degree personally familiar with Papias's writings. Regarding Papias's knowledge of the New Testament, this fragment provides no objective reference to any specific New Testament book. Nevertheless, it does affirm that Papias was "flourishing" during the lifetime of the apostle John.

FRAGMENT 16

> And others also in Pergamum, among whom was also Papias and many others, and about which the writings bear their martyrdoms.
>
> *Chronicon Paschale*, ca. early seventh century.[434]

The *Chronicon Paschale* is an anonymous early seventh-century chronicle of the world's history beginning with the creation and running to 630.[435] It surveys history through a Christian paradigm, using the Crucifixion as the turning point and standard for properly interpreting human history. Regarding the historic value of this work, Michael and Mary Whitby wrote,

> Particular attention is paid in *CP* to the dating of major church feasts, especially Easter, and to their connection with the

432. Apollinaris of Laodicea of the fourth century is also considered by some to have been a millenarian, see Newman, "Jerome's Judaizers," 441–43.

433. See fragment 1 of this book.

434. *Chronicon Paschale* (PG 92: 628). This fragment in Greek reads as follows: "καὶ ἐν Περγάμῳ δὲ ἕτεροι, ἐν οἷς ἦν καὶ Παπίας καὶ ἄλλοι πολλοί, ὧν καὶ ἔγγραφα φέρονται τὰ μαρτύρια." It is absent from the lists of Ehrman, Schoedel, Körtner, Kürzinger, and Kleist. Lightfoot dated the *CP* as originating "in the first half of the seventh century." Lightfoot, *Essays*, 147.

435. *Chronicon Paschale* 284–628, xi.

chronology of the Creation, but the text set out to be much more than a treatise on biblical chronology and computation since the author chose to include a substantial amount of historical information as well. This material is arranged annalistically by individual years, being dated throughout by consuls, emperors, indications, and Olympiads, and sometimes by Antiochene or other local Eras, and Ascension dates; a large number of entries also contain specific dates (by Roman and/ or Greek, and occasionally Egyptian months), so that all events are located as accurately as possible.[436]

The Whitbys concluded that the author's "attempt at chronological precision distinguishes" the CP from other known chronologies.[437] This fragment, as previously discussed, is the earliest extant reference to Papias having suffered a martyr's fate. It will not, however, be the last. The context in which this fragment is found is the author's summary of Polycarp's death, which according to the CP occurred in 163 during the reign of Marcus Aurelius. The author asserted regarding Papias's martyrdom that documentation existed that also testified to Papias's death as having occurred in the city of Pergamum.[438] This fragment provides no objective evidence that Papias was aware of any New Testament books. Consequently, its primary value is that it may shed some light, albeit rather dimly, upon the death of Papias of Hierapolis.

FRAGMENT 17

. . . taking their cue from the great Papias of Hierapolis, who was a disciple of the Bosom-Friend, and Clement, from Pantaenus, the priest of the Alexandrians, and Ammonius, the most learned scholar, those ancient and earliest interpreters who agree with each other in understanding the whole "six days" to refer to Christ and the church.

Anastasius of Sinai (d. ca. 700)
Considerations on the Hexaemeron I[439]

---

436. Ibid., ix–x.

437. Ibid., x.

438. For a more thorough discussion regarding the possible martyrdom of Papias see the discussion on the death of Papias in chapter 3.

439. Holmes, *The Apostolic Fathers: Diglot Edition*, 578–79.

Very little is known about Anastasius of Sinai. He is generally thought to have been a monk who later became the abbot of the monastery of Mount Sinai.[440] He is also believed to have written several treatises defending orthodoxy against the Monophysite and Monothelite heresies. He was referred to by some as "the New Moses," and is best known for writing a book titled "*Hodegos*." The above fragment is taken from an introduction he wrote to the *Hexaemeron*. This fragment does not provide demonstrable evidence that Papias was aware of any books of the New Testament. Anastasius did, however, believe that Papias knew the apostle John, whom he referred to as the "Bosom-Friend."[441] Holmes rightly saw the title "Bosom-Friend" as a reference to John 13:23, 25; 21:20.[442] Other references to this particular disciple of Jesus are also found in John 19:26 and 20:2. Anastasius later wrote that Papias was a "follower" of "John the Evangelist."[443] It seems reasonable to conclude, therefore, that he was referring to the same person, who was none other than the apostle John.[444]

Although this fragment does not contain a direct quote from Papias's *Exposition*, it does provide some evidence that Anastasius was familiar with Papias's work. This is observable from his reference to Papias's explanation of the creation account. Anastasius stated that Papias implied that the "six day" creation account as found in the book of Genesis was also a reference to Christ and his church.[445] If Anastasius was accurate regarding what Papias wrote, then it reveals that there were occasions when Papias employed a hermeneutic of typology or allegory when dealing with certain Old Testament passages. This is evident from Anastasius's alignment of Papias with other patristic leaders who are commonly associated with the "Alexandrian school."[446] There is little evidence from the other fragments, however, that Papias was thoroughly committed to the Alexandrian method of interpreting

440. Krueger, "Anastasius of Sinaita," 164–65.

441. The exact phrase is ἐν τῷ ἐπιστηθίῳ φοιτήσαντος, which is literally translated, "the one frequenting upon the breast." Consequently, "Bosom-Friend" is a good translation. LSJ, s.v. "στήθειος." Schoedel stated that this was a common "epithet for John the Evangelist in the Greek Fathers." Schoedel, *The Fragments*, 114.

442. Holmes, *The Apostolic Fathers: Diglot Edition*, 579.

443. See the following fragment.

444. Keener, *John*, 1:81–115; Blomberg, *Reliability of John's Gospel*, 22–35. For the argument that the "Bosom-Friend" or "Beloved Disciple" was not John, a son of Zebedee, see Culpepper, *John*, 72–85.

445. See Schoedel, *The Fragments*, 114–16 for a more detailed discussion of how Papias might have believed the creation account referred to both Christ and the church.

446. Kleist, *Papias*, 209; Schoedel, *The Fragments*, 114.

the Old Testament. That is not to say, however, that he did not at times employ typology in his exposition of certain Old Testament texts. Anastasius is not the only author to note Papias's employment of the Old Testament.[447] Regarding the reference to Papias's association of the church with the six day creation account, without a direct quote from *Exposition* it is hard to determine if Anastasius had properly understood Papias or had possibly confused him with a different author. If, however, he had read *Exposition*, and if he correctly understood Papias's exposition concerning the creation account in Genesis, then it appears that one of Papias's purposes in his five-volume work was to exposit the "oracles of the Lord" while interacting with passages from the Old Testament. This theory will be developed further in the discussion of fragment 23. Papias's exposition of specific Old Testament passages and Jesus' teachings might explain Eusebius's admiring remarks about his knowledge of the "Scriptures" in his earlier edition of *Ecclesiastical History*.[448]

Some clarification is in order regarding Anastasius's opinion that Papias was a "disciple" of the "Bosom-Friend." First, Anastasius did not use the more commonly known word "μαθητής" to describe Papias's relationship to the apostle John. He instead employed only the genitive article "τοῦ" to indicate Papias's relationship to the "Bosom-Friend;" nonetheless, calling him John's "disciple" is not entirely inappropriate.[449] Anastasius, however, used in the next fragment a more specific word while describing Papias's relationship to the apostle John. Regardless of his vocabulary, Anastasius, unlike Eusebius, believed Papias knew the "Bosom-Friend" of Jesus, who Anastasius also identified as "John the Evangelist." While it is possible that Anastasius relied upon the opinions of others regarding Papias's relationship to the apostle John, it is equally possible that he came to this conclusion by his personal reading of Papias *Exposition*. How Anastasius more precisely described the relationship between the two will be more thoroughly developed in the discussion of the next fragment.

Fragment 18

> So then, the more ancient interpreters of the churches—I mean
> Philo, the philosopher and contemporary of the apostles, and the
> famous Papias of Hierapolis, the disciple of John the Evangelist,

447. See fragment 23, p. 248.

448. See fragment 4, p. 116.

449. For an explanation of the genitive of relationship see Wallace, *The Basics*, 47, 105.

Irenaeus of Lyons and Justin the martyr and philosopher, Pantaenus the Alexandrian and Clement the Stromateus, and their associates—interpreted the sayings about Paradise spiritually, and referred them to the church of Christ.

Anastasius of Sinai, *Considerations on the Hexaemeron* 7[450]

It may appear to the casual observer that Anastasius did not have an adequate grasp of Philo or his writings since he associated Philo with other Christian authors. Schoedel, however, explained that Anastasius was "vividly conscious of the gulf that separates the Jewish philosopher Philo from Christianity (*Vtae Dux* 14; PG, LXXXIX, 244–45); but he does not hesitate to refer to him as a man with a sound (allegorical) sense for scriptural interpretation (cf. *In Hexaem.* 7; PG, LXXXIX, 956)."[451] Anastasius clearly held Papias in high regard, referring to him as "the great Papias" in the previous fragment,[452] while in this fragment he called him "famous."[453] He also associated Papias with some of the most respected men in patristic history. Given his admiration for Papias as a leader of the patristic church, it seems reasonable to assume that Anastasius had at some point read Papias's writings for himself. He also called Papias one of the more ancient "interpreters of the churches,"[454] indicating that he perceived Papias was far more than a collector of potentially soon to be forgotten church traditions. Instead, he understood him as one who explained their meanings and significance.[455]

Regarding Papias's relationship to the apostle John, Anastasius called him a "φοιτητής" of John the Evangelist, which is literally translated as referring to one who "frequently comes and goes" or has access to another. It is especially used with reference to a pupil's access to his or her teacher; consequently, "disciple" is an appropriate translation.[456] There is greater precision, however, in Anastasius's vocabulary then some might infer from the

---

450. Holmes, *The Apostolic Fathers: Diglot Edition*, 578–79.

451. Schoedel, *The Fragments*, 115.

452. "Παπίας ὁ πολὺς"

453. "Παπίου τοῦ πάνυ"

454. The Greek word Anastasius used for "interpreters" is "ἐξηγητικῶν." Regarding this entire phrase "ἐκκλησιῶν ἐξηγητικῶν," Holmes argued that the text should read as, "εκκηγοσιαστικων εξηγητικων." See note 13 on Holmes, *Apostolic Fathers*, 3rd ed., 750. Schoedel likewise translated the phrase as "the ecclesiastical interpreters," Schoedel, *The Fragments*, 115.

455. There is also the possibility that Anastasius simply inherited a tradition from others who valued Papias.

456. LSJ, s.v. "φοιτητής."

word "disciple," for the term "φοιτητής" communicates that Papias was not simply one who followed in the teachings of the apostle John, but rather that he was one who had regular access to his mentor. Clearly, therefore, Anastasius believed that Papias knew the apostle John. What makes Anastasius's opinion about Papias's relationship with the apostle John so important is that he, unlike Eusebius, was not threatened by Papias's eschatology, even though he clearly appreciated the "Alexandrian" tradition of interpreting the Scriptures. One can discern from this fragment, in conjunction with fragment 17, a strong inference that Papias was an exegete of biblical narratives rather than one who simply collected oral traditions. However, as with fragment 17, there is no objective evidence indicating Papias's knowledge of any specific New Testament book.

FRAGMENT 19

> After Domitian, Nerva reigned one year. He re-called John from the island and allowed him to live in Ephesus. At that time he was the sole survivor of the twelve disciples, and after writing the Gospel that bears his name was honored with martyrdom. For Papias, the bishop of Hierapolis, who had seen him with his own eyes, claims in the second book of the *Sayings of the Lord* that he was killed by the Jews, thus clearly fulfilling, together with his brother, Christ's prophecy concerning them and their own confession and agreement about this.
>
> For when the Lord said to them, "Are you able to drink the cup that I drink?" and they eagerly assented and agreed, he said: "You will drink my cup and will be baptized with the baptism with which I am baptized." And this is to be expected, for it is impossible for God to lie. Moreover the encyclopedic Origen also affirms in his interpretation of the Gospel According to Matthew that John was martyred, indicating that he had learned this from the successors of the apostles. In addition, the well-informed Eusebius says in his *Ecclesiastical History*: "Thomas was allotted Parthia, while John received Asia, where he made his residence and died in Ephesus."

> George the Sinner (ninth c.), *Chronicle*[457]

---

457. Holmes, *The Apostolic Fathers: Diglot Edition*, 573–75.

George "the Sinner," was a ninth-century monk who is also known as George "Hamartolus."[458] Little is known about him save what can be gleaned from his chronicle of world history in which he asserted that at the time of his writing Michael III was reining in Constantinople (842–867). As with several others, the author of this fragment testified that Papias associated with the apostle John. He also believed, however, that John and his brother James were killed by the Jews.[459] Schoedel has aptly demonstrated that the author of this particular fragment in all probability was not Hamartolus, explaining that;

> All MSS of George's *Chronicon* (ninth century) except Coislin-ianus 305 have "John the Theologian" (the Evangelist) go "to his rest in peace." The composer of the exceptional MS, whose text we translate, seems to have gone out of his way to collect references concerning John's end. In (1) he follows the opening sentences found in all the other MSS, changing "went to his rest in peace" to "was honored by martyrdom." In (2) the reason for the change becomes clear: our author has information from Papias and has reflected on Mark 10:38–39. In (3) he makes reference to Origen's remarks on Mark 10:35–40 in his *Commentary on Matthew* 16:6 (ed. Klostermann, I, 486). This is followed by a quotation from Eusebius, *H.E.* 3.1.1, which is to be found also in the other MSS.[460]

This fragment, therefore, does not appear to be from the hand of Hamartolus but from the hand of an unknown redactor. Whether this redactor had read Papias for himself, or was relying upon a manuscript associated with Philip of Side regarding the martyrdom of the apostle John is not clear, for he provided no direct quote from Papias to validate his observation. Moreover, he failed to provide any demonstrable evidence that he had independently read Papias's *Exposition* for himself. This is evident since all the data he provided is also found in the fragments preserved by both Eusebius and Philip of Side. Consequently, it is not clear whether his statement that Papias "had seen him (the apostle John) with his own

---

458. Hereafter, "Hamartolus."

459. For a discussion concerning possibilities of the apparent martyrdom of the apostle John see fragment 11, p. 215. As can be observed above, Lightfoot, Harmer, and Holmes dated Hamartolus's work as from the ninth century. Consequently, this fragment is obviously later then the ninth century since it appears to be an insertion into Hamartolus's work. Carl Clemen dated the manuscript containing this insertion as originating in the tenth or eleventh century. Clemen, "John at Ephesus," 645–46.

460. Schoedel, *The Fragments*, 120. Origen's comments can be found in Origen *Commentary on Matthew* 16.6 (PG 13:1385).

eyes," was a conclusion he borrowed from another author (e.g., Philip of Side) or a conviction he arrived at by his own investigation. Without clear evidence, therefore, that he had personally read Papias's *Exposition*, certitude about the validity of his opinion regarding Papias's relationship to the apostle John and John's death is unattainable.

This redactor, however, unlike in fragment 11 explained the theological capital to be gained from John's supposed martyrdom, contending that it was the fulfillment of Jesus' prophecy concerning the sons of Zebedee.[461] Lightfoot argued that the importance of the potential martyrdom of both of the sons of Zebedee was consistent with Papias's exegetical purpose; consequently, he believed that Papias was the "ultimate" source for "Hamartolus," although he had either misunderstood or misread Papias. Lightfoot explained his position by writing,

> Here we have an obvious error. The fate which really befell James is attributed to John. Georgius Hamartolos therefore cannot be quoting directly from Papias, for Papias cannot have reported the martyrdom of John. But, on the other hand, Papias seems plainly to have been the ultimate source of his information. The work is precisely and correctly quoted. The general tenor accords with the main object of Papias' book—the exposition of a saying of Christ, and the illustration of it by a story derived from tradition. This being so, the error is most easily explained by a lacuna.[462]

Lightfoot continued by explaining that Hamartolus seems to have read a manuscript in which several lines were missing, or that he had accidentally skipped over several lines; consequently, he misattributed Papias's reference to James's death as having also befallen the apostle John. This theory is attractive; however, it is unverifiable. More importantly, however, whether this mistake was caused by lost text or the misreading of a text, it does not appear to have come from Hamartolus but from a later redactor. Regarding this redactor, Schoedel observed that he had relied heavily upon other patristic authors for his conclusion concerning the death of the apostle John; and even when dealing with these sources he

---

461. See Mark 10:35–38. This passage does not demand death as the fulfillment of Jesus' prophecy. The idea that apostle John had not died as a martyr was apparently viewed by some as evidence of failed prophecy. This seems to have created a challenge to the trustworthiness of the Scriptures. Ironically, as the first century drew to a close there were some in the church who were concerned that the apostle John might not live long enough to see the return of Jesus (see John 21:20–23).

462. Lightfoot, *Essays*, 212.

apparently lacked the ability to correctly interpret them. Schoedel noticed with respect to his handling of Origen's writings that this redactor failed to notice that Origen saw "the fulfillment of the prophecy of Mark 10:35–40 in James's death and *John's later exile to Patmos!*"[463]

It is again worth noting that this redactor, however "uncritical" he may have been, disagreed with Eusebius regarding Papias's association with the apostle John. Contra Eusebius, he believed that Papias had in fact seen him "with his own eyes." Given his uncritical approach to his data it is hard to place a great deal of confidence in his conclusion about Papias's relationship to the apostle John. Nevertheless, his motivation was no better or worse than that of Eusebius, for while Eusebius desired to distance Papias from the apostle John because of Papias's eschatology, this redactor wished to connect Papias and the apostle in order to vindicate Jesus' prophecy concerning the sons of Zebedee. Their motivations, therefore, were less then admirable since both were driven by different apologetical issues. Regardless of this redactor's motives, he failed to provide any quote from Papias or any data indicating that he had independently read Papias's *Exposition* for himself, thus this fragment provides no independent evidence that Papias was aware of any New Testament books. This fragment's significance, consequently, for learning more about Papias and his knowledge of specific New Testament writings is marginal.

FRAGMENT 20

> Indeed, [Stephen Gobarus follows] neither Papias, the bishop and martyr of Hierapolis, nor Irenaeus, the holy bishop of Lyons, when they say that the kingdom of heaven is the enjoyment of certain material foods.
>
> Photius (ninth c.), *Bibliotheca* 232[464]

This fragment comes from Photius's work titled *Bibliotheca*.[465] Photius was the Patriarch of Constantinople during much of the last half of the ninth

463. Schoedel, *The Fragments*, 120.

464. Holmes, *The Apostolic Fathers: Diglot Edition*, 582–83.

465. For brief biographies on the life of Photius see René Henry's introduction to Photius, *Bibliothèque*, 1:ix–xxv, and Schaff, *History of the Church*, 4:312–16, 636–42. Some, such as Burton, believe the reference to Papias's martyrdom actually came from Stephen Gobarus, an obscure late sixth-century theologian (Burton, *Lectures*, 392). Since Photius did not provide an exact quote from him, it is unclear whether Gobarus

century. The context in which this fragment is found is his explanation of Stephen Gobarus's position regarding Papias's and Irenaeus's eschatology. Very little is known about Stephen, most of which is drawn from Photius's comments concerning him. He appears to have lived in the sixth century, and was an "Aristotelian" and "tritheist" whose writings exposed apparent contradictions in the church's theological traditions.[466] It is Photius's statement regarding Papias that is germane to the focus of this book. His comments provide no objective evidence that Papias was aware of any writings found in the New Testament. He does, however, refer to Papias as a martyr. It is not possible to confirm that his opinion about Papias's death came from his own investigation or his reading of the *CP*.[467] It is not unreasonable to think that Photius, a ninth-century Patriarch of Constantinople, had access to the *CP*, a Byzantine historiography written ca. 630. While this fragment does not challenge the thesis of this book, it also provides no additional independent data.

FRAGMENT 21

> . . . and the great Methodius . . . and also Irenaeus, bishop of Lyons, and Papias, bishop of Hierapolis; the first won the crown of martyrdom, while the latter two were men of apostolic character. . . . But we do not follow them whenever they treated the truth too lightly and were lead to speak against the generally accepted ecclesiastical teaching. We do not at all, however, take anything away from their patristic honor and glory.
>
> Photius, *Letter to Archbishop and Metropolitan Aquileias*[468]

This fragment, as in the case of the preceding fragment, provides no objective evidence that Papias knew of any New Testament writings;

---

was the writer who originally referred to Papias as a martyr, or if he had depended upon an earlier source.

466. Harnack, *Dogma*, 3:221, 4:240.

467. See fragment 16, p. 233. Schoedel suggested that Photius may have obtained his information about Papias from Irenaeus. Schoedel, *The Fragments*, 117.

468. Holmes, *The Apostolic Fathers: Diglot Edition*, 586–87. Kürzinger included this fragment but passed over it without comment, Kürzinger, *Papias*, 120–21; as did Preuschen (Preuschen, *Antilegomena*, 97, 201. Körtner simply addressed a few textual variations. Körtner, *Papias*, 69, 252–53. It is absent from the lists of Schoedel, Kleist, and Ehrman.

therefore, it does not seriously challenge or aid the thesis of this book. It may be inferred from this fragment that Photius believed that Papias was of the same generation as Irenaeus, although this would be incorrect. As previously discussed, Irenaeus may have been considered by some as a participant of the era of the "apostolic fathers" since he was a disciple of Polycarp. Such a classification, however, would be viewed as inaccurate by today's scholarship. Compared to Methodius, who died ca. 311, both Irenaeus and Papias would certainly have been considered as members of a more senior generation. Consequently, Photius regarded these two earlier bishops as honorable because of their antiquity, while Methodius was honored for his martyrdom. Such classifications by Photius seems rather awkward since he referred to Papias as a "martyr" in the previous fragment, while here he only recognized Methodius as having been martyred. Photius's intent, however, was to focus upon Papias's association with the church's earliest generation, rather than any honor Papias may have also possessed as a martyr. Photius had a rather healthy view of Papias and his importance. While not agreeing with some aspects of Papias's theology, such as his eschatology, he was unwilling in the manner of Eusebius to marginalize Papias and his significance to the history of the early church.

Fragment 22

> Here begins the summary of the Gospel According to John:
>
> The Gospel of John was made known and given to the churches by John while he was still in the flesh, as a man of Hierapolis by the name of Papias, a beloved disciple of John, has related in the exoteric—that is, the last—part of his five books. Indeed, he wrote down the Gospel correctly as John dictated.
>
> Codex Vaticanus Alexandrinus 14 (ninth c.)[469]

This fragment is commonly referred to as one of the "anti-Marcionite prologues." It is anonymous and generally inspires little confidence regarding

---

469. Holmes, *The Apostolic Fathers: Diglot Edition*, 585. Schoedel included this fragment but included additional material unrelated to Papias. Schoedel, *The Fragments*, 122. Holmes in the initial diglot edition included this same material in Latin but did not translate it into English. He removed it, however, in the third edition. Holmes, *Apostolic Fathers*, 3rd ed., 756–57. This fragment is also included in the lists of Kleist, *Papias*, 124; *Papias and Quadratus* (LCL 25:117–18); Kürzinger, *Papias*, 124–25; and Körtner, *Papias*, 69–70.

factual information about Papias or what he might have written. Some, however, may have underestimated its value. The prologue certainly contains data that creates challenges to its credibility, but this should not be construed as proof that it is completely worthless with respect to all the historical information contained in it.[470] It is assigned at this position in this list of Papian fragments since it is viewed as originating from the ninth century, primarily because that is the estimated date of the manuscript in which it is found. Some, however, have estimated it to be considerably older.[471] Regarding its actual age and origin Schoedel wrote, "Its clumsy Latin suggests a Greek original; some of the Latin phraseology is characteristic of fourth century writers."[472] If Schoedel's estimation is correct, then it should be moved forward in this list of Papian fragments; however, it is kept here because certitude regarding its age is tenuous.

Although this fragment provides no direct quote from Papias's writings, it is significant because it intimately associates Papias with the apostle John and his Gospel. This fragment states that John authored the Fourth Gospel, and that it was not the work of later compilers and redactors, which is also consistent with a tradition found in the Muratorian Fragment.[473] Evidence for the assertion that John authored the Fourth Gospel was apparently to be found in the fifth book of Papias's *Exposition*.[474] Since

470. For the view that this fragment has little historical value see Schoedel, *The Fragments*, 121–23.

471. Culpepper, *John*, 129–30.

472. Schoedel, *The Fragments*, 121.

473. Bruce, *The Canon*, 159–61.

474. There is some confusion regarding the Latin word *exotericis* in fragment 22, p. 243. Schoedel argued that it seems to be a mistake since it does not appear to be a word at all. Consequently, it should read as "exegetical." Schoedel, *The Fragments*, 123. Lightfoot, however, while correctly understanding that *exotericis* was a Latin word, also believed it was a mistake; Lightfoot, *Essays*, 213. Ruppert Annand argued that the word referred to the "outermost part" or "original outer wrappings enclosing Papias own Five Books, or possibly to the cover protecting the original copy of the Fourth Gospel." Annand, "Four Gospels," 58. To argue that the author of this fragment, which is no later than ninth-century and may be as early as the fourth century, could possibly have had access to information contained on the "original wrapping" of Papias's work or the original manuscript of the Gospel of John taxes the imagination. Consequently, Schoedel's assessment that Annand's theory is "farfetched" is justified. Alexander, however, may have the best explanation of the meaning of this Latin word, for he stated that "exoteric were treatises designed for a wider public (cf., e.g., EN 1102a26)." Alexander, "The Living Voice," 238. Consequently, this word appears not to be a translation to any word in Papias's title (e.g., of the Greek word ἐξηγήσεως), but rather it is a Latin description of his work, thus it should be translated as "treatise."

Papias's work is no longer extant, confirmation of this particular reference is not possible. By referring to Papias as the apostle's amanuensis, this fragment contradicts a tradition claiming that the Gospel of John was dictated by John to a disciple named Prochorus during John's exile on Patmos.[475] The tradition of Prochorus's involvement with the writings of the apostle John is tenuous at best. Prochorus is associated with John predominantly through a redaction of a work known as *The Acts of John*. Regarding Prochorus's potential relationship with the apostle, Pieter J. Lalleman wrote,

> Until far into the last century, episodes from the AJ were only preserved because they had been incorporated in manuscripts of a more recent story about John. The later account, the so-called *Acts of John by Prochorus*, dates from the fifth century and was popular in the Byzantine Church. In several medieval copies of this text, there appear episodes that are considerably older than the fifth century and which, taken together, forms a rather homogeneous text, the early AJ.
>
> Nowadays the division of the episodes belonging to the AJ and those belonging to the *Acts of John by Prochorus* is beyond dispute. The differences in doctrinal stance between the post-Nicene Prochorus-text and the heterodox AJ are clear to everyone who reads the texts; besides, most of the action in Prochorus is concentrated on the Isle of Patmos, which is never mentioned in the early AJ.[476]

Some speculate that this is the same Prochorus who is mentioned in Acts 6.5, in which he and six others were selected to be deacons by the Jerusalem church in order to oversee the caretaking of the church's widows. How and when he became associated with the apostle John during his exile at Patmos has never been substantially documented; consequently, it is unclear if he actually associated with John. When analyzing this fragment there are several questions about its author that are worthy of consideration: did he originally write in Latin or Greek, is it a later copy of the original, and if it is a copy does it reflect the education of the copyist or of the original author? If the author of this fragment has correctly understood Papias, then it appears that Papias served as an amanuensis for the apostle John as he composed a part or the whole of the Fourth Gospel.[477]

475. For a brief summary of Prochorus's supposed relationship to the Gospel of John see Taniguchi, Bovon, and Antonopoulos, "John the Theologian," 338.

476. Lalleman, *The Acts of John*, 5–6. Lalleman dated the *Acts of John* as originating in the early to mid second century, see pages 268–73.

477. Zahn recognized the possibility that Papias could have served as an amanuensis

If one were pressed to conjecture as to which of these two figures possibly served as an amanuensis of the apostle John at one point or another, then Papias would have a better claim to such a position since the tradition concerning Prochorus is in all probability is spurious, as well as later than Papias's *Exposition*.[478]

Concerning the likelihood of Papias having served as the amanuensis of the apostle John, Lightfoot speculated that the author of this fragment may have misunderstood what Papias might have written, arguing that he misinterpreted the aorist form of the verb "ἀπογράφω" as a first person singular instead of a third person plural, in which case if the "ν" were incorrectly dropped at the end of the third person plural it would have the identical form as the first person aorist.[479] This would mean that the author might have possibly understood Papias to have written, "I wrote the Gospel as John dictated," instead of "They wrote the Gospel as John dictated."[480] While this conjecture has some merit, two important observations must be made; first, such a view demands that the author of this fragment possessed at least a portion of the fifth book of Papias's *Exposition*;

---

for John, writing that "it is almost self-evident that John, like Paul, dictated extended portions of Greek writings to an amanuensis; and Papias, the friend of Polycarp, and a companion of the same age, can just as well as he would have been twenty-five or more years of age when the Fourth Gospel was written." Zahn, *Introduction*, 3:197.

478. Badham wildly conjectured that the author of this fragment was terribly confused and conflated traditions from Eusebius, Papias, and the *Acts of John by Prochorus*. Badham, "The Martyrdom of St. John," 737. Schoedel considered this an "anachronism," thereby discrediting this fragment. Schoedel, *The Fragments*, 122. He assumed, however, a conjecture that has not been proven, which is either that Papias was not an associate of John or that John's Gospel was written earlier in his life before he associated with Papias. If Papias had received a formal education and was a "beloved disciple" of the apostle John in his early twenties, there is nothing that prohibits him from having served as the apostle John's amanuensis. This possibility, however, would mean that John wrote his Gospel very near the close of the first century. Some have argued for a pre-70 AD composition for this Gospel, which would make it impossible for Papias to have served in such a capacity. Robinson, *Redating*, 254–311; also Wallace, "The Fourth Gospel," 177–205.

479. Lightfoot, *Essays*, 213–14; see also 214 n. 1.

480. The verb ἀπογράφω in the first person singular aorist active appears as ἀπέγραψα, while the third person plural aorist active form is ἀπέγραψαν. However, if the final "ν" were dropped then its form would be identical to the first person singular. Lightfoot's theory essentially depends upon a mistake by either Papias or a scribe who erred as he copied a manuscript of *Exposition*. While Lightfoot believed this theory provided the most probable explanation regarding this question of who served as John's secretary, to his credit he confessed that "no weight can be attached" to it. Lightfoot, *Essays*, 214.

and secondly, even if the author misunderstood this particular verb (i.e., whether the verb was singular or plural), his observation demands that Papias was aware of the Gospel of John.

There is some question regarding the credibility of the author of this fragment when handling historical material. It should be noted, however, that he was not inaccurate with respect to everything he wrote concerning Papias. He correctly noted, for example, that Papias was from Hierapolis and that he had written a five-volume work. It is his comment about Papias's last book, however, that is most compelling.[481] In a similar manner of footnoting found among other ancient authors (such as Eusebius's reference to Papias's preface), this author stated that in Papias's fifth book two important observations could be made; first, that a man named John wrote the Fourth Gospel, which the author believed to be the apostle John; and secondly, that Papias knew of this Gospel and even served as John's amanuensis. The implications are obvious; first, he believed that Papias knew the apostle John, referring to Papias as his "beloved disciple;"[482] and secondly, that Papias knew of the Fourth Gospel. Schoedel made a great deal out of certain anachronistic material contained in the second section of this fragment. The "possible" anachronism concerns Marcion rather than Papias. More specifically, this material states that Marcion had met and was rejected by the apostle John, which seems extremely unlikely, although not entirely impossible, since Marcion appears to have been a contemporary of Papias and Polycarp.[483] Kleist suggested that the author of this fragment may have confused Marcion's possible confrontation with the apostle John with other well known confrontations, such as Marcion's own confrontation with Polycarp, or the apostle John's confrontation with

481. The phrase in Latin is *quinque libris retulit*, which literally reads, "fifth of the book sees it." A more fluent translation would be "it can be seen in the fifth book." Holmes, *Apostolic Fathers*, 3rd ed., 756.

482. It seems appropriate to refer to a disciple of the apostle John as the "beloved disciple" since John, the son of Zebedee, was in all probability the "beloved disciple" of Jesus. See the discussion on fragment 17, p. 234, for a more thorough explanation of this phrase and its significance in the Gospel of John. For a survey of the possible identities of the "beloved disciple," see Culpepper, *John*, 56–84.

483. For a summary of Marcion's life see Frend, *The Rise of Christianity*, 212–18. Schoedel called any confrontation between the apostle John and Marcion impossible. Schoedel, *The Fragments*, 121. Frend estimated Marcion to have been born ca. 85 and to have died ca. 165. Regarding Marcion's possible association with Polycarp, Eusebius preserved an encounter between the two see Eusebius *Ecc. Hist.* IV.14.6–7 (LCL 153:337–39).

Cerinthus.[484] Körtner speculated that the author may have been referring to Papias rather than the apostle John regarding this confrontation with Marcion.[485] Concerning the historical accuracy of some of the data found in this fragment, at worse this author was incorrect regarding his information about Marcion, and at best he was simply unclear. There is nothing in this fragment, however, that demands one come to the same conclusion concerning his information about Papias.

If one surveys and combines all the surviving data available from the writings of Papias, data from his preface to his fifth book, one would find information about the origins of the first Gospels, i.e., Matthew's Hebraic Gospel and Mark's Greek Gospel (contained in his preface), and information about the church's martyrs and early leaders (contained in his second book), as well as other previously unrecorded traditions of the Lord's oracles (contained in his fourth book). It does not seem unreasonable, therefore, that Papias may have waited until his fifth and final book to discuss the writings of the last surviving apostle, who in all probability was the apostle John. In summary, while certain material contained in this fragment requires critical analysis, this fragment should not be unnecessarily marginalized as having no historical value.[486] Its value is especially important with respect to information found in Papias's fifth book and his knowledge of the apostle John and the Fourth Gospel.

FRAGMENT 23

And Papias spoke in the following manner in his treatise:

"Heaven did not endure his earthly intentions, because it is impossible for light to communicate with darkness. He fell to earth, here to live; and when mankind came here, where he was, he did not permit them to live in natural passions; on the contrary, he led them astray into many evils. But Michael and his legions, who are guardians of the world, were helping mankind, as Daniel learned; they gave laws and made the prophets wise. And all this was war against the dragon, who was setting stumbling blocks for men. Then their battle extended into heaven, to Christ himself. Yet Christ came; and the law, which was impossible for anyone else, he fulfilled in his body, according to the

---

484. Kleist, *Papias*, 210; see also Lightfoot, *Essays*, 212.
485. Körtner, *Papias*, 69–70; see also Kleist, *Papias*, 210.
486. Contra, Lightfoot, *Essays*, 214.

apostle. He defeated sin and condemned Satan, and through his death he spread abroad his righteousness over all. As this occurred, the victory of Michael and his legions, the guardians of mankind, become complete, and the dragon could resist no more, because the death of Christ exposed him to ridicule and threw him to earth, concerning which Christ said: 'I was seeing Satan fallen from heaven like a lightning bolt.'"

In this sense the teacher understood not his first fall, but the second, which was through the cross; and this did not consist of a spatial fall, as at first, but rather judgment and expectation of a mighty punishment. . . .

Andrew of Caesarea, *On the Apocalypse*, on Rev 12:7–9[487]

Before analyzing the content of this fragment, it is necessary to discuss its author, as well as its length. Holmes indicated that this fragment is actually found in an Armenian translation of Andrew's commentary, *On the Apocalypse*; however, it does not appear in his commentary as found in *PG*. It has been translated into German by Folker Siegert, who stated that the manuscript containing this fragment "deviates considerably from the Greek version," of Andrew's commentary.[488] It appears, therefore, that it is misleading to attribute this fragment to Andrew; consequently, it is not grouped with the other Papian fragments originating from him. Lightfoot suggested that this text is a catena, while Siegert wrote that it came from Constantine, a metropolitan of Hierapolis who flourished approximately four hundred years after Andrew.[489] This is not to say, however, that this fragment holds no value for researching Papias and his knowledge of the New Testament, for the author appears to have provided a lengthy quote from Papias. Regarding its length, Holmes, Siegert, and Kürzinger end this Papian fragment with the quote of Luke 10:18.[490]

---

487. Holmes, *The Apostolic Fathers: Diglot Edition*, 588–91. This fragment is absent in Schoedel edition.

488. Siegert, "Papiaszitate," 605–6.

489. Ibid., 611. Ramsey, relying on L. Campbell, dated Constantine to have lived ca. 1000. Ramsay, *Cities and Bishoprics of Phrygia*, vol. 1.1, 120 n. 14. Lightfoot appeared to have a slightly different version of this "catena" (maybe even Greek), which he stated bears "the names Ecumenius and Artheas." Lightfoot, *Essays*, 201. Lightfoot also elaborated on some interesting similarities in what this catena records regarding Papias's interpretation of Luke 10.18 and with what Anastasius of Sinai, who had read Papias's *Exposition* wrote about this same verse (see Lightfoot, *Essays*, 200–201).

490. Holmes, *The Apostolic Fathers: Diglot Edition*, 589; Siegert, "Papiaszitate," 607; and Kürzinger, *Papias*, 129. I wish to thank Timothy Michael Law, a D.Phil. candidate

The significance of a Papian fragment possibly containing a passage from Luke should not be considered insignificant. Regrettably, the text does not state that the quote of Jesus came from Luke's Gospel, or from "the Scriptures."[491] It is possible, therefore, that Papias employed a well memorized "oral" tradition that was being circulated by Christian communities of Asia Minor. It is equally as possible, however, that Papias did in fact rely upon Luke's Gospel for this "oracle of the Lord." Certainly, by the middle of the first quarter of the second century some Christian communities were orally transmitting "oracles" of Jesus that were embedded within the canonical Gospels. Since the text is only preserved in Armenian, not knowing the exact vocabulary and structure of Papias's quote makes it difficult for determining whether he had relied upon the Third Gospel or an oral tradition. The fragment as it stands now can provide a multitude of conjectures regarding Papias's source. For example, even if Papias referred to Jesus' words as found in Luke's Gospel there is no guarantee that he had not relied upon his own memory, and as a result he may have loosely quoted Jesus as he remembered it from the Gospel of Luke. Consequently, this would make it difficult to prove conclusively that he had relied upon Luke, since a "loose" quote could also be perceived as the product of an "oral tradition" rather than a direct quote from a literary source. Regardless of the many possibilities and conjectures concerning what Papias's source(s) may have been, this fragment creates a serious challenge to the contention that Papias had no knowledge of Luke's Gospel.[492]

This fragment is also helpful for observing one of Papias's purposes for his *magnum opus*. It clearly reveals, as his title suggests, that he intended to "explain" Jesus' "oracles." In this particular fragment Papias "exposited" Jesus' teaching about Satan's meteoric fall from heaven. In order to do so he interpreted Jesus' words in light of other well-known biblical themes, themes such as God—who is the true light—is intolerant of all that is unholy, which in the Scriptures is often described as darkness. The

in Oriental Studies at Oxford University for his help in understanding more about this text. It is his opinion its author believed that Papias had quoted Luke 10:18. He also observed that the writing style is consistent with other writings from the medieval period.

491. The possibility that material in Luke's Gospel might be considered "Scripture" is not without warrant as can be observed in the quote of Luke 10:7 in 1 Tim 5:18.

492. Lightfoot contended that "great stress" cannot be laid upon this fragment as evidence Papias knew Luke's Gospel. In spite of his tenuous acknowledgment, he did admit that "it must indeed seem highly improbable that Papias should have been unacquainted with a Gospel which Marcion, a contemporary and native of Asia Minor, thought fit to adapt to his heretical teaching." Lightfoot, *Essays*, 186.

author of this fragment explained that "it is impossible for light to communicate with darkness," which touches upon one of the more significant themes contained in the writings of the apostle John (John 1:4–8; 3:19; and 1 John 1:5–7). While this theme is common in Johannine literature, it is also commonly found throughout the Scriptures (see Gen 1:1–4; Ps 18:28; Isa 42:6–7; 1 Cor 6:14; 1 Pet 2:9). Next, he associated Satan's fall with the angelic warfare found in the book of Daniel.[493] It is at this point that the author referred to Satan as "the dragon." While acknowledging that a similar reference to Satan may also possibly be found in Isaiah 27:1 and 51:9, it is much more likely that the author relied upon the book of Revelation for this description of Satan.[494] Consequently, assuming Papias was in fact the author of this fragment, one could reasonably infer that he was familiar with the book containing the apocalyptic visions of the apostle John.

The sentence, "Yet Christ came; and the law, which was impossible for anyone else, he fulfilled in his body, according to the apostle. He defeated sin and condemned Satan, and through his death he spread abroad his righteousness over all," is significant since it is attributed to one called "the apostle." Unfortunately, one is left to wonder which apostle Papias was referring to since a specific identity was not provided. The text appears to be a condensation of several New Testament passages. The phrase "Christ came" is found in Galatians 3:24; Ephesians 2:17; and Hebrews 9:11 and 10:5. The theme of human inability to satisfy the law is found in Galatians 2:16, 3:11, 3:13, and Colossians 2:14. That Christ's physical death satisfied the requirement of the Law is also addressed in Romans 7:4, Colossians 1:22 and 2:15, Hebrews 10:10, and 1 Peter 2:24. His defeat of sin is especially evident in 1 Corinthians 15:54–57 and Colossians 2:13–14. That he has secured condemnation for Satan is found in John 12:31; Luke 10:18; Ephesians 1:19–23 and 6:10–12; as well as Colossians 2:15. And finally, the theme that Jesus' impact is expanding "over all" is specifically found in Colossians 1:6, 23. Nielsen, armed with only silence, conjectured that Papias had rejected the writings of Paul as being on a par with "Holy Scripture," contending that he "encountered Paul in the person and writings of Polycarp of Smyrna and that Polycarp had done something with the Pauline corpus which caused Papias' polemical reaction."[495] Additionally, that "Papias himself, of course, does not admit that the Pauline collection

---

493. See Dan 10:1–14; 12:1–4.

494. See Rev 12:3, 4, 7, 9, 13, 16–18; 13:2; 16:13; and 20:2.

495. Nielsen, "Papias," 530.

is Holy Scripture, but he takes unfavorable notice of the fact that writings of Paul are so designated by others, and especially by Polycarp and his circle."[496] Concerning the close association of Papias and Polycarp in the many histories of the church, Lightfoot wrote, "As regards Papias therefore, it is reasonable to infer, in the absence of direct evidence, that his views were, at all events, in general accordance with his friends."[497] Given this fragment's Pauline characteristics, and the lack of Papian material indicating a clear anti-Pauline sentiment, and that the whole of church history witnesses to his close association with Polycarp, there appears to be little reason for accepting Nielsen's theory.

Having addressed the spiritual warfare found in the book of Daniel, Papias turned to theological themes found throughout the New Testament that state that the inevitable and final victory over Satan was secured by "Christ's" incarnation, death, and resurrection. Lightfoot speculated that Papias was probably familiar with Paul's letters to the churches of Asia Minor, but provided no evidence to support this theory.[498] It can be argued that this fragment provides this missing evidence. While the themes found in this fragment can be found throughout the New Testament, they are particularly evident in Paul's letter to the church at Colosse (or Colossae). Interestingly, Colossians is the only New Testament book that mentions Hierapolis, revealing that the church there had a connection with the apostle Paul through his associate Epaphras (Colossians 1:7; 4:12–13). Moreover, Paul made it clear that his letter to the Colossian church was also to be sent to the church at Laodicea (Col 4:16), which only lay approximately twelve miles from Colosse and 6 to 8 miles across the valley from Hierapolis. It is not a dramatic stretch of imagination to believe that Paul's letters to the churches at Laodicea and Colosse were also read and preserved at the church in Hierapolis, letters which Papias would have access to some fifty years later.[499]

As to the identity of "the apostle," Eusebius stated that Papias had utilized "testimonies" from both John and Peter.[500] It is conceivable, therefore, that he may have had either of these two apostles in mind as he wrote about Christ's bodily sacrifice fulfilling the requirement of the law. Nevertheless, one cannot ignore the real possibility that Papias was

496. Ibid., 532.

497. Lightfoot, *Essays*, 154.

498. Ibid., 151.

499. Hill, "Papias," 312.

500. See section 17 of fragment 15, p. 232.

referring to the apostle Paul since the sentence in question is extremely Pauline.[501] If one were pressed to conjecture as to the source of Papias's Pauline theology, then one need only to read Paul's letter to the Colossians to see not only a theological connection,[502] but also a relational connection between Paul and the church at Hierapolis. There is a very real possibility, consequently, that Papias had direct access to or a personal copy of Paul's letter to the Colossians.

Having surveyed the theology found in both the Old Testament and in the apostolic writings, Papias next harmonized the significance of Jesus' victory through the cross with the eschatological thought found in Revelation 12:7–9 and Jesus' declaration regarding Satan's fall in Luke 10:18. Consequently, what is observable in this fragment is that Papias attempted to systematically explain Jesus' proclamation regarding the judgment of Satan with the rest of the authoritative writings of the church, which were the Old Testament and certain apostolic writings. Regarding which apostolic writings this fragment reveals that Papias was aware of, an argument could be made that he knew the Gospel of Luke,[503] the book of the Revelation, and possibly Colossians.[504]

The entire fragment ends with the author clarifying which fall of Satan the "teacher" had in mind, which he understood to be a second fall of condemnation that secured the final eschatological demise of Satan. Who the author was referring to as the "teacher" is not entirely clear. He may have been referring to Jesus or Papias since both seem to fit the context. The title "teacher" as a reference to the Lord Jesus Christ seems extremely mundane, and since the author was predominately quoting Papias it seems more reasonable to conclude that he had Papias in mind. Regardless of who the author was referring to, analyzed in its entirety this fragment is extremely helpful for understanding how Papias "exposited" oracles of the Lord throughout his writings, as well as discovering what New Testament books Papias may have known.

---

501. Both Siegert and Kürzinger referenced several New Testament passages with respect to this fragment, most of which are Pauline. Kürzinger, *Papias*, 133. Siegert, "Papiaszitate," 611.

502. See particularly Col 1:6, 22–23; 2:13–15.

503. Hill, "Papias," 311.

504. For discussions regarding the authorship of Colossians see Polhill, *Paul*, 334–35; O'Brien, *Colossians, Philemon*, xli–xliv; Lightfoot, *Colossians*, 73–126.

FRAGMENT 24

> At this time there lived in Hierapolis a prominent teacher and author of many treatises; he wrote five treatises about the Gospel. In one of these treatises, which he wrote concerning the Gospel of John, he relates that in the book of John the Evangelist there is a report about a woman who was an adulteress. When the people led her before Christ our Lord, he spoke to the Jews who had brought her to him: "Whoever among you is himself certain that he is innocent of that of which she is accused, let him now bear witness against her." After he had said this, they gave him no answer and went away.

> Agapius of Hierapolis, (tenth c.), *World History*[505]

This fragment possesses material also found in fragment 22; however, before discussing their commonalities, an introduction to clarify its author and origin are in order. Agapius was a ninth-century Melkite bishop of Hierapolis in present-day northern Syria. He was not a bishop of Hierapolis in Asia Minor (present-day Turkey). Little is known about him other than he wrote a book titled, *World History*, which dealt with the history of the world until ca. 942. Although Agapius did not mention Papias by name, it seems evident that he was referring to him, since Papias is the only known bishop at Hierapolis known to have composed a five-volume work. There is a question regarding the accuracy of Kürzinger's translation as cited by Holmes; therefore, an alternative translation is here provided:

> And it came to be around that time in Hierapolis a teacher of theology who authored many treatises on the Bible. And he mentioned in the treatise that he wrote on the Gospel of John that in the book of John the Evangelist that a woman fornicated. So, when they brought her before our Lord the Christ—all the glory be to Him—(to) all the Jews that brought her *he said to them* whoever among you knows that he is innocent of what this *woman* committed, let him bear testimony against her. When he said that to them, no one of them did assault her with anything, so, he left.[506]

505. Holmes, *The Apostolic Fathers: Diglot Edition*, 589; Kürzinger, *Papias*, 126–27. This fragment is absent from the lists of Schoedel, Holmes, Kleist, and Körtner.

506. I would like to thank Dr. Ihab Griess of Washington D.C. and Dr. Peter Gentry (a professor at the Southern Baptist Theological Seminary in Louisville, Kentucky) for assisting me in translating this Arabic text. Arabic is beyond my expertise; consequently, their help was very instrumental. The words in italics indicate words not in the

It appears that Agapius had access to Papias's *Exposition* that gave him certain impressions about Papias and his writings. First, he was of the opinion that Papias was a "teacher of theology," thus indicating that Papias was not simply interested in only collecting and preserving oral traditions. As with other early Christian authors, such as the Gospel writers, Papias wanted to influence his audience. His theology is known to have influenced other Christian authors and apologists such as Irenaeus, Justin Martyr, and Apollinaris.[507] Agapius also believed that Papias's work was about "the Bible,"[508] which is a rather interesting distinction; generally speaking, most Papian fragments describe Papias's work as focusing upon the "oracles" or "sayings" of the Lord. Holmes's translation of the clause, "he wrote five treatises about the Gospel,"[509] might be better translated as, "he wrote five treatises about the Bible." Agapius's statement implies that Papias had also interacted with other canonical sources and that his work was not only a loose collection of oral traditions. Regarding Agapius's anachronistic use of the term "Bible," it seems reasonable to assume that he was not referring to the canon as we know it today, but rather he was referring to the apostolic writings that Papias had access to, writings that were inevitably recognized by the church as Scripture. Without further material from Papias, however, an evaluation of the accuracy of Agapius's summary is not possible.

Agapius also indicated that the Gospel of John was a major focus in one of Papias's books, thus corroborating data found in fragment 22 which also states that Papias was aware of the Fourth Gospel. What some might find troubling about his assertion is Agapius's example regarding Papias's knowledge of the John's Gospel, which was the *pericope adulterae*. Nevertheless, the idea that some might link this pericope to Papias, or his knowledge of the Gospel of John should not be surprising. Eusebius confirmed that Papias was aware of this pericope, Eusebius, however, associated it with *The Gospel according to the Hebrews*.[510] It should be noted that he never objectively validated or denied that the *pericope adulterae* could be found in some manuscripts of the Gospel of John, on this subject

---

original text; nevertheless, they are provided in order to create a smoother translation.

507. See fragments 18 and 15.

508. Dr. Griess informed me that the Arabic word used in the text, "*'nǧl* " when used alone is properly translated "Bible." If it is constructed with a proper name, however, such as "John," e.g., "*'nǧl yhn*," then it is translated "the Gospel of John." For the Arabic text see Kürzinger, *Papias*, 126; and Holmes, *Apostolic Fathers*, 3rd ed., 760.

509. Holmes, *Apostolic Fathers*, 3rd ed., 761.

510. See fragment 5, p. 119.

he was silent. Consequently, one could easily infer that Eusebius was either ignorant of its association with John's Gospel, or that he knew it was present in some manuscripts of the Fourth Gospel but viewed is as not authentically part of John's autograph. Nevertheless, such conclusions are at best only conjectures, since they are predominantly based upon silence.

Eusebius was not the only writer who confirmed Papias's awareness of this account. As will be seen below, a Papian fragment by Vardan Vardapet also associated it with Papias and the Fourth Gospel. Vardan, however, stated that Papias was the reason this pericope was embedded in the Gospel of John. It is not clear whether the fragment above provides a direct quote of Papias or whether Agapius had relied upon his memory concerning what Papias had actually wrote.[511] Although being rather brief, his summary is generally consistent with the account as it is found in John's Gospel. However, because of its brevity and the fact that it is in Arabic, its value for answering text critical issues regarding this pericope as it is found in the Gospel of John is minor.[512] In conclusion, this fragment provides additional evidence, albeit not definitive, that Papias was aware of the Fourth Gospel.

Fragment 25

But concerning the aloe which people brought [to Jesus' tomb; cf. John 19:39], some say that it was a mixture of oil and honey, but the aloe is certainly a kind of incense. The Geographer and Papias report that there are fifteen kinds of aloe in India. . . .

Vardan Vardapet (thirteenth c.),
Explanations of Holy Scripture[513]

511. It is possible that Agapius has quoted Papias. If, however, Agapius quoted the Gospel of John, then it appears that he did so in a rather loose fashion.

512. Lightfoot included the *pericope adulterae* among his list of Papian fragments as it is found in John 7:53—8:11, Holmes, *Apostolic Fathers*, 3rd ed., 741–43. While it is understandable that he might desire to acknowledge this pericope, or provide a version of it in the form of an appendix or footnote, it probably should not be listed as a Papian fragment since there appears to be more than one version of this event. Holmes provided an insightful discussion about other traditions of this pericope. Holmes, *Apostolic Fathers*, 3rd ed., 724–27. Regarding the possibility of multiple traditions of this event, Cadbury attempted to make a case that the pericope is actually Lukan. Cadbury, "Lukan Authorship," 237–45. For a thorough analysis about the textual questions concerning this pericope and other related issues see Metzger, *A Textual Commentary*, 187–90; and Burge, "The Woman Caught in Adultery," 141–48.

513. Holmes, *The Apostolic Fathers: Diglot Edition*, 591. Kürzinger also cited this

The above fragment is preserved by a late thirteenth-century Armenian scholar named Vardan of Vardapet, who at the request of King Hethum of Armenia wrote a book titled, *Explanations of Holy Scripture*.[514] Some have inferred that the above reference to aloe was an allusion drawn from the Gospel of John. While this may very well be true, this fragment provides no objective evidence that Papias was aware of any writings of the New Testament.[515] In reality, it is not even certain that Vardan cited Papias at all. Folker Siegert explained that because the name found in the text was apparently "unrecognizable," there is a significant question as to whether Papias's name is the correct translation of the original text.[516] Papias apparently became associated with the fragment through the hand of a "French" translator.

Concerning the different kinds of aloe found in "India," Vardan's first source was an individual that he referred to as "The Geographer." This was a common Armenian reference to a fifth-century Armenian scholar named Moses of Chorenensis (or Chorene).[517] He is best known as a disciple of Mesrop and as one of Armenia's most celebrated poets and grammarians. Moses was apparently well traveled and educated, having received part of his education in Alexandria. One of his main sources for data was an Alexandrian geographer named "Pappos." It appears, therefore, that the fragment above is not actually Papian.[518] The confusion appears to be the result of a later translator who, when confronted with an illegible name, incorrectly guessed that the source for Moses' information was a "Papias," apparently forgetting that Moses had previously mentioned a "Pappos" as the one who had provided him with much of his geographical information. If, however, this is truly a Papian fragment it still holds little value, since it provides no historical information about Papias. Additionally, it only indirectly associates Papias with

---

fragment, but provided little analysis of it. See Kürzinger, *Papias*, 132–34.

514. Siegert, "Papiaszitate," 607. Siegert provided the actual Armenian text for this fragment and the one to follow. He dated Vardan to have written sometime between 1274 and 1276.

515. Siegert concluded the reference to aloe is an allusion to John 19.39, apparently basing his decision on the Greek work "ἀλόη" Siegert, "Papiaszitate," 608. Why this Greek word has significance for a text written in Armenian Siegert did not explain. See also Holmes, *Apostolic Fathers*, 3rd ed., 765.

516. Concerning the confusion of names in this text Siegert stated that "die folgende Papias-Stelle ist in dieser Übersetzung durch Änderung des Namens unkenntlich geworden." Siegert, "Papiaszitate," 608.

517. Ibid.

518. A bishop in Hierapolis of Asia Minor hardly makes a likely candidate for being an expert of aloes and ointments of India.

the Gospel of John; consequently, it provides no material support indicating that Papias was aware of any writings of the New Testament.

FRAGMENT 26

> The story of the adulterous woman, which the other Christians have written in their gospel, was written by a certain Papias, a disciple of John, who was declared and condemned as a heretic. Eusebius said this.

Vardan Vardapet, *Explanations of Holy Scripture*[519]

This fragment is certainly interesting, however, its value regarding the life and writings of Papias is questionable. It is the only fragment that attributes the authorship of the *pericope adulterae* to Papias, an accusation not even made by Eusebius.[520] What Eusebius actually wrote was that Papias had "related also another tradition concerning a woman accused of many sins before the Lord, which *The Gospel according to the Hebrews* contains."[521] Vardan, writing in the last quarter of the thirteenth century, failed to respect the fact that manuscript evidence for this pericope predated him by more than seven hundred years. This is not to say that there were not others who shared Vardan's opinion, but only that Papias was not the only reason that this pericope was included in the canon. He was, however, convinced that Papias was the reason why some Christians "have written" this pericope into their Bibles. Unfortunately, he failed to precisely identify where and in which Gospel this pericope had been inserted. A survey of early Armenian translations of the New Testament reveal that when this pericope is found it is located either after John 7:52 or at the end of John's Gospel.[522] This makes sense given Papias's association with the apostle John. While Vardan's angst regarding this pericope provides no hard evidence that Papias was familiar with John's Gospel, his next statement makes it almost certain that he believed Papias knew of the Fourth Gospel, for he asserted that Papias was a disciple of John. Siegert rightly understood Vardan as referring to the apostle John.[523]

---

519. Holmes, *The Apostolic Fathers: Diglot Edition*, 590–91.

520. See fragment 5, p. 119.

521. Holmes, *The Apostolic Fathers: Diglot Edition*, 568–69.

522. Metzger, *A Textual Commentary*, 188. Early Armenian translations do not associate this pericope with the Gospel of Luke.

523. Although Siegert did not give attention to this statement by Vardan, he did

A second misunderstanding of Vardan concerns his declaration of Eusebius's opinion of Papias. Eusebius did not, as far as we know, label Papias as a "heretic." He may have evaluated Papias as a simpleton,[524] he did not, however, refer to Papias as a heretic. Nevertheless, in spite of Eusebius's defamation of Papias, Vardan still believed that Papias was a disciple of the apostle John. While it should be assumed that Vardan was referring to Papias, one is left to wonder if Vardan had not confused Papias with other early second-century heretics such as Victorinus or Cerinthus. Consequently, given his haphazard references to this apostolic father, it is hard to feel comfortable about placing much weight on his testimonies about Papias.

FRAGMENT 27

> For the last of these, John, surnamed "the Son of Thunder,"
> when he was a very old man (as Irenaeus and Eusebius and a
> succession of other trustworthy historians have handed down
> to us) and about the time when terrible heresies had cropped
> up, dictated the Gospel to his own disciple, the virtuous Papias
> of Hierapolis, to complete the message of those before him who
> had preached to the peoples of the whole world.
>
> Anonymous comment from a commentary on the Gospel
> of John consisting of comments drawn from the writings of
> various Greek fathers[525]

Like several other fragments, the above fragment provides no direct quote of Papias employing any passage of the New Testament. Holmes indicated that this fragment originated not from one but "various" unknown "Greek fathers." Consequently, its value for providing verifiable data is extremely limited. As with fragment 22, however, it refers to Papias as not only a personal disciple of the apostle John, but also as the amanuensis that John employed while composing his Gospel.[526] This fragment is unfortunately anonymous; therefore, one can only speculate about its author, his education, and his

---

refer to Papias as an "Apostelschüler." Siegert, "Papiaszitate," 610.

524. "σφόδρα γάρ τοι σμικρὸς ὤν τὸν νοῦν" Holmes, *Apostolic Fathers*, 3rd ed., 738.

525. Holmes, *The Apostolic Fathers: Diglot Edition*, 584–85. This fragment is absent from the lists of Schoedel, Ehrman, and Kleist. It was published by B. Corder in 1630, but its actual origin(s) and age(s) are unknown. Although it apparently is a compilation of statements from several Greek "fathers," for the sake of discussion, however, it will be addressed as having one author.

526. For a more thorough discussion of this possibility see fragment 22, p. 243.

exposure to his sources. As a result, some may find it difficult to give this fragment a great deal of credibility.

Regardless of what weight one might place upon this fragment, its author(s) was confident in his opinion concerning who wrote the Fourth Gospel, identifying him as John, "the Son of Thunder," who was most certainly a son of Zebedee and an apostle.[527] This fragment also clearly reveals that he held Papias in high regard. Additionally, he claimed that one of the factors that motivated the apostle John to write a fourth biography upon the life and teachings of Jesus was the presence of "heresies." The author was not specific in his charge, but it is likely that he was referring to Cerinthus, a late first-century heretic known by the apostle John.[528] His account, as he admitted, is consistent with other accounts concerning the origin of the Fourth Gospel. If it were not for his statement concerning Papias's involvement in the composition of the Gospel of John, it could be argued that this fragment provides no independent data concerning Papias. It is conceivable that the traditions found in the anti-Marcionite Prologues were accessible to this author as well. One could justifiably contend, therefore, that this fragment provides no independent witness concerning Papias's service to the apostle John.

That such a tradition existed and was accessible to this author should not be surprising. The more intriguing question, however, is what was the original source of this tradition? Could it have been Papias's own writings? If so, then it is just as possible that this author had read Papias's *Exposition* and had arrived at his conclusion independently of the tradition contained in fragment 22, which was that Papias had at some point and to some degree served as the apostle John's secretary. Incontrovertible proof for either position is regrettably not available; thus, certitude concerning this issue remains elusive. Consequently, that Papias may have served as an amanuensis of the apostle John remains a possibility.

527. Mark 3:17.

528. See Eusebius *Ecc. Hist.* III.28.1.6 (LCL 153: 263–67).

5

Papias and His Witness to the New Testament

COMMON CONJECTURES ABOUT PAPIAS

FEW FIGURES IN THE church's history have been more misunderstood than Papias, and examples of such confusion are not difficult to find. Carl Clemen wrote concerning the association of the apostle John with the city of Ephesus that "Nevertheless it might be possible also, that the presbyter John of Papias to whose existence we must hold fast, although he is mentioned by no one again until the time of Eusebius, actually lived in Asia Minor, but that Papias did not meet him, either because he had died earlier or had lived in another locality. And, further, since Irenaeus seems to have heard Polycarp only as a boy, it might also be conceived that he had only misunderstood the latter, but that he himself had in mind that very presbyter."[1]

Support for such conjectures can be found in the faulty explanations of ancient historians, such as Eusebius, and modern scholars who in spite of evidence to the contrary, and with almost religious fervor, demand that Papias not be associated with the apostle John. Johannes Munck is an example among several who, while recognizing that the data could very well support a different conclusion, rejected that Papias had any direct connection with the apostle John. Although Munck was aware that Eusebius's treatment of Papias was "entirely one-sided," and that Papias was able to travel in order to receive instruction from those he believed to be

1. Clemen, "John at Ephesus," 673–74.

the most trustworthy sources, and that he applied the term "presbyter" to seven of the twelve apostles, and that his use of it was not as broad as that of Irenaeus, Munck still contended that Papias should not be associated with the apostle John.[2] He defended this position by arguing that

> It is true that the two Fathers knew far more than we do, since they read—or could have read—the whole of Papias' work, and in addition to this Irenaeus must have known a good deal about Papias' generation through his connection with Asia Minor, especially through Polycarp. *Nevertheless, it may be of importance here to disregard all this,* which cannot lead to greater clarity, being merely guesswork. Let us instead assume that the interpretation given here describes what Irenaeus found in Papias' preface, and what made him call Papias "John's hearer." Eusebius found something different because he was interested in the otherwise unknown presbyter John. On the other hand, Eusebius probably remains right in thinking that there were two men called John, although it is not certain that the other lived in Ephesus. The reason given him by Dionysios for such an assumption is without value. But the attempts that have been made to identify John the apostle with "John the presbyter" in ll.18–20 *must be rejected.* It would be unnatural to describe the same person in this way with an interval of barely more than a line.[3] It seems to be no reason for such an artificial device. . . . *We must assume* that the other John, who was both a "disciple of the Lord" and a "presbyter," but not an apostle (nor an apostle's disciple), being the only duplicated in the list of names, had to be distinguished from his great namesake by a description that indicated that this was John the non-apostle.[4]

2. Munck, "Presbyters," 226, 229, 231, 233, 235. Concerning the possibility that Papias used the word "presbyter" when referring to the apostles, Munck wrote that "this last reflection takes us straight on to Papias' text, since it is obvious from the above that the word presbyter does *not* mean disciples of the apostles, *although it can quite well be used to describe them,* also when the context makes it clear. And this vaguer definition, in which antiquity and authority are the basic meaning, shows that *we cannot exclude the possibility that 'presbyters' might be used of the apostles,* even though there is instance of it in later literature. *But this could in fact not occur in the later literature, but only in Papias' generation.*" Munck, "Presbyters," 236. Italics mine.

3. This line of argument indicates that either Munck had no understanding of the anaphoric use of a Greek article, or he lacked the objectivity to recognize it.

4. Munck, "Presbyters," 237–38. Italics mine.

There are others, of course, who also have employed the most questionable Papian fragments to support their superficial knowledge of Papias and his writings. An example of such is J. Merle Rife, who wrote,

> Following the example of Eusebius, later scholars have made endless attempts to get at the meaning of Papias. His statements about our First and Second Gospels are reported in coalescing with these Gospels. Irenaeus used Papias in a desperate attempt to prove the Fourth Gospel was written by the son of Zebedee.[5] He too has had many followers.
>
> Other Papias fragments report legends about Judas Iscariot, the fallen angels, views on the authenticity of Revelation, the martyrdom of John at the hand of Jews in fulfillment of Jesus' prophecy that he and James would indeed drink the cup he was going to. It is from Papias that the idea that two Johns at Ephesus is derived.[6]

Statements such as those made by Clemen, Munck, and Rife suggest an inability on the part of some to interact objectively with the data concerning Papias and his relationship with the apostle John. The fact remains that if Eusebius had never written his thirty-ninth chapter of *Ecclesiastical History* few would doubt Irenaeus's claim that Papias was a hearer of the apostle John and a companion of Polycarp, which is a claim that even Eusebius himself affirmed earlier in his life in his work titled *Chronicle*.[7] In order to illustrate the weight of evidence that associates Papias with the apostle John and his knowledge of certain books of the New Testament, a brief summary of the Papian fragments is here provided.[8]

EVIDENCE FROM THE PAPIAN FRAGMENTS

The earliest reference to Papias is from the hand of Irenaeus who wrote that Papias had heard the apostle John and was a companion of Polycarp, and had authored a five-volume work (fragment 1). Eusebius, also relying upon Irenaeus, wrote that the apostle John survived until the reign of Trajan and that both Papias and Polycarp had heard him (fragment 2).

---

5. To date I have found no evidence supporting this assertion.

6. Rife, *The New Testament*, 135–36.

7. See the discussion concerning fragment 2, p. 111.

8. Refer to chapter 4 for in-depth analysis of each fragment. It is assumed that all references to Papias's five-volume work are references to *Exposition* regardless of how the title is worded.

He again referred to Papias as a bishop of Hierapolis who provided corroboration to the tradition that Mark composed the Second Gospel based upon the reminiscences of the apostle Peter. Eusebius also stated that Papias quoted 1 Peter 5:13 as proof of Mark's association with Peter. Consequently, he attested that Papias was aware of the Gospel of Mark and 1 Peter (fragment 3). He also wrote that at the time of Polycarp's ascension to the bishopric at Smyrna Papias was also a well known bishop at Hierapolis (fragment 4). Lastly, Eusebius confirmed that Papias composed a five-volume work titled *Exposition*. It was at this point in his *Ecclesiastical History*, however, that he rejected Irenaeus's claim that Papias was a hearer of the apostle John and provided three quotes from Papias's writings.

The first quote was Papias's claim that he had successfully learned and remembered certain traditions of the apostolic elders and that he was committed to their instructions. He also stated that he regularly examined the "words" or teachings of visiting itinerants who claimed to have associated with any apostolic elders. A portion of this quote can be understood as Papias's claim to have personally heard the apostle John and a second disciple of Jesus named Aristion. Although Eusebius rejected Papias's claim to have heard the apostle John, he did interpret his statement as a claim to have heard two specific disciples of Jesus, and stated that they were important sources for his five-volume work. He also indicated that Papias preserved certain oral traditions that he had received from the daughters of the apostle Philip. He claimed that Papias's belief in a literal millennial kingdom was based upon oral sources that Papias believed originated from Jesus. Eusebius questioned Papias's intelligence because of his eschatology and his approach to apostolic material. He also recognized, however, that Papias had influenced several significant Christian leaders, his primary example being Irenaeus.

After stating that Papias had quoted traditions from "John the elder,"[9] Eusebius provided a second quote from Papias that in reality is a quote from an individual that Papias referred to as "the Elder." This quote corroborates Mark's association with the apostle Peter and his part in the composition of the Second Gospel. Papias's source indicated that Mark alone was the compiler of his materials, materials that came exclusively from the testimonials and sermons of the apostle Peter, testimonials that Mark was careful not to falsify or contaminate with his own imaginative stories.

---

9. Understood as the apostle John.

In the last Papian quote provided by Eusebius Papias wrote that Matthew's initial Gospel was written in Aramaic. Lastly, Eusebius claimed that Papias "utilized testimonials" from 1 John and 1 Peter, and that he also recorded an account of the event commonly referred to as the *pericope adulterae*. Consequently, with respect to certain canonical books of the New Testament, Eusebius attested that Papias was aware of the Gospel of Mark, 1 Peter, and 1 John (fragment 5).

Fragment 6 is attributed to Apollinaris of Laodicaea.[10] This fragment states that Papias was a disciple of John. It is devoted to a tradition concerning the death of Judas Iscariot, which appears to be a gross embellishment of the tradition of his demise as found in the book of Acts. It does not, however, provide concrete evidence proving that Papias was aware of any books of the New Testament.

The great church doctor Jerome referred to Papias as a disciple of the apostle John and the bishop of Hierapolis who authored *Exposition* (fragment 7). He also believed that Papias had mentioned Eusebius's character known as John the elder; however, there is little evidence to suggest that Jerome believed this individual to have authored any canonical writings. Jerome also corroborated that Papias's eschatology was millenarian. Jerome's descriptions imply that he was personally familiar with *Exposition* (fragment 8). However, in fragment 9 he only indicated that Papias was an author and provided no information about his relationship to the apostle John or his awareness of any New Testament books. Nevertheless, in fragment 10 he again affirmed Papias was "a hearer" of the apostle John, although he provided no indication that Papias any had knowledge of any New Testament writings in this fragment. One could also infer, however, from this fragment that Jerome believed that Irenaeus had personally known Papias. There is, however, no additional evidence within this fragment corroborating this possibility.

Fragment 11 is attributed to Philip of Side and provides no direct quote from Papias.[11] This fragment affirms that Papias's bishopric was at Hierapolis and that he was also a "hearer" of the apostle John and a companion of Polycarp. It also states that Papias preserved certain oral traditions. The author of this fragment appears to have been familiar with Papias's *Exposition*. It is most famous for stating that Papias claimed that

10. There are considerable questions concerning the exact author and extent of this fragment.

11. There is some question concerning the identity of this fragment's author, as well as whether all of the information it contains is accurate, or was actually drawn directly from Philip's *Church History*.

the apostle John suffered the same fate as his brother James and was martyred by the "Jews." It provides no evidence that Papias was aware of any New Testament writings.

Andrew of Caesarea wrote one of the earliest extant commentaries on the book of Revelation. He affirmed in his preface that Papias was aware of the book of Revelation (fragment 12). In another fragment (fragment 13), he provided a direct quote from Papias concerning Satan's fall from heaven as commentary on Revelation 12:7–8. This quote, however, provides no additional evidence proving that Papias was aware of any other books of the New Testament.

Fragments 14 and 15 are both attributed to Maximus the Confessor. In fragment 14 Maximus affirmed that Papias wrote *Exposition*. His reference to the first volume of *Exposition* implies that he was personally acquainted with the work, and from his reference one can infer that Papias was familiar with 1 John, and possibly 2 and 3 John, although this is not a certainty. Maximus indicated in fragment 15 that Papias was a bishop at Hierapolis who "flourished" in the days of the apostle John. He also recognized that Papias's eschatology had influenced other leading Christian thinkers in later generations.

Fragment 16 is from an unknown author who wrote an early seventh-century chronology. His chronology gives no indication that Papias was aware of any New Testament writings. It does, however, refer to Papias as having been martyred in Pergamum.

Fragments 17 and 18 are from Anastasius of Sinai, neither of which contains a direct quote from Papias. Anastasius referred to Papias in both fragments as a disciple of the apostle John, as well as stating that Papias believed that certain Old Testament passages should be interpreted as references to the church. The implication of these statements is that Papias was not unilaterally opposed to employing typology in his approach to the Scriptures. Neither fragment, however, provides evidence that Papias was aware of any New Testament writings.

Fragment 19 has been associated with George the Sinner, but in all probability he is not its author. This fragment contains no direct quote from Papias, or any evidence that the author had independently read *Exposition*. Moreover it provides no evidence that Papias was aware of any books of the New Testament. Consequently, this fragment is one of the least credible of all the Papian fragments. It does, however, affirm that Papias was a bishop at Hierapolis, that he wrote *Exposition*, and that he had seen the apostle John. This fragment, as with the one associated with

Philip of Side, is most famous for stating that Papias claimed that the apostle John was "killed" by the Jews.

A scholar known as Photius also provided two brief references to Papias, and in both he affirmed that Papias was a bishop in Hierapolis. He did not, however, quote Papias or provide evidence that he was aware of any New Testament books. Photius stated in his first reference to Papias that he was a martyr and corroborated Papias's chiliastic beliefs (fragment 20). Photius affirmed in his second reference to Papias his orthodoxy, as well as his own respect for Papias as an early church leader, even though he disagreed with some of Papias's theological positions (fragment 21).

The author of fragment 22 is unknown. This fragment is drawn from material that is commonly referred to as the anti-Marcionite prologues to the Gospels. The author claimed, in the prologue to the Gospel of John, that Papias of Hierapolis was not only a disciple of the apostle John and aware of the Fourth Gospel, but that he also served as John's amanuensis as he dictated his Gospel. The author indicated that this information could be found in the last volume of *Exposition*, thus implying that to some degree he was familiar with Papias's writings. His statement about Papias's knowledge of the Gospel of John, whether based upon a misunderstanding of a verb in the first person singular (e.g., "I wrote") or third person plural (e.g., "they wrote") demands that Papias was aware of the Fourth Gospel.[12] While the information found within this fragment is intriguing, some doubt its credibility because its author is unknown and because he failed to provide a direct quote from *Exposition* supporting his claim.

Fragment 23 is attributed to Andrew of Caesarea, but it is unlikely that he was in fact its author. This fragment is found in an Armenian translation of Andrew's commentary on the book of Revelation and is an anonymous "catena" expositing Revelation 12:7–9. Its author, however, claimed to provide an exact quote from *Exposition*, thus making this fragment of considerable importance. Regrettably, he did not identify where it could be found in Papias's five-volume work. This fragment, in a similarly fashion to fragment 1, appears to provide an excellent example of how Papias "exposited" certain "oracles" of Jesus. It reveals that Papias was not only aware of the Old Testament Scriptures (e.g., the book of Daniel) but quite possibly some writings from the New Testament, the most likely candidates being Colossians and the Gospel of Luke. The author's quote of Papias indicates that Papias drew some of his theology about Christ's

---

12. See the discussion on fragment 22, p. 243, in the previous chapter for a more comprehensive analysis of this issue.

eschatological victory over Satan from an individual that Papias referred to as "the apostle." Which apostle Papias meant is uncertain, however, the apostle Paul appears to be the more probable candidate. This fragment also concludes with a quote of Luke 10.18; consequently, it provides evidence that Papias was aware of the Third Gospel.

Fragment 24 was written in Arabic. Its author is Agapius of Hierapolis, which was located in present-day Syria.[13] Agapius stated that Papias devoted one of his "treatises" or volumes to the Gospel of John, thus indicating that Papias had knowledge of the Fourth Gospel. Agapius, however, also associated the *pericope adulterae* with the John's Gospel. This should not be surprising since Papias's knowledge of this account was corroborated by Eusebius, although he never records that Papias associated it with any specific canonical Gospel. Concerning this pericope, it is not clear whether Agapius provided an exact quote from Papias's *Exposition* or whether his discussion of the pericope was drawn from his memory. Agapius version of the pericope differs somewhat from the account that is traditionally associated with the Gospel of John. Nevertheless, he openly stated that Papias was aware of the Fourth Gospel.

Fragments 25 and 26 are from an Armenian scholar named Vardan Vardapet. Fragment 25 in all probability should not be associated with Papias. Regardless of its possible connection to Papias, it provides no quote from him or concrete evidence that he was aware of any books of the New Testament. Even though Vardan clearly disdained Papias he affirmed that Papias had been a disciple of John (fragment 26). He also claimed that Papias was the composer of the *pericope adulterae* and that he was the one responsible for motivating "other Christians" to place it into "their gospel." Unfortunately he did not identify the Gospel(s) into which it had been inserted. Early Armenian manuscripts, however, indicate that it was only associated with the Gospel of John, being found either after John 7:52, at the end of the Gospel of John, or omitted altogether.[14] Fragment 26, as with Vardan's other fragment, provides neither a Papian quote or any demonstrable evidence that Papias was aware of any books of the New Testament.

Fragment 27 is an anonymous catena found in a Greek commentary on the Gospel of John. It also associates Papias with the apostle John, calling him John's disciple and amanuensis as he "dictated" his Gospel. Its author(s) and date are unknown. The author openly stated his dependence

---

13. Which is not to be confused with Hierapolis of Asia Minor.

14. Metzger, *A Textual Commentary*, 188.

upon other patristic sources and provided no evidence that he was personally familiar with Papias's writings.

Conclusions Drawn from These Fragments

Although some fragments are clearly more credible than others, there are several conclusions that may be drawn from them regarding Papias and his knowledge of books found within the New Testament. They are as follows. Papias appears to have been a Phrygian who was born at or near the beginning of the last quarter of the first century (ca. 75). He became a bishop of the church at Hierapolis in Asia Minor around the commencement of the second century. He was a contemporary of Polycarp who was also the bishop of the church(s) at Smyrna during the same time. There is no demonstrable evidence suggesting that the two were anything but companions and important leaders of the Asiatic church during the first half of the second century. Papias was literate and appeared to have attained an acceptable level of education, both pagan and Christian. Papias claimed with respect to his Christian training that he had received from the specific apostles "trustworthy" traditions that he had perceptively understood and accurately remembered.

Papias wrote a five-volume work titled *An Exposition of the Oracles of the Lord* in which he attempted to explain certain sayings of Jesus Christ, some of which were from oral sources while others were from literary sources. His eschatology was millenarian and he influenced other important pastors and Christian apologists who came after him (such as Irenaeus). Concerning those who immediately followed Papias's generation we know of only one person that spoke of Papias who could have also personally known him. He is Irenaeus of Lyons, and he claimed that Papias had "heard" the apostle John. Eusebius corroborated that Papias claimed to have heard personal disciples of Jesus. He appears to have had a long and successful ministry, and to have died around the middle of the third quarter of the second century, possibly as a martyr in Pergamum. Given his place in the patristic time line it is very probable that many of the traditions he received about Jesus and the apostolic writings originated deep within the first century.

One of the more debated issues with respect to Papias is his possible association with the apostle John and the possible existence of a second individual that some refer to as "John the Elder." Of the twenty-seven fragments listed in this book, twelve different fragments from ten different authors claimed that Papias had to some degree personally known the apostle John. It is recognized that some of these authors depended upon others for their knowledge of Papias's connection to the apostle. Nevertheless, some of the more credible witnesses of the apostle John's mentoring of Papias are Irenaeus, Eusebius, Jerome, and Anastasius of Sinai. The only person that questioned Papias's association with the apostle was Eusebius, who later in his life unashamedly and unjustifiably displayed gross prejudice towards Papias for his eschatology and hermeneutical approach to the Scriptures. Only Eusebius denied Papias's knowledge of the apostle John, and in his stead he claimed that Papias had known a second church leader also named John. Eusebius's support for his contention, however, was poorly defended and reflects badly upon his own credibility rather than the credibility of Papias. Concerning the existence of Eusebius's second John, Petrie aptly wrote,

> For here we have the genesis of "John the Elder," that elusive mythical figure that for long has bedevilled students of the Fourth Gospel. We must see just how Eusebius brings him into the picture and why; and then, after wondering at the fuss he has been allowed to cause, consign him to oblivion. In conjuring up this "John the Elder," Eusebius is indulging in what these days is called "cross-talk," and for those who read with reasonable care he does not conceal his motive. Perhaps he anticipated those moderns who hold that the bigger the bluff, the more likely it is to succeed. At any rate, he has met with extraordinary success in having the figure of his imagination so widely accepted, and in some quarters having him regarded as rather more respectable than the brother of James son of Zebedee. The persistence with which the "John the Elder" has reared his head is probably due in no small measure to the manner in which the Papias extract is so often quoted—with, at most, only *part* of Eusebius' comments.[15]

Consequently, it is only upon the baseless conjectures of Eusebius—who built his theory about this mythical second John upon the equally speculative theory that originated from Dionysius of Alexandria—that the legend of "John the Elder" continues today.

Some authors were more familiar with Papias and his writings than others. Several of them displayed a personal knowledge of *Exposition* by providing either an actual citation or allusion to four different volumes of

---

15. Petrie, "Matthew," 20.

Papias's five-volume *magnum opus*.[16] Papias shows no evidence of a New Testament canon as it is known today. He does, however, attest to a period when certain leaders of the church discerned that the foundation of the Christian faith was laid out in the very words of Jesus and the instructions he gave to his immediate followers. Before the close of the first century these "traditions" were being coalesced into a recognized body of instruction and church dogma, a coalescing that was supervised by some of the actual followers of Jesus (e.g., the apostle John and Aristion) and their disciples (e.g., Mark, Luke, Polycarp, and Papias). Papias did have knowledge of some books of the New Testament. The authors of the Papian fragments stated that Papias was aware of the canonical Gospels of Mark and John. Moreover, there is credible evidence indicating that he was also aware of the Gospel of Luke (fragment 23).

Some have inferred from Papias's reference to an Aramaic Gospel written by Matthew that he must have known about the canonical Gospel of Matthew. This, however, is not a certainty. Setting aside the questionable theory that Matthew wrote his canonical Gospel in a Jewish rhetorical style rather than in the Aramaic language as Papias stated, there are three other reasonable conclusions concerning the relationship of Matthew's Aramaic Gospel and the canonical Gospel of Matthew. The first is that the two Gospels have absolutely nothing in common with respect to their author or content.[17] The second is that the canonical Gospel of Matthew is actually a Greek translation of Matthew's original Aramaic work, a translation supervised by someone other than Matthew.[18] The last alternative is that Matthew wrote both Gospels. The more probable chronology of these two works is that he first wrote a Gospel in Aramaic very early in the church's history (ca. 50) for an Aramaic speaking audience that was presumably in Jerusalem or its surrounding area (which is supported by the historical data preserved by Eusebius). Regrettably this document, whatever its literary style may have been, has not survived the erosion of time. Later in Matthew's ministry, however, he moved to a location that was primarily Greek speaking, as a result he also wrote a second Gospel in Greek that appears to have depended not only on his own memories of Jesus, but

16. There is no reference to vol. 3 in any of the Papian fragments.

17. This conjecture has little historical support.

18. A survey of the majority of Gospel scholars suggests that the Gospel of Matthew is not a translation of an Aramaic original but was originally written in Greek. See Carson and Moo, *Introduction*, 143–44; Morris, *Matthew*, 12–15, Stein, *Synoptic Gospels*, 143–45.

also relied heavily upon the Gospel of Mark.[19] Regardless of the question concerning the relationship of Matthew's Aramaic and Greek Gospels, the fragments only confirm that Papias understood that Matthew wrote for an Aramaic audience a Gospel in their own language. Regrettably, therefore, they provide no definitive answer to the question concerning which of these three theories most accurately reflects the origin of the canonical Gospel of Matthew.

Although there is no evidence that Papias held to a fourfold Gospel corpus, it appears that he valued Gospels that originated from the apostles or their personal followers above all other sources (fragment 5.3). Papias also provided no evidence that the early church understood the canonical Gospels to be anything other than the accurate reminiscences of their apostolic sources, rather than compilations of serial redactors who finally sewed together multiple gospel traditions into four separate volumes sometime during the second century. While Papias's exposition in fragment 23 displayed some affinities with Pauline theology, we have no concrete evidence indicating he had knowledge of a Pauline corpus. If one were to conjecture about whether Papias was aware of any of the Pauline epistles, then Colossians appears to have the best claim, since specific themes and subject matter in fragment 23 are also found in Colossians 2:14–15. Colossians is also the only epistle that actually documents Paul's awareness of and connection to the church at Hierapolis. There is also no concrete reference to indicate that Papias knew of the book of Acts. Concerning the catholic epistles, the Papian fragments provide no indication that Papias knew of Hebrews, James, 2 Peter, or Jude; although there is some evidence that he was possibly familiar with 2 and 3 John. They do indicate, however, that he employed passages from 1 Peter and 1 John, as well as an awareness of the book of Revelation.

That the fragments of Papias show no demonstrable evidence of the majority of the books of the New Testament should not be a major concern. So little of his writings have survived and so few references to him are known that to conclude he only knew of a few canonical New Testament books would be an unwarranted assumption based upon silence. At best one can only recognize that the evidence is insufficient to suggest that he knew of any New Testament books other than the Gospels of Mark, John, and Luke, the epistles of 1 Peter and 1 John, the book of Revelation, and lastly possibly Colossians as well as 2 and 3 John.

---

19. This theory seems the most attractive with respect to the historical evidence. It is, however, only a theory.

Papias may have also known about certain debatable materials that are currently included within the New Testament. He was aware of an account of the *pericope adulterae*. One can only conjecture about what part if any he may have had in its association with the Gospel of John. Whether or not he knew of the traditional ending of Mark's Gospel, or whether his *Exposition* influenced its composition or employed common source material from it is equally as speculative.

When researching the apostolic fathers Polycarp, Clement, Ignatius, and Papias, the most mischaracterized and least understood figure is Papias. Along with Polycarp, Papias began his ministry on the cusp of the first era without living apostles, i.e., the original twelve disciples of Jesus. It was his contention, however, that the Lord had given commandments to and for the Christian faith. He believed that these commandments were from the essence of Truth itself, and thus they were by their very nature truth. He understood that Jesus had divinely spoken and had passed on his "oracles" to his immediate followers, and that if one wanted to know truth and the truth about Jesus one must adhere not only to the words of Jesus and his followers, but also to their correct meanings as well, meanings that Papias confessed that he had well learned and accurately remembered.

At some point in Papias's ministry, possibly because of growing confusion concerning the exact meanings of some of Jesus' teachings, Papias felt the need to write a five-volume work that attempted to accurately exposit certain sayings of Jesus, some of which he had received through oral transmissions, while others were contained in apostolic narratives, narratives that we know of today as the canonical Gospels. One of the themes that Papias was most interested in was the return of the risen Christ and the establishment of his earthly kingdom. His work also appears to have had a historical concern. Papias also interacted with certain Old Testament passages in *Exposition*. Evidence indicates that his hermeneutical approach was predominately Antiochene, although he was not opposed to employing typology while interpreting Old Testament passages.

Those who interacted with his writings thought of him variously as an honorable apostolic leader, a teacher, a theologian, a buffoon, and a heretic. Regardless of how they described him, Papias said his greatest concern was the preservation of the truth of Christ, both the truth that was found in the words that Jesus spoke as well as the truth about him. Papias claimed to have only employed what in his opinion were the most trustworthy apostolic sources—both oral and written—in order to accurately explain Jesus and his meanings. Walls, writing about Papias's highest concern, stated that "for him, authenticity meant apostolicity; and apostolicity was patient of historical verification. Far from being uninterested in the literary preservation of the tradition, he is wrestling manfully with the problems involved in it."[20]

Some conclusions based upon the evidence found within the fragments of Papias are that Papias witnesses to a period of time in which the church was collecting authoritative literature that would be foundational to its future. The materials and traditions most valued were those known to have been received from Jesus via his immediate followers. Papias's witness does not testify to the "creation" of this literature, but to the "collection" of apostolic writings and traditions that were already in existence during the period in which he ministered and wrote. His witness also testifies to a period in which oral traditions that originated from trustworthy sources were still being investigated and valued. Some of these traditions were viewed as accurate preservations of the words of Jesus (fragment 1); consequently, for some they were viewed as authoritative. Other "traditions" appeared to have been provided for their historical importance or to confirm that certain prophetic oracles of Jesus (possibly those contained in written sources) had been fulfilled (e.g., Barsabbas's drinking of poison in fragment 5.9 and Luke 10:19; or Jesus' words in Matt 10:8 and the raising of some from the dead, also in fragment 5.9).

Oral traditions, however, were not the only source of authority in Papias's church. Papias also valued "apostolic" writings. Consequently, he reflects a segment of the early church and her leadership that viewed the apostolic writings and traditions as the source of truth and the basis of her authority. Apostolic material was considered trustworthy if it came from those known to have been personal disciples of Jesus (e.g., Aristion and the apostle John), or who were from their immediate circle of influence (e.g., Mark and the daughters of the apostle Philip). While this was not the opinion of everyone in the early church in Papias's day (cf. 3 John 9–10; Rev 2:15, 20; fragment 5.3), it was the opinion of orthodox bishops such as Papias, Polycarp, and Clement. Papias is, therefore, an important witness to a period of time in the Asiatic church in which literature that would inevitably form today's New Testament canon was viewed as authoritative sources for truth and the reservoir from which recognized orthodox traditions should be drawn. He displayed values that were consistent with criteria that someday would be used to determine which books would comprise the New Testament canon, criteria such as "apostolic authority"

20. Walls, "Papias," 139.

and "antiquity."[21] Papias quite literally believed in a canon, but for him that canon was found in the "oracles" of Jesus, which could be found in the Old Testament and materials originating from Jesus' personal disciples and their immediate followers, materials that were both written and oral. We have no evidence to suggest that Papias knew of today's New Testament canon. Nevertheless, in him we have an early second-century Christian leader who provided evidence that several books of the New Testament were viewed as authoritative, as well as one whose approach towards those writings was consistent with the values that the church later used to collect, determine, and close what is commonly recognized today as the New Testament canon.

21. For a more complete discussion of the factors that were used in the canonical debate see Bruce, *The Canon*, 255–69.

APPENDIX 1

Eusebius's Marginalization of Papias

INTRODUCTION

A SEGMENT OF NEW TESTAMENT scholarship in America has for more than a century based much of its conclusions regarding the first-century church and the origins of its literature on theories that have been criticized as being based on a philosophy of religion rather than the historical data.[1] It now appears that within the last couple of decades some outside of American Evangelicalism are seriously considering these criticisms; one example of such consideration is Richard Bauckham's book, *Jesus and the Eyewitnesses*. A significant reason for the questionable presuppositions of some New Testament scholars regarding the origins of the New Testament is the lack of surviving literature immediately following the apostolic period. Time, persecutions, and ecclesiastical politics have unfortunately taken their toll on literature from this period, the result being that much of this material is no longer extant. One particular victim of these attacks is material from Papias the bishop of Hierapolis. Because Papias's work is no longer extant he is often misunderstood. This misunderstanding can be largely attributed to Eusebius of Caesarea, as well as the lack of critical investigation concerning his interpretation of Papias and other Papian material. The purpose of this appendix is to demonstrate that since there are serious flaws in Eusebius's method, as well as theological bias on his

1. For examples of evangelical scholars that have competently addressed the Tübingen School and other similar approaches to the origins of the church and its early literature see Stein, *Synoptic Gospels*; Carson and Moo, *An Introduction*; Warfield, *Inspiration and Authority*.

part, then he should not be consider a credible witness to understanding Papias and his meanings. Consequently, he should not be uncritically followed with respect to interpreting Papias and his possible value as a witness to the apostles and their times.

EUSEBIUS'S VALUE

Eusebius is without question an invaluable resource for gaining access to the historical events of the church and the Roman Empire from the time of Jesus of Nazareth to the end of the Diocletian persecutions. This appendix, therefore, should not be understood as an attempt to completely repudiate Eusebius as a valuable resource regarding the first three centuries of the church's existence. He is indispensable because he documents events that occurred before his lifetime, and for gaining insights into how some in the church in his day interpreted those events. Fredrick John Foakes-Jackson wrote regarding Eusebius's value that "This pioneer in our subject possessed two indispensable qualifications, an indefatigable power of research and an excellent library. He can be censured for his opinions, and criticised [sic] for his style, nevertheless, the Christian Church owes him a debt which can hardly be exaggerated; for without him its rise and progress could never be properly known, and many of his predecessors have been rescued from complete oblivion, to enjoy a fame to which their lives and writings had justly entitled them."[2]

Similarly, William Bright wrote, "No reader of his history can ignore this: and no Christian ought to name him without cordially recognizing it in conjunction with his energy and industry in performance of an arduous and sacred task. These are merits which, in spite of literary defects, theological errors, and personal faults, have secured to Eusebius of Caesarea a high place among the great benefactors of Christendom—among the great benefactors of mankind."[3] It can hardly be overemphasized, therefore, that although Eusebius had questionable methods and at times biased perspectives, nevertheless, he is an important resource for understanding the history of the early church and its impact upon the Roman Empire.

Eusebius's work is especially valuable in at least three important areas. First, he is important because if it had not been for him a significant amount of important historical material would not have survived to our time. Second, he exemplifies theologies that were commonly propagated

2. Foakes-Jackson, *Church History*, 56.
3. Eusebius *Ecc. Hist.* ed. Bright, l.

by a segment of the church in his time. Finally, he is an example of the scholarship of his time. As Robert Grant has stated, "Eusebius's work is important not just because of the documents he used but because of the ways in which he used them. These ways illuminate the history of the Christian Church in one of its most important transitions, a transition in which Eusebius himself played a prominent role."[4] Consequently, even though one may criticize Eusebius's approach to his subject matter or how he employed and interpreted his materials, such weaknesses should not negatively affect his overall contribution to the church and students of history. Simply put, scholars both great and small occasionally make errors, and it would be unjust, not to mention ridiculous, if their peers judged them as completely unqualified because of such mistakes. What is true today, therefore, is equally true for Eusebius. With this in mind, I now turn to some of Eusebius's observable weaknesses.

EUSEBIUS'S WEAKNESSES

That Eusebius was at times biased in his interpretations of the events of his time or his treatment of his subject matter is not a secret to students of historiography. Norman F. Cantor and Richard I. Schneider, in their book *How to Study History*, used Eusebius as an example of the problems associated with researching "contemporary formal histories."[5] These authors employed Eusebius not as an example of inaccuracy with regard to the reporting historical events, but as an example of an author who portrayed his interpretation of the significance of those events as "truth" or "reality." Cantor and Schneider implied in their discussion of Eusebius that he would be an extremely valuable source of information concerning events that occurred within the church during Constantine's rise to power. Eusebius's interpretation of the church's history, however, should be critically evaluated and not necessarily perceived as accurate or truthful. Cantor and Schneider wrote concerning to the use of contemporaneous histories such as Eusebius's *Ecclesiastical History* that "Because of the contrived and conscious nature of treatises and contemporary histories, the student will be on his guard against accepting any statements at face value in these formal sources. He will look for implicit assumptions, hidden conflicts, and ulterior motives . . . you must avoid the temptation to engage in a simple literal-minded acceptance of the statements in this kind of material. Here too, you

4. Grant, *Eusebius*, 164.
5. Cantor and Schneider, *Study History*, 59.

must consider the values and assumptions of the author. . . ."[6] Even though the hazards regarding Eusebius's interpretation of history have been transparently apparent to historians, they have not always been correctly recognized by New Testament scholars. Many of them, as well as some patristic scholars, have at times have relied too heavily upon Eusebius's interpretation of Papias and his relevance to the history of the early church.[7] This is a mistake because it assumes more about Eusebius's use of Papias than is defendable.

One reason why scholars should be cautious in depending heavily upon Eusebius is that he is known to have used redacted material or to have misquoted his sources. An example of this type of error by Eusebius is observable in his *Ecclesiastical History* I.XI.6, in which he employed a text from Josephus's *Antiquities of the Jews*. Kirsopp Lake, regarding Eusebius's quote of Josephus, observed that he modified Josephus's text, the impact of which is that Josephus's meaning has been "slightly altered."[8] John R. Frank stated on the subject of Eusebius's freedom with his sources that

> Another shortcoming of the work is found in Eusebius' handling of his sources. A careful comparison of his *History* with the documents used as sources discloses several problems. When Eusebius paraphrases, he freely rewrites passages so as to alter the emphasis of the original. When he quotes extant writers directly, he often truncates the source and in many ways alters the meaning. Over fifty quotations, other than citations of Scripture, have been mutilated. In at least thirty-five instances the mutilation obscures the sense of the passage cited. One might also assume that citations from lost documents have been similarly mutilated or altered. In addition, Eusebius sometimes unknowingly used forged or altered documents, as when he failed to detect Christian interpolations in Josephus. Hence, although the *History* contains a wide

6. Ibid., 62–63.

7. Carson and Moo, *An Introduction*, 233–35; Kümmel, *Introduction*, 241–44; Metzger, *The Canon*, 53–56. These citations are not referenced because these authors are right or wrong regarding their opinions about Papias; they are provided only as examples of scholars who discussed Papias while relying heavily upon Eusebius. In many instances, scholars attempt to debate Eusebius by employing only Eusebius. By doing so modern scholars fall right into Eusebius's hands, and as a result they are no longer debating Papias's significance on a level playing field.

8. Eusebius *Ecc. Hist.* I.11.4–9 (LCL 153: 81). For the significance of this redaction see Lake's note 1, which begins on page 80.

range of important material, it cannot be taken at face value and must be studied critically.[9]

Frank's exhortation to exercise caution with respect to Eusebius's employment of lost material is especially apt concerning Eusebius's handling of Papias since the vast majority of his writings are lost.

Not only are there examples of Eusebius using redacted sources, whether intentionally or unintentionally, there were also times that he employed unverifiable sources.[10] This is especially true regarding his position that Papias was personally unfamiliar with the apostle John. Eusebius, in order to buttress his position, provided an "external source" that in his mind "proved" that there were two different "Johns" in Asia. His conclusion was "So that [Papias] hereby also proves their statement to be true who have said that two persons in Asia have borne the same name, and that there were two tombs in Ephesus, each of which is still to this day said to be John's."[11] And what was Eusebius's source for this assertion? It appears to be Dionysius of Alexandria, an anti-chiliast author with whom Eusebius was quite familiar, which is observable by his extensive quotations of Dionysius in *Ecclesiastical History* VII.24–26.[12] The context of Eusebius's quote of Dionysius in book VII is Dionysius's debate about the proper hermeneutical approach to the book of Revelation (a book that Dionysius did not "reject") and its possible association with the heretic Cerinthus.[13]

Dionysius, in order to distance the book of Revelation from apostolic authorship, discussed both internal and external evidence concerning it, and concluded that it should be attributed to someone else rather than to the apostle John. Some of Dionysius's arguments are weighty while others are not. After Dionysius's discussion of John Mark as a possible author, Eusebius quoted Dionysius as stating, "But I think that there was

9. Franke, "Eusebius of Caesarea," 72. For examples of some of these infractions by Eusebius, as well as other errors, see William Bright's introductory remarks to Eusebius, *Ecc. Hist.,* xlvii–l.

10. Although McGiffert's praise of Eusebius regarding his discrimination of "reliable and unreliable sources" has its merits, the fact remains that at times—as McGiffert admits—Eusebius chose poorly with respect to his use of certain sources. Eusebius's writings, therefore, as with any other historical document should be confirmed by the principle of multiple attestations. For the entirety of McGiffert's comments see his "Prolegomena" in Eusebius *Church History* (NPNF2 1:48–49).

11. Stevenson, *Eusebius,* 50–51.

12. Barnes, *Constantine and Eusebius,* 140.

13. Kelly, *Early Christian Doctrines,* 466.

a certain other John among those that were in Asia, since it is said both
that there were two tombs at Ephesus, and that each of the two is said to
be John's."[14] It should be noted that Dionysius did not state that there was
verifiable evidence that there were two Johns, but rather that he was basing
his argument on nothing more than his own conjecture. Eusebius quoted
Dionysius as having stated, "But I think . . ." and not "I know that there
were two Johns because. . . ." And what did Dionysius provide to warrant his conjecture? He supplied only hearsay evidence from an unknown
source or sources that there were apparently two tombs in Ephesus. What
is more confusing is that Dionysius's unnamed source(s) claimed that each
of these two tombs was supposed to be the tomb of the apostle John—that
is, *not belonging to two different Johns who were both leaders in the church
at Ephesus, but rather that both tombs were thought to be that of the John
who was a son of Zebedee and one of the original twelve apostles of Jesus.* It is
ironic that not only was Dionysius vague about the identity of his source,
but also that his source could only confirm confusion about which tomb
was actually occupied by the apostle John the beloved disciple of Jesus. It
is this confusion about the tomb of the apostle John that led Dionysius to
conjecture that there were two different Johns in Ephesus.

Armed with Dionysius's conjecture, Eusebius apparently felt the
freedom to conjecture additionally that Papias was not an associate of the
apostle John, but rather that he knew a different John, a conclusion that
he argued was conclusively proven by Papias's own preface.[15] Such conjectures would not be tolerated in a court of law, nor would they be accepted
by most reasonable historians, and they should not be given credence by
New Testament scholars. Nevertheless, to a significant degree these very
conjectures have provided a hearing to the theory that there were two different Johns functioning as leaders among the churches at Ephesus during
the transition from the first to second century.[16]

What makes Eusebius's conclusions especially egregious is his willingness to accept Dionysius's conjecture in spite of Irenaeus's contemporaneous witness to Papias and his writings. Dionysius was not born
until the beginning of the third century (ca. 200), approximately forty-five

14. Eusebius *Ecc. Hist.* VII.25.16 (LCL 265:202). In the Greek the name "John" is in
the singular (καὶ ἑκάτερον Ἰωάννου). This is true in both Eusebius's quote of Dionysius,
and in Eusebius's conjecture found in his discussion about Papias.

15. Gundry, *Older Is Better*, 58. Gundry argued that Eusebius was the first to make
the unwarranted distinction between Papias's apostle John and the character commonly referred to as "John the elder."

16. Culpepper, *John*, 241–43.

years after the death of Polycarp. Irenaeus on the other hand was a disciple of Polycarp who was himself a "hearer" of the apostle John. Eusebius did affirm that Papias was a "contemporary" of Polycarp (see *Ecc. Hist.* III.36.1). He also provided evidence that Irenaeus lived during the later part of Papias's life. Some scholars, however, have preferred Eusebius's acceptance of Dionysius's unsubstantiated conjecture and have chosen to marginalize Irenaeus's memories as the vague recollections of a "child."[17] Irenaeus, however, in his letter to Florinus was adamant that his memories of Polycarp and his times were anything but the vague recollections of a small child but rather that of a diligent student—a claim that Eusebius was well aware of and incorporated in his own *Ecclesiastical History*.[18] Eusebius himself referred to Irenaeus as a hearer of Polycarp in his "early youth."[19] The salient point for this appendix is that Irenaeus is either a better witness to Papian material than Dionysius and Eusebius, or he is at least their equal since he claimed to be familiar with Papias and his writings—which again is a point that Eusebius was aware of and chose to ignore (*Ecc. Hist.* III.39.1-2). Regarding the value of Irenaeus's witness to Papias and his writings, Chapman concluded that "St. Irenaeus not only was acquainted with the work of Papias, but looked upon it as a fountain-head of apostolical [*sic*] tradition and of theological wisdom. He was certainly more familiar with it than was Eusebius, who despised it. His evidence is, therefore, from this point of view alone, at least equally important with that of Eusebius."[20]

Another weakness of Eusebius was his tendency to castigate those who did not share his own theological biases.[21] This weakness is magnified when confronted with reality that theology was not a particular strength of Eusebius. Consequently, he was often unjustifiably prejudicial towards those that found themselves on the wrong side of the aisle with respect to his personal theological convictions. It should not be forgotten that Eusebius not only defended and aggressively politicked for Arius,[22] but

17. Kümmel, *Introduction*, 241.

18. Eusebius *Ecc. Hist.* V.20.4-8 (LCL 153: 497-99).

19. Ibid., V.5.6 (LCL 153:448). The Greek term is "νέαν ἡλικίαν." On the different uses of ἡλικία that referred to maturity beyond that of a mere child see Luke 2.52; John 9.21; and Eph 4.13.

20. Chapman, *John the Presbyter*, 41.

21. Lawlor and Oulton, *Eusebius*, 2:29.

22. Arius became a leading proponent for the theological position that Jesus the Son of God was not co-eternal with God the Father. This position is commonly referred to as "Arianism." For the origins of this heresy and Arius's relationship to it see González, *The Story of Christianity*, 1:158–67.

that he also lobbied to dispose Athanasius of Alexandria. It was Eusebius's inability to appreciate the theological import of Arius's Christology and its impact upon the apostolic faith as revealed in the Scriptures that caused the synod of Antioch to provisionally excommunicate Eusebius in January 325. Consequently, because of the synod's actions at Antioch, Eusebius had to defend himself at Nicea, and ultimately, albeit begrudgingly, affirm his support for what is now known as the Nicene Creed. Whether Eusebius was truly Arian one can only speculate, but as McGiffert has written, "It is a useless endeavor to clear Eusebius of all sympathy with and leaning toward Arianism."[23]

An example of Eusebius's prejudicial marginalization of someone who did not share his theological views is obvious in his treatment of Papias. Eusebius wrote in *Ecclesiastical History* that Papias "was a man of very little intelligence as is clear from his books."[24] What proof did Eusebius offer for Papias's apparent lack of intellectual acumen? Primarily it was Papias's convictions regarding a literal physical millennial kingdom rather than any apparent lack of grammar, vocabulary, or writing skills.[25] Nevertheless, that Papias was literate and wrote a five-volume work that influenced men such as Irenaeus argues against him being a man of average intelligence. Ironically, modern scholars are generally sensitive to the inappropriate castigation of others for the sake of productive dialogue and healthy academic debate. Many scholars, however, for unknown reasons completely ignore Eusebius's lack of objective treatment and demonstrable marginalization of Papias. They instead assume that his treatment of Papias is entirely trustworthy, as was the case with A. C. Perumalil, who wrote, "There is no reason to doubt the truth of the statement of Eusebius on Papias' relation with the apostles."[26] Such uncritical acceptance of Eusebius's commentary concerning Papias and what he meant, as well as his possible associations with certain apostles is not well defended. If, for example, I questioned another scholar's intelligence on the basis that he or she was theologically "Arminian," it is very likely that I would receive rebukes from my peers, and rightfully so. Many scholars, however, do not pause when confronted by Eusebius's assessment of Papias; instead, they appear to take Eusebius at his word, concluding that he is the most reliable source for understanding Papias and his writings.

23. McGiffert's "Prolegomena" in Eusebius *Church History* (NPNF2 1:13).
24. Eusebius *Ecc. Hist.* III.39.13 (LCL 153:297).
25. Altaner, *Patrology*, 113.
26. Perumalil, "Papias and Irenaeus," 333.

Consequently, Eusebius's lack of objectivity while handling some of his sources is a glaring weakness of his *Ecclesiastical History*. Regarding this weakness, Doron Mendels wrote, "He was not an objective writer; indeed, objectivity does not appear to have been high on his list of priorities. Eusebius himself seems, unlike Thucydides, not even to have attempted to write an objective narrative."[27] Mendels later detailed why he assessed Eusebius so harshly, stating that "media scholars evaluate the sensationalism vs. impartiality factor by applying two subcriteria [*sic*], 'balance' and 'neutrality.' On both these counts, Eusebius would fail the test."[28] This is not to say that Eusebius did not think of himself as objective. Given the events that had transpired before his very own eyes, his commitment to Christianity, and his theological perspective, Eusebius probably felt he was completely objective while dealing with his sources, as well as accurate in his interpretation of their significance. Modern scholars, however, should not have this same confidence when dealing with certain topics that Eusebius addressed.

Finally, in order to appreciate why Eusebius felt justified in his handling of Papias it is important to discuss a significant purpose and weakness of Eusebius's *Ecclesiastical History*. Eusebius's approach to his "historical treatise" was not purely academic; it also possessed an apologetic aspect as well. McGiffert wrote concerning Eusebius's apologetic purpose that

> The reasons which led him to undertake its composition seem to have been both scientific and apologetic. He lived, and he must have realized the fact, at the opening of a new age in the history of the Church. He believed, as he frequently tells us, that the period of struggle had come to an end, and that the Church was now about entering upon a new era of prosperity. He must have seen that it was a peculiarly fitting time to put on record for the benefit of posterity the great events which had taken place within the Church during the generations that were past, to sum up in one narrative all the trials and triumphs which had now emerged in this final and greatest triumph, which he was witnessing. He wrote, as any historian of the present day would write, for the information and instruction of his contemporaries and of those who should come after, and yet there was in his mind all the time the apologetic purpose,

---

27. Mendels, *The Media Revolution*, 19. While there are problems with Mendel's methods and conclusion; nevertheless, he is qualified to assess whether Eusebius was an objective writer and historian.

28. Ibid., 25.

the desire to exhibit to the world the history of Christianity as a proof on its divine origin and efficacy.[29]

Eusebius made it clear in his preface that his purpose was not simply to record but also to interpret and convince (*Ecc. Hist.* I.1.1–3). An example of Eusebius's apologetic purpose is observable in his statement, "To this I will add the fate which has beset the whole nation of the Jews from the moment of their plot against the divine word."[30] Eusebius was of the opinion that everything that the nation of Israel had experienced under Roman oppression was directly from the hand of God as punishment for their betrayal of the savior, and he contended for this position throughout *Ecclesiastical History*. The demise of Israel, however, did not mean the demise of God's people, for in *Ecclesiastical History* Eusebius portrays the church as ever advancing in victory under the superintendence of God. He was, in the words of Bovon, "a theologian of salvation history, rather than of history as such."[31] Eusebius, therefore, in *Ecclesiastical History* ultimately attempted to convince his audience that the kingdom of God had finally come to earth as promised in the Scriptures, and it had literally come in a real and tangible way through the reign of his great advocate Constantine the Great.

Eusebius was, in a very real sense, the first theologian to propagate a "now not yet" eschatology within the context of complete political victory. Eusebius actually witnessed the transition of the Roman Empire from a pagan institution that mercilessly sought to eradicate Christians and their faith to a kingdom whose emperor proclaimed allegiance to the Lord of lords. Bovon aptly described Eusebius's perspective on the significance of Constantine's ascension as "The 'already and not yet' of the New Testament thus finds itself again in Eusebius. . . . [The] Christian faith is in the process of visibly conquering the world; already the kingdom of God is partly manifest in plain sight."[32] What was once a distant eschatological hope for Eusebius was suddenly an "objective" reality, and all that he had been taught through the allegorical hermeneutic of the Alexandrian school about the deeper meanings of eschatological prophecies was now daily being clearly displayed before his very eyes.

It is not in the purview of this appendix to recount Eusebius's employment of biblical imagery of Constantine as a Christ-like type of hero

29. McGiffert's "Prolegomena" in Eusebius *Church History* (NPNF2 1:46).
30. Eusebius *Ecc. Hist.* I.1.2 (LCL 153:7).
31. Bovon, *Early Christianity*, 273.
32. Ibid., 278–79.

for the faith, or the eschatological promises that he believed were fulfilled in Constantine's "Christian" empire. Let it be sufficient for the moment to state that with Constantine's ascension to the throne of the Roman Empire that nothing appeared on the horizon to indicate to Eusebius that he should vigilantly await the imminent return of the Lord Jesus Christ. Regarding Eusebius's lack of concern for the literal return of Christ, Bovon wrote, "His indifference toward a future-oriented eschatology draws attention to the small role the second coming plays in his thought, to his negative disposition toward the book of Revelation, and to his hatred of millenarianism."[33] Barnes wrote in a similar vein that "The idea that a different John wrote Revelation derived from Dionysius of Alexandria, whose arguments against the traditional attribution to the apostle Eusebius quotes at some length. The cause of Eusebius' unease can readily be diagnosed. Revelation breathes an atmosphere of persecution, with an oppressed minority in a hostile world hoping for a glorious vindication in heaven; Eusebius believed that God intended his Church to prosper on earth."[34] Given his Alexandrian pedigree and his anti-literal eschatology, it is not surprising that Papias suffered poor reviews from Eusebius. This is not to argue that Papias did not deserve some of these criticisms, for if students will survey the surviving Papian material it is more than likely that they will sense the need to lift an eyebrow. That being said, however, Eusebius should not be excused for his poor treatment of Papias and his witness to the close of the apostolic period.

A proper understanding of who Papias was for many scholars often appears to be settled by whether they find Irenaeus or Eusebius more convincing. If one believes that this issue can only be settled by ferreting out the possibilities based upon the statements of these two patristic figures then one may feel a degree of confidence in agreeing with one or the other. The truth is, however, that these two are not the only witnesses to Papias and his writings, although this often appears to be the case as one surveys literature that addresses the apostolic fathers and the origins of books in the New Testament. Since Irenaeus and Eusebius provide conflicting statements about Papias's relationship to the apostle John, the principle of multiple attestations should play an important role in deciding who was correct about Papias and his witness to the apostolic period. Such evidence can be found in other Papian fragments.

33. Ibid., 281–82.

34. Barnes, *Constantine and Eusebius*, 140.

A survey of this material reveals that there are at least fourteen different fragments from known authors and two anonymous sources that associate Papias with the apostle John. Given the previous analysis of the Papian fragments provided throughout this book and in this appendix only a few of the more important witnesses will be addressed at this point. The first witness to be discussed that associates Papias with the apostle John is Eusebius himself. In his *Chronicle* Eusebius wrote that Papias was a "hearer" of the apostle John. Jerome's Latin translation of Eusebius reads roughly as follows, "John, the apostle, all the way to Trajan's time, Irenaeus the most excellent bishop writes. Afterwards of whom his hearers became famous, Papias the bishop of Hierapolis and Polycarp of Smyrna and Ignatius of Antioch."[35] It is interesting to note that Papias was listed as a "hearer" of the apostle John before Polycarp. Robert Grant questions whether this reference to Papias reflects Eusebius's view of Papias or Jerome's view, implying that Jerome inserted his own opinion regarding Papias while translating Eusebius's work into Latin.[36] Grant's argument was not based on any textual variants but on Jerome's descriptions of Papias in his treatise, *De viris illustribus* (hereafter, *Illustrious Men*). Grant, in order to support his conjecture, observed that in *Illustrious Men* Jerome only referred to Papias as "*a Iohannis auditor*—of the presbyter, not the apostle . . . and only Polycarp is *Iohannis apostoli disciple.*"[37]

It should not be ignored, however, that the descriptions of Polycarp and Papias are found in separate chapters of *Illustrious Men*, and nowhere does Jerome indicate that he intended to compare Papias's and Polycarp's relationship with the apostle John. Clearly, therefore, Grant has taken Jerome's descriptions of the two out of their original context and has assigned to them meanings that Jerome never intended. Additionally, Grant failed to address the significance of Jerome's description of Papias in his letter to Theodora, in which he described Papias as "the hearer of evangelist John."[38] Jerome's description of Papias in Latin is: "*et Papiæ, auditoris Evangelistæ Johannis.*"[39] Consequently it is clear that Jerome at one time believed that Papias was a "hearer" of the author of the Gospel of John.

35. Eusebii Pamphili *Chronici*, 275–76. The text in Latin appears as follows: "Johannem apostolum usque ad Traiani tempora Hireneus episcopus permansisse scribit, post quem auditores eius insignes fuerunt Papias Hierapolitanus episcopus et Polycarpus Zmyrnaeus et Ignatius Antiochenus."

36. Grant, "Papias in Eusebius," 210.

37. Ibid.

38. Jerome *Letter 75: To Theodora* (NPNF2 6:156).

39. Holmes, *Apostolic Fathers*, 3rd ed., 748.

Regarding Grant's proposal that Jerome may have felt the freedom to redact Eusebius's work, Alden Mosshammer has done an extensive study regarding the textual history of Jerome's translation of Eusebius's *Chronicle*, and concluded that:

> For antiquity and continuity alone, the early manuscript tradition of Jerome has a strong claim to authentic representation of the original format of the *Chronicle* of Eusebius. Although Jerome did augment the text by entering some additional historical notices drawn from Latin authors, he gives no indication that he made any significant changes in the format of the original. On the contrary, he says that apart from his additions to the historical text he carried out the duties of the translator as faithfully as possible. . . . [To] preserve with great care the format and relative spacing of the original tables. Not only are significant changes unlikely, but there is also much in the organization of the tables as preserved in the oldest manuscript that answer directly to Eusebius' chronographic purposes and much that suggests that it derives from Greek, rather than Latin, predilection.[40]

Given the absence of substantial evidence that Jerome significantly redacted Eusebius's Greek portion of his *Chronicle*, it appears safe to conclude that the reference to Papias in *Chronicle* is authentic to Eusebius's original composition. The question arises, however, why would Eusebius describe Papias as a hearer to the apostle John and then later defame Papias and reject him as John's student? Ironically the most reasonable explanation may have been provided by Grant, who in his book *Eusebius as Church Historian* argued that

> Beyond this, we must note that according to Irenaeus, cited in III.39.1, Papias was definitely a hearer of John and a companion of Polycarp and an "ancient man." This, as we have just seen, was the view of Papias which Eusebius accepted when he wrote his *Chronicle*. The link between Papias and John, author [of *sic*] the Apocalypse, was important for all who valued the literal interpretation of apocalyptic eschatology. Irenaeus was one of such enthusiasts. At one time Eusebius was another. . . . Eusebius changed his mind about the work and traces of the change are present in Book III of the *Church History*.[41]

---

40. Mosshammer, *The Chronicle of Eusebius*, 67–68.

41. Grant, *Eusebius*, 131.

It appears, therefore, that between the first edition of Eusebius's *Chronicle* and his final edition of his *Church History* one can find evidence of development within Eusebius regarding Papias's value as a witness to the apostolic period. If one chooses to disregard Eusebius's conflicting attestations of Papias's relationship to the apostle John, this would still leave Irenaeus and Jerome as witnesses to Papias's relationship to the beloved disciple.

The last source to be discussed concerning Papias's relationship to the apostle John is that of Philip of Side and his work *Church History*. What makes Philip an important witness to Papias and what he meant is that he was familiar with Eusebius's conclusion about Papias's relationship to the apostle John, as well as Papias's five-volume work. Philip wrote regarding Papias that

> Papias, bishop of Hierapolis, who was a disciple of John the Theologian and a companion of Polycarp, wrote five books on the sayings of the Lord. In them he made a list of apostles, and after Peter and John, Philip and Thomas and Matthew, he included among disciples of the Lord Aristion and another John, whom he also called "the Elder." So, some think that this John is the author of the two short catholic epistles which circulate under the name John, because the men of the earliest period accept only the first epistle. And some have mistakenly thought that the Apocalypse was also his. . . . Papias says in his second book that John the Theologian and James his brother were killed by the Jews.[42]

The salient observation from Philip's quote of Papias is that although he was aware of Eusebius's exegesis of Papias's preface and his conclusion that Papias knew of a second John who Eusebius referred to as "the Elder," Philip disagreed with Eusebius's conclusion that Papias was not a disciple of the apostle John. What would lead Philip to such a conclusion? It is very possible that he came to this conclusion by his own study of Papias's writings. Other Papian fragments also suggest that Papias indicated in his five-volume work that he knew the apostle John.[43] As previously discussed, Philip is not the only early church writer whom came to this same conclusion, there are over a dozen other similar references that provide multiple attestations that Papias knew the apostle John and was a witness to the late

42. Holmes, *The Apostolic Fathers: Diglot Edition*, 571–73. There are questions regarding the authorship of this fragment. For a more thorough discussion concerning this issue see the analysis of fragment 11 in this book.

43. Ibid., 584–85, see fragments 19 and 20.

apostolic period. In fact, as one surveys all of the Papian fragments it becomes obvious that Eusebius is in the minority regarding Papias's relationship to the apostle John. Given this data and the glaring bias that Eusebius displayed in his treatment of Papias, it is a wonder that anyone considers him a credible source with respect to Papias and his value as a witness of the church's history in the last quarter of the first century.

SOME CONCLUDING RECOMMENDATIONS

Faced with demonstrable evidence of Eusebius's weaknesses in his method and his biases for his own theological perspectives, and the fact that his treatment of Papias objectively displays these flaws, a few recommendations are justified. First, New Testament and patristic scholars should not uncritically rely upon Eusebius and his exegesis as providing the correct understanding of what Papias meant. Regarding Eusebius's exegesis of Papias, James A. Kleist and Johannes Munck have aptly demonstrated that his interpretation of Papias was at least questionable if not certainly flawed.[44] Secondly, New Testament and patristic scholars should not assume that Eusebius is the sole witness of Papian material. Thirdly, scholarship in both fields should consider the very real possibility that Eusebius's opinion of Papias was not constant but changed as he wrote throughout the period of the church's transition from an oppressed illegal religion to a protected institution of the state, which for Eusebius was a period that spanned decades. Fourthly, New Testament scholarship should remember that Eusebius was theologically biased and politically committed to an eschatology that no longer saw a need for Papias's brand of chiliasm, but instead attempted to apply a "now more than ever" realized eschatology based upon a belief that the kingdom of God had come to earth through the reign of Constantine. Eusebius's association and loyalty to Constantine can hardly be questioned. This loyalty wedded to Eusebius's eschatology is but one of the reasons that led Eusebius to unjustly marginalize Papias and his witness to the apostolic period. We cannot afford, therefore, to assume Eusebius was simply an unbiased historian. Fifthly, scholarship should not assume that Eusebius was completely familiar with all of Papias's writings. It should be noted that Eusebius quoted predominately from Papias's preface, and reported only a few other smaller passages that contained the more spectacular events recorded in Papias's writings. If one surveys the whole of the Papian fragments, one will discover other citations of Papias's

44. Kleist, *Papias*, 105–13; Munck, "Presbyters," 236–37.

five-volume work that clearly contradict Eusebius's conclusions. It is possible, therefore, that Eusebius did not closely examine the whole of Papias's work, or that he had not even read it in its entirety. As many a professor and student can attest, Eusebius would not be the first scholar who missed a nugget of important information that was critical to his thesis simply because he failed to examine closely or to have completely read a source that he had already concluded was marginal.

In conclusion, regarding Eusebius's value McGiffert has appropriately written,

> The whole Christian world has reason to be thankful that there lived at the opening of the fourth century a man who, with his life spanning one of the greatest epochs that has occurred in the history of the Church, with an intimate experimental knowledge of the old and of the new condition of things, was able to conceive so grand a plan and possessed the means and the ability to carry it out. Had he written nothing else, Eusebius' *Church History* would have made him immortal; for if immortality be a fitting reward for large and lasting services, few possess a clearer title to it than the author of that work.[45]

Although this appendix has been rather blunt in its criticism of Eusebius, the fact remains that his service to the church will endure long after the echoes of his critics have subsided, and rightfully so. Nevertheless, New Testament and patristic scholarship should be reminded of William Bright's insightful analogy, especially in the case of Eusebius's handling of Papias, that Eusebius is the frame that contains the masterpiece, which we call the history of the early church—he is not the picture.[46] Consequently, when researching Papias and his writings, limited as they are, Eusebius should not be viewed as the definitive resource for correctly interpreting Papias, or understanding his value as a witness to the church's history at the end of the first century and the beginning of the second century.

45. McGiffert's "Prolegomena" in Eusebius *Church History* (NPNF2 1:46).
46. Bright's introduction in Eusebius *Ecc. Hist.*, ed. Bright, l.

Appendix 2

Who Has Confused Whom?

Which Philip Lived in Hierapolis

WHEN RESEARCHING PAPIAS ONE commonly finds discussions concerning the possibility that Papias may have met or known the apostle Philip. Many, however, believe that Eusebius inadvertently mistook Philip the Evangelist of Acts 6:5; 8:4–40; 21:7–9; for Philip the apostle.[1] If Eusebius erred, the source of his error is easily traceable. He does not often mention either Philip, but in *Ecclesiastical History* III.31.1–5 he discussed either one or both at some length, drawing largely from a letter from Polycrates, a bishop of Ephesus, and the debate between Gaius and the Montanist Proclus. An English translation of the text in question is here provided.

> The time and manner of the death of Paul and of Peter, and the place where their corpses were laid after their departure from this life, have been already described by us. The date of the death of John has also been already mentioned, and the place of his body is shown by a letter of Polycrates (he was bishop of the diocese of Ephesus) which he wrote to Victor, bishop of Rome. In this he mentions both John, Philip the Apostle, and Philip's daughters as follows: "For great luminaries sleep in Asia, and they will rise again at the last day of the advent of the Lord, when he shall come with glory from heaven and call back all the saints, such as was Philip, one of the twelve apostles, who sleeps at Hierapolis with his two daughters who

1. Matthews, *Philip*, 31.

grew old as virgins and his third daughter who lived in the Holy Spirit and rests in Ephesus. And there is also John, who leaned on the Lord's breast, who was a priest wearing the mitre, and martyr and teacher, and he sleeps at Ephesus." So far concerning their deaths. And in the dialogue of Gaius, which we mentioned a little earlier, Proclus, with whom he was disputing, speaks thus about the death of Philip and his daughters and agrees with what has been stated. "After him the four daughters of Philip who were prophetesses were at Hierapolis in Asia. Their grave is there and so is their father's." So he says. And Luke in the Acts of the Apostles mentions the daughters of Philip who were then living with their father at Caesarea in Judaea and were vouchsafed the gift of prophecy. He says as follows: "We came to Caesarea and entered into the house of Philip the Evangelist, one of the seven, and remained with him. And he had four daughters who were prophetesses.[2]

Before continuing it should first be duly noted that Eusebius was convinced that at least one Philip was buried in Hierapolis, and that the one buried there was none other than the apostle Philip. He clearly stated in *Ecclesiastical History* III.39.9 that the apostle had resided in Hierapolis, and in V.24.2 he documented that Hierapolis was the city where the apostle Philip was buried. However, some reasonable questions still remain. The first is, was Eusebius confused; and secondly, did the apostle Philip actually live and die in Hierapolis. As to the second question, there is no concrete evidence to suggest that the apostle Philip was not buried at Hierapolis. There is, in fact, no evidence that demands that both Philips could not have been buried at Hierapolis. The coincidence of their names, however, and that fact that they were both blessed with multiple daughters causes some to pause and conjecture that an error has occurred, either on the part of Polycrates, Proclus, Eusebius, or any combination of the three.

Christopher Matthews wrote an entire monograph on this subject in which he concluded that Philip the apostle and Philip the evangelist was the same person.[3] He theorized that Luke never intended to communicate that there were two Philips. Luke created the confusion between the two because by the time he wrote Acts the vocabulary of the early church had changed. As a result of Philip's missionary activities he was no longer identified as an apostle, but instead became known as an evangelist.[4]

2. Eusebius *Ecc. Hist.* III.31.1–5 (LCL 153: 269–73).

3. Matthews, *Philip*, 3, 33.

4. Ibid., 8.

Matthews argued, therefore, that the confusion between the two Philips is completely the fault of Luke, writing that

> In the second century of the Christian era, whenever Chris-
> tian sources mention Philip, it is the apostle of the same name
> who is in view. There is no evidence to suggest the existence
> of competing or parallel traditions of two early, influential
> Christian figures that happened to share the name Philip.
> Both the later ecclesiastical view that carefully distinguishes
> the "deacon" Philip from the apostle of the same name and the
> pervasive modern assumption that there were two high profile
> Philips in the earliest days of the church are based solely on
> Luke's presentation in Acts. Were it not for Acts, there would
> be no clue that a problem existed with respect to Philip's
> identity.[5]

While it is possible that there is some confusion on the part of patristic and modern authors regarding these two Philips, an error or ambiguity
on the part of Luke has not been proven and, therefore, should not be
assumed. Matthews's theory ignores the fact that Luke associated Philip
the apostle with the apostolic colloquium and distinguished Philip the
deacon and evangelist as separate from the twelve. In Acts 1:13 Philip is
named among the eleven apostles (pre-Matthias). In Acts 6:2, however,
Luke referred to "the twelve" (post-Matthias) who called the Jerusalem
congregation and commissioned them to choose spiritual men to solve the
crisis concerning the distribution of food to widows. Consequently, the
apostle Philip should be assumed to be among the twelve. The congrega-
tional search led to the selection of seven men, one of which was a Philip
who later became known as the evangelist who settled in Caesarea along
with his four prophetic daughters (Acts 21:8–9). A closer study of Acts,
therefore, reveals that Luke was not confused nor did he create confusion by being ambiguous. Luke knew that there was one Philip, who was a
member of the apostolic tribe, he also knew of another Philip who served
widows and initiated the Gentile mission; consequently, this Philip was
identified as "the evangelist" (Acts 21:8). The apostle Philip as a member of
the apostolic colloquium was to be devoted to prayer and the "ministry of
the word" (Acts 6:4); while Philip the evangelist undertook the ministry of
service to the Hellenistic widows. And, as Luke recorded, this was the entire purpose for the division of their ministries, so that the apostle Philip
could be free to focus upon the ministry that Jesus had commissioned

5. Ibid., 15.

him. It would have been a dereliction of the apostle Philip's divine calling from Jesus Christ to allow himself to be entangled in a different ministry. Coincidentally, however, both of them came to have several daughters, and both of them apparently settled in Hierapolis. If anyone was confused about which Philip lived in Hierapolis it does not appear to have been Luke, for on this topic Luke is completely silent, nor is there any evidence indicating that he was ever aware of where both Philips may have settled in their later years.

The previously provided Eusebian quote indicates that Eusebius stated that both Philips were buried in Hierapolis. Relying upon Polycrates, Eusebius believed that Philip the apostle was buried there with two of his daughters, while another daughter was buried in Ephesus. After his initial reference to Philip the apostle, Eusebius recorded that a second Philip was also buried in Hierapolis. For the tradition of this Philip, however, he relied upon the Montanist Proclus. Eusebius identified Proclus's Philip with the Philip of Acts 21:7-9, and his identification may be correct since Proclus claimed this second Philip had four prophetic daughters, indicating that this Philip was the evangelist and not the apostle. Proclus also claimed that the graves of Philip's daughters were also in Hierapolis with their father's grave. This is not so concerning the graves of the daughters of the apostle Philip, for one had apparently married and was buried in Ephesus. Knowing Eusebius's disdain for the Montanists, it is understandable that he might attempt to distance the apostle Philip from any association with the Montanists or their heritage.[6] However, the fact that Eusebius never inadvertently quoted a Gospel text (e.g., John 1:43)[7] while referring to the evangelist should cause one to realize that Eusebius was not confused and knew exactly which of the two Philips he was discussing.

Apparently both Philips had daughters, and it is this coincidence that aids in the confusion concerning which Philip may have lived and died in Hierapolis. The apostle Philip appears to have had at least three daughters, two of which lived out their devotion to Christ as virgins, while a third, although being a spiritual woman, married, died, and was buried in Ephesus.[8] Additionally, Eusebius reported that Clement of Alexandria

6. For Eusebius's reporting on Montanism see *Ecc. Hist.* V.14-18 (LCL 153:471-93).

7. John 1:43 reads as "The next day He purposed to go into Galilee, and he found Philip. And Jesus said to him, 'Follow me.'" This particular text clearly refers to the apostle Philip and not Philip the evangelist.

8. Eusebius recorded that "such as was Philip, one of the twelve apostles, who sleeps at Hierapolis with this two daughters who grew old as virgins and his third daughter who lived in the Holy Spirit and rests in Ephesus." Eusebius *Ecc. Hist.*

corroborated this tradition, stating that both Peter and Philip "begat children, and Philip even gave his daughters to husbands."[9] Luke, however, reported that all four of the daughters of Philip the evangelist were virgins (Acts 21:9). If a mistake has occurred, then it is either that the apostle Philip had more than three daughters, four of whom did not marry and migrated with him to Asia Minor, or that Clement was mistaken when he suggested that a daughter of the apostle Philip had married. Such errors, however, seem unlikely. Consequently, demanding that a mistake has occurred does not appear to be the best explanation to this conundrum. Moreover, there is no record that daughters of Philip the apostle were ever described as being "prophetesses." That description was only applied to the daughters of the evangelist. It is interesting that Eusebius's two other references to the evangelist actually focus upon his daughters rather than Philip.[10] Regardless of Eusebius's other references to the evangelist, it is his inclusion of Proclus's statement about the Philip the evangelist in the context of a discussion about Philip the apostle that is most likely the source of most of the confusion regarding both Philips, their daughters, and Papias's possible association with any of them. If Eusebius had not included Proclus's comments about the second Philip then there would be no debate regarding which Philip had lived and died in Hierapolis, nor would there be any discussion concerning which Philip Papias may have known.[11] Nevertheless, it appears that both Philips eventually lived, died, and were buried in Hierapolis.

Some may balk at the idea that two influential Philips, both of whom had multiple daughters, could have migrated to Hierapolis, and were inevitably buried there. Many, however, have no problem believing that there resided in Ephesus two Johns who were influential leaders of the Asiatic church. But of Eusebius's mythical John the elder, we have no clear reference of him until Dionysius's blind conjecture originating in the early third century. Concerning both Philips, however, we have sound historical data, from both the New Testament and other church historians, that both were active in the life of the church. The data seems to suggest that the apostle Philip did indeed migrate to Hierapolis, and that Papias did receive some traditions from his daughters, and possibly from the apostle

---

III.31.2–3 (LCL 153: 269–71). It seems reasonable to assume, therefore, that one of Philip's daughters had married since she was not identified as a "virgin."

9. Ibid., III.30.1 (LCL 153: 269).

10. Ibid., III.37.1; V.17.3 (LCL 153: 287, 485).

11. Lawlor and Oulton, *Eusebius*, 2:114–18.

Philip as well. This same data also suggests that Philip the evangelist also migrated to Hierapolis. Although such a migration seems rather coincidental, there is nothing to demand that it could not have occurred.[12] Asia Minor proved to be fruitful soil for the expansion of the church during the late first century and well into the second century. It is not unreasonable, consequently, to believe that men so wonderfully blessed with charismatic daughters might want to locate in an area that provided their families with the greatest opportunity for peaceful lives and fruitful ministry.

12. Matthews, *Philip*, 32 note 66.

Bibliography

Abbott, Edwin A. "The 'Elders' of Papias." *The Expositor* 1 (1895) 333–46.

Alexander, Loveday. "The Living Voice: Skepticism towards the Written Word in Early Christian and in Graeco-Roman Texts." In *The Bible in Three Dimensions*, edited by David J. A. Clines, Stanley E. Porter, and Stephen E. Fowl, 221–47. Sheffield, UK: Sheffield Academic Press, 1990.

Altaner, Berthold. *Patrology*. Translated by Hilda C. Graef. New York: Herder and Herder, 1960.

Anderson, R. Dean Jr. *Ancient Rhetorical Theory and Paul*. Rev. ed. Leuven: Peeters, 1999.

Andrew of Caesarea. *The Apocalypse of John the Theologian*. Edited by J.-P. Migne. Patrologia Graeca, vol. 106. Paris: J.-P. Migne, 1860.

Annand, Rupert. "Papias and the Four Gospels." *Scottish Journal of Theology* 9 (1956) 46–62.

Augustine. *Teaching Christianity: De Doctrina Christiana*. Translated by Edmund Hill. Vol. 11 of *The Works of Saint Augustine: A Translation for the 21st Century*. Hyde Park, NY: New City, 1996.

Bacon, B. W. "The Elder John, Papias, Irenaeus, Eusebius and the Syriac Translator." *Journal of Biblical Literature* 27 (1908) 1–23.

———. "An Emendation of the Papias Fragment." *Journal of Biblical Literature* 17 (1898) 176–83.

Bacon, Benjamin W. *Studies in Matthew*. New York: Holt, 1930.

Badham, F. P. "The Martyrdom of St. John." *The American Journal of Theology* 3 (1899) 729–40.

———. "The Martyrdom of John the Apostle." *The American Journal of Theology* 8 (1904) 539–53.

Barnes, Jonathan. *Early Greek Philosophy*. London: Penguin, 1988.

Barnes, Timothy. *Constantine and Eusebius*. Cambridge: Harvard University Press, 1981.

Bartlet, Vernon. "Papias." In *A Dictionary of Christ and the Gospels*, vol. 2, edited by James Hastings. New York: Scribner's Sons, 1908.

———. "Papias's 'Exposition': Its Date and Contents." In *Amicitiae Corolla*, edited by H. G. Wood, 15–44. London: University of London Press, 1933.

Bauckham, Richard. *Jesus and the Eyewitnesses: The Gospels as Eyewitness Testimony*. Grand Rapids: Eerdmans, 2006.

———. "Papias and Polycrates on the Origin of the Fourth Gospel." *The Journal of Theological Studies* 44 (1993) 24–69.

Bauer, Walter. *A Greek-English Lexicon of the New Testament*. 2nd ed. Edited and translated by F. Wilber Gingrich William F. Arndt, and Frederick W. Danker. Chicago: University of Chicago Press, 1979.

————. *Orthodoxy and Heresy in Earliest Christianity*. Edited by Robert A. Kraft and Gerhard Krodel. Translated by Philadelphia Seminar on Christian Origins. Philadelphia: Fortress, 1971.

Baum, Armin Daniel. "Der Presbyter des Papias über einen 'Hermeneuten' des Petrus." *Theologische Zeitschrift* 56 (2000) 21–35.

Beard, Mary, John North, and Simon Price. *Religions of Rome: A History*. Vol. 1. Cambridge: Cambridge University Press, 1999.

Bernard, J. H. *Studia Sacra*. London: Hodder and Stoughton, 1917.

Beyer, Hermann W. "ἐπίσκοπος." In *Theological Dictionary of the New Testament*, vol. 2, edited by Gerhard Kittel and translated and edited by Geoffrey W. Bromiley. Grand Rapids: Eerdmans, 1980.

Bihlmeyer, Karl. *Die Apostolischen Väter: Neubearbeitung der Funkschen Ausgabe*. Mit einem Nachtrag von Wilhelm Schneemelcher, 2nd ed. Tübingen: Mohr [Siebeck], 1956.

Bingham, Jeffrey. "Development and Diversity in Early Christianity." *Journal of the Evangelical Theological Society* 49 (2006) 45–66.

Bisbee, Gary A. *Pre-Decian Acts of the Martyrs and Commentarii*. Philadelphia: Fortress, 1988.

Black, David Alan. *Learn to Read New Testament Greek*. Nashville: Broadman & Holman, 1994.

Black, Matthew. "The Use of Rhetorical Terminology in Papias on Mark and Matthew." *Journal for the Study of the New Testament* 37 (1989) 31–41.

Blázquez, José M. "Relations between Hispania and Palestine in the Late Roman Empire." *Assaph* 3 (1998) 163–78.

Blomberg, Craig L. *The Historical Reliability of John's Gospel*. Downers Grove, IL: InterVarsity, 2001.

Bock, Darrell L. *Luke 1:1—9:50*. Baker Exegetical Commentary on the New Testament 1. Grand Rapids: Baker, 1999.

Bornkamm, Günther. "πρεσβύτερος." In *Theological Dictionary of the New Testament*, vol. 6, edited by Gerhard Kittel and translated and edited by Geoffrey W. Bromiley. Grand Rapids: Eerdmans, 1975.

Bosio, Guido. *I Padri Apostolici, Parte II*. Torino: Societa Editrice Internazionale, 1940.

Bovon, François. *Studies in Early Christianity*. Translated by Laura Beth Bugg. Grand Rapids: Baker, 2003.

Bruce, F. F. *The Book of Acts*. The New International Commentary on the New Testament. Grand Rapids: Eerdmans, 1988.

————. *The Canon of Scripture*. Downers Grove, IL: InterVarsity, 1988.

————. *The Epistles to the Colossians, to Philemon, and the Ephesians*. The New International Commentary on the New Testament. Grand Rapids: Eerdmans, 1984.

————. *New Testament History*. Garden City, NY: Doubleday, 1972.

Brunt, P. A. "Marcus Aurelius and the Christians." In *Studies in Latin Literature and Roman History*, edited by C. Deroux, 483–520. Brussels: Latomus, 1979.

Burge, Gary M. "A Specific Problem in the New Testament Text and Canon: The Woman Caught in Adultery (John 7:53—8:11)." *Journal of the Evangelical Theological Society* 27 (1984) 141–48.

Burnet, John. *Early Greek Philosophy*. London: Black, 1948.

Burton, Edward. *Lectures upon the Ecclesiastical History of the First Three Centuries*. 4th ed. London: Parker, 1855.

Cadbury, Henry J. "A Possible Case of Lukan Authorship (John 7.53—8.11)." *The Harvard Theological Review* 10 (1917) 237–45.

Cantor, Norman F., and Richard I. Schneider. *How to Study History*. Wheeling, IL: Davis, 1967.

Carson, D. A., and Douglas J. Moo. *An Introduction to the New Testament*. 2nd ed. Grand Rapids: Zondervan, 2005.

Chapman, John. *John the Presbyter and the Fourth Gospel*. Oxford: Clarendon, 1911.

Chronicon Paschale. Edited by J.-P. Migne. Patrologia Graeca, vol. 92. Paris: J.-P. Migne, 1860.

Chronicon Paschale 284-628. Edited and translated by Michael Whitby and Mary Whitby. Liverpool: Liverpool University Press, 1989.

Clemen, Carl. "The Sojourn of the Apostle John at Ephesus." *The American Journal of Theology* 9 (1905) 643–76.

Coenen, L. "Bishop, Presbyter, Elder." In *New International Dictionary of New Testament Theology*, vol. 1, edited by Colin Brown. Grand Rapids: Zondervan, 1986.

Collins, Adela Yarbro. "Pergamon in Early Christian Literature." In *Pergamon: Citadel of the Gods*, edited by Helmut Koester, 163–84. Harrisburg, PA: Trinity, 1998.

Colson, F. H. "Τάξει in Papias." *The Journal of Theological Studies* 14 (1913) 62–69.

Culpepper, R. Alan. *John, the Son of Zebedee: The Life of a Legend*. Edinburgh: T. & T. Clark, 2000.

Deardorff, James W. "A Recently Discovered Document Indicating That Immanuel (Jesus) Taught of the Individual Spirit: Is It Papias' Logia?" *Journal of Religion and Psychical Research* 15 (1992) 115–26.

Deeks, David G. "Papias Revisited: Part I." *Expository Times* 88 (1977) 296–301.

———. "Papias Revisited: Part II." *Expository Times* 88 (1977) 324–29.

deSilva, David A. *Introducing the Apocrypha*. Grand Rapids: Baker Academic, 2002.

Didache. Translated and edited by Bart D. Ehrman. Loeb Classical Library, vol. 24. Cambridge: Harvard University Press, 2005.

Dillion, Richard, J. "Preview Luke's Project from His Prologue (Luke 1:1–4)." *Catholic Biblical Quarterly* 43 (1981) 205–27.

Dionysius the Pseudo-Areopagite. *The Ecclesiastical Hierarchy*. Translated and edited by Thomas L. Campbell. Lanham, MD: University Press of America, 1981.

Donaldson, James. *A Critical History of Literature and Doctrine*. Vol. 1. London: Macmillan, 1864.

Epistle of Barnabas. Edited and translated by Bart D. Ehrman. In *The Apostolic Fathers II*. Loeb Classical Library, vol. 25. Cambridge: Harvard University Press, 2005.

Eusebi. *Chronicorum Canonum*. Edited by Alfred Schoene. Translated by H. Petermann. Dublin: Weidmann, 1875.

Eusebii Pamphili. *Chronici Canones*. Edited and compiled by Johannes Knight Fotheringham. London: Milford, 1923.

Eusebius. *The Church History of Eusebius*. Translation by and prolegomena with notes by Arthur Cushman McGiffert. American ed. Nicene and Post-Nicene Fathers, vol. 1. 1895. Reprint. Peabody, MA: Hendrickson, 2004.

———. *Ecclesiastical History*. Edited with introduction by William Bright. Oxford: Clarendon, 1872.

———. *Ecclesiastical History I*. Translated by Kirsopp Lake. Loeb Classical Library, vol. 153. Cambridge: Harvard University Press, 1980.

———. *Ecclesiastical History II*. Translated by J. E. L. Oulton and H. J. Lawlor. Loeb Classical Library, vol. 265. Cambridge: Harvard University Press, 1980.

Bibliography

————. *The Ecclesiastical History of Eusebius Pamphilus*. Translated by Christian Frederick Cruse. Grand Rapids: Baker, 1989.

————. *Eusebius Werke*. Vol. 2, pt. 1. *Die Kirchengeschichte*. Edited by Eduard Schwartz and Theodor Mommsen. Berlin: Akademie-Verlag, 1999.

————. *Die Griechischen Christlichen Schriftsteller der Ersten Jahrhunderte*. Vol. 7, *Die Chronik des Hieronymus*. Edited by Rudolf Helm. Berlin: Akademie-Verlag, 1956.

————. *Historica*. Edited and translated by J.-P. Migne. Patrologia Graeca, vol. 20. Paris: J.-P. Migne, 1857.

First Enoch. Translated by E. Isaac. In *The Old Testament Pseudepigrapha*, vol. 1. Garden City, NY: Doubleday, 1983.

First Enoch: A New Translation. Translated by George W. E. Nickelsburg and James C. VanderKam. Minneapolis: Fortress, 2004.

Foakes-Jackson, Fredrick John. *A History of Church History*. Cambridge: Heffer & Sons, 1939.

Fragments of Papias. Translated and edited by Alexander Roberts and James Donaldson, with notes by A. Cleveland Coxe. American ed. Ante-Nicene Fathers, vol. 1. 1885. Reprint. Peabody, MA: Hendrickson, 2004.

The Fragments of Papias. Translated by James C. Kleist. In *Ancient Christian Writers: The Works of the Fathers in Translation*, vol. 6, edited by Johannes Quasten and James C. Plumpe, 103–24. New York: Newman, 1948.

The Fragments of Papias. Translated by William R. Schoedel. In *The Apostolic Fathers: A New Translation and Commentary*, vol. 5, edited by Robert M. Grant, 87–130. Camden, NJ: Thomas Nelson, 1967.

Franke, John R. "Eusebius of Caesarea." In *Historians of the Christian Tradition*, edited by Michael Bauman and Martin L. Klauber, 59–78. Nashville: Broadman & Holman, 1980.

Frend, W. H. C. *The Rise of Christianity*. Philadelphia: Fortress, 1984.

Froehlich, Karlfried, editor and translator. *Biblical Interpretation in the Early Church*. Sources of Early Christian Thought Series. Philadelphia: Fortress, 1984.

Gebhardt, Oscar de, Adolfus Harnack, and Theodorus Zahn. *Patrum Apostolicorum Opera*. Leipzig: Hinrichs, 1902.

Giles, K. N. "Church Order, Government." In *Dictionary of the Later New Testament*, edited by Ralph P. Martin and Peter H. Davids. Downers Grove, IL: InterVarsity, 1997.

Gill, David W. J., and Bruce Winter. "Acts and Roman Religion." In *The Book of Acts in Its Graeco-Roman Setting*, edited by David W. J. Gill and Conrad Gempf, 79–92. Grand Rapids: Eerdmans, 1994.

González, Justo L. *The Story of Christianity*. Vol. 1. New York: HarperCollins, 1984.

Goodspeed, Edgar J. *The Apostolic Fathers: An American Translation*. New York: Harper, 1950.

Goppelt, Leonhard. *Apostolic and Post-Apostolic Times*. Translated by Robert Guelich. London: Black, 1970.

Grant, Robert M. *Eusebius as Church Historian*. Oxford: Clarendon, 1980.

————. *Irenaeus of Lyons*. London: Routledge, 1997.

————. "Papias in Eusebius' Church History." In *Mélanges d'histoire des religions offerts à Henri-Charles Puech*, edited by André Bareau, 209–13. Paris: Presses Universitaires de France, 1974.

Gregory, Caspar René. *Canon and Text of the New Testament*. Edinburgh: T. & T. Clark, 1907.

Gregory, Joel Cliff. *The Chiliastic Hermeneutic of Papias of Hierapolis and Justin Martyr Compared with Later Patristic Chiliasts.* Ann Arbor, MI: University Microfilms International, 1992.

Gundry, Robert H. *Mark: A Commentary on His Apology for the Cross.* Grand Rapids: Eerdmans, 1993.

———. *Matthew: A Commentary on His Literary and Theological Art.* Grand Rapids: Eerdmans, 1982.

———. *Older Is Better.* Tübingen: Mohr Siebeck, 2005.

Gunther, John J. "The Elder John, the Author of Revelation." *Journal for the Study of the New Testament* 11 (1981) 3–20.

Hall, Edward H. *Papias and His Contemporaries: A Study of Religious Thought in the Second Century.* New York: Riverside, 1899.

Hamell, Patrick J. *Handbook of Patrology.* Staten Island, NY: Alba House, 1968.

Harnack, Adolf. *Geschichte der Altchristlichen Literatur bis Eusebius.* Vol. 1.1. Leipzig: Hinrichs, 1958.

———. *History of Dogma.* Vol. 2–5. Translated by Neil Buchanan. New York: Dover, 1961.

———. *The Mission and Expansion of Christianity: In the First Three Centuries.* Translated by James Moffatt. New York: Harper, 1962.

Harris, W. Hall. *Background to the Study of John* [on-line]. Accessed 8 August 2007. Online: http://www.bible.org.

Heard, Richard. "Papias' Quotations from the New Testament." *New Testament Studies* 1 (1955) 130–34.

Hengel, Martin. *The Johannine Question.* Translated by John Bowden. London: SCM, 1989.

Hiebert, D. Edmond. *The Epistles of John.* Greenville, SC: Bob Jones University Press, 1991.

"Hierapolis" [on-line]. accessed 11 April 2007. Online: http://www.ourfather lutheran. net /biblehomelands/ sevenchurches/hierapolis/ hierapolis.htm.

"Hierapolis" [on-line]. Accessed 11 April 2007. Online: http://www.sacred-destinations. com/turkey/hierapolis-pamukkale.htm.

Higgins, Ronald V. "I Dislike Doing Family Genealogy." Paper presented at the annual meeting of the Evangelical Theological Society, San Diego, CA, 15 November 2007.

Hill, Charles E. "Papias of Hierapolis." *Expository Times* 117 (2006) 309–15.

———. "What Papias Said about John (and Luke)." *The Journal of Theological Studies* 49 (1998) 582–629.

Hock, Ronald F., "General Introduction to Volume 1." In *The Chreia in Ancient Rhetoric: Volume 1 The Progymnasmata,* edited by Ronald F. Hock and Edward N. O'Neil, 1–60. Texts and Translations 27, Graeco-Roman Religions Series 9 of Society of Biblical Literature. Atlanta: Scholars, 1986.

Hoehner, Harold W. "Evidence from Revelation 20." In *A Case for Premillennialism,* edited by Donald K. Campbell and Jeffery L. Townsend, 235–62. Chicago: Moody, 1992.

Holmes, Michael W., editor. *The Apostolic Fathers: Greek Texts and English Translations.* Updated ed. Grand Rapids: Baker Academic, 1999.

———. *Apostolic Fathers: Greek Texts and English Translations.* 3rd ed. Grand Rapids: Baker Academic, 2007.

Hunter, A. M. "Recent Trends in Johannine Studies." *Expository Times* 71 (1959) 219–22.

Hunter, James Davison. *Cultural Wars: The Struggle to Define America.* New York: Basic, 1991.

Ignatius. *Letters of Ignatius.* Translated and edited by Bart D. Ehrman. In *The Apostolic Fathers I.* Loeb Classical Library, vol. 24. Cambridge: Harvard University Press, 2005.

Irenaeus. *Against Heresies.* Translated by Alexander Roberts and W. H. Rambaut. American ed. Ante-Nicene Fathers, vol. 1, 307–578. 1885. Reprint. Peabody, MA: Hendrickson, 2004.

———. *Contra Haereses.* Edited by J.-P. Migne. Patrologia Graeca, vol. 7. Paris: Migne, 1857.

———. *On the Detection and Refutation of the Knowledge Falsely So Called.* Translated and edited by Robert M. Grant. London: Routledge, 1997.

Jefford, Clayton N. *The Apostolic Fathers: An Essential Guide.* Nashville: Abingdon, 2005.

Jerome. *Letters and Selected Works.* Translated by W. H. Fremantle. American ed. Nicene and Post-Nicene Fathers, vol. 6. 1890. Reprint. Peabody, MA: Hendrickson, 2004.

———. *Lives of Illustrious Men.* Translated and edited by Earnest Cushing Richardson. American ed. Nicene and Post-Nicene Fathers, vol. 3. 1895. Reprint. Peabody, MA: Hendrickson, 2004.

Jonas, Hans. *The Gnostic Religion: The Message of the Alien God and the Beginnings of Christianity.* 2nd ed. Boston: Beacon, 1963.

Josephus, Flavius. *The Works of Flavius Josephus.* Translated by William Whiston. In *Antiquities of the Jews*, vol. 4. Nashville: Baker, 1994.

Joslin, Barry. "Getting up to Speed: An Essential Introduction to 1 John." *The Southern Baptist Journal of Theology* 10 (2006) 4–26.

Kampmann, Ursula. "*Homonoia* Politics in Asia Minor: The Example of Pergamon." In *Pergamon: Citadel of the Gods*, edited by Helmut Koester, 373–93. Harrisburg, PA: Trinity, 1998.

Keener, Craig S. *The Gospel of John: A Commentary.* Vol. 1. Peabody, MA: Hendrickson, 2003.

Kelly, J. N. D. *Early Christian Doctrines.* Rev. ed. New York: Harper Row, 1978.

———. *Jerome: His Life, Writings, and Controversies.* New York: Harper and Row, 1975.

Keresztes, Paul. "Marcus Aurelius a Persecutor?" *Harvard Theological Review* 61 (1968) 321–41.

Kinzig, Wolfram. "The Greek Christian Writers." In *Handbook of Classical Rhetoric in the Hellenistic Period, 330 B.C.–A.D. 400*, edited by Stanley Porter, 633–70. Leiden: Brill, 1997.

Kittel, Gerhard. "λόγιον." In *Theological Dictionary of the New Testament*, vol. 4, edited by Gerhard Kittel and translated and edited by Geoffrey W. Bromiley. Grand Rapids: Eerdmans, 1967.

Kleist, James A. "Rereading the Papias Fragment on St. Mark." In *Saint Louis University Studies, Series A, Humanities* 1 (1945) 1–17.

Körtner, Ulrich H. J. *Papias von Hierapolis.* Göttingen: Vandenhoeck & Ruprecht, 1983.

Krueger, Hermann Gustav Eduard. "Anastasius of Sinaita." In *The New Schaff-Herzog Encyclopedia of Religious Knowledge*, edited by Samuel Macauley Jackson. Grand Rapids: Baker, 1949.

Kümmel, Werner Georg. *Introduction to the New Testament.* Translated by A. J. Matill. Nashville: Abingdon, 1966.

Kürzinger, Josef. *Papias von Hierapolis und die Evangelien des Neuen Testaments.* Regensburg: Pustet, 1983.

Lalleman, Pieter J. *The Acts of John: A Two-Stage Initiation into Johannine Gnosticism.* Leuven: Peeters, 1998.

Lampe, G. W. H. *A Patristic Greek Lexicon.* Oxford: Clarendon, 1978.

Lawlor, Hugh Jackson. *Eusebiana.* Amsterdam: Philo, 1973.

———. "Eusebius on Papias." *Hermathena* 43 (1922) 167–222.

Lawlor, Hugh Jackson, and John Ernest Leonard Oulton. *Eusebius.* Vol. 2. London: SPCK, 1928.

Lewis, Frank Grant. *Fourth Gospel: Its Extent, Meaning, and Value.* Chicago: The University of Chicago Press, 1908.

Liddell, Henry George, and Robert Scott. *A Greek Lexicon.* Revised and augmented by Henry Stuart Jones. Oxford: Clarendon, 1996.

Lightfoot, J. B. *The Apostolic Fathers Part I. S. Clement of Rome. A Revised Text with Introductions, Notes, Dissertations, and Translations.* London: Macmillan, 1890.

———. *The Apostolic Fathers Part II. S. Ignatius. S. Polycarp. Revised Texts with Introductions, Notes, Dissertations, and Translations.* London: Macmillan, 1885.

———. *Essays on the Work Entitled: Supernatural Religion.* London: Cambridge University Press, 1889.

———. *Saint Paul's Epistles to the Colossians and to Philemon.* Grand Rapids: Zondervan, 1970.

———. "Supernatural Religion: Papias of Hierapolis." *Contemporary Review* 26 (1875) 377–403.

Lightfoot, J. B., and J. R. Harmer. *Apostolic Fathers: Revised Greek Texts with Introductions and English Translations.* 1891. Reprint. Grand Rapids: Baker Academic, 1984.

———. *Apostolic Fathers.* Edited and revised by Michael W. Holmes. 2nd ed. Grand Rapids: Baker Academic, 1989.

Louth, Andrew. *Denys the Areopagite.* Wilton, CT: Morehouse-Barlow, 1989.

———. *Maximus the Confessor.* London: Routledge, 1996.

Mackenzie, Iain M. *Irenaeus's Demonstration of the Apostolic Preaching: A Theological Commentary and Translation.* Aldershot, UK: Ashgate, 2002.

Mansfeld, Jaap. "Galen, Papias, and Others." In *Things Revealed*, edited by Esther G. Chazon, 317–29. Leiden: Brill, 2004.

The Martyrdom of Polycarp. Translated and edited by Bart D. Ehrman. In *The Apostolic Fathers I.* Loeb Classical Library, vol. 24. Cambridge: Harvard University Press, 2005.

Matthews, Christopher R. *Philip: Apostle and Evangelist, Configurations of a Tradition.* Leiden: Brill, 2002.

McGuckin, John A. "Cyril of Alexandria: Bishop and Pastor." In *The Theology of St. Cyril of Alexandria*, edited by Thomas G. Weinandy and Daniel A. Keating, 205–36. London: T. & T. Clark, 2003.

Mendels, Doron. *The Media Revolution of Early Christianity.* Grand Rapids: Eerdmans, 1999.

Methodius. *The Symposium: A Treatise on Chastity.* Translated and edited by Herbert Musurillo. Ancient Christian Writers, vol. 27. London: Longmans, Green and Co, 1958.

Metzger, Bruce M. *The Canon of the New Testament: Its Origin, Development, and Significance*. Oxford: Clarendon, 1997.

———. *Lexical Aids for Students of New Testament Greek*. Princeton, NJ: Bruce Metzger, 1971.

———. *The Text of the New Testament: Its Transmission, Corruption, and Restoration*. 2nd ed. New York: Oxford University Press, 1968.

———. *A Textual Commentary on the Greek New Testament*. Stuttgart: Biblia-Druck, 1994.

Mosshammer, Alden A. *The Chronicle of Eusebius and Greek Chronographic Tradition*. Cranbury, NJ: Associated University, 1979.

Morris, Leon. *The Gospel according to Matthew*. Grand Rapids: Eerdmans, 1992.

Mullins, Terence Y. "Papias on Mark's Gospel." *Vigiliae Christianae* 14 (1960) 216–24.

Munck, Johannes. "Presbyters and Disciples of the Lord in Papias." *The Harvard Theological Review* 52 (1959) 223–43.

Musurillo, Herbert. *The Acts of the Christian Martyrs*. Oxford: Clarendon, 1972.

Nash, Henry S. "Supernatural Religion." In *The New Schaff-Herzog Encyclopedia of Religious Knowledge*, edited by Philip Schaff. Grand Rapids: Baker, 1954.

Newman, Hillel I. "Jerome's Judaizers." *Journal of Early Christian Studies* 9 (2001) 421–52.

Nielsen, Charles M. "Papias: Polemicist against Whom?" *Theological Studies* 35 (1974) 529–35.

Norris, Fredrick W. "Andrew of Caesarea." In *Encyclopedia of Early Christianity*, Vol. 1., 2nd ed., edited by Everett Ferguson. New York: Garland, 1997.

O'Brien, Peter. *Colossians, Philemon*. Waco, TX: Word, 1982.

Origen. *Commentary on Matthew*. Edited by J.-P. Migne. Patrologiae Graeca, vol. 13. Paris: J.-P. Migne, 1857.

Osborn, Eric. *Irenaeus of Lyons*. Cambridge: Cambridge University Press, 2001.

Papias and Quadratus. Translated and edited by Bart D. Ehrman. Loeb Classical Library, vol. 25. Cambridge: Harvard University Press, 2005.

Parke, H. W. *The Oracles of Apollo in Asia Minor*. London: Croom Helm, 1985.

Perumalil, A. C. "Are Not Papias and Irenaeus Competent to Report on the Gospels?" *Expository Times* 91 (1980) 332–37.

———. "Papias." *Expository Times* 85 (1974) 361–66.

Petrie, C. Stewart. "The Authorship of 'The Gospel of Matthew': A Reconsideration of the External Evidence." *New Testament Studies* 14 (1968) 15–33.

Photius. *Bibliothéque*. Vol. 1. Translated and edited by René Henry. Paris: Société D'Édition Les Belles Lettres, 1959.

———. *Bibliothéque*. Vol. 5. Translated and edited by René Henry. Paris: Société D'Édition Les Belles Lettres, 1967.

Plummer, Alfred. "Bishop, Elder, Presbyter." In *Dictionary of the Apostolic Church*, edited by James Hastings. Edinburgh: T. & T. Clark, 1915.

Polhill, John B. *Acts*. The New American Commentary, vol. 26. Nashville: Broadman, 2001.

———. *Paul and His Letters*. Nashville: Broadman and Holman, 1999.

———. "The Setting of 2 John and 3 John." *The Southern Baptist Journal of Theology* 10.3 (2006) 28–39.

Polybius. *Histories*. Accessed 9 November 2007. Online: http://www.perseus.tufts.ed.

Polycarp. *To the Philippians*. Translated and edited by Bart D. Ehrman. Loeb Classical Library, vol. 24. Cambridge: Harvard University Press, 2005.

———. *To the Philippians*. Translated by William R. Schoedel. In *The Apostolic Fathers: A New Translation and Commentary*, vol. 5, edited by Robert M. Grant, 1–43. Camden, NJ: Thomas Nelson, 1967.

Preuschen, Erwin. *Antilegomena*. Gieszen: Töpelmann, 1905.

Quasten, Johannes. *Patrology*. 3 vols. Westminster, MD: Newman, 1950–60.

Ramsay, W. M. *Cities and Bishoprics of Phrygia*. Vol. 1.1. Oxford: Clarendon, 1895.

———. *Cities and Bishoprics of Phrygia*. Vol. 1.2. Oxford: Clarendon, 1897.

A Reply to Dr. Lightfoot's Essays. London: Longmans, Green, 1889.

Rife, J. Merle. *The Nature and Origin of the New Testament*. New York: Philosophical Library, 1975.

Rigg, Horace Abram. "Papias on Mark." *Novum Testamentum* 1 (1956) 161–83.

Robertson, A. T. *A Grammar of the Greek New Testament: In the Light of Historical Research*. Nashville: Broadman, 1934.

Robinson, John A. T. *Redating the New Testament*. Philadelphia: Westminster, 1976.

Routh, Martin Joseph. *Reliquiæ Sacræ*. Vol. 1. Oxford: Oxford, 1846.

Rowe, Galen O. "Style." In *Handbook of Classical Rhetoric in the Hellenistic Period: 330 B.C.–A.D. 400*, edited by Stanley E. Porter, 122–57. Leiden: Brill, 1997.

Salmon, G. "Apollinaris." In *A Dictionary of Early Christian Biography*, edited by William Piercy. Peabody, MA: Hendrickson, 1999.

Schaff, Philip. *History of the Christian Church*. Vols. 2–4. Grand Rapids: Eerdmans, 1910.

Schenkeveld, Dirk M. "Philosophical Prose." In *Handbook of Classical Rhetoric in the Hellenistic Period: 330 B.C.–A.D. 400*, edited by Stanley E. Porter, 196–264. Leiden: Brill, 1997.

Schoedel, William R. "Papias." In *Anchor Bible Dictionary*, edited by David Noel Freedman. New York: Doubleday, 1992.

———. "Papias." In *Principat* 27.1. *Vorkonstantinisches Christentum; Apostolische Väter und Apologeten*, edited by Wolfgang Hasse, 235–70. Berlin: de Gruyter, 1993.

Second Baruch. Translated by A. F. J. Klijn. In *The Old Testament Pseudepigrapha*, vol. 1, edited by James H. Charlesworth, 615–52. New York: Doubleday, 1983.

Showers, Renald E. *There Really Is a Difference*. Bellmawr, NJ: The Friends of Israel Gospel Ministry, 2005.

Siegert, Folker. "Unbeachtete Papiaszitate Bei Armenishcen Schriftstellern." *New Testament Studies* 27 (1981) 605–14.

Simonetti, M. "Andrew of Caesarea." In *Encyclopedia of the Early Church*, edited by Angelo Di Berardino. Translated by Adrian Walford. New York: Oxford University Press, 1992.

Simpson, E. K., and F. F. Bruce. *Commentary on the Epistles to Ephesians and Colossians*. Grand Rapids: Eerdmans, 1975.

Smith, Carl B. *No Longer Jews: A Search for Gnostic Origins*. Peabody, MA: Hendrickson, 2004.

Smith, Leonhard. "Galli." In *A Dictionary of Greek and Roman Antiquities*, edited by William Smith. London: Murray, 1875.

Smyth, Herbert Weir. *Greek Grammar*. Revised by Gordon M. Messing. Cambridge: Harvard University Press, 2002.

Socrates. *Ecclesiastical History.* Translated and edited by A. C. Zenos. American ed. Nicene and Post-Nicene Fathers, vol. 2. 1895. Reprint. Peabody, MA: Hendrickson, 2004.

Stein, Robert H. *Studying the Synoptic Gospels: Origin and Interpretation.* 2nd ed. Grand Rapids: Baker Academic, 2003.

Stevenson, J. *A New Eusebius.* London: SPCK, 1974.

Stewart-Sykes, Alistair. "Τάξει in Papias: Again." *Journal of Early Christian Studies* 3 (1995) 487–92.

Stott, John R. *The Epistles of John.* Leicester, UK: InterVarsity, 1983.

Strathmann, H. "μάρτυς." In *Theological Dictionary of the New Testament*, edited by Gerhard Kittel and translated and edited by Geoffrey W. Bromiley. Grand Rapids: Eerdmans, 1981.

Streeter, Burnett Hillman. *The Four Gospels: A Study of Origins.* London: Macmillan, 1924.

Supernatural Religion: An Inquiry into the Reality of Divine Revelation. London: Longmans, Green, 1874.

Syncelli, Georgii. *Ecloga Chronographica.* Edited by Alden A. Mosshammer. Leipzig: Teubner, 1984.

Synkellos, George. *The Chronography of George Synkellos.* Translated and edited by William Alder and Paul Tuffin. Oxford: Oxford University Press, 2002.

Taniguchi, Yuko, and François Bovon. "The Memorial of Saint John the Theologian" (BHG 919fb). In *The Apocryphal Acts of the Apostles*, edited by Ann Graham Brock, François Bovon, and Christopher R. Matthews, 333–42. Cambridge: Harvard University Press, 1999.

Tatian. *Diatessaron.* Translated by Hope W. Hogg. American ed. Ante-Nicene Fathers, vol. 9. 1886. Reprint. Peabody, MA: Hendrickson, 2004.

Taylor, R. O. P. *The Groundwork of the Gospels.* Oxford: Alden, 1946.

Tertullian. *On Prescriptions against Heresies.* Translated by Peter Holmes. American ed. Anti-Nicene Fathers, vol. 3. 1885. Reprint. Peabody, MA: Hendrickson, 2004.

Thornton, T. C. G. "Jerome and the 'Hebrew Gospel according to Matthew.'" *Studia Patristica* 28 (1993) 118–22.

Tischendorf, Constantine. *When Were Our Gospels Written?* London: The Religious Tract Society, 1896.

Tracey, Robyn. "Syria." In *The Book of Acts in Its Graeco-Roman Setting*, edited by David W. J. Gill and Conrad Gempf, 223–78. Grand Rapids: Eerdmans, 1994.

Trebilco, Paul. "Asia." In *The Book of Acts in Its Graeco-Roman Setting*, edited by David W. J. Gill and Conrad Gempf, 291–362. Grand Rapids: Eerdmans, 1994.

Turner, C. H. *The Day and Year of St. Polycarp's Martyrdom.* Piscataway, NJ: Gorgias, 2006.

von Campenhausen, Hans. *The Formation of the Christian Bible.* Translated by J. A. Baker. Philadelphia: Fortress, 1972.

Wallace, Daniel B. *The Basics of New Testament Syntax.* Grand Rapids: Zondervan, 2000.

———. *Greek Grammar beyond the Basics.* Grand Rapids: Zondervan, 1996.

———. "John 5:2 and the Date of the Fourth Gospel." *Biblica* 71 (1990) 177–205.

———. "Reconsidering 'The Story of Jesus and the Adulteress Reconsidered.'" *New Testament Studies* 39 (1993) 290–96.

Walls, A. F. "Papias and Oral Tradition." *Vigiliae Christianae* 21 (1967) 137–40.

Warfield, B. B. *The Inspiration and Authority of the Bible*. Philadelphia: Presbyterian and Reformed, 1970.

Weiss, Johannes, and Rudolf Knopf. *Earliest Christianity: A History of the Period A.D. 30–150*. Vol. 2. Translated by Paul Stevens Kramer. New York: Harper, 1959.

Wenham, John. *The Elements of New Testament Greek*. London: Cambridge University Press, 1956.

———. *Redating Matthew, Mark and Luke*. Downers Grove, IL: InterVarsity, 1992.

Willett, Tom W. *Eschatology in the Theodicies of 2 Baruch and 4 Ezra*. Sheffield, UK: Sheffield Academic Press, 1989.

Wright, Arthur. "Τάξει in Papias." *The Journal of Theological Studies* 14 (1913) 298–300.

Yarbrough, Robert W. "The Date of Papias: A Reassessment." *Journal of the Evangelical Theological Society* 26 (1983) 181–91.

———. "The Date of the Writings of Papias of Hierapolis." M.A. thesis, Wheaton College, 1982.

Younger, E. M. "Apollinaris the Elder." In *A Dictionary of Early Christian Biography*. Edited by William Piercy. Peabody, MA: Hendrickson, 1999.

Zahn, Theodor. *Forschungen zur Geschichte des neutestamentlichen Kanons und der altkirchlichen Literatur*. Vol. 6. Leipzig: Deichert, 1900.

———. *Introduction to the New Testament*. Vol. 2–3. Translated by Melancthon Williams Jacobus. Edinburgh: T. & T. Clark, 1909.

39317762R00182

Made in the USA
San Bernardino, CA
19 June 2019